Applications of Artificial Neural Networks for Nonlinear Data

Hiral Ashil Patel
Ganpat University, India

A.V. Senthil Kumar
Hindusthan College of Arts and Science, India

A volume in the Advances in
Computational Intelligence and
Robotics (ACIR) Book Series

Published in the United States of America by
IGI Global
Engineering Science Reference (an imprint of IGI Global)
701 E. Chocolate Avenue
Hershey PA, USA 17033
Tel: 717-533-8845
Fax: 717-533-8661
E-mail: cust@igi-global.com
Web site: http://www.igi-global.com

Library of Congress Cataloging-in-Publication Data

Names: Patel, Hiral Ashil, 1988- editor. | Kumar, A. V. Senthil, 1966-
    editor.
Title: Applications of artificial neural networks for nonlinear data /
    Hiral Ashil Patel and A.V. Senthil Kumar, editors.
Description: Hershey, PA : Engineering Science Reference, an imprint of IGI
    Global, [2020] | Includes bibliographical references and index. |
    Summary: "This book is a collection of research on the contemporary
    nature of artificial neural networks and their specific implementations
    within data analysis"-- Provided by publisher.
Identifiers: LCCN 2019059548 (print) | LCCN 2019059549 (ebook) | ISBN
    9781799840428 (hardcover) | ISBN 9781799851509 (paperback) | ISBN
    9781799840435 (ebook)
Subjects: LCSH: Quantitative research--Data processing. | Nonlinear
    systems--Data processing. | Neural networks (Computer science)
Classification: LCC QA76.9.Q36 .A 2020 (print) | LCC QA76.9.Q36 (ebook) |
    DDC 001.4/20285632--dc23
LC record available at https://lccn.loc.gov/2019059548
LC ebook record available at https://lccn.loc.gov/2019059549

This book is published in the IGI Global book series Advances in Computational Intelligence and Robotics (ACIR) (ISSN: 2327-0411; eISSN: 2327-042X)

British Cataloguing in Publication Data
A Cataloguing in Publication record for this book is available from the British Library.

All work contributed to this book is new, previously-unpublished material.
The views expressed in this book are those of the authors, but not necessarily of the publisher.

For electronic access to this publication, please contact: eresources@igi-global.com.

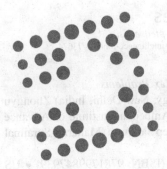

Advances in Computational Intelligence and Robotics (ACIR) Book Series

ISSN:2327-0411
EISSN:2327-042X

Editor-in-Chief: Ivan Giannoccaro, University of Salento, Italy

MISSION

While intelligence is traditionally a term applied to humans and human cognition, technology has progressed in such a way to allow for the development of intelligent systems able to simulate many human traits. With this new era of simulated and artificial intelligence, much research is needed in order to continue to advance the field and also to evaluate the ethical and societal concerns of the existence of artificial life and machine learning.

The **Advances in Computational Intelligence and Robotics (ACIR) Book Series** encourages scholarly discourse on all topics pertaining to evolutionary computing, artificial life, computational intelligence, machine learning, and robotics. ACIR presents the latest research being conducted on diverse topics in intelligence technologies with the goal of advancing knowledge and applications in this rapidly evolving field.

COVERAGE

- Automated Reasoning
- Cyborgs
- Synthetic Emotions
- Intelligent control
- Adaptive and Complex Systems
- Evolutionary Computing
- Algorithmic Learning
- Fuzzy Systems
- Agent technologies
- Computational Intelligence

IGI Global is currently accepting manuscripts for publication within this series. To submit a proposal for a volume in this series, please contact our Acquisition Editors at Acquisitions@igi-global.com or visit: http://www.igi-global.com/publish/.

Titles in this Series

For a list of additional titles in this series, please visit:
http://www.igi-global.com/book-series/advances-computational-intelligence-robotics/73674

Intelligent Computations Applications for Solving Complex Problems
Naveen Dahiya (Maharaja Surajmal Institute of Technology, New Delhi, India) Zhongyu
Lu (University of Huddersfield, UK) Vishal Bhatnagar (Ambedkar Institute of Advance
Communication Technologies & Research, India) and Pardeep Sangwan (Maharaja Surajmal
Institute of Technology, New Delhi, India)
Engineering Science Reference • © 2021 • 300pp • H/C (ISBN: 9781799847939) • US
$225.00

Artificial Intelligence and the Journey to Software 2.0 Emerging Research and Opportunities
Divanshi Priyadarshni Wangoo (Indira Gandhi Delhi Technical University for Women, India)
Engineering Science Reference • © 2021 • 150pp • H/C (ISBN: 9781799843276) • US
$165.00

Practical Applications and Use Cases of Computer Vision and Recognition Systems
Chiranji Lal Chowdhary (Vellore Institute of Technology, India) and B.D. Parameshachari
(GSSS Institute of Engineering and Technology for Women, India)
Engineering Science Reference • © 2020 • 300pp • H/C (ISBN: 9781799849247) • US
$195.00

Machine Learning Applications in Non-Conventional Machining Processes
Goutam Kumar Bose (Haldia Institute of Technology, Haldia, India) and Pritam Pain (Haldia
Institute of Technology, India)
Engineering Science Reference • © 2020 • 300pp • H/C (ISBN: 9781799836247) • US
$195.00

Handbook of Research on Smart Technology Models for Business and Industry
J. Joshua Thomas (UOW Malaysia KDU Penang University College, Malaysia) Ugo Fiore
(University of Naples Parthenope, Italy) Gilberto Perez Lechuga (Autonomous University
of Hidalgo State, Mexico) Valeriy Kharchenko (Federal Agroengineering Centre VIM ,
Russia) and Pandian Vasant (University of Technology Petronas, Malaysia)
Engineering Science Reference • © 2020 • 491pp • H/C (ISBN: 9781799836452) • US
$295.00

For an entire list of titles in this series, please visit:
http://www.igi-global.com/book-series/advances-computational-intelligence-robotics/73674

701 East Chocolate Avenue, Hershey, PA 17033, USA
Tel: 717-533-8845 x100 • Fax: 717-533-8661
E-Mail: cust@igi-global.com • www.igi-global.com

Editorial Advisory Board

Table of Contents

Section 1
Concepts and Categorization

Section 2
Applications and Analytics

Detailed Table of Contents

Section 1
Concepts and Categorization

Chapter 1
    Pooja Deepakbhai Pancholi, Ganpat University, India
    Sonal Jayantilal Patel, Ganpat University, India

The artificial neural network could probably be the complete solution in recent decades, widely used in many applications. This chapter is devoted to the major applications of artificial neural networks and the importance of the e-learning application. It is necessary to adapt to the new intelligent e-learning system to personalize each learner. The result focused on the importance of using neural networks in possible applications and its influence on the learner's progress with the personalization system. The number of ANN applications has considerably increased in recent years, fueled by theoretical and applied successes in various disciplines. This chapter presents an investigation into the explosive developments of many artificial neural network related applications. The ANN is gaining importance in various applications such as pattern recognition, weather forecasting, handwriting recognition, facial recognition, autopilot, etc. Artificial neural network belongs to the family of artificial intelligence with fuzzy logic, expert systems, vector support machines.

Chapter 2
    Meghna Babubhai Patel, Ganpat University, India
    Jagruti N. Patel, Ganpat University, India
    Upasana M. Bhilota, Ganpat University, India

An artificial neural network (ANN) is an information processing modelling of the human brain inspired by the way biological nervous systems behave. There are about 100 billion neurons in the human brain. Each neuron has a connection point between 1,000 and 100,000. The key element of this paradigm is the novel structure of the information processing system. In the human brain, information is stored in such a way as to be distributed, and we can extract more than one piece of this information when necessary from our memory in parallel. We are not mistaken when we say that a human brain is made up of thousands of very powerful parallel processors. It is composed of a large number of highly interconnected processing elements (neurons) working in union to solve specific problems. ANN, like people, learns by example. The chapter includes characteristics of artificial neural networks, structure of ANN, elements of artificial neural networks, pros and cons of ANN.

The new era of the world uses artificial intelligence (AI) and machine learning. The combination of AI and machine learning is called artificial neural network (ANN). Artificial neural network can be used as hardware or software-based components. Different topology and learning algorithms are used in artificial neural networks. Artificial neural network works similarly to the functionality of the human nervous system. ANN is working as a nonlinear computing model based on activities performed by human brain such as classification, prediction, decision making, visualization just by considering previous experience. ANN is used to solve complex, hard-to-manage problems by accruing knowledge about the environment. There are different types of artificial neural networks available in machine learning. All types of artificial neural networks work based of mathematical operation and require a set of parameters to get results. This chapter gives overview on the various types of neural networks like feed forward, recurrent, feedback, classification-predication.

Ever since the advent of modern geo information systems, tracking environmental changes due to natural and/or manmade causes with the aid of remote sensing applications has been an indispensable tool in numerous fields of geography, most of the earth science disciplines, defense, intelligence, commerce, economics, and administrative planning. Remote sensing is used in science and technology, and through it, an object can be identified, measured, and analyzed without physical presence for interpretation. In India remote sensing has been using since 1970s. One among these applications is the crop classification and yield estimation. Using remote sensing in agriculture for crop mapping, and yield estimation provides efficient information, which is mainly used in many government organizations and the private sector. The pivotal sector for ensuring food security is a major concern of interest in these days. In time, availability of information on agricultural crops is vital for making well-versed decisions on food security issues.

Chapter 5

    Satyen M. Parikh, Ganpat University, India
    Mitali K. Shah, Ganpat University, India

A utilization of the computational semantics is known as natural language processing or NLP. Any opinion through attitude, feelings, and thoughts can be identified as sentiment. The overview of people against specific events, brand, things, or association can be recognized through sentiment analysis. Positive, negative, and neutral are each of the premises that can be grouped into three separate categories. Twitter, the most commonly used microblogging tool, is used to gather information for research. Tweepy is used to access Twitter's source of information. Python language is used to execute the classification algorithm on the information collected. Two measures are applied in sentiment analysis, namely feature extraction and classification. Using n-gram modeling methodology, the feature is extracted. Through a supervised machine learning algorithm, the sentiment is graded as positive, negative, and neutral. Support vector machine (SVM) and k-nearest neighbor (KNN) classification models are used and demonstrated both comparisons.

Section 2
Applications and Analytics

Chapter 6

    Yakup Akgül, Alanya Alaaddin Keykubat University, Turkey

This chapter aims to determine the main factors of mobile payment adoption and the intention to recommend this technology. An innovative research model has been proposed with the advancement of the body of knowledge on this subject that combines the strengths of two well-known theories: the extended unified theory of acceptance and use of technology (UTAUT2) with the innovation characteristics of the diffusion of innovations (DOI) with perceived security and intention to recommend the technology constructs. The research model was empirically tested using 259 responses from an online survey conducted in Turkey. Two techniques were used: first, structural equation modeling (SEM) was used to determine which variables had significant influence on mobile payment adoption; in a second phase, the neural network model was used to rank the relative influence of significant predictors obtained by SEM. This study found that the most significant variables impacting the intention to use were perceived technology security and innovativeness variables.

Higher penetration of the most widely used mobile technology applications and 3G and 4G mobile networks have led to the higher usage of smartphones for mobile banking activities in recent times. Data were collected from 395 mobile banking users and analyzed using an innovative two-staged regression and neural network (NN) model. In the first stage, structural equation modeling was employed to test the research hypotheses and identify significant antecedents influencing mobile banking acceptance. In the second stage, the significant antecedents obtained from the first stage were input to a neural network model for ranking. The results revealed that autonomous motivation and perceived ease of use are the two main predictors influencing mobile banking acceptance. Theoretical and practical implications of findings are discussed. Policy makers can find significant results in this chapter for implementing future service design. Limitations and future research scope are also discussed.

Electrical induction machines are widely used in the modern wind power production. As their repair cost is important and since their down-time leads to significant income loss, increasing their reliability and optimizing their proactive maintenance process are critical tasks. Many diagnosis systems have been proposed to resolve this issue. However, these systems are failing to recognize accurately the type and the severity level of detected faults in real time. In this chapter, a remote automated control approach applied for electrical induction machines has been suggested as an appropriate solution. It combines developed Fast-ESPRIT method, fault classification algorithm, and fuzzy inference system interconnected with vibration sensors, which are located on various wind turbine components. Furthermore, a new fault severity indicator has been formulated and evaluated to avoid false alarms. Study findings with computer simulation in Matlab prove the satisfactory robustness and performance of the proposed technique in fault classification and diagnosis.

Chapter 9

Wavelet neural networks are a class of single hidden layer neural networks consisting of wavelets as activation functions. Wavelet neural networks (WNN) are an alternative to the classical multilayer perceptron neural networks for arbitrary nonlinear function approximation and can provide compact network representation. In this chapter, a tutorial introduction to different types of WNNs and their architecture is given, along with its training algorithm. Subsequently, a novel application of WNN for equalization of nonlinear satellite communication channel is presented. Nonlinearity in a satellite communication channel is mainly caused due to use of transmitter power amplifiers near its saturation region to improve efficiency. Two models describing amplitude and phase distortion caused in a power amplifier are explained. Performance of the proposed equalizer is evaluated and compared to an existing equalizer in literature.

Chapter 10

Artificial neural networks (ANN) are often more suitable for classification problems. Even then, training of ANN is a surviving challenge task for large and high dimensional natured search space problems. These hitches are more for applications that involves process of fine tuning of ANN control parameters: weights and bias. There is no single search and optimization method that suits the weights and bias of ANN for all the problems. The traditional heuristic approach fails because of their poorer convergence speed and chances of ending up with local optima. In this connection, the meta-heuristic algorithms prove to provide consistent solution for optimizing ANN training parameters. This chapter will provide critics on both heuristics and meta-heuristic existing literature for training neural networks algorithms, applicability, and reliability on parameter optimization. In addition, the real-time applications of

ANN will be presented. Finally, future directions to be explored in the field of ANN are presented which will of potential interest for upcoming researchers.

Chapter 11
Meghna Babubhai Patel, Ganpat University, India
Jagruti N. Patel, Ganpat University, India
Upasana M. Bhilota, Ganpat University, India

ANN can work the way the human brain works and can learn the way we learn. The neural network is this kind of technology that is not an algorithm; it is a network that has weights on it, and you can adjust the weights so that it learns. You teach it through trials. It is a fact that the neural network can operate and improve its performance after "teaching" it, but it needs to undergo some process of learning to acquire information and be familiar with them. Nowadays, the age of smart devices dominates the technological world, and no one can deny their great value and contributions to mankind. A dramatic rise in the platforms, tools, and applications based on machine learning and artificial intelligence has been seen. These technologies not only impacted software and the internet industry but also other verticals such as healthcare, legal, manufacturing, automobile, and agriculture. The chapter shows the importance of latest technology used in ANN and future trends in ANN.

Preface

Neural systems are propelled design acknowledgment calculations fit for removing complex, nonlinear connections among factors. This examination looks at those abilities by displaying nonlinearities in the activity fulfillment work execution association with multilayer perceptron what's more, spiral premise work neural systems. A system for examining nonlinear connections

With neural systems is utilized. It is actualized utilizing the activity fulfillment work execution association with results characteristic of unavoidable examples of nonlinearity.

The essential distinction between neural systems and regular factual techniques is that ANNs are versatile. That is, information are gone through by organizing ordinarily to such an extent that each go of information results in an anticipated worth that is contrasted with a known result. Changes are made to lessen blunder, and information is gone through the system until a worthy decrease in mistake is achieved. This procedure is alluded to as learning on the grounds that as information go through the system, mistake is diminished. Learning happens in the shrouded layer where information is summed and weighted with factual capacities to create an anticipated worth that is then passed on to the yield layer as a rule with a direct exchange work. Example acknowledgment is refined as loads are balanced with each go of information through the system design. To display nonlinear connections, the neurons in the shrouded layer must utilize nonlinear measurable capacities. In particular, it has been appeared whenever summed determined data sources are changed into a yield utilizing a nonlinear factual capacity, the outcome is a model with genuine nonlinear parameters

This procedure is influenced by the sort of measurable exchange capacity utilized and the number of neurons in the shrouded layer. Accordingly, extraordinary neural system designs or potentially diverse exchange capacities can deliver particularly various outcomes. Moreover, it ought to be noticed that neural systems are not limited to one shrouded layer, and occasions where at least two concealed layers are more qualified to mapping nonlinearities in information are normal. All the more explicitly, one concealed layer probably won't be adequate to demonstrate complex nonlinear connections with the goal that at least two shrouded layers are important to precisely demonstrate connections among factors. It is the obligation of the analyst to show that the number of shrouded layers in an ANN is suitable for the current issue.

ORGANIZATION OF CHAPTERS

Chapter 1 aims to carried out the literature survey of ANN. This chapter is devoted to the major applications of artificial neural networks and the importance of the e-Learning application. It is necessary to adapt to the new intelligent e-learning system to personalize each learners. The result focused on the importance of using neural networks in possible applications and its influence on the learner's progress with the personalization system. The number of ANN applications has considerably increased in recent years, fueled by theoretical and applied successes in various disciplines. This chapter presents an investigation into the explosive developments of many artificial neural network related applications.

Chapter 2 illustrates modelling and structure of ANN. The key element of this paradigm is the novel structure of the information processing system. In the human brain, information is stored in such a way as to be distributed, and we can extract more than one piece of this information when necessary from our memory in parallel. We are not mistaken when we say that a human brain is made up of thousands of very, very powerful parallel processors It is composed of a large number of highly interconnected processing elements (neurons) working in union to solve specific problems. ANN is like people, learn by example. The proposed chapter includes Characteristics of Artificial Neural Networks, Structure of ANN, Elements of Artificial Neural Networks, Pros and Cons of ANN.

Chapter 3 gives the introductory and categories of ANN in brief. ANN is working as non linear computing model which based on activities perform by human brain such as classification, prediction, decision making, visualization just by considering previous experience. Ann use to solve complex, hard to manage problem, by accruing knowledge about their environment, comply internal and outmost parameter. There are different types of Artificial neural network available in Machine learning. All types of Artificial neural network work on based of mathematical operation and required set of parameters to get result. In propose chapter give overview on various types of neural network like feed forward, recurrent, feedback, classification-predication.

Chapter 4 purely focus on the ANN role in agriculture domain One among these applications is the crop classification and yield estimation. Using remote sensing in Agriculture for crop mapping and yield estimation provides efficient information which is mainly used in many government organizations and private sectors. The pivotal sector for ensuring food security is major concern of interest in these days. In time availability of information on agricultural crops is vital for taking well-versed decisions on food security issues.

Chapter 5 focuses on one most classification application through ANN on text data in the form of tweets. A utilization of the computational semantics is known as Natural Language Processing or NLP. Any people's opinion through the attitude, feelings and thoughts can be communicated is identified as sentiment. The overview of people against specific events, brand, things or association can be recognized through sentiment analysis. Positive, negative and neutral are each of the premises that can be grouped into three separate categories. Also applied comparative study for selection of classifier.

Chapter 6 aims to determine the main factors of mobile payment adoption and the intention to recommend this technology. An innovative research model has been proposed with the advancement of the body of knowledge on this subject that combines the strengths of two well-known theories; the extended unified theory of acceptance and use of technology (UTAUT2) with the innovation characteristics of the diffusion of innovations (DOI), with perceived security and intention to recommend the technology constructs. The research model was empirically tested using 259 responses from an online survey conducted in Turkey. It is utilize the concept of SEM NN.

Chapter 7 analyses the effects of Higher penetration of the most widely used mobile technology applications and 3G and 4G mobile networks have led to the higher usage of smartphones for mobile banking activities in recent times. Data were collected from 395 mobile banking users and analyzed using an innovative two-staged regression and neural network (NN) model. In the first stage, structural equation modeling was employed to test the research hypotheses and identify significant antecedents influencing mobile banking acceptance. In the second stage, the significant antecedents obtained from the first stage were input to a neural network model for ranking. The results revealed that autonomous motivation and perceived ease of use are the two main predictors influencing mobile banking acceptance. Theoretical and practical implications of findings are discussed. Policy makers can find significant results in this paper for implementing future service design. Limitations and future research scope are also discussed.

Chapter 8 discusses one more application of ANN. Electrical induction machines are widely used in the modern wind power production. As their repair' cost is important and since their down-time lead to significant income loss, increasing their reliability and optimizing their proactive maintenance process are critical tasks. Many diagnosis systems has been proposed to resolve this issue. However, these systems are failing to recognize accurately the type and the severity level of detected faults in real time. In this paper, a remote automated control approach applied for electrical induction machines has been suggested as an appropriate solution. It combines developed Fast-ESPRIT method, fault classification algorithm and fuzzy inference system interconnected with vibration sensors which are located on various wind turbine components. Furthermore, a new fault severity indicator has been formulated and evaluated to avoid false alarms. Study findings with computer simulation in Matlab prove the satisfactory robustness and performance of the proposed technique in fault classification and diagnosis.

Chapter 9 discusses on WNN another type of ANN application. A novel application of WNN for equalization of nonlinear satellite communication channel is presented. Nonlinearity in a satellite communication channel is mainly caused due to use of transmitter power amplifiers near its saturation region to improve efficiency. Two models describing amplitude and phase distortion caused in a power amplifier are explained. Performance of the proposed equalizer is evaluated and compared to an existing equalizer in literature.

Chapter 10 discusses the ANN Usage and adoptability. Artificial Neural Networks (ANN) are often more suitable for classification problems. Even then training of ANN is a surviving challenge task for large and high dimensional natured search space problems. These hitches are more for applications that involves process of fine tuning of ANN control parameters: weights and bias. There is no single search and optimization method which suits the weights and bias of ANN for all the problems. The traditional heuristic approach fails because of their poorer convergence speed and chances of ending up with local optima. In this connection, the meta-heuristic algorithms prove to provide consistent solution for optimizing ANN training parameters. This chapter will provide critics on both heuristics and meta-heuristic existing literature for training neural networks algorithms, applicability and reliability on parameter optimization. In addition the real time applications of ANN will be presented. Finally, future directions to be explored in the field of ANN are presented which will of potential interest for upcoming researchers.

Chapter 11 summaries the applications and scopes of ANN. Nowadays, the age of smart devices dominates the technological world, and no one can deny their great value and contributions to mankind. As seen dramatic rise in the platforms, tools, and applications based on Machine learning and artificial intelligence. These technologies not only impacted software and the Internet industry but also other verticals such as healthcare, legal, manufacturing, automobile and agriculture. The proposed chapter so the importance of latest technology used in ANN and future trends in ANN.

CONCLUSION

Artificial NN is become very comprehensive approach to deal with real time problem solving and atomization as well. This book focus on basic part of ANN to live case study of ANN. It also covers the ANN structural and application-based study. It also describes the features and applicability of ANN. The section one basically focuses on the brief overviews and categories of ANN in terms of applicability and strength. Second part focus on analytical study and experimental study of ANN. The book written with very basic level.

Hiral Ashil Patel
Ganpat University, India

Acknowledgment

I would like to thank IGI Global for offering me the opportunity to edit this book on Applications of Artificial Neural Networks for Nonlinear Data. I am grateful to Editorial Advisory Board Members and all the valuable contributing authors of this book for the support, assistance, suggestions and contribution. My sincere thanks extends to all reviewers for their extended support during the tiring review process.

I will not have completed this work in time unless continuous support came from my husband, son and family members.

Finally, my regards go to the colleagues and friends for their supports and encouragements, without which, I would not have been able to complete this research publication. I specially thank to my guide for motivate me.

Hiral Ashil Patel
Ganpat University, India

Section 1
Concepts and Categorization

Chapter 1
Literature Survey for Applications of Artificial Neural Networks

Pooja Deepakbhai Pancholi
Ganpat University, India

Sonal Jayantilal Patel
Ganpat University, India

ABSTRACT

The artificial neural network could probably be the complete solution in recent decades, widely used in many applications. This chapter is devoted to the major applications of artificial neural networks and the importance of the e-learning application. It is necessary to adapt to the new intelligent e-learning system to personalize each learner. The result focused on the importance of using neural networks in possible applications and its influence on the learner's progress with the personalization system. The number of ANN applications has considerably increased in recent years, fueled by theoretical and applied successes in various disciplines. This chapter presents an investigation into the explosive developments of many artificial neural network related applications. The ANN is gaining importance in various applications such as pattern recognition, weather forecasting, handwriting recognition, facial recognition, autopilot, etc. Artificial neural network belongs to the family of artificial intelligence with fuzzy logic, expert systems, vector support machines.

DOI: 10.4018/978-1-7998-4042-8.ch001

CHARACTER RECOGNITION APPLICATION

Now a day, character recognition has become important because portable devices like Palm Pilot are becoming more and more famous. NN can be used to identify the latter.

Given the ability of ANN to receive a large amount of information and process them to derive hidden, complex and non-linear relationships, ANNs play an significant role in character recognition.

The classification of character recognition is as shown in Figure 1.

Figure 1. Classification of character recognition

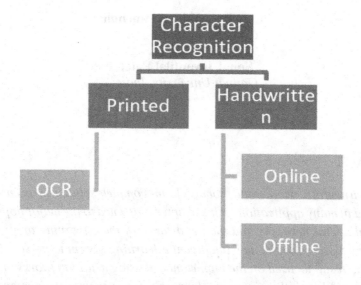

OPTICAL CHARACTER RECOGNITION (OCR)

- OCR is a procedure that converts a printed document or a page scanned into ASCII characters that a computer can identify. Computer systems prepared with such an OCR system improve the input speed, reduce certain person error and allow solid storage space, speedy recovery and additional file manipulations. Accurateness, elasticity and velocity are the major characteristics of a excellent OCR system. Some character recognition algorithms based on feature selection have been developed. The performance of the systems was limited by police dependence, size and orientation. The recovery rate in these algorithms depends on the choice of features. Most existing algorithms involve complete image processing before feature extraction, which increases the calculation time. In this topic, discuss a method of character recognition based on a neural network that would efficiently shrink picture processing time though maintaining effectiveness and flexibility. The parallel computing efficiency of NN ensure big identify rate, which is essential for a mercantile domain. The neural network access has been recycled for character identify, although entire system that beset totally the characteristics of a pragmatic OCR system has not still been developed. The main elements besmeared in the execution are: an optimum collecting of characteristics that indeed define the expansion of the alphabets, the count of characteristics and a reduced image processing time (Mani 1997).

Figure 2. Optical character recognition example

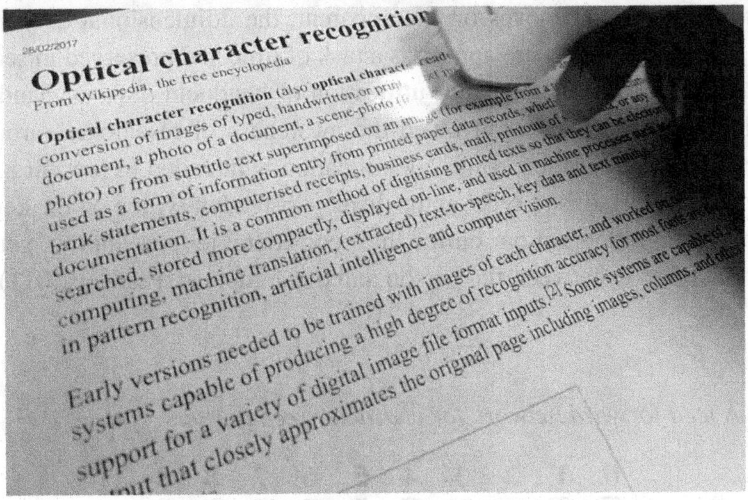

HANDWRITTEN CHARACTER RECOGNITION

- Character recognition is an art of detecting, segmenting and identifying characters in an image. One of the main purposes of recognizing handwritten characters is to imitate human reading abilities therefore that the computer can read, perceive and performance in the same way as text. The identity of handwriting has been different majorities like charming and difficult analysis domain in the scope of picture processing and pattern indentify in nearly season. It greatly devotes to progress of the automatism procedure and

3

rectified the interface among person and device in huge applications. Some analysis studies have focused on recent technology and schemes to decrease processing period and provide superior identity accuracy. Letter identity is mostly dual types: one is online and other is offline. At the time of online letter identity, data is cached at the time of writing procedures using a particular pen on an electronic level. At the time of offline identity, the prewritten content commonly written on a page of document is scanned. In usual, everything printed or written letters are sorted as offline. Offline manuscript identity refers to as process of character recognition in scanned document from a surface like paper sheet and stored digitally in grayscale formation. The repository of scanned documents must be huge and major processing applications, such as content search, modifying, preservation are difficult or not possible. The online identification style is generally use for identify simply handwritten letters. Here in case, the writing is caught and preserved in digital appearance through various ways. Generally, a special pen through computerized surface is used. When pen moves on the apparent, the 2dimensional coordinate of the succeeding points are appear as a task of time and preserved in sequence. In recent times, because major utilization of handheld devices, handwritten online identification has involved the awareness of researchers around the world. The handwritten online identification is intended to present a natural interface for persons to type on the display instead of typing on the keyboard. Handwriting recognition online has considerable possible to get better communication between the person and the computer (Pradeep 2011).

Figure 3. A feed-forward network for character recognition.

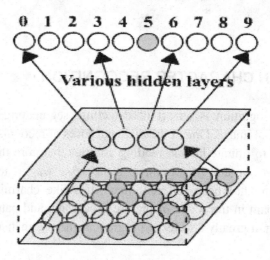

Feed-Forward Networks - Character Recognition

- Another one idea of using feed forward networks to recognize handwritten characters is quite simple. As in most supervised exercise, the bitmap pattern of the handwritten character is treated as an input, with the correct letter or number as the desired output. Normally, such programs require the user to form the network by providing handwritten design.
- Many applications like mail sorting, bank processing, document reading and postal address identification require handwriting recognition systems offline. As a result, recognition of manual writing offline remains an active area of research to explore new techniques that can improve recognition accuracy.

Pattern Recognition Application

The Pattern recognition of forms involves studying how equipment can monitor the surroundings and study to differentiate the motives of concern from their origins. And from them build sensible and practical conclusion in relation to the group of form. Despite approximately 50 years of investigate, the drawing of an ordinary-intent equipment-shaped recognition device stays a difficult ambition to achieve. The most excellent model identifiers in every case are human, but don't know how as human being identify structure. Here our main ambition is to establish pattern identification by the use of ANN. For that the greatest achievable method to make use of the different sensors, domain knowledge and processors are available to create choice automatically.

Till now discussion, the pattern identification are mainly use for direct calculation by machines. This direct calculation is depending on mathematical methods. After that topic will introduce idea related to bionics in pattern identification. The meaning of bionics is the application of biological concept to electronic equipment. The neural methods implement biological idea to equipment to identify the structure. So the achievement after this processes the innovation of the network of artificial neurons.

A neural network is known as an information processing system. These are simple and massive working element with a high level of interlinking among every element. The working element work in cooperation with altogether and allow corresponding cluster distributed processing. The drawing and purpose of NN imitate several functionality of biological brain power and neuronal structure. NNs have the different benefits like self –organization, error acceptance and their adaptive learning skill. Because of these different exceptional abilities, NNs are used for pattern identification purpose. Several most excellent neuronal models are backscatter, high order networks, moment delay NNs and recurring networks.

Generally, pattern identification is done by only progress networks. The meaning of feed-forward is no comments on the post. Just like humans taught from fault, NNs can also learn from their fault by giving response to input models. So this kind of return would be utilized to rebuild participation models and eliminate them from any errors; as a result increasing the work of NNs. Clearly, it is extremely difficult to construct this kind of NNs. These types of networks are called self-associating NNs.

Figure 4. Pattern recognition example

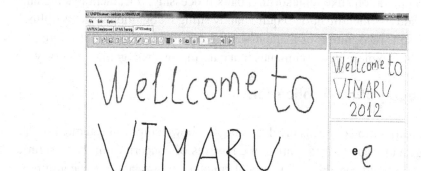

Face Recognition Application

Face recognition is a problem of recognition of visual forms. In detail, a facial recognition system with the entry of an arbitrary image will search the database to produce the identification of the people in the input image. A facial recognition system generally comprises four modules: detection, alignment, feature extraction and matching, with location and normalization (face detection and alignment) that are processing steps before facial recognition (removal and matching of facial features).

Face detection segments the areas of the background face. In the case of a video, it may be necessary to follow the detected faces using a face tracking component. Face alignment aims to achieve a more precise location and normalization of faces, while face detection provides approximate estimates of the location and scale of each face detected. The components of the face are located, such as the eyes, the nose, the mouth and the contour of the face; Depending on the location points, the image of the participation face is normalized by value to geometric properties, like size and pose, through geometric alteration. The features are generally more standardized through esteem to picture metric effects like lighting and grayscale. Once a face is geometrically and picture metrically normalized, characteristic taking out is executed to give useful information to distinguish faces of people who are different and constant from geometric and photometric variations. For face matching, the characteristic vector extracted from the participation face is compared with those faces which registered in the record; returns the identity of the face when a equal is establish through enough confidence or indicates an unidentified face (Le 2011).

Figure 5. Face recognition

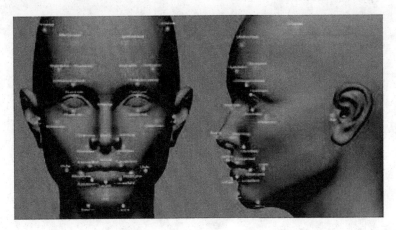

Spelling Check Application

ANN are a hopeful technology for natural language process because one of ANN's strengths is its "sensible" ability to make reasonable decisions even in the face of new information, even as the limitation of natural language process applications is weakness in the problem of ambiguous situations. Word is a part where ambiguity is excellent, words can be spell wrongly, they can have different legal spelling and can be homologous. Strong term identification functions may get better applications that involve text comprehension and form core component of applications, like spell examination and given name search. For artificial neural networks to identify variation and homologous word style, words have to be changed into a style that makes sense to artificial neural networks. The edge with the ANN consists of enter and production layers, each one consisting of unchanging number of nodes. Every node is linked through a number assessment, generally among 0 and 1. Therefore, words, variable length of strings, symbols, must be transformed into tables of preset length statistics so that ANNs can process them. The resulting verbal illustration should preferably: I) In the form, that allows an ANN to recognize likeness and spelling variation; 2) characterize every letters of the words; 3) Brief sufficient to permit the dealing out of a big digit of terms in a sensible moment. To date, ANN investigate has unseen these low- stage enter problems, still they have a critical impact on "superior stage processing. A general opinion have that various methods of representation don't have a significant effect on the presentation of ANN. However, this topic presents word representations that considerably improve artificial NN performance in NL words (Lewellen 1998).

Figure 6. Spelling check

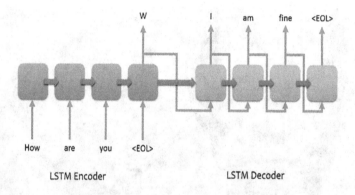

Autopilot Application

The main obligation of the autopilot is to keep the ship heading in a predefined direction using mainly the rudder. Transport safety and efficiency depend directly on the performance of the autopilots. For this, many techniques such as proportional-integral-derivative controller, optimal control theory, adaptive control and non-linear control are used to improve the performance of the autopilot. The main feature of these approaches is that they require accurate knowledge of the dynamics of controlled objects, which is difficult to obtain in practice due to the complexity of the hydrodynamics of ships. For adaptive and nonlinear control, there are some disadvantages, such as difficult design and stability analysis. The above mentioned drawbacks can be overcome through the use of an artificial neural network (ANN) due to its ability to approximate arbitrary smooth functions with the required precision. The first way of application of ANN to ship steering is to use a conventional controller for training the neural network (NN) controller. Another way to develop an NN controller is to integrate NN with other control techniques for adaptive control. The structure of this article is organized as shown in Figure 7 (Unar 1999).

Voice Recognition Application

Figure 7. Autopilot

Lecture and vocal identification is the upcoming defense and verification field for the future. Wording and picture password nowadays are subject to assault. In majority case common wording passwords applied, person must handle various passwords for email, Internet banking, etc. Therefore, they pick secret code those are simple to keep in mind. However they are sensitive in region of privacy. In case of illustrated secret code, they are sensitive to shoulder navigation and additional hacking methods. Moving forward in vocal technology has aroused great attention in the realistic appliance of voice detection. So, this structure provides person by way of the suitable and valuable technique of verification system based on volume identification. The vocal is as well a physiological characteristic for the reason that each human has a various voice, although the vocal identification is based primarily on the learning of how a human speaks, usually categorized as behavioral. The lecturer verification focuses on the vocal features that the speech produces and not on the vocal or pronunciation of the speech itself. The sound features rely on the measurement of the sound zone, the mouth, the nasal cavities and the additional verbal communication processing method of the human body. Biometric voice systems can be classified into two category one is voice processing and other one is biometric security. This double affiliation has powerfully influenced the function of biometric voice tools in the real world. Speech therapy, like other speech therapies, tools, voice biometrics extracts information from the voice flow to perform its work. They can be configured to operate on many of the same acoustic parameters as their closest relative voice recognition. Voice recognition has two categories that depend on the text and are independent of the text. Text-dependent sound identification recognizes the speaker facing the sentence that was specified at the moment of registration. The sound identification independent of the text identifies the speaker regardless of what person say. This technique is extremely repeatedly used in sound identification because it requires incredibly few calculations, although it requires additional support from speakers. In this matter, the content in the authentication stage is variant from that in the training or registration stage. An important application of audio processing is the recognition of the voice and the speaker used in the investigation of voice texts, human-machine interactions and autonomous robots. Several related research studies have been published, each of which differs in the applied algorithms. These include dynamic neural networks based on Synapse for the classification of temporal patterns found in speech to perform verification and recognition of the speaker at normal noise levels, as well as the genetic algorithm (GA) (Mansour 2015).

Figure 8. Voice recognition

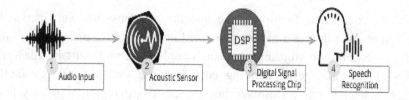

| 1
Audio Input | 2
Acoustic Sensor | 3
Digital Signal
Processing Chip | 4
Speech
Recognition |

Weather Forecasting Application

Climate prediction is a procedure of recognizing and forecasting weather conditions with some precision using various technologies. Many living systems depend on weather conditions to make the essential adjustments to the systems. Quantitative forecasts such as temperature, moisture and rainfall are important in the agricultural area and for traders in the commodity market. Today, we use many approaches for climate prediction. Mathematical modeling, statistical modeling and AI methods are among them. The mathematical models of the climate to forecast future climate conditions based on present climate situation are digit climate prediction. It requires information of dynamics atmosphere and include calculations with a huge number of variables and data sets. With advances in modern computer hardware, many improvements have been made in the prediction of the digital climate. We use ANN, which is based on an intelligent analysis of the trend based on past records. The additional models are precise in the calculations although not in the prediction, they cannot adapt the irregular data structures that cannot be written as a function or deduced in the form of a formula. Climate prediction report need ingenious computing that can read nonlinear information and make regulation and models to practice from inspect record to forecast future climate conditions. The utilization of artificial NN will provide a additional perfect outcome. At this point, the mistake may or may not be absolutely reduced. However, accurateness will get better compared to earlier prediction. The forecast and weather forecast (WRF) models, common forecast model, seasonal weather forecast, global data prediction model, are at present admissible models for climate forecasting. In addition, the calculation of all these forecasting models is extremely costly due to the intensive nature of the calculation. In contrast, data mining models operate with past records, probability models and / or similarity. For every forecast categories, the model workings similarly and expects moderate accuracy. In weather forecasts, model output may be needed for a on a daily basis climate guide or weekly basis or monthly basis climate scheduling. Therefore, the accurateness of the outcome is extremely essential feature of the forecast in order to provide the most excellent outcome amongst the entire additional climate forecast models (Bashir 2009).

The Traveling Saleman's Problem Application

There are two methods to solve the Sales Passenger (TSP) problem. First of all the ant system (Ant colony system (ACS)). Second, Neural Network (Hopfield Neural Network).At ACS a number of cooperating agents, called ants, work together to find good solutions for TSPs. Ants work together using an indirect form of pheromone-mediated communication that they deposit on the edges of the TSP chart while building solutions. A proposed algorithm and a standard algorithm are derived that are applied to the sales traveler problem (TSP). ACS study represented by conducting experiments to understand how it works. Many algorithm that uses a continuous neural network from Hopfield to resolve the TSP. To enable N neurons in the TSP network to calculate a solution to the problem, the network must be described by an energy function in which the lowest energy state (the most stable state of the network) corresponds to the best path.

Figure 9. Weather forecasting

5-day forecast
8/23 - 8/27

Today 8/23	Tomorrow 8/24	Sat 8/25	Sun 8/26	Mon 8/27
Rain	Rain	Rain	Cloudy	Rain
29°C	29°C	29°C	29°C	27°C
25°C	25°C	24°C	25°C	24°C
Cloudy	Rain	Cloudy	Cloudy	Cloudy
Southwest Force 4	Southwest Force 3	Southwest Force 4	Southwest Force 3	Southwest Force 3

Figure 10. Weather forecasting

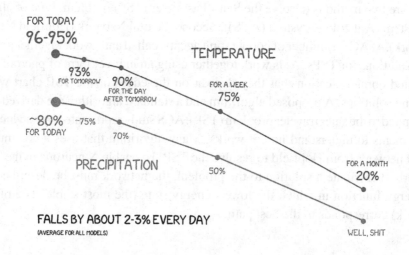

ACCURACY OF MODERN WEATHER FORECAST MODELS
YEAR 2018

FOR TODAY
96-95%

TEMPERATURE

93%
FOR TOMORROW **90%**
FOR THE DAY
AFTER TOMORROW

FOR A WEEK
75%

~80% ~75%
FOR TODAY   70%

PRECIPITATION   50%

FOR A MONTH
20%

FALLS BY ABOUT 2-3% EVERY DAY
(AVERAGE FOR ALL MODELS)

WELL, SHIT

Figure 11. The traveling saleman's problem

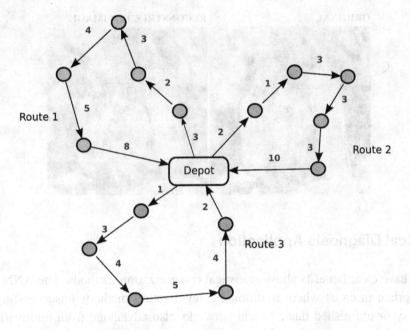

Image Processing Application

ANN are supporting tools for image processing. The pre-processing of images with neural networks generally falls into one of two categories: image reconstruction and restoration. The Hopfield neural network is one of the most widely used neural works for image reconstruction. Artificial neural networks retain their role as non-parametric classifiers, non-linear regression operators or extractors of monitored functions.

The purpose of image recovery is noise removal (sensor noise, movement shadow, and so on.) on or after the pictures. The easiest probable way used for noise elimination is different kinds of filters, like low-pass filters or median filters. Many advanced techniques take a representation of how local picture formation seems to be distinguished from noise. By initial examine the image records in terms of local picture construction, like lines or edges, and then controlling the filtering based on local information from the investigation phase, we usually get a better level of noise removal than most approaches. Simple an example in this area is painting.

Figure 12. Image processing

ORIGINAL   RECONSTRUCTED IMAGE

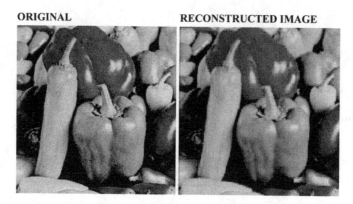

Medical Diagnosis Application

ANN have clear benefits above statistical categorization methods. The ANNs are appropriate in cases where traditional categorization methods unsuccessful due to noisy or unfinished data. Neural networks also advantage from multivariable categorization troubles with a high degree of correlation. The analysis of diseases is excellent example of such difficult classification troubles. Through correctly applying artificial neural networks in this region to achieve symptom interdependence and correct diagnosis, this dependence can be generalized, depend on this generalized model. So after that categorize the input models that represent different symptoms of diseases. In the application procedure, however, it is not required to specify the algorithm or otherwise recognize the disease. The application just requires input schedules. The entire diagnostic procedure of diseases in medical exercises is exposed in Figure 13.

The entire diagnostic procedure of diseases can be separated into training and diagnostic part. Mostly the training procedure starts through the selection of target diseases to which the classification trouble will be correlated. After an adequate selection of the disease, it is essential to determine the exact parameters, symptoms and laboratory outcome that explain the nature of this disease in detail. In the next step, a database is created based on this data that must be validated and the extreme values removed outside the range. The neural network is trained via this database and then the outcome obtained in this practice are verified. If the outcome of the trained neural network are true, the neural model can be applied in medical practice. The diagnostic procedure starts with this step. Patient data is processed via the neural network, which determines the likely diagnosis. This outcome is then validated with the treating physician. The concluded diagnosis is the outcome of the doctor's

Figure 13. Medical diagnosis

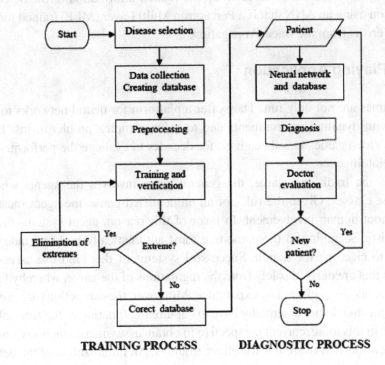

TRAINING PROCESS　　　　**DIAGNOSTIC PROCESS**

decision, who evaluates every facts of the disease and the outcome of the neural network categorization based on his own experiences.

Object Recognition Application

Object recognition is one of the most fascinating skills that people have easily possessed since childhood. With a simple glance at an object, people can tell their identity or category, despite the changes in appearance due to the change in posture, enlightenment, consistency, distortion and occlusion. Moreover, people can easily generalize from observing a series of objects to recognizing objects that have never been seen before. Considerable efforts have been made to develop representation schemes and algorithms aimed at recognizing generic objects in images created under different imaging conditions (for example, viewpoint, illumination, and occlusion).

The approach based on the artificial neural network for the recognition of different objects is investigated via various functions. The aim is to configure and teach an ANN to recognize an object using a set of functions consisting of Principal Component Analysis (PCA), Frequency Domain and Discrete Cosine Transform (DCT) components. The proposal is to use these different components to create a unique hybrid function set to catch up the related information of the objects for recognition using an ANN that is a Perceptron Multi Layer (MLP) trained for work in learn (error) from the Back Propagation.

Game Playing Application

Video games are not only fun. They offer a platform for neural networks to learn to deal with dynamic environments and to solve complex problems, just like in real life. Video games have been used for decades to evaluate the performance of artificial intelligence.

Unlike the traditional game, the general game involves the agents who can play game classes. Given the rules of an unidentified game, the agent must play well without human involvement. In favor of this reason, agent systems that use deterministic searching in the game tree must automatically build a grade value function to cicerone the search. Successful systems of this kind use assessment functions that are derived solely from the regulations of the game, whereby further improvements are neglected by experience. Moreover, these functions are preset in their outline and do not essentially have to capture the function of the true value of the game. In this topic, current perspective to obtain assessment functions based on neural networks that overcome the above troubles. An initialization of the network extracted from the game regulations guarantees proper behavior without prior training. However, the subsequent training can lead to important improvements in the excellence of the assessment, as our results point out.

Signature Verification Application

Signatures are one of the mainly convenient traditions to authorize and authenticate a person in lawful communication. The signature proof procedure is a non-vision based method. In support of this application, the first approach is to take out the function, or somewhat, the set of geometric features that represent the signature. By way of these function sets, we must train neural networks with an efficient neural network algorithm. This educated neural network classifies the signature as authentic or fake in the confirmation phase.

REFERENCES

Bashir, Z. A., & El-Hawary, M. E. (2009). Applying wavelets to short-term load forecasting using PSO-based neural networks. *IEEE Transactions on Power Systems*, *24*(1), 20–27. doi:10.1109/TPWRS.2008.2008606

Basu, J. K., Bhattacharyya, D., & Kim, T. H. (2010). Use of artificial neural network in pattern recognition. *International Journal of Software Engineering and Its Applications, 4*(2).

Burns, R. S. (1995). The use of artificial neural networks for the intelligent optimal control of surface ships. *IEEE Journal of Oceanic Engineering, 20*(1), 65–72. doi:10.1109/48.380245

Chow, T. W. S., & Leung, C. T. (1996). Neural network based short-term load forecasting using weather compensation. *IEEE Transactions on Power Systems, 11*(4), 1736–1742. doi:10.1109/59.544636

Le, T. H. (2011). Applying artificial neural networks for face recognition. *Advances in Artificial Neural Systems, 2011*, 15. doi:10.1155/2011/673016

Lewellen, M. (1998, August). Neural network recognition of spelling errors. In *Proceedings of the 36th Annual Meeting of the Association for Computational Linguistics and 17th International Conference on Computational Linguistics-Volume 2* (pp. 1490-1492). Association for Computational Linguistics.

Mani, N., & Srinivasan, B. (1997, October). Application of artificial neural network model for optical character recognition. In *1997 IEEE International Conference on Systems, Man, and Cybernetics. Computational Cybernetics and Simulation* (Vol. 3, pp. 2517-2520). IEEE. 10.1109/ICSMC.1997.635312

Mansour, A. H., Zen, G., Salh, A., Hayder, H., & Alabdeen, Z. (2015). *Voice recognition Using back propagation algorithm in neural networks*. Academic Press.

Pao, Y. (1989). *Adaptive pattern recognition and neural networks*. Academic Press.

Pradeep, J., Srinivasan, E., & Himavathi, S. (2011, March). Neural network based handwritten character recognition system without feature extraction. In 2011 international conference on computer, communication and electrical technology (ICCCET) (pp. 40-44). IEEE. doi:10.1109/ICCCET.2011.5762513

Schürmann, J. (1996). *Pattern classification: a unified view of statistical and neural approaches*. Wiley.

Unar, M. A., & Murray-Smith, D. J. (1999). Automatic steering of ships using neural networks. *International Journal of Adaptive Control and Signal Processing, 13*(4), 203–218. doi:10.1002/(SICI)1099-1115(199906)13:4<203::AID-ACS544>3.0.CO;2-T

Chapter 2
Comprehensive Modelling of ANN

Meghna Babubhai Patel
Ganpat University, India

Jagruti N. Patel
Ganpat University, India

Upasana M. Bhilota
Ganpat University, India

ABSTRACT

An artificial neural network (ANN) is an information processing modelling of the human brain inspired by the way biological nervous systems behave. There are about 100 billion neurons in the human brain. Each neuron has a connection point between 1,000 and 100,000. The key element of this paradigm is the novel structure of the information processing system. In the human brain, information is stored in such a way as to be distributed, and we can extract more than one piece of this information when necessary from our memory in parallel. We are not mistaken when we say that a human brain is made up of thousands of very powerful parallel processors. It is composed of a large number of highly interconnected processing elements (neurons) working in union to solve specific problems. ANN, like people, learns by example. The chapter includes characteristics of artificial neural networks, structure of ANN, elements of artificial neural networks, pros and cons of ANN.

DOI: 10.4018/978-1-7998-4042-8.ch002

INTRODUCTION

Features of Artificial Neural Network

- It's an impartially applied scientific model.
- Its contains vast figure of interrelated handling components named neurons to do all operations.
- Information put in storage in the neurons are basically the weighted linkage of neurons.
- The input signals reach at the processing components through associates and attaching masses.
- It has the capability to study, remember and simplify from the given data by suitable assignment and adjustment of weights.
- The mutual activities of the neurons define its computational power, and no single neuron transmits explicit data.

Structure of ANN

An ANN is recognized as a Neural Network, it is mainly based on mathematical model based on the arrangement and roles of natural neural networks. This is almost a non-natural human nervous system to receive, process and transmit information in Computer Science (Mehrotra et al., 1997) (Agatonovic-Kustrin & Beresford, 2000).

The ANN idea is created on the certainty of the functioning of the People mind in creation the accurate influences can be copied for use of silicon and cables like neurons and active a short branched extension of a nerve cell.

The People mind is ready up of 86 billion nerve cells is known as neurons. neurons connected to a multiple other cells by Axons. A short branched extension of a nerve cell accepts the provocations of the outside atmosphere or the assistances of the physical structures.

The inputs generate electrical compulsions, which are transmit through the neural network. A neuron cannot send any message to some other neuron to solve the any difficulties. (Mehrotra et al., 1997)[2].

ANNs are made up of multiple nodes that mimic the genetic neurons of the People mind. Neurons associated with bonds and interrelate to each other.

The intersection is takings contribution information and do basic Process on the information. The outcome of these processes is spread to next neurons. The productivity on individually intersection applies to the beginning or importance of the node.

Separately connection is connected to a weight. ANNs are skilled of learning and altering weight values.

The structure of an ANN contains of artificial neurons in a clustered layer. The ANN structure contains three layer like: an input layers, hidden layers, and an output layers (Agatonovic-Kustrin & Beresford, 2000; Artificial Neural Networks in Data Mining, n.d.; Maind & Wankar, 2014; Mehrotra et al., 1997; Papantonopoulos, 2016; Sharma et al., 2012; Xenon Stack, n.d.).

Details of layers in a neural network see in below Figure 1.

1. **Input Layer:** Every input is sent to the prototypical through this layer.
2. **Hidden Layer:** There are many masked layers used to procedure the input acknowledged from the input layers.
3. **Output Layer:** Post-processing data is accessible at the output layer.

Figure 1. Structure of ANN

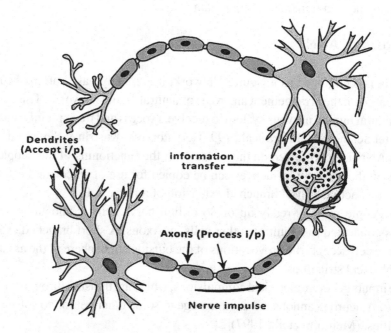

- **Input Layer:** Input layer is the starting layer of the neural network. The layer links to the outside atmosphere that offerings a strategy of the neural network. This layer handles only input. Gets the input and transfers it to hidden layers and detailed in the Hidden layer. The input layers have to signify the form for working in the neural network. Each inputs neuron has to mean approximately autonomous variable that influences the outcome of the neural network. It does not calculations on the given values like no weight and preference value connected. In figure there are four input signals x1, x2, x3, x4 (Agatonovic-Kustrin & Beresford, 2000; Artificial Neural Networks in Data Mining, n.d.; Maind & Wankar, 2014; Mehrotra et al., 1997).

- **Hidden Layers:** It is one type bridge layer that lies of the input layers and the output layers. That is why the layer is answerable for extract the essential features from the input data. The layer works on to get the input value from the previous layer. The hidden layer of the group of neurons that have the startup function applied. This layer has devices that put on altered transformations in the given data. A hidden layer is a group of straight up arranged neurons (Rendering) (Agatonovic-Kustrin & Beresford, 2000; Artificial Neural Networks in Data Mining, n.d.; Maind & Wankar, 2014; Mehrotra et al., 1997; Papantonopoulos, 2016; Sharma et al., 2012; Xenon Stack, n.d.).

Given figure shows 5 hidden layers. In that, the layer contains 4, 5 and 6 devices respectively first, second and third, the 4th consumes 4, and the 5th consumes 3 devices. In the last layer passes the values to the output layer. All devices in middle layer are linked to every device in the last layer. Finally, the hidden layers were completely connected (Maind & Wankar, 2014)[5].

Much research has been done to assess the quantity of neurons in the hidden layer, but none of them has managed to find the exact outcome. on that they define how the problem arise in middle layer. Assume that the information is in linearly separated, without use of middle layer the trigger function can be applied on the input layer, for solve the problem.

When complex decisions create for some problems, we can access 3, 4 and 5 middle layer dependent on the notch of difficulty of the problematic or the notch of accuracy essential. It certainly does not mean that if we continue to increase the number of layers, the neural network will provide great accuracy! A phase occurs when the accuracy matures constant or cuts when we enhance a further layer! In adding, we also necessity to compute the amount of neurons in the network.

If the problem is bigger than the neurons, In the hidden layer there are less neurons to identify signals in a complex database. If they have avoidable neurons in the network, an over-adjustment can occur. So far, various procedures have not provided the particular method for computing the amount of hidden layers, as well as the number of neurons in each hidden layer. (Agatonovic-Kustrin & Beresford, 2000; Artificial Neural Networks in Data Mining, n.d.; Maind & Wankar, 2014; Papantonopoulos, 2016; Xenon Stack, n.d.).

- **Output Layer:** This layer is last layer in the linkage and receives the inputs from the last hidden layer. The last layer of the neural network gathers and

Figure 2. Processing elements

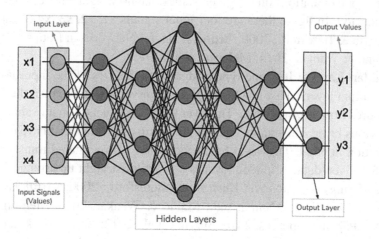

transfers the data consequently, in the method it was planned for. The design offered by the last layer can be drawn straight to the input layer. The number of neurons in this layer must be straight connected to the form of effort performed by the neural network. To control the number of neurons in this layer, initial reflect the planned use of the neural network. With this layer we can obtain the preferred values and preferred series. In last, we given 3 neurons and get three outputs like y1,y2,y3 (Artificial Neural Networks in Data Mining, n.d.)[5-7].

Components of Artificial Neural Networks

Posture in mind the discussed features, we can gather the basic components of any non-natural neural network as follows (Agatonovic-Kustrin & Beresford, 2000; Artificial Neural Networks in Data Mining, n.d.; Maind & Wankar, 2014; Mehrotra et al., 1997; Xenon Stack, n.d.):

- Handling Components
- Topology
- Learning Algorithm

Handling Components

The Ribonucleic Acid (RNA) is a basic computer prototypical of a biotic neuron network, an RNA contains of simple treatment parts or components like to neurons in the mind.

The Figure 2 displays the general configuration of processing elements

In common, a processing unit is composed of a summation part trailed by a productivity part see in Figure 3. The basic purpose is to summation of takings n input and weight for every input then compute the weighted sum of these inputs.

Figure 3. Composed of a summation unit

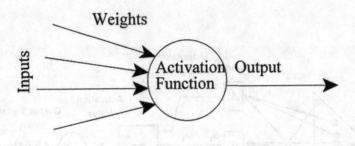

On the basis of the symbol of the weight of every entry, it is resolute whether the entrance has an +ve or -ve weight. The weighted amount of the summation entity is called the initiation worth and, depending on the sign after the beginning value, the outcome is generated.

Entry and exit may be continuous or discrete, as well as deterministic or uncertain.

Topology

The ANN will develop suitable only when all the processing elements are appropriately prepared, so that the pattern recognition task can be performed.

This association or organization of the handling components, their mutual connections, inputs and outputs, is called a topology.

Typically, in an ANN, handling parts are layered and entirely elements in a specific level have the similar beginning and amount produced values. The assembly between the layers can be made in some ways, for example, a part to procedure a layer associated to a part to alternative layer, a part to procedure a layer associated to a part to the similar layer, etc.

Nearly of the topologies normally used in ANN:

- Instar
- Outstar
- Group of Instars
- Group of Outstar
- Bidirectional Associative Memory

•   Autoassociative Memory

The below figure displays an procedure of two layers F1 and F2 with an M and N number of handling parts, each in the Instar and Outstar topologies.

Learning Algorithm

Figure 4.

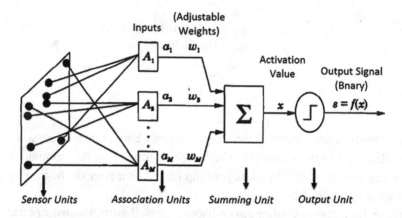

The last main components of any ANN are learning algorithms or laws. The functioning of any neural network is ruled by neural subtleties, which includes both the subtleties of the activation state and the dynamics of synaptic weight.

The procedures or learning rules are executions of synaptic subtleties and are defined in terms of primary derived weights. The learning rules can be managed, unverified or a mixture of the two.

Figure 5.

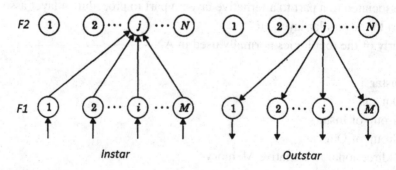

Approximately the top recognized learning processes are:

- Hebb's Law
- Perception Learning Law
- Delta Learning Law
- Wildrow & Hoff LMS Learning Law
- Correlation Learning Law
- Instar Learning Law
- Outstar Learning Law

Pros and Cons of ANN

ANN have marched in the world of 20th era is developing fast. Today, in present day examine the ANN advantages and disadvantages means problems encountered during the use of ANN. It is not forgeable that day by day problems in ANN is going to reduce and advantages of ANN is increasing. So, now a days ANN become incredible part of live. The following section discuss the advantages and drawbacks of ANN (Kohli et al., 2014; Mijwel, 2018; Mohamed, 2016).

Advantages of ANN

ANN has benefits that best suitable based on particular problems and situations:

Storage of Information

Like traditional programming, the information is stored in the network instead of the database. Losing little information from one location does not prevent the network from connecting.

Capability of Working with Lack Knowledge

The ANN is established on adaptive learning. In ANN the output is generated even with partial knowledge after ANN training. The performance depends on significance of missing data. The ANN has ability to learn itself so it doesn't need to be reprogrammed.

Having Superior Fault Tolerance

Compare to traditional network, ANN provide superior potential for fault tolerance because the network is capable for regenerating a failure of any component, without loss of stored information. It means the ANN able to found missing information or nodes or servers which cannot communicate in the case when the network proportion done on multiple server and machines.

Easy Implementation

ANN can be easily implemented without any complications. It is adaptable and flexible because neural networks are robust for cracking difficulties. Neural networks are efficient in their software design and experts agree that the benefits of using ANN balance the possibilities.

Distributed Memory ANN

In order for the ANN to learn, it is essential to define the examples and teach the network based on the desired result, showing the cases to the network. The success of the network is directly relational to the instances selected and, if the experience cannot be exposed to the network in all its facets, the network may generate an incorrect outcome.

Corruption Progressive

A network decreases over time and undertakes relation poverty. The network problem is not corrected instantly.

Capability to do Machine Learning

ANN study procedures and do choices by remarking on comparable procedures. ANN are flexible and take the ability to learn, generalize and adapt to situations based on its results.

ANNs Can Generalize

ANN can learn organically. This means that the outputs of an ANN are not entirely limited by the inputs and that the results are initially provided by a proficient method. Artificial neural networks have the capability to simplify their inputs. This capability is invaluable for automation and pattern recognition systems.

Later knowledge the original contributions and their relations, it can also conclude unseen relations from unseen information, allowing the prototypical to simplify and guess unseen information. Generalize knowledge to produce appropriate responses to unknown situations.

Parallel Processing Capability

ANN have the capability to absorb and prototypical non-linear and difficult relations, which is actually main as in actual lifecycle, various relations among contributions and productions are non-linear and complex.

Non-Linearity

A neural network can do duties that a linear program cannot do. This functionality permits the network to obtain information efficiently while learning. This is a different benefit above a usually linear network, which is insufficient for showing non-linear information. ANN have a numerical power proficient of deed many jobs in same time. When a part of the neural network breakdowns down, it can continue smoothly due to its parallel nature. Nonlinear systems have the ability to find shortcuts to get exclusive resolutions in computation. The systems can also derive associates between statistics facts, rather than waiting for records from a data source to be clearly associated. This nonlinear shortcut tool is used in artificial neural networks, which kinds it valued for profitable analysis of large information.

Self-Repair

Artificial neural networks can do more than route around parts of the network that no longer work. If they are asked to find specific data that no longer communicate, these artificial neural networks can regenerate large amounts of data by inference and help determine which node is not working. This attribute is useful for networks that require their users to be aware of the current state of the network and result in self-debugging and network diagnostics.

Scientists are now trying to understand the capabilities, assumptions, and applicability of various approaches that can dramatically improve the performance of artificial neural network systems.

Disadvantages of ANN

Dependency on Hardware

ANN require processor accordingly its structure. The processor must contain the power of parallel processing. That's why, the recognition of the tackle is dependent.

Inexplicable Network Performance

The main vital disadvantage of ANN because when ANN generate an exploratory solution then it doesn't give hint for how and why it's generated like this. That's why it degrades the trust factor on network.

Define Appropriate Network Structure

The rules are not defined for ANN structure. So, based on trial and error and with experience, proper network structure is generating.

Trouble to Showing Problems to the Network

The problems should be translated in numerical value before presented to ANN because ANN can purely work with numeric standards. Network performance is directly influenced by the display mechanism which is confirmed and depends on the capacity of the user.

The Unknown Time Duration

The training will be considered as completed because the system compacts to assured importance of a fault on samples and because of this value cannot obtain finest result. So, for large network ANN requires high processing time.

REFERENCES

2. Agatonovic-Kustrin, S., & Beresford, R. (2000). Basic concepts of artificial neural network (ANN) modeling and its application in pharmaceutical research. *Journal of Pharmaceutical and Biomedical Analysis, 22*(5), 717–727. doi:10.1016/S0731-7085(99)00272-1 PMID:10815714

4. *Artificial Neural Networks in Data Mining.* (n.d.). Computer & Information System, Sadat Academy for Management Sciences.

8. Kohli, S., Miglani, S., & Rapariya, R. (2014). Basics of Artificial Neural Network. *International Journal of Computing Science and Mobile Computing, 3*(9), 745-751.

3. Maind, S. B., & Wankar, P. (2014). Research paper on basic of artificial neural network. *International Journal on Recent and Innovation Trends in Computing and Communication, 2*(1), 96–100.

1. Mehrotra, K., Mohan, C. K., & Ranka, S. (1997). *Elements of artificial neural nets*. Academic Press.

9. Mijwel, M. (2018). *Artificial neural networks advantages and disadvantages*. Academic Press.

10. Mohamed, N. E. (2016). Artificial Neural Networks in Data Mining. *IOSR J Comput Eng*, *18*(6), 55–59.

6. Papantonopoulos, G. (2016). *On the use of complexity methods in*. Personalized Periodontology and Implant Dentistry.

7. Sharma, V., Rai, S., & Dev, A. (2012). A comprehensive study of artificial neural networks. *International Journal of Advanced Research in Computer Science and Software Engineering*, *2*(10).

5. Xenon Stack. (n.d.). https://www.xenonstack.com/blog/artificial-neural-network-applications/

Chapter 3
Fundamental Categories of Artificial Neural Networks

Arunaben Prahladbhai Gurjar
Ganpat University, India

Shitalben Bhagubhai Patel
Ganpat University, India

ABSTRACT

The new era of the world uses artificial intelligence (AI) and machine learning. The combination of AI and machine learning is called artificial neural network (ANN). Artificial neural network can be used as hardware or software-based components. Different topology and learning algorithms are used in artificial neural networks. Artificial neural network works similarly to the functionality of the human nervous system. ANN is working as a nonlinear computing model based on activities performed by human brain such as classification, prediction, decision making, visualization just by considering previous experience. ANN is used to solve complex, hard-to-manage problems by accruing knowledge about the environment. There are different types of artificial neural networks available in machine learning. All types of artificial neural networks work based of mathematical operation and require a set of parameters to get results. This chapter gives overview on the various types of neural networks like feed forward, recurrent, feedback, classification-predication.

DOI: 10.4018/978-1-7998-4042-8.ch003

CONVOLUTIONAL NEURAL NETWORKS

A CNN architecture consists of different ConvNet stages. For each degree winding of the following comparison module / Sub sampling order module. While the traditional clustering ConvNet modules conceal the average or most of the groups, this grouping uses LP. Ordinance and that, unless it is to become a parameter, as opposed to subtractive. Subtractive is not division, that is, on the average of the value of each of its immediate surroundings; own extended withdrawn(Lawrence,1997). Finally, as is known, also multi-stage the functions that are used in place of the same rank.

One-dimensional convolution is an operation between a vector of weight m 2 Rm and vector entries seen as a series of s 2 Rs. The carrier m is the convolution filter. In particular, we think of it as an insertion phrase and yes 2 R is a unique function value associated with the ith word of the phrase. The idea behind the one-dimensional convolution is to take the point product of the vector m with every m-gram in the sentence s another series c:

$$c_j = m \mid s_j - m + 1 : j \tag{1}$$

Equation 1 gives rise to two types of convolutions according to the scope of the J. Lo strait index the type of convolution requires that s ≥ give me a series c 2 Rs-m + 1 with j going from m one s. The broad type of convolution does not have this requirements for s or m and give a series of c 2 Rs + m-1 where the index j varies from 1 to s +m - 1. Enter out of range values where i <1 where i> s are considered zero. The result of the narrow convolution is a partial sequence of the result of wide convolution (Cireşan,2011). Two types of one dimensional convolution are illustrated in Fig. 1.

Figure 1. Narrow and wide types of CNN
m=5

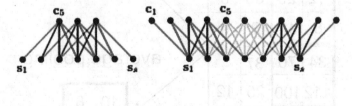

Why ConvNets Over Feed-Forward Neural Nets?

An image is just a matrix of values in pixels, isn't it? So why not paste the image (for example a description of 3x3 images into a 9x1 vector) and send it to a multi-part Perceptron for processing?

Figure 2. A classic convolutional network

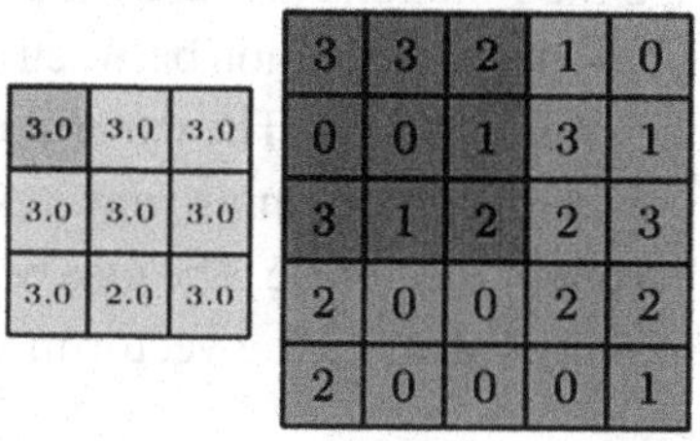

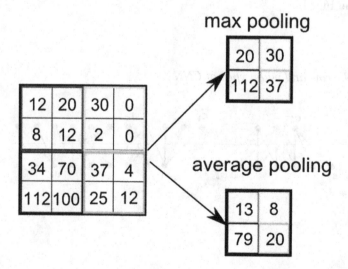

In the case of high quality imagery(Kalchbrenner,2014), the method may show sufficient scale during class imaging, but is low or poorly organized for complex images with pixel dependencies.

ConvNet is able to efficiently capture spatial and model dependencies in the image through the use of appropriate filters. The architecture is more efficient for the data

Figure 3. Flattening of a 3x3 image matrix into a 9x1 vector

structure due to the reduced number of parameters involved and the overload of the load. In other words, the network can be formed to better understand image stability.

Input Image

In the figure we have a separate RGB image of the three color areas: red, green and blue. There are many color spaces that contain images: grayscale, RGB, HSV, CMYK, and so on.

Figure 4. 4x4x3 RGB Image

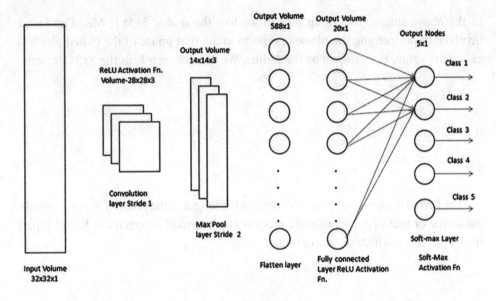

Figure 5. Convoluting a 5x5x1 image with a 3x3x1 kernel to get a 3x3x1 convolved feature

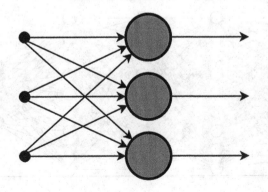

You can imagine the intensity of the calculation when the images are the desired size, for example 8K (7680 × 4320). The role of ConvNet is to shrink the images into a simpler form to process, without losing the essential functions to get a good prediction. This is important when designing an architecture that is not only powerful for learning functions, but also scalable for large data sets.

Convolution Layer — The Kernel

Image Dimensions = 5 (Height) x 5 (Breadth) x 1 (Number of channels, e.g. RGB)

In the above image, the green part looks like the image 5x5x1, Me. The factor involved in performing the phase operation in the first phase of the called phase is called the value, K, is shown by the radius. We have chosen K as the 3x3x1 matrix.

Core / Filter, K = 1 0 1

0 1 0

1 0 1

The kernel moves 4 or 9 times because of the length of the process = 1 (unsigned), each time or matrix multiplication process is performed between the K and P part of the image on which the kernel falls.

Figure 6. Movement of the Kernel

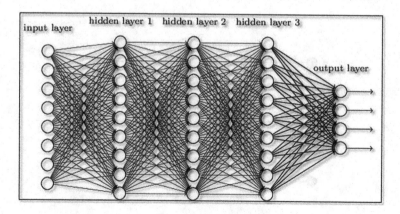

The filter moves to the right with the column type until it fills the width. As you progress, it moves down to the start (left) of the image as well as melting the value and adjusting the function so that the whole image is in good shape.

For multichannel (ie RGB) images, the kernel has a depth similar to that of the input image. Matrix multiplication is performed between Kn and In ([K1, I1], [K2, I2], [K3, I3]) and the total output is added along the ring to obtain an entity output joining a single-depth channel.

Figure 7. Convolution operation on a MxNx3 image matrix with a 3x3x3 Kernel

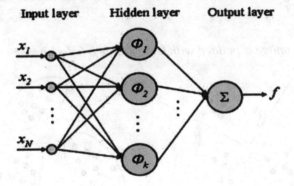

The purpose of the design is to remove high-step tasks, as a process, from a low-level image. ConvNets doesn't just need to be locked on one platform. In fact, the first

Figure 8. Convolution Operation with Stride Length = 2

Linear separability

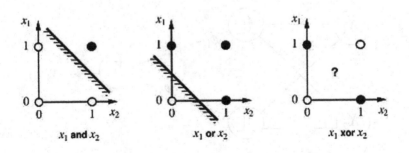

ConvLayer was responsible for capturing small-scale events such as location, color, grid path, and so on. With the addition of a wall, design is like high-performance, so finding a network that is good at integrating images into a store is the way to go.

There are two types of service costs: one is that the link is decreasing relative to participation, the other is increasing in size or similarity. This is done by applying for an Undergraduate Degree in either a Secondary agreement or a Secondary degree.

Same Padding (Boureau, 2010)

If we add the 5x5x1 image to the 6x6x1 image, write the 3x3x1 graph above and see that the only gene shown is the size of 5x5x1. That is why the name - paragraph

Figure 9. 5x5x1 image is padded with 0s to create a 6x6x1 image

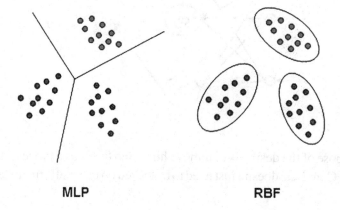

MLP   RBF

Figure 10. 3x3 pooling over 5x5 convolved features

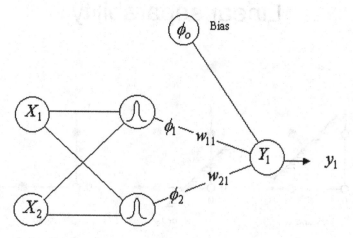

is paper. On the other hand, if we perform the same operation without a table, we get a square with the same kernel components (3x3x1) - Advanced Manufacturing.

The following functions include various functions such as GIF files to help you better understand why we need to work with People and virtualization to deliver the best results for us.

Pooling Layer

Like the bonding layer, the polar layer is responsible for reducing the size of the bonding process. This will reduce the processing power required to process the data by reducing the size. In addition, it is advisable to take in the main features of the visitors of rotation and positioning, thus keeping them in good working position of the model.

Figure 11. Types of pooling

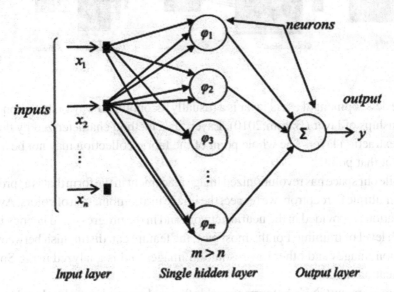

m > n

Input layer   **Single hidden layer**   **Output layer**

There are two types of pooling: max pooling and average pooling. Max Pooling returns the maximum value of the image segment covered by the kernel. On the other hand, drawing compression returns an average of the total value of the part of the image that contains the kernel.

Noise suppressant is also done by Max pooling. Generally it helps to remove noisy activations and do de-noising with region decrement. At next end Average pooling operate for dimensionality reduction as a noise suppressing system. The output is Average pooling is less effective than Max Pooling.

The broad layer and the cluster layer form an i-th tool of convolutional neuron networks. Depending on the complexity of the images, the number of components may be greater, but depending on the severity of the stress.

After following the above, we conducted a mod to understand the behavior. Moving forward, we will move on to the final version and feed the neural network for treatment.

Figure 12. Classification — fully connected layer (FC Layer)

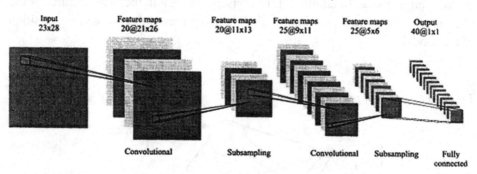

The development of a real layer is a (usually) economical way to study non-linear relationships of layer (Baroni,2010). Layers as a method characterized by the flow of the extraction layer. The whole point of the fabric collection may not be a linear design at that point.

While our space has revolutionized image placement in the form that is appropriate for our multiple Perceptron, we respect the image in a combination of colors. Aviation information is provided in the neural network and in the progress, and latency is used for each level of training. For the most part, the feature can distinguish between high resolution images and other low resolution images and is analyzed using Softmax classification method.

There are many CNN platforms available that are become key to develop algorithms that are powerful and powerful for all AI anticipated future.

Feed Forward Neural Network

This neural network is one of the simplest simple networks, while data or inputs work in the same way. The data passes through the input and output fields at the output.

This network of neurons may not be secret. In simple terms, it has an avant-garde interface and does not extend using standard classification functions.

Below are the networking and networking sites. Here, the price of a product or a product is calculated and the output is given. The result can be seen if it is higher than the price, ie the initial neuron (usually 0) as well as the active neuron with a positive output (usually 1) if it does not burn and eliminating the potential value (usually -1).

Figure 13. A classic feed forward neural network

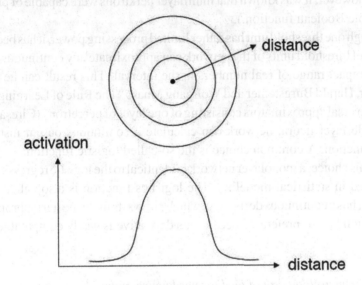

The anticipated neural network is an artificial neural network to which the connections between the nodes do not form a cycle. (Sermanet,2012) As such, it differs from recurrent neural networks.

The direct-acting neural network was the first and simplest type of artificial neural network designed. On this network, the information is only moved one way forward, from the input nodes to the hidden nodes (if any) and to the output nodes. No cycles or loops on the net.

One of the output nodes; tickets are fed directly to departures via a series of pesos. The sum of the products of weights and inputs is calculated in each node, and if the value is above the threshold (usually 0), the neurons are turned on and the value takes activation (usually 1); otherwise, the value is removed (usually -1). Neurons with this kind of activation function are also called artificial neurons or linear threshold units. In literature, the term perceptron often refers to networks that consist only of one of these units.

You can create a perctron using any value for enabled and disabled states whenever the threshold value is between the two.

The tax collectors can be trained by a simple learning algorithm commonly called delta rule. Calculate the errors between the calculated output data and the output samples and use this option to create a weight adjustment, thus implementing a gradient descent form.

Single-layer perceptors can only study linearly separable patterns; in 1969, in a well-known monograph called Perceptrons, Marvin Minsky and Seymour Paper showed that it was impossible to study the XOR function of a single-layer drum network (however, it was known that multilayer perktrons were capable of producing any possible Boolean function.).

Although one threshold unit has rather limited processing power, it has been shown that parallel threshold units of the network can approximate any continuous function from a compact range of real numbers in the interval. This result can be found in Peter Auer, Harald Burgsteiner and Wolfgang Maass "The Rule of Learning for very simple universal approximators consisting of one layer of percetron" (Cireşan,2011).

A single layer neural network can calculate a continuous output instead of a passage function. A common choice is the so-called logistic function:

With this choice, a monolayer network is identical to the logistic regression model widely used in statistical modeling. The logistics function is also called sigmoid function. It has a continuous derivative, which allows its use in posterior propagation. This function is also preferable because its derivative is easily computable:

Figure 14. The architecture of feed forward neural network

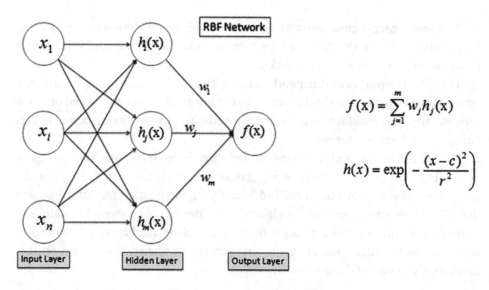

{\displa{ystyle $f'(x) = f(x)(1 - f(x))$}$f(x) = 1$

(The fact that f satisfies the differential equation above can easily be shown by applying the Chain Rule)

A feed-forward neural network is classification algorithm galvanize by biological concept. There are number of simple neuron like refine unit formulated in layers and every entity in layer coherent with all other entity in preceding layer. There is no equality in all connections, every connection might have various potency or density. The knowledge of network are encode by weights on these connections.

The cost of training for the training sessions reflects the difference between the estimate made by our model and the exact target value that we are trying to achieve, which is a one-time price, he says the network is reviewing everything. Similar to machine learning cycles, manual control networks have also been created using slower learning. In this teaching method, an algorithm is used, such as the gradient.

To choose an exercise that I think increasingly worth taking another example of traditional models.

In cases where we compare the distribution model $p(j \mid i, \Sigma)$, and we use this for us in terms of information transfer between the train and the model is an affordable price. You can also choose to add to this number for x and y not modify in any part, in a way, in order to predict differs of distribution.

The distribution and use of the process is to be turned again because they are in the best of the two Properties. As it is written, the average cost function should be possible.

From the output of the activation depends on the price of the same is not part of the investors.

A particular form of cost function 100 (W, B, S Onan Sela), where W is the weight of the neural network, the network is destroyed R, S has entered the exercise is one of ideal is the desired exit from training him cf.

Some functions can be taken:

Quadratic Cost Function

$$C_{MST}(W, B, S^r, E^r) = 0.5 \sum_j (a_j^L - E_j^r)^2$$

This function is also namely like squared error, maximum likelihood, and sum squared error.

Cross-Entropy Cost Function

$$C_{CE}\left(W, E, S^R, E^R\right) = -\sum_J \left[E_j^r \ln a_j^L + \left(1 - E_j^r\right) \ln \left(1 - a_j^L\right)\right]$$

Exponential Cost Function

$$C_{EXP}\left(W, B, S^r, E^r\right) = \Gamma \exp\left[\frac{1}{\Gamma} \sum_j \left(a_j^L - E_j^r\right)^2\right]$$

Hellinger Distance Cost Function

$$C_{HD}\left(W, B, S^r, E^r\right) = \frac{1}{\sqrt{2}} \sum_j \left(\sqrt{a_j^L} - \sqrt{E_j^r}\right)^2$$

This is a function is also referred to as the statistical distance.

The output of those units that output layer. Their job is to get us the desired output or forecast to complete the operation so that the neural network to run. The output will be close to the selection function is taken. Nothing can be hidden from drive to drive the neural network can also be as a monitor.

The output is equally chosen;

The Linear Units

The proportions of the output unit used for an output of linear Gaussian output distributions, these are connected, according to a transformation that does not propose the compatible output level. Given the functions h, a linear vector layer of output of the generator:

$$\hat{Y} = W^{\mathrm{T}}h + b$$

Linear Function Unit

This is tantamount to maximizing the linear minimize the superposition of bars with ignorance of the average, and the propaganda street makes it easier for most likely to support the Gaussian covariance distribution(Blunsom,2006).

The usefulness of these units is to say, that the lines do not become saturated, that is to say, what is the same as He is always, and does not come: there is not them. These units can therefore be a problem because according to their algorithms.

Sigmoid Unit Function

$$S(x) = \frac{1}{1+e^x} = \frac{e^x}{e^x + 1}$$

To solve the above question of a binary kind, as we combine the top and the bottom of the output units have no probability. The Gulf components of the output unit 2, which uses a linear layer consists of calculating $z = w * h$ B uses the activation function and then transformed into z are opposite. When at any time the loss of all rights and without hesitation others, such as the level of a square at the same time a little bit of error, it may be useful to saturate the experience of loss. Therefore, the most desirable.

Softmax Unit

The units are used for softmax output distributions multitudinali, because of the probability distribution of a discrete variable with n possible values, this function can also be considered as a bay associated with it, general manager of the probability distribution of the binary variable. Softmax. The function is defined as follows:

$$soft\max(z)_i = \frac{\exp(z_i)}{\sum_j \exp(z_i)}$$

When Sigmoid is running, the Softmax feature may also be weak, which means it can reduce obstacles to learning. In the case of Softmax, the outputs being larger, the units can always be filled when the entered values change.

These groups are dominated by the stock market because they are generally at Level 1 and not so much, and its value for one, is clear that other units of production are closer to value 0.

Hidden Units

Searching for the hidden unit type is also a powerful finding that no unit can ensure that everything is in order for every problem, but we still have units with a clear choice in the beginning. For example, the line numbers are changed or called Relu. It is widely used, because of this knowledge, rather than test cases, which, on the other hand, cannot be predefined before they work. Selecting the hidden option option will include trial and error, which requires a specific type of corrector to be properly managed and tested.

Possible options for hidden options are:

ReLU(Rectified Linear Units)

These functions use the activation function defined by g(z)

$$g\left(z\right) = \max\{0, z\}$$

Optimize similar to the linear rails are easy, and only 0. Since their role is always the case with a hearty side in unison. The direction of development of learning useful for the activation features that characterize the effects of second order.

Relu is able to have the disadvantage that they do not know the method of gradient is activated, in which there is none.

Radial Basis Function Neural Network

Typically, an RBFN is composed of three layers: the input layer, the RBF layer (masked layer), and the output layer. The masked layer inputs are the linear combinations of scalar weights and the input vector x=[ ] x1, x2, L, xn T, where the scalar weights are usually assigned. Thus, the complete input vector appears for each neuron of the hidden layer. Inbound vectors are mapped by radial base functions on each hidden node. The output layer produces a vector y = [ ] y1, y2, L, ym for m outputs by linearly combining the outputs of the hidden nodes to produce the final output. Figure 1 shows the structure of a single output RBF network; the network output can be obtained via

$$y = f(x) = \sum_{i=1}^{k} w_i \varphi_i (x)$$

where f (x) is the final output,)(i). denotes the radial basis function of the i-th hidden node, w_i denotes the hidden weight at the output corresponding to the hidden i-node, and k is the number total hidden nodes (Sun et al.,2009)

Figure 15. A typical radial basis function neural network

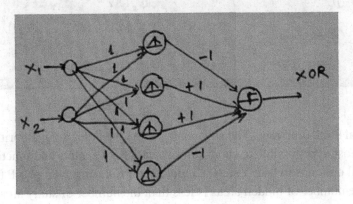

Ligament function, which describes the distance function between the center and the passenger multidimensional approach and a predefined vector. There are other types of radial basic functions. Q1 "RBFNN general education is divided into two stages

1. Determine the parameters of the radius functions, namely the Gaussian center and the propagation width. In general, the grouping method k-means, as a rule, here.
2. In real time, determine the way out of the weight management training process. Usually shorter mean square (LM) or recursive (RLS) squares are smaller.
3. Everything, the scene, first of all, is very important, and the place where, under the passage above, and from the moment of the number of centers, the performance of RBFNN itself.

One of the great benefits of RBF networks is learning (Zaremba,2014) The algorithm involves solving a linear problem and is therefore faster. Because of the linearity of the basic function, the network can do it. Create complex non-linear mappings. Theoretical learning strategies Can be created with changes of place and

Figure 16. Chart for Linear separability.

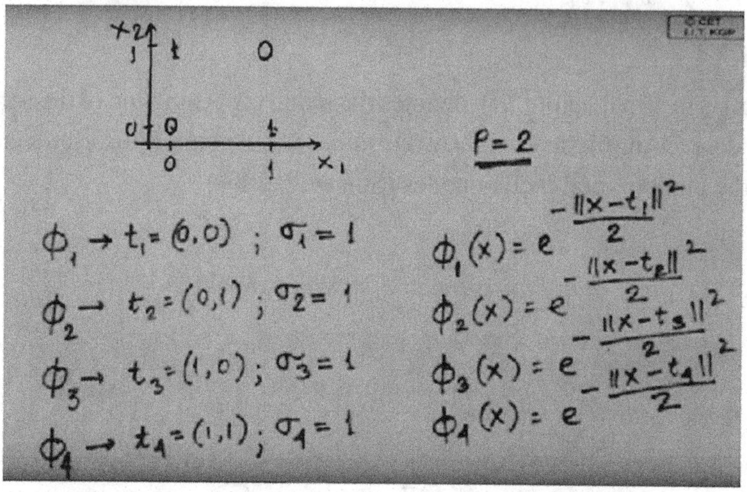

form Radial basic functions. The advantages of the linear learning algorithm it will always be lost. It is possible to choose from a variety of centers and functions Way. The natural option is to take Yi as the input vector Creating data, or XP time of its traffic. The number of hidden areas is less than the number of study areas.

If the network is used as a grouping model, the base number usually the operations are considered to be larger in size .

Inclusion criteria. Then, the hidden units plan the input vectors instead of the line.

The size of the quantity. Work can be divided into tasks

This is an upward trajectory even if it does not divide the root

Especially In this case, a layer of weight differs between the hidden values

Figure 17. Distinction between MLP and RBF

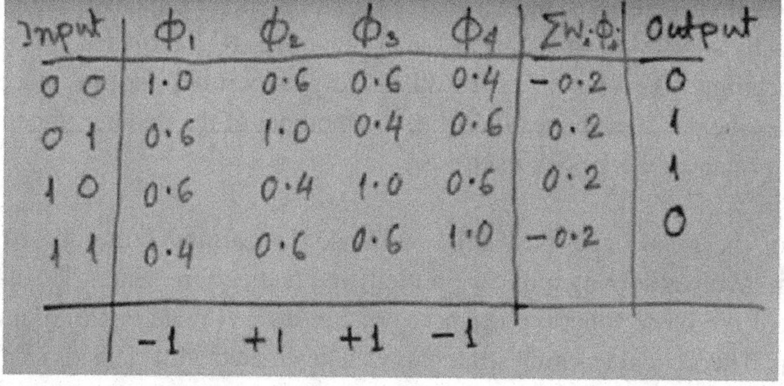

Input	ϕ_1	ϕ_2	ϕ_3	ϕ_4	$\sum w_i \phi_i$	Output
0 0	1.0	0.6	0.6	0.4	-0.2	0
0 1	0.6	1.0	0.4	0.6	0.2	1
1 0	0.6	0.4	1.0	0.6	0.2	1
1 1	0.4	0.6	0.6	1.0	-0.2	0
	-1	+1	+1	-1		

And the output components are good at giving accurate signals

[Improving the Generalization Properties of Radial Basis Function Neural Networks]

In a single perceptron / multi-layer perceptron (MLP), we have only linear segmentation because it contains input and output levels (multiple layers hidden in MLP).

Figure 18. RBNN increases extents of feature vector.

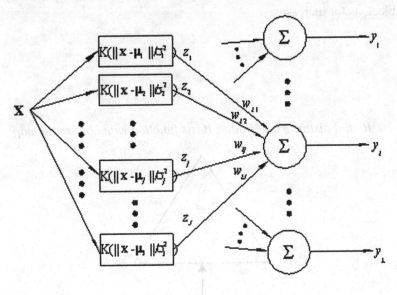

For example, functions and, or are linearly separated and the function XOR is not linearly different.

To separate non-linearities, at least one hidden layer is required.

Figure 19. Simplest diagram shows the architecture of RBNN

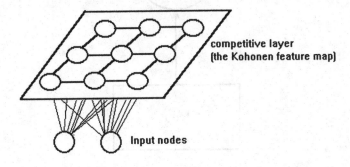

What R RBNN does is convert the input signal to another format and feed it into the network to achieve linear separation.

B RBNN is structurally similar to perceptron (MLP)

RBNN is temperate of input, hidden, and output layer. RBNN is strictly limited to have exactly one hidden layer. We call this hidden layer as feature vector.

Before starting the classification problem, we apply a nonlinear transfer function to the function vector.

- When we increase the size of the object vector, the linear separability of the object vector increases.

Figure 20. Radial distance and Radial Basis function with confrontal map

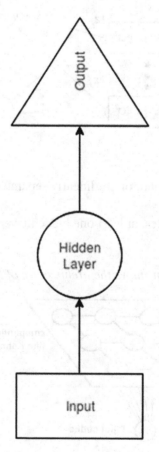

The problem of separable non-linearity (the problem of classification of models) is strongly separable in a multidimensional space with respect to a space of small dimension.

[Cover's Theorem]

What is the function of the radial base?

In the middle we define the receiver = T

We map the conflict around the receiver.

Radian Basis Function(confront mapping) conventionally used by Gaussian Functions . So we define the radial distance r = ‖x- t‖.

Gaussian Radial Function:= $\phi(r) = \exp(-r^2/2\sigma^2)$

where $\sigma > 0$

$$f\left(x\right) = \sum_{j=1}^{m} w_j h_j\left(x\right)$$

$$h\left(x\right) = \exp\left[-\frac{(x-c)^2}{r^2}\right]$$

This is not only a division in the period when the linear combination of functions leads to the hidden output layer.

Example. XOR function:-

- I have 4 inputs and I will not increase dimension at the feature vector here. So I will select 2 receptors here. For each transformation function $\phi(x)$, we will have each receptors t.

Now consider the RBNN architecture,

- P:= # of input features/ values.
- M = # of transformed vector dimensions (hidden layer width). So M ≥ P usually be.
- Each node in the hidden layer, performs a set of non-linear radian basis function.
- Now consider the RBNN architecture,
- := # of input features/ values.

Figure 21. Formula of RBF network

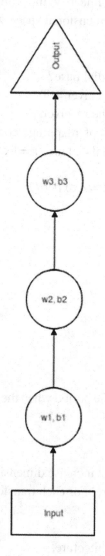

- M = # of transformed vector dimensions (hidden layer width). So M ≥ P usually be.
- Each node in the hidden layer, performs a set of non-linear radian basis function.

Output C will remain the same as for classification problems (a number of predefined class tags).

Figure 22. Architecture of XOR RBNN

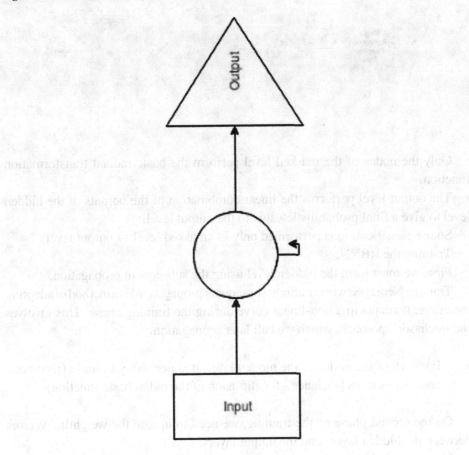

Figure 23. Transformation function with receptors and variances

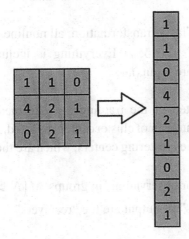

Figure 24. Output → linear combination of transformation function is tabulated

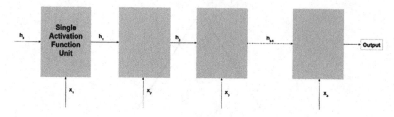

Only the nodes of the masked level perform the basic radiant transformation function.

The output level performs the linear combination of the outputs of the hidden level to give a final probabilistic value to the output level.

So the classification is performed only @ (masked level → output level)

Training the RBNN:-

First, we must form the hidden level using the subsequent propagation.

Training Neural network training (subsequent propagation) is a method of adapting the curve. It adapts to a non-linear curve during the training phase. This involves the stochastic approach, which we call later propagation.

- For each of the nodes of the hidden layer, it is necessary to find t (receivers) and variance (σ) [variance - the diffusion of the radial basic function]

On the second phase of the training, we need to update the weighting vectors between the hidden layers and the output layers.

Layers In hidden layers, each node represents each basic function of the transformation. Any of the functions could satisfy the non-linear separability OR even the combination of a set of functions could satisfy the non-linear separability.

- Then, in our hidden layer transformation, all nonlinearity terms are included. Let's say that $x^2 + y^2 + 5xy$; Everything is included in a hyper-surface equation (X and Y are inputs).

Therefore, the first step of the training is performed using a classification algorithm. We define the number of cluster centers we need. And using the clustering algorithm, we calculate the clustering centers, which are then assigned as receptors to each hidden neuron.

Do group N samples or observations in groups $M\left(N > M\right)$.

Therefore, the "groups" of output are the "receivers".

For each receiver, I can find the variance as "the square sum of the distances between the respective receiver and each nearest cluster sample": $= 1/N * \| x - t \|^2$

- The interpretation of the first phase of training is that the "characteristic vector is projected onto the transformed space".

Training with RBNN is much faster than the multilayer Perceptron (MLP) → requires many interactions with MLP.

Figure 25. Complex diagram depicting the RBNN

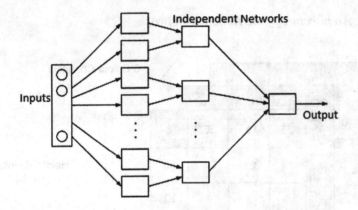

We can define what is the function / function of each node in the RBNN encryption layer. This is very difficult in MLP.

(what should be the number of hidden positions and the number of hidden points) is this parameterization difficult in MLP. But this was not found on RBNN.

The configuration will take longer in RBNN than in MLP.

Kohonen Self Organizing Networks

Among various network Kohonen's networks is one of diverse of self-organizing neural networks. The strength of self-organize offers new possibilities - adaptation to previously unknown input data. It look like the way of natural learning and that is used in our brains, where patterns are not defined. These patterns take shape during the learning process associated with normal work(Kiang,2001). Kohonen's networks are synonymous with a whole group of networks that use self-organizing, competitive learning methods. We set up signals at the entrances of the network and then select the winning neuron, the one that best matches the input vector. There are many rivalry-based subtypes that differ in precise self-organizing algorithms.

Architecture of the Kohonen Network

The Kohonen network consists of an input layer, which distributes the inputs to each node in a second layer, so it is called competitive layer.

Each of the nodes at this level acts as an output node.

Each neuron in the competitive layer is connected to other neurons in its neighborhood and feedback is restricted to neighbors through these lateral connections. Figure 26 show the Architecture of the kohonen network.

Figure 26. Architecture of the Kohonen Network

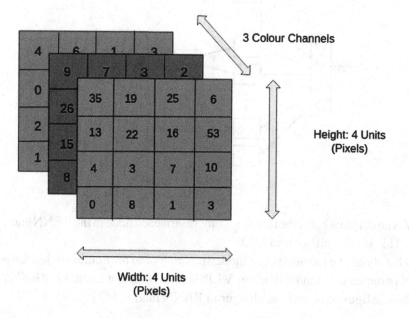

The neurons of the competitive layer have stimulating connections to the immediate neighbors and inhibitory connections to more distant neurons.

All neurons in the competitive layer receive a mixture of stimulating and inhibitory signals from the neurons of the input layer and other neurons of the competitive layer.

The Kohonen Network in Operation

When an input model is presented, some of the neurons are sufficiently enabled to produce outputs that are returned to other neurons in their vicinity.

The node whose weighting vector is closest to the input pattern vector (called the "winning node") produces the largest output. During training, the input weights of the winning neuron and its neighbors are adjusted to make them look even more like the input model.

At the end of training, the weighting vector of the winning node is aligned with the input pattern and produces the strongest output when presenting that particular pattern.

The weighting of the nodes in the neighborhood of the winning node has also been changed to give an average representation of that pattern class. As a result, even invisible patterns belonging to this class are correctly classified (generalization).

The m neighborhoods corresponding to the m possible pattern classes are to form a topological map representing the patterns(Kohonen,2007).

At above we mentioned the initiative size of neighbourhood and the fixed values of excitatory (positive) and inhibitory (negative) weights to neurons in the neighbourhood are among the design decisions to be made.

Learning Rule for the Kohonen Network

The square sum error for pattern p for all neurons in the output layer can be written as (Gregor,2015)

$$E_p = \frac{1}{2} \sum_j \left(w_{ij} - x_j^p \right)^2 \tag{2}$$

where x_j^p is the ith component of the p pattern for neuron j. The addition is made on all neurons j. Any Δw_{ij} change in weight is conventional to cause a reduction in the error E_p.

Now E_p is a function of all weights, so its exchange rate with respect to any w_{ij} weight value must be measured by calculating its partial derivative with respect to w_{ij}. (For that we have use the small delta δ, instead of d in the below equation for the derivative)

$$\Delta_p w_{ij} = -\eta \frac{\delta E_p}{\partial w_{ij}} \tag{3}$$

whereη is a constant of proportionality.

Now we have to calculate the partial derivative of E_p. Using (2):

$$\frac{\delta E_p}{\partial w_{ij}} = w_{ij} - x_j^p \tag{4}$$

Combining (3) and (4), we get

$$\Delta_p w_{ij} = -\eta \frac{\delta E_p}{\partial w_{ij}} = -\eta(w_{ij} - x_j^p) = \eta(x_j^p - w_{ij})$$

The Kohonen Algorithm

1. Initialiseweights: Each node's weights are initialized.
2. Present new input: A vector is chosen at the random from the set of data and presented to the network.
3. Compute distances to all nodes:

To calculate distances d_j between input and every output node j by using

$$d_j = \sum_{i}^{n-1} \left(x_i(t) - w_{ij}(t) \right)^2$$

where $x_i(t)$ is the input to node i at time t and $w_{ij}(t)$ is the weight from input node i to output node j at time t.

4. Select output node with minimum distance:

Select output node j* as the output node with minimum d_j.

5. Update weights to node j* and neighbours

Weights updated for node j* and all nodes in the neighbourhood defined by $N_j^*(t)$. New weights are

$$w_{ij(t+1)} = w_{ij}(t) + \eta(t)\left(x_i^{(t)} - w_{ij}^{(t)}\right) \ .$$

for j in N_j^*, $0 \le i \le N-1$

The term $\eta(t)$ is a gain term $0 \le \eta \le 1$. Both η and $N_j^*(t)$ decrease with time.

6. Repeat by going to step 2

Issue in Kohonen Neural Nets Algorithm

- **Vector normalization:** In order to compare the vectors independently of the scales and depend only on the orientation, the vectors are normalized by their scaling. It also helps to reduce exercise time.
- **Weight initialization:** A random distribution of the initial weights may not be optimal, resulting in sparsely populated trainable nodes and poor classification performance. Possible assistance:
  a. Initialization of weights at the same value and grouping of input vectors to a similar orientation. This increases the probability that all nodes are closer to the pattern vector. Entries slowly returned to the original orientation with training.
  b. Adding random noise to the inputs to distribute vectors in a larger pattern space.
  c. Using a large initial neighborhood slowly changing.

Decreasing the Size of Neighbourhood

The shape of the neighborhood may vary by application. For example, circular or hexagonal instead of rectangular.

Applications of the Kohonen Network

The Kohonen network is used in speech and image processing and has potential for statistical and database applications.

Speech Processing - Kohonen's Phonetic Typewriter

Unlimited, speaker-independent vocabulary, continuous speech recognition has not yet been achieved using conventional techniques. The problem is made difficult by the fact that the same word is pronounced with different pronunciations, volume levels, accent and background noise. In addition to analyzing individual sound units (phonemes), the human brain uses stored speech patterns, context, and other clues to effectively recognize speech (Campos,2009).

Kohonen Phonetic Typewriter Combines Digital Signal Processing Techniques and Using a Rule Base with a Kohonen Network to Achieve 92-97% Accuracy with Unlimited Vocabulary for Multiple Speakers in Finnish and Japanese.

RECURRENT NEURAL NETWORK (RNN)

Today, different Machine Learning techniques are used to handle different types of data. One of the most difficult types of data to handle and forecast is sequential data. Sequential data is different from other types of data in the sense that, although it can be assumed that all the characteristics of a typical data set are independent of order, this cannot be assumed for a sequential data set. To handle this type of data, the concept of recurrent neural networks was conceived. It is different from other artificial neural networks in its structure. While other networks "travel" in a linear direction during the feedback process or the backward propagation process, the recurring network follows a recurrence relationship instead of a feedback pass and uses backward propagation over time to learn.

The recurrent neural network (RNN) is a type of neural network in which the outputs of the previous step are fed into the input of the current step. In traditional neural networks, all inputs and outputs are independent of each other, but in cases such as when it is required to predict the next word in a sentence, the previous words are required and, therefore, it is necessary to remember the previous words(Mikolov,2010).

The recurrent neural network consists of multiple units of fixed activation function, one for each time step. Each unit has an internal state that is called the hidden state of the unit.

Thus, RNN came into existence, which solved this problem with the help of a hidden layer. The main and most important feature of RNN is the hidden state show in Figure 27, in which remembers certain information about a sequence.

RNN has a "memory" that remembers all the information about what has been calculated. Use the same parameters for each entry as it performs the same task on all hidden inputs or layers to produce the output. This reduces the complexity of the parameters, unlike other neural networks.

How RNN Work

The working of a RNN can be understood with the help of below example:

Suppose there is a deeper network, with its have one input layer, three hidden layers and one output layer. In each hidden layer will have its own set of weights and

Figure 27. Hidden layer in RNN

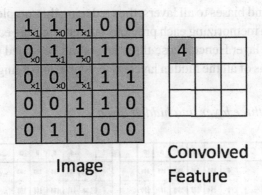

Image   Convolved Feature

biases. In first hidden layer weights and biases are (w1,b1), second layer consists (w2,b2) and third layer consists (w3,b3). This means that each of these layers are independent of each other, i.e. they do not memorize the previous outputs. The below Figure 28 shows work of RNN.

Now the RNN will do the following:

Figure 28. Example of RNN work

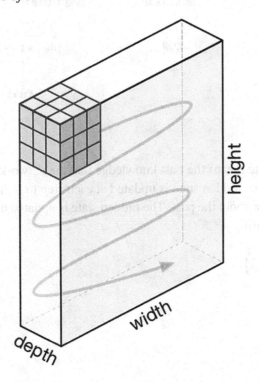

RNN converts independent activations into dependent activations by providing the same weights and biases to all layers, thus reducing the complexity of increasing the parameters and memorizing each previous output by giving each output as input to the next hidden layer.Hence, these three layers can be joined together such that the weights and bias of all the hidden layers is the same, into a single recurrent layer.

Figure 29. Joined three layer into hidden layer

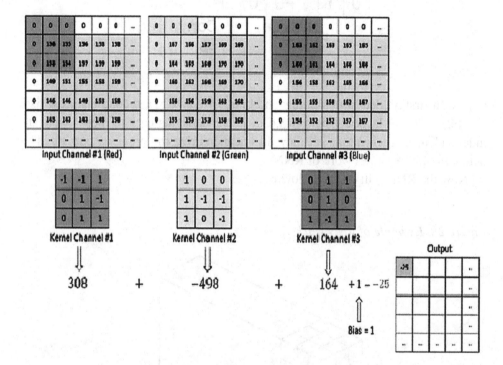

This hidden state means the past knowledge that the network currently has in a given time step. This hidden state is updated at each step to indicate the change in network knowledge about the past. The hidden state is updated using the following recurrence relationship: -

$$h_t = fw\left(x_t - h_t - 1\right)$$

Where

h_t -> current state

$h_t - 1$ -> previous state

x_t -> input state

fw -> The fixed function with trainable weights

At each time step, the new hidden state is calculated using the recurrence relation as given above. This new generated hidden state is used to generate indeed a new hidden state and so on(Sreekanth,2010).

The basic work-flow of a Recurrent Neural Network is as follows in Figure 30.

Figure 30. The basic work-flow of a RNN

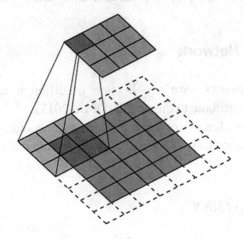

Training Through RNN

1. A single time step of the input is provided to the network.
2. Then calculate its current state using set of current input and the previous state.
3. The current ht becomes ht-1 for the next time step.
4. One can go as many time steps according to the problem and join the information from all the previous states.
5. Once all the time steps are completed the final current state is used to calculate the output.
6. The output is then compared to the actual output i.e the target output and the error is generated.
7. The error is then back-propagated to the network to update the weights and hence the network (RNN) is trained.

Advantages of Recurrent Neural Network

- An RNN remembers each and every information through time. It is useful in time series prediction only because of the feature to remember previous inputs as well. This is called Long Short Term Memory.
- Recurrent neural network are even used with convolutional layers to extend the effective pixel neighborhood.

Disadvantages of Recurrent Neural Network

- Gradient vanishing and exploding problems.
- Training an RNN is a very difficult task.
- It cannot process very long sequences if using tanh or relu as an activation function.

Modular Neural Network

Modular neural networks have a collection of different networks that work independently and contribute to the output (Devin,2017).

Each neural network has a set of inputs that are unique compared to other networks that build and perform subtasks. These networks do not interact or point to each other

Figure 31. The work of MNN

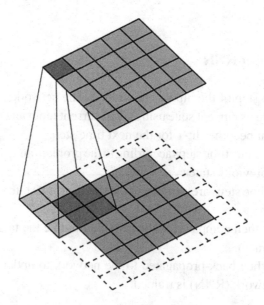

to perform the tasks. The advantage of a modular neural network is that it breaks down a large computational process into smaller components, decreasing complexity.

This breakdown will help decrease the number of connections and deny the interaction of these networks with each other, which in turn will increase the speed of calculation. However, the processing time will depend on the number of neurons and their participation in the calculation of the results(Kourakos,2009). Figure 31 shows the work of Modular neural networks.

REFERENCES

Baroni, M., & Zamparelli, R. (2010, October). Nouns are vectors, adjectives are matrices: Representing adjective-noun constructions in semantic space. In *Proceedings of the 2010 conference on empirical methods in natural language processing* (pp. 1183-1193). Academic Press.

Blunsom, P., Kocik, K., & Curran, J. R. (2006, August). Question classification with log-linear models. In *Proceedings of the 29th annual international ACM SIGIR conference on Research and development in information retrieval* (pp. 615-616). ACM.

Boureau, Y. L., Ponce, J., & LeCun, Y. (2010). A theoretical analysis of feature pooling in visual recognition. In *Proceedings of the 27th international conference on machine learning (ICML-10)* (pp. 111-118). Academic Press.

Campos, B. R. (2009). *Character recognition in natural images*. VISAPP.

Cireşan, D., Meier, U., Masci, J., & Schmidhuber, J. (2011, July). A committee of neural networks for traffic sign classification. In *The 2011 international joint conference on neural networks* (pp. 1918–1921). IEEE. doi:10.1109/IJCNN.2011.6033458

Danisman, K., Dalkiran, I., & Celebi, F. V. (2006). Design of a high precision temperature measurement system based on artificial neural network for different thermocouple types. *Measurement*, *39*(8), 695–700. doi:10.1016/j.measurement.2006.03.015

Devin, C., Gupta, A., Darrell, T., Abbeel, P., & Levine, S. (2017, May). Learning modular neural network policies for multi-task and multi-robot transfer. In *2017 IEEE International Conference on Robotics and Automation (ICRA)* (pp. 2169-2176). IEEE. 10.1109/ICRA.2017.7989250

Gregor, K., Danihelka, I., Graves, A., Rezende, D. J., & Wierstra, D. (2015). *Draw: A recurrent neural network for image generation*. arXiv preprint arXiv:1502.04623

Kalchbrenner, N., Grefenstette, E., & Blunsom, P. (2014). *A convolutional neural network for modelling sentences.* arXiv preprint arXiv:1404.2188

Kangas, J. A., Kohonen, T. K., & Laaksonen, J. T. (1990). Variants of self-organizing maps. *IEEE Transactions on Neural Networks, 1*(1), 93–99. doi:10.1109/72.80208 PMID:18282826

Kiang, M. Y. (2001). Extending the Kohonen self-organizing map networks for clustering analysis. *Computational Statistics & Data Analysis, 38*(2), 161–180. doi:10.1016/S0167-9473(01)00040-8

Kohonen, T., & Honkela, T. (2007). Kohonen network. *Scholarpedia, 2*(1), 1568. doi:10.4249cholarpedia.1568

Kourakos, G., & Mantoglou, A. (2009). Pumping optimization of coastal aquifers based on evolutionary algorithms and surrogate modular neural network models. *Advances in Water Resources, 32*(4), 507–521. doi:10.1016/j.advwatres.2009.01.001

Lawrence, S., Giles, C. L., Tsoi, A. C., & Back, A. D. (1997). Face recognition: A convolutional neural-network approach. *IEEE Transactions on Neural Networks, 8*(1), 98–113. doi:10.1109/72.554195 PMID:18255614

Mikolov, T., Karafiát, M., Burget, L., Černocký, J., & Khudanpur, S. (2010). Recurrent neural network based language model. In *Eleventh annual conference of the international speech communication association.* Academic Press.

Sermanet, P., Chintala, S., & LeCun, Y. (2012). *Convolutional neural networks applied to house numbers digit classification.* arXiv preprint arXiv:1204.3968

Sreekanth, J., & Datta, B. (2010). Multi-objective management of saltwater intrusion in coastal aquifers using genetic programming and modular neural network based surrogate models. *Journal of Hydrology (Amsterdam), 393*(3-4), 245–256. doi:10.1016/j.jhydrol.2010.08.023

Sun, T. Y., Liu, C. C., Lin, C. L., Hsieh, S. T., & Huang, C. S. (2009). A radial basis function neural network with adaptive structure via particle swarm optimization. In *Particle Swarm Optimization.* IntechOpen. doi:10.5772/6763

Zaremba, W., Sutskever, I., & Vinyals, O. (2014). *Recurrent neural network regularization.* arXiv preprint arXiv:1409.2329

Chapter 4
Applications of ANN for Agriculture Using Remote Sensed Data

Geetha M.
Bapuji Institute of Engineering and Technology, India

Asha Gowda Karegowda
(iD) https://orcid.org/0000-0002-1353-4293
Siddaganga Institute of Technology, India

Nandeesha Rudrappa
Siddaganga Institute of Technology, India

Devika G.
(iD) https://orcid.org/0000-0002-2509-2867
Government Engineering College, K. R. Pet, India

ABSTRACT

Ever since the advent of modern geo information systems, tracking environmental changes due to natural and/or manmade causes with the aid of remote sensing applications has been an indispensable tool in numerous fields of geography, most of the earth science disciplines, defense, intelligence, commerce, economics, and administrative planning. Remote sensing is used in science and technology, and through it, an object can be identified, measured, and analyzed without physical presence for interpretation. In India remote sensing has been using since 1970s. One among these applications is the crop classification and yield estimation. Using remote sensing in agriculture for crop mapping, and yield estimation provides efficient information, which is mainly used in many government organizations and the private sector. The pivotal sector for ensuring food security is a major concern of interest in these days. In time, availability of information on agricultural crops is vital for making well-versed decisions on food security issues.

DOI: 10.4018/978-1-7998-4042-8.ch004

INTRODUCTION

In India more than 60% of population is depending on agriculture. In agriculture, crop yield estimation before harvesting is a challenging task. Many models have been developed in Asia, USA, Europe and elsewhere in the country, but due to the complexity of agriculture ecosystem, yield prediction is still based on the traditional methods or the statistical methods. Artificial Neural Network (ANN) is one of the most powerful and self-adaptive model for crop yield estimation using remote sensing. This method employs a nonlinear response function that iterates many times in a special network structure in order to learn the complex functional relationship between input and output training data. Once trained, an ANN model can remember a functional relationship and be used for further calculation. For these reasons, the ANN concept has been widely used to develop models, especially in strongly nonlinear, complicated systems. Since Remote sensing provides the availability of large data in time with respect to the crop season would be combined with ANN to develop an efficient model for predicting the yield before harvesting. ANN and satellite remote sensing has got an unlimited scope in the sector of agriculture these days as it is being used for land resource mapping, weed detection, pesticide management, soil health mapping, crop yield estimation, and for assessment of natural calamities. In India the technology is being promoted by ministry of agriculture through MGNREGA scheme for rural area to assist farmers remotely.

The chapter is presented as follows. Section II covers overview of ANN, followed by detailed study of remote sensing in section III. Applications of ANN in agriculture using remote sensed data is briefed in section IV, followed by contribution to chapter, future scope for research and conclusions in the remaining sections.

Overview of ANN

Most of recent innovations and advances in statistical technology are conveyed through computational model artificial neural networks (ANN). ANN concept will be briefed in this section. The ANN model functions similar to nervous systems in human beings, where neurons are connected in complex patterns. It is not a new concept, but it has underwent gradual change because of which the current ANN does not certainly same as to that of its inception C. Stergiou (1996). As Howard Rheingold's explanation on ANN "The neural networks is these days technology is not an algorithm, it is a network that has weights on it, and you can adjust the weights so that it learns. You teach it through trails." ANN can be hardware or software that is carved of functioning to that of human brains. Few of researchers define ANN has a mathematical model of human neural network architecture with learning and generalization functions. The figure 1 gives comparison between actual neurons and synapses in human brain. The neurons are termed as perceptron in ANN during 1960 by McCulloch while presenting McCulloch –Pitt's neurons model V.S. Dave, K. Dutta (2014).

Figure 1. Comparison between actual neurons and synapses in human brain

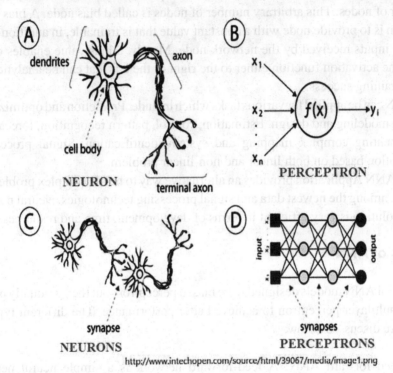

http://www.intechopen.com/source/html/39067/media/image1.png

A typical ANN consist of large number of perceptrons, they operate parallel even though organized in the form of layers. As human brains receive information similarly in ANN first layer receives input, process and forward it to next layer, same sequencing happens until input reaches last layer T.J. Huang (2017). The working process is divided into three layers; input, hidden and output layers. ANN will consist of single and equal perceptron numbered input and output layer, and multiple hidden layers as in figure 2(a). Every perceptron in network will receive weighted input from its preceding perceptron known as synapses. The perceptron will process received inputs to generate output based on activation function of a perceptron. The single perceptron is shown in figure 2(b). The sum of weights and inputs generates output in form of activation signal. The most commonly used activation functions are linear, step, sigmoid, tan and rectified linear unit (ReLu) functions as in figure 3.

Each perceptron contribute in ANN for processing, as they are individually capable of contributing to ANN with their knowledge including rules that which has been programmed and learnt by itself. Each perceptron are extremely adaptive and learn quickly. Each perceptron will weight for its importance of input it receives from its preceding perceptrons based on it the current perceptron contribute towards the right output in order to give the highest weight. A specific layer can have an arbitrary number of nodes. This arbitrary number of nodes is called bias node. A bias major function is to provide node with a constant value that is trainable, in addition to the normal inputs received by the network node. Mainly, a bias value enables one to move the activation function either to the right or the left that can be analytical for ANN training success.

ANN can be applied for various tasks which include: Prediction and optimization, System modeling and design, Estimation, control, pattern recognition, forecasting, Implementing complex mapping and system identification, Signal processing, Application based on both linear and non-linear problem.

An ANN Application provides an alternative way to tackle complex problems as they are among the newest data and signal processing technologies. Neural network based solution is very efficient in terms of development, time and resources.

Types of ANN

The initial ANN models designed were biased perceptron, but then gradually moved on to multilayer perceptron to achieve better performance. The different types of ANN are discussed below:

- Feed forward ANN: A feed-forward network is a simple neural network consisting of an input layer, an output layer and one or more layers of neurons. Through evaluation of its output by reviewing its input, the power of the network can be noticed base on group behavior of the connected neurons and the output is decided. The main advantage of this network is that it learns to evaluate and recognize input patterns.
- Feedback ANN: In this type of ANN, the output goes back into the network to achieve the best-evolved results internally. The feedback network feeds information back into itself and is well suited to solve optimization problems, according to the University of Massachusetts, Lowell Center for Atmospheric Research. Feedback ANNs are used by the internal system error corrections.
- Radial Basis ANN: In this type of ANN inner layer the featured are combined with the radial basis function. The output is taken into consideration in calculation of weights of next layer.

Figure 2. (a) Layered structure of ANN; (b) Typical perceptron view

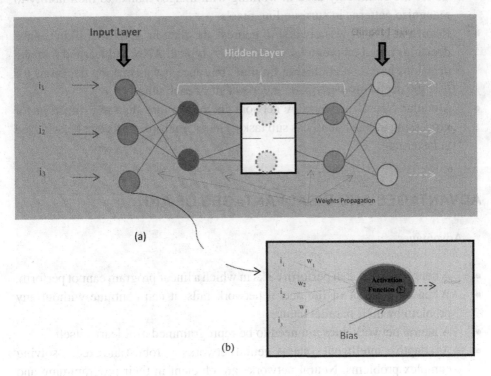

Figure 3. Activation function

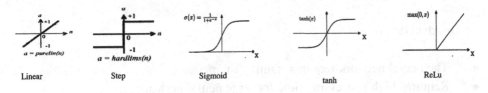

- Multilayer perceptron: Here the perceptron's are fully connected with more than three layers. Each node is connected to another node in the next layers, used maximum in speech recognition and machine translation technologies.
- Convolution neural network (CNN): CNN sometimes called LeNets (named after Yann LeCun), are artificial neural networks where the connections between layers appear to be somewhat arbitrary. However, the reason for the synapses to be setup the way they are is to help reduce the number of parameters that need to be optimized. This is done by noting certain symmetry in how the neurons are connected, and so you can essentially "re-use" neurons to have identical copies without necessarily needing the same number of synapses.

CNNs are commonly used in working with images thanks to their ability to recognize patterns in surrounding pixels.

- Recurrent NN: It was created to address the flaw in ANN that didn't make decisions based on previous knowledge. A typical ANN had learned to make decisions based on context in training, but once it was making decisions for use, the decisions were made independent of each other.
- Modular Neural network: A network includes more than one function for processing independently as sub tasks. Hence, multiple tasks can be achieved at faster rate.

ADVANTAGES AND DISADVANTAGES OF ANN

Advantages

- A neural network can perform tasks in which a linear program cannot perform.
- When an element of the neural network fails, it can continue without any problem by their parallel nature.
- A neural network does not need to be reprogrammed as it learns itself.
- As adaptive, intelligent systems, neural networks are robust and excel at solving complex problems. Neural networks are efficient in their programming and the scientists agree that the advantages of using ANNs outweigh the risks.
- Can handle noisy and incomplete data.

Disadvantages

- The neural network requires training to operate.
- Requires high processing time for large neural networks.
- The architecture of a neural network is different from the architecture and history of microprocessors so they have to be emulated.

REMOTE SENSING

This section mainly covers the various remote sensing methodologies for agriculture related data acquisition. Remote sensing is defined as the science and technology using which specified objects properties, size, area, or it's a phenomenon that can be used to identify, measure, and analyze the objects without direct contact to provide useful decision making. With the development of computer technology,

Figure 4. (a) Feed forward (b) Feedback (c) Radial basis function (d) Multi- layer (e) Recurrent (f) Convolution neural network (g) Modal network

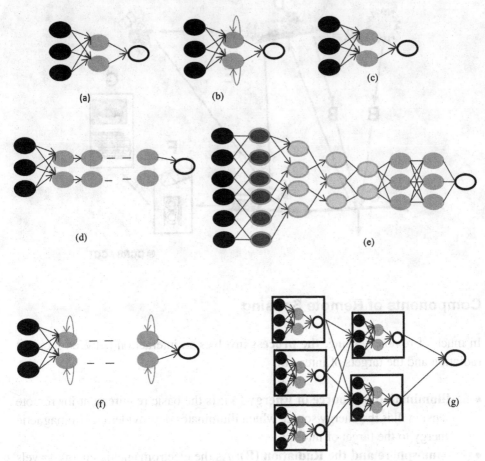

Geographical Information System (GIS), remote sensing and various satellite image processing tools a new era has been evolved since from 1970's. It is a phenomenon that has various applications which includes photography, geology, monitoring earth resources, forestry, change detection, surveying, flood assessment, droughts, fire in forest, and classification of crops in agriculture and many more.

The main source of remote sensing data is the electromagnetic radiations which are emitted or reflected by the object, which will helps in their identification and classification.

Figure 5. The Process of Remote Sensing (http1)

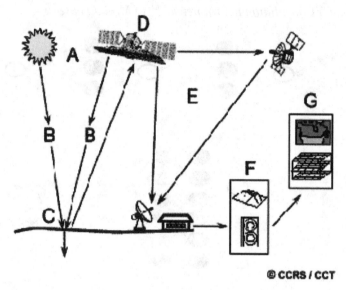

© CCRS / CCT

Components of Remote Sensing

In much of remote sensing, **the process** involves an interaction between incident radiation and the targets of interest.

- **Illumination or Source of Energy (A)**: Is the basic requirement for remote sensing .It is the energy source which illuminates or provides electromagnetic energy to the target of interest.
- **Atmosphere and the Radiation (B)**: As the electromagnetic energy travels from its source to the target, it will come in contact with and interact with the atmosphere as it passes through.
- **Interaction with the Target (C)**: Once the energy from the source reaches its target through the atmosphere, it interacts with the target depending on the both target and radiation properties.
- **Footage of Energy by the Sensor (D)**: The scattered or emitted energy from the target is collected and recorded using the sensors.
- **Transmission, Reception, and Processing (E)**: The recorded energy by the sensor will be transmitted to a receiving and processing station in electronic form where the processed data will in an image format (hardcopy and/or digital).

- **Interpretation and Analysis (F)**: The transmitted and processed image is interpreted, visually and/or electronically or digitally, to extract information of the illuminated target.
- **Application (G)** – Finally we can extract the information from the element of remote sensing process, for better understanding provide some additional information or assist in solving a specific problem.

Platforms for Remote Sensing

- Platform: A Platform is defined as the carrier for remote sensing sensors. There are three major remote sensing platforms: ground-level platform (towers and cranes), aerial platforms (Helicopters, low altitude aircraft, high altitude aircraft), and space borne platforms (space shuttles, polar-orbiting satellites, and geostationary satellites).

Figure 6. Platforms for Remote sensing

Types of remote sensing instruments are

- **Active sensor:** Active sensors provide their own energy in order to scan objects and areas whereupon a sensor then detects and measures the radiation that is reflected or backscattered from the target.

Ex: RADAR and LiDAR (SAR or microwave data) Sentinel 2A, Awifis etc.

- **Passive sensor:** Passive sensors detect natural energy that is reflected by the object scene being observed (Optical Data).

Ex: Photography, Charge-Coupled Devices and Radiometers, Landsat, sentinel-2B etc.

Figure 7. Difference between Active and Passive sensors
(www.nrcan.gc.ca)

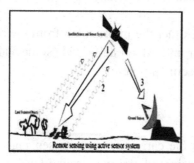 

- **Active sensing** sends the energy towards the object then measure and detects the radiation that is reflected or backscattered from the object.
- **Passive sensing** is a collection of energy that is reflected or emitted from the surface of the earth.

Figure 8. The electromagnetic spectrum
(https://link.springer.com/chapter/10.1007/978-3-319-58039-5_3)

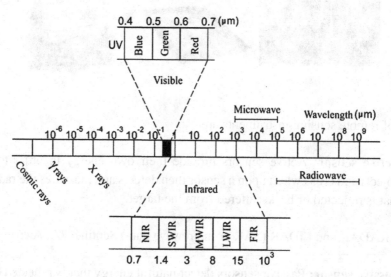

- **Optical Remote Sensing:** It makes use of visible, near infrared and short-wave infrared sensors to form images of the earth's surface by detecting the solar radiation reflected from targets on the ground. Different materials reflect and absorb differently at different wavelengths. Thus, the targets can be differentiated by their spectral reflectance signatures in the remotely sensed images. Optical remote sensing systems are classified into the following types, depending on the number of spectral bands used in the imaging process.

- **Panchromatic Imaging System:** The sensor is a single channel detector sensitive to radiation within a broad wavelength range. If the wavelength ranges coincide with the visible range, then the resulting image resembles a "black-and-white" photograph taken from space. The physical quantity being measured is the apparent brightness of the targets. The spectral information or "colour" of the targets is lost. Examples of panchromatic imaging systems are: IKONOS PAN,SPOT HRV-PAN
- **Multispectral Imaging System:** The sensor is a multichannel detector with a few spectral bands. Each channel is sensitive to radiation within a narrow wavelength band. The resulting image is a multilayer image which contains both the brightness and spectral (colour) information of the targets being observed. Examples of multispectral systems are:
  - LANDSAT MSS
  - LANDSAT TM
  - SPOT HRV-XS
  - IKONOS MS
  - SENTINEL 2B
- **Super Spectral Imaging Systems:** A super spectral imaging sensor has many more spectral channels (typically >10) than a multispectral sensor. The bands have narrower bandwidths, enabling the finer spectral characteristics of the targets to be captured by the sensor. Examples of super spectral systems are: MODIS, MERIS
- **Hyperspectral Imaging Systems:** A hyperspectral imaging system is also known as an "imaging spectrometer". It acquires images in about a hundred or more contiguous spectral bands. The precise spectral information contained in a hyperspectral image enables better characterization and identification of targets. Hyperspectral images have potential applications in such fields as precision agriculture (e.g. monitoring the types, health, moisture status and maturity of crops), coastal management (e.g. monitoring of phyto planktons, pollution, bathymetry changes). An example of a hyperspectral system is: Hyperion on EO1 satellite (https://crisp.nus.edu.sg/).
- **Synthetic Aperture Radar** (SAR) image data provide information different from that of optical sensors operating in the visible and infrared regions of the electromagnetic spectrum. SAR data consist of high-resolution reflected returns of radar-frequency energy from terrain that has been illuminated by a directed beam of pulses generated by the sensor. The radar returns from the terrain are mainly determined by the physical characteristics of the surface

features (such as surface roughness, geometric structure, and orientation), the electrical characteristics (dielectric constant, moisture content, and conductivity), and the radar frequency of the sensor. By supplying its own source of illumination, the SAR sensor can acquire data day or night without regard to cloud cover. Characteristics of SAR are:

◦ The unique information of surface roughness, physical structure, and electrical conduction properties

◦ The high spatial resolution

◦ The 24-hour, all-weather data-acquisition capability; and

◦ The now-realizable long-term continuity of the data that enables repetitive (seasonal) coverage of major global land regions. (http://www.ciesin.org/TG/RS/sarsens.html).

Table 1. Details of Indian satellites and its tasks

SN	Satellite	No. of Bands, Resolution and Revisit	Task
1.	Resourcesat-2A LISS III LISS IV AWiFs	4,23.5m,24 Days 3,5.8m,5 Days 4,56m,5 Days http://lps16.esa. int/posterfiles/ paper1213/[RD13]_ Resourcesat-2_ Handbook.pdf	To provide multispectral images for inventory and management of natural resources, Crop production forecast, wasteland inventory, Land & Water Resources development, and Disaster Management Support. (https://directory.eoportal.org/web/eoportal/satellite-missions/r/resourcesat-2)
2.	Cartosat-1	4,2.5m,5 Days(http://www.eotec. com/images/ IRS_-_Current_and_ Future_-_Web.pdf)	To provide high resolution images for Cartographic mapping, Stereo data for Topographic Mapping & DEM, and host of DEM Applications – Contour, Drainage network, etc.
4.	RISAT-1	3-4,1-50m,5 Days http://www.eotec. com/images/ IRS_-_Current_and_ Future_-_Web.pdf	To provide all weather imaging capability useful for agriculture, particularly paddy and jute monitoring in kharif season and management of natural disasters.
5.	Kalpana-1	3,2km, 16 Days https://nssdc.gsfc. nasa.gov/nmc/ spacecraft/display. action?id=2002-043A	To provide meteorological data to enable weather forecasting services.

Some of Indian satellite details of launching, characteristics of these satellites, along with tasks are given in table 1. Satellite launched by other countries is mentioned in table 2.

Table 2. Foreign satellite and its tasks

SN	Satellite	No. of Bands, Resolution and Revisit	Task
1	Sentinel 2	13 10,30,60 5 Days	The objective of SENTINEL-2 is land monitoring, and the mission will be composed of two polar-orbiting satellites providing high-resolution optical imagery. Vegetation, soil and coastal areas are among the monitoring objectives. (https://sentinel.esa.int)
2	MODIS	36, 250,500,1000 16 Days	MODIS is playing a vital role in the development of validated, global, interactive Earth system models able to predict global change accurately enough to assist policy makers in making sound decisions concerning the protection of our environment. (https://modis.gsfc.nasa.gov)
3	Landsat 8	8,30,16 Days	The objective of scheduling and data collection is to provide cloud-free coverage of the global landmass on a seasonal basis. (https://earth.esa.int)

Basic Steps Involved in Remote Sensing

- Data acquisition (energy propagation, platforms)
- Processing (conversion of energy pattern to images)
- Analysis (quantitative and qualitative analysis)
- Analysis (quantitative and qualitative analysis)
- Information distribution to users

IV Remote Sensing Applications

It is a phenomenon that has numerous applications including photography, surveying, geology, forestry, land-use land Cover Mapping, weather forecasting, environmental study, natural hazards study, and crop classification, yield monitoring and Estimation, monitoring earth resources, change detection, flood assessment, droughts, fire in forest and many more.

- Land Use Mapping: Remote sensing data is useful in obtaining up-to-date land use pattern of large areas at any given time and also monitor changes that occur from time to time. It can be used for updating road maps, asphalt conditions, and wetland delineation. This information is used by regional planners and administrators to frame policy matters for all-round development of the region.

- Weather Forecasting: Remote sensing is extensively used in India for weather forecasting. It is also used to warn people about impending cyclones.
- Environmental Study: It can be used to study deforestation, degradation of fertile lands, pollution in atmosphere, desertification, eutrophication of large water bodies and oil spillage from oil tankers.
- Study of Natural hazards: Remote sensing can be used to study damages caused by earthquakes, volcanoes, landslides, floods and melting of ice in polar regions. Many times remote sensing will be helpful to predict the occurrence of natural hazards.
- Resource exploration: Remote sensing data is helpful for updating existing geological maps, rapid preparation of lineament and tectonic maps, identifying the sites for quarrying the minerals and helpful in locating fossil fuel deposits.

Applications of Remote Sensing in Agricultural Sector

- **Crop Production Forecasting:** Remote sensing is used to forecast the expected crop production and yield over a given area and determine how much of the crop will be harvested under specific conditions. Researchers can be able to predict the quantity of crop that will be produced in a given farmland over a given period of time.
- **Assessment of Crop Damage and Crop Progress:** In the event of crop damage or crop progress, remote sensing technology can be used to penetrate the farmland and determine exactly how much of a given crop has been damaged and the progress of the remaining crop in the farm.
- **Horticulture, Cropping Systems Analysis:** Remote sensing technology has also been instrumental in the analysis of various crop planting systems. This technology has mainly been in use in the horticulture industry where flower growth patterns can be analyzed and a prediction made out of the analysis.
- **Crop Identification:** Remote sensing has also played an important role in crop identification especially in cases where the crop under observation is mysterious or shows some mysterious characteristics. The data from the crop is collected and taken to the labs where various aspects of the crop including the crop culture are studied.
- **Crop Acreage Estimation:** Remote sensing has also played a very important role in the estimation of the farmland on which a crop has been planted. This

is usually a cumbersome procedure if it is carried out manually because of the vast sizes of the lands being estimated.

- **Crop Condition Assessment and Stress Detection:** Remote sensing technology plays an important role in the assessment of the health condition of each crop and the extent to which the crop has withstood stress. This data is then used to determine the quality of the crop.

- **Identification of Planting and Harvesting Dates:** Because of the predictive nature of the remote sensing technology, farmers can now use remote sensing to observe a variety of factors including the weather patterns and the soil types to predict the planting and harvesting seasons of each crop.

- **Crop Yield Modeling and Estimation:** Remote sensing also allows farmers and experts to predict the expected crop yield from a given farmland by estimating the quality of the crop and the extent of the farmland. This is then used to determine the overall expected yield of the crop.

- **Identification of Pests and Disease Infestation:** Remote sensing technology also plays a significant role in the identification of pests in farmland and gives data on the right pests control mechanism to be used to get rid of the pests and diseases on the farm.

- **Soil Moisture Estimation:** Soil moisture can be difficult to measure without the help of remote sensing technology. Remote sensing gives the soil moisture data and helps in determining the quantity of moisture in the soil and hence the type of crop that can be grown in the soil.

- **Irrigation Monitoring and Management:** Remote sensing gives information on the moisture quantity of soils. This information is used to determine whether a particular soil is moisture deficient or not and helps in planning the irrigation needs of the soil.

- **Soil Mapping:** Soil mapping is one of the most common yet most important uses of remote sensing. Through soil mapping, farmers are able to tell what soils are ideal for which crops and what soil require irrigation and which ones do not. This information helps in precision agriculture.

- **Monitoring of Droughts:** Remote sensing technology is used to monitor the weather patterns including the drought patterns over a given area. The information can be used to predict the rainfall patterns of an area and also tell the time difference between the current rainfall and the next rainfall which helps to keep track of the drought.

- **Land Cover and Land Degradation Mapping:** Remote sensing has been used by experts to map out the land cover of a given area. Experts can now tell what areas of the land have been degraded and which areas are still intact. This also helps them in implementing measures to curb land degradation.

- **Identification of Problematic Soils:** Remote sensing has also played a very important role in the identification of problematic soils that have a problem in sustaining optimum crop yield throughout a planting season.
- **Crop Nutrient Deficiency Detection:** Remote sensing technology has also helped farmers and other agricultural experts to determine the extent of crop nutrients deficiency and come up with remedies that would increase the nutrients level in crops hence increasing the overall crop yield.
- **Reflectance Modeling:** Remote sensing technology is just about the only technology that can provide data on crop reflectance. Crop reflectance will depend on the amount of moisture in the soil and the nutrients in the crop which may also have a significant impact on the overall crop yield.
- **Determination of Water Content of field Crops:** Apart from determining the soil moisture content, remote sensing also plays an important role in the estimation of the water content in the field crops.
- **Crop Yield Forecasting:** Remote sensing technology can give accurate estimates of the expected crop yield in a planting season using various crop information such as the crop quality, the moisture level in the soil and in the crop and the crop cover of the land. When all of this data is combined it gives almost accurate estimates of the crop yield.
- **Flood Mapping and Monitoring**: Using remote sensing technology, farmers and agricultural experts can be able to map out the areas that are likely to be hit by floods and the areas that lack proper drainage. This data can then be used to avert any flood disaster in future.
- **Collection of Past and Current Weather Data**: Remote sensing technology is ideal for collection and storing of past and current weather data which can be used for future decision making and prediction.
- **Crop Intensification**: Remote sensing can be used for crop intensification that includes collection of important crop data such as the cropping pattern, crop rotation needs and crop diversity over a given soil.
- **Water Resources Mapping**: Remote sensing is instrumental in the mapping of water resources that can be used for agriculture over a given farmland. Through remote sensing, farmers can tell what water resources are available for use over a given land and whether the resources are adequate.
- **Precision Farming**: Remote sensing has played a very vital role in precision agriculture. Precision agriculture has resulted in the cultivation of healthy crops that guarantees farmers optimum harvests over a given period of time.
- **Climate Change Monitoring**: Remote sensing technology is important in monitoring of climate change and keeping track of the climatic conditions which play an important role in the determination of what crops can be grown where.

- **Compliance Monitoring:** For the agricultural experts and other farmers, remote sensing is important in keeping track of the farming practices by all farmers and ensuring compliance by all farmers. This helps in ensuring that all farmers follow the correct procedures when planting and when harvesting crops.

- **Soil Management Practices**: Remote sensing technology is important in the determination of soil management practices based on the data collected from the farms.

- **Air Moisture Estimation**: Remote sensing technology is used in the estimation of air moisture which determines the humidity of the area. The level of humidity determines the type of crops to be grown within the area.

- **Crop Health Analysis**: Remote sensing technology plays an important role in the analysis of crop health which determines the overall crop yield.

- **Land Mapping**: Remote sensing helps in mapping land for use for various purposes such as crop growing and landscaping. The mapping technology used helps in precision agriculture where specific land soils are used for specific purposes.https://grindgis.com/remote-sensing/remote-sensing-applications-in-agriculture#

Remote Sensing for Yield Estimation

Remote sensing is commonly used to monitor and estimating yield crops in large areas. K. Kuwataa, R. & Shibasakib (2016) have used MODIS data with daily input dataset and 5-days accumulation input dataset with surface reflectance from https://lpdaac.usgs.gov and calculated Enhanced Vegetation Index(EVI) using the following equation(1): EVI=G*NIR-R/NIR+C1*R-C2*B+L, where G=Gain Factor, R=MODIS band1,NIR= MODIS band2,B= MODIS band3, C1C2=Aerial resistance weights, L=the canopy background adjustment factor, with G=2.5, L=1,C1=6 &C2=7.5. They developed a model for estimation corn Yield using an Artificial Neural Network, Support Vector Machine (SVM) and deep Neural Network (DNN). The performance of crop yield estimation model was evaluated based on the Root Mean Square Error (RMSE) and the coefficient of determination (R^2). Nearly 80% of the dataset is used for training and the remaining 20% is used to evaluate the accuracy of the models. The comparison between the two models shows that the DNN with six hidden layers produce higher accuracy than SVM.

Yield estimation is very essential for decision making in food and agriculture economic growth of a country as well as for import and export of food grains. Mohammad Saleem Khan et.al (2019) acquired multispectral satellite Landsat8 OLI (Operational Land Imager) data for the month of May 2019 and derived different vegetation Indices like NDVI(Normalized Difference Vegetation Index),

ENDVI(Enhanced Normalized Difference Vegetation Index), TNDVI(Transformed Normalized Difference Vegetation Index), GVI(Green Vegetation Index) etc., for the yield estimation of Menthol crops along with the Artificial Neural Network techniques of Multi-Layer Perceptron. This algorithm is used to optimize the dependent variables (field biomass) with respect to independent variables (Vegetation Indices). The figure 9 shows the ANN topology used for predicting Menthol mint crop biomass.

Figure 9. The architecture of ANN model used to estimate the Menthol mint crop biomass
(Mohammad Saleem Khan et.al (2019))

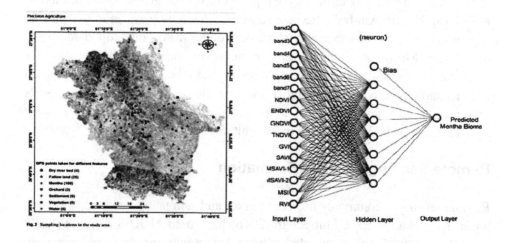

ANN was implemented to identify the important predictors from amongst spectral bands, indices and they collected field data for estimation of the crop biomass which has a good relationship (R2 = 0.785 and root mean square error (RMSE) = 2.74 t/ha) with field-measured biomass. Linear regression method was used further to calculate regression coefficients and the empirical equation thus developed was used to visualize biomass variability in the study area (Barabanki). The Artificial Neural Network model with the various vegetation Indices of satellite data coupled with collection of field sampling during crop maturity enabled the menthol mint yield estimation with high accuracy.

With the rapid development of Precision Agriculture (PA) promoted by high-resolution remote sensing, it makes significant sense in management and estimation of agriculture through crop classification of high-resolution remote sensing image. Due to the complex and fragmentation of the features and the surroundings in the circumstance of high-resolution, the accuracy of the traditional classification methods has not been able to meet the standard of agricultural problems. In this case, Yao Chunjing et.al(2017) proposed a classification method for high-resolution agricultural remote sensing images based on convolution neural networks (CNN). For training, a large number of training samples were produced by panchromatic images of GF-1 high-resolution satellite of China. In the experiment, through training and testing on the CNN under the toolbox of deep learning by MATLAB, the crop classification finally got the correct rate of 99.66% after the gradual optimization of adjusting parameter during training. Through improving the accuracy of image classification and image recognition, the applications of CNN provide a reference value for the field of remote sensing in Precision Agriculture.

Rice is a globally used staple food. Forecasting and yield estimation of Boro Rice in Bangladesh plays a crucial role in economy of agro departments. Due to rapid increase in population and reduction in agricultural land area has become a key issue in Bangladesh economy to maintain the food security for its large population. Kawsar Akhand et.al (2018) have developed a model for predicting Boro Rice crop using ANN and Advanced Very High Resolution radiometer(AVHRR) satellite data and calculated NDVI using the formula NDVI= (NIR-VIS) / (NIR+VIS) for vegetation health Indices.

The temperature Condition index (TCI) and Vegetation Condition Index (VCI) are used as input to the forward back propagation ANN network and the obtained crop yield is predicted by comparing the yield with the actual Boro Rice yield statistical data.

Thus, the results obtained shows that this model is highly promising by giving 90% accuracy & this type of models are important to the agricultural departments, Governments, Planning crop production, Policy makers for monitoring food security and for agricultural stake holders. The Figure 10 shows ANN yield prediction model.

Machine Learning approaches such as ANN and Random Forest algorithms are used to develop a model for Kharif Rice yield prediction in Purulia and Bankura

Figure 10. NARX Neural network Boro rice yield prediction model simulated diagram (Kawsar Akhand et.al (2018))

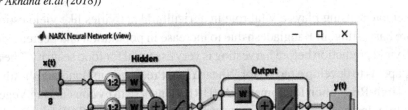

district, West Bengal. Aditi Chandraet.al(2019),have developed a model by integrating Non-weather variables at block level for the period from 2006 to 2015 with monthly NDVI. The correlation obtained from the model was 0.702 with MSE 0.01.

The various model like Weather Variables vs Yield Models, Weather Variables vs NDVI Models, NDVI vs Yield Models, Weather Variables & NDVI vs Yield, Weather Variables, Fertilizer and NDVI vs Yield. The study reveals that NDVI alone may not yield the desired model for rain fed kharif rice yield prediction, combining non-weather predictor variables improve the model accuracy up to 70%.

Now-a-days a growing number of applications of machine learning techniques in agriculture are required for which a large amount of data currently available from many resources can be analyzed to find the hidden knowledge. This is an advanced researched field and is expected to grow in the future. The integration of computer science with agriculture helps in forecasting agricultural crops. It is required to build on objective methodology for pre-harvest crop forecasting. Building up a suitable model will have certain merits over the traditional forecasting method. A detail about the study is which has been developed by Subhadra Mishra et.al(2016) is shown in table3.

Table 3. Applications of various models

Fusion Type	Application Area
Non Linear Regression	Forecasting Corn Yields
Markov Chain Approach	Forecasting Cotton Yields
Linear Regression	Estimating Grain Yield of Maturing Rice
Modified K-Means Clustering	Crop Prediction
Polynomial Regression	Factors Affecting the Yield of Winter Cereals in Crop Margins
Decision Tree	Soybean Productivity Modeling

(Subhadra Mishra et.al(2016))

Remote sensing plays a vital role in agricultural activities like yield estimation before harvesting, in Bangladesh due to increase in population and decrease in crop land, yield prediction before harvesting is very essential for food security. The aim of this paper is to develop a model for Wheat Yield Prediction in Bangladesh Advanced Very High-Resolution Radiometer (AVHRR) sensor data by considering Vegetation condition Index (VCI) and Temperature Condition Index (TCI) and Multilayer Perceptron Network (MLP) of ANN by training the model by Back Propagation algorithm, which reduces error using weights and bias adjustments. The obtained results are compared with the actual statistics of the yield, the predicted results shows the more than 90% accuracy.

Figure 11. Comparison graph of actual and predicted wheat yield in Bangladesh (Subhadra Mishra et.al(2016))

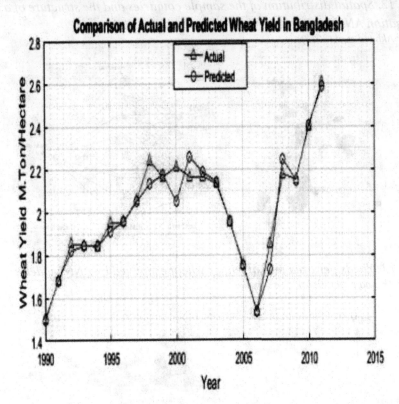

Results in figure 11prove that Artificial Neural Network is a potential tool for wheat yield prediction model development using AVHRR satellite data by considering vegetation indices of crops health TCI and VCI characterizing thermal and moisture conditions respectively.

ANN has proved to be a powerful tool for yield estimation compared to simple non-linear and traditional linear analysis. This study demonstrated that it is possible to develop a yield estimation model using remote sensing images and ANN techniques. Kawsar Akhand et.al (2018) developed a model to predict winter wheat yield estimation in north China, during winter yield is affected by many factors like temperature, water stress, soil conditions and sunlight supply. Five Indices has been selected to represent the above factors such as NDVI, absorbed photosynthesis active radiation

(APAR), surface temperature (Ts), water stress index and average crop yield over the last 10 years. 1 km*1 km resolution NOAA AVHRR dataset is used for yield estimation along with back propagation model as shown in below figure 12. Thus it

Figure 12. Spatial distribution of the sample countries and the structure of a back-propagation ANN model
(Kawsar Akhand et.al (2018))

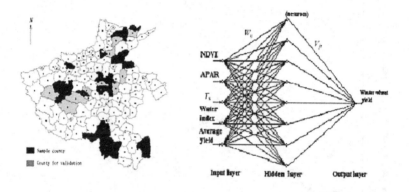

Figure 13. Yields per area unit of winter wheat estimated by ANN model
(Kawsar Akhand et.al (2018))

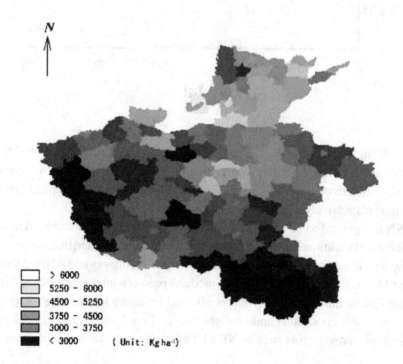

has been confirmed from the survey that ANN yield estimation model with remote sensing plays a vital role in agriculture from several characteristics (1) capabilities of ANN itself, such as self-learning, compatibility and flexibility; (2) integrated use of remotely sensed data together with historical statistical information. Parameters retrieved from satellite images were coalesced by the main growing season of the crop; and (3) precise division of the study area based on agricultural knowledge and careful selection of sample data. This model has been implemented in the Nan province in 1999. The model has only been applied in the He Nan province in 1999. Further studies may focus on the test and calibration of this model in larger areas and over longer temporal scales.

Figure 12 and 13 represents Spatial distribution of the sample countries in He Nan province and the structure of a back-propagation ANN model used for winter wheat yield estimation by using various indices like NDVI, NDWI etc., as input layers.

Table 4 represents the comparison results of ANN model and Multi-Regression model which shows that ANN model provides an better results in comparison with regression model.

Table 4. Comparison of results of ANN model and multi-regression model

County name	NDVI	T_s (°C)	Water index	APAR (MJ m^{-2})	Average yield (kg ha^{-1})	Actual yield (kg ha^{-1})	Result of ANN	Result of MR	Relative error (ANN)	Relative error (MR)
Qi Xian	3329.1	3466.8	100.5	3664.2	3950.6	4807.1	5194.7	4742.0	−8.06	1.35
Luan Chuan	2121.7	3606.2	78.5	3460.8	2634.6	4215.9	4269.9	3466.8	−1.28	17.8
Lu Shan	1635.3	3974.1	57.6	2555.5	2483.0	3593.4	3414.9	2389.9	4.97	33.5
Jia Xian	2401.2	3852.8	83.5	3018.0	4087.2	4686.5	4482.6	3815.7	4.35	18.6
JunXian	2918.2	3495.9	117.3	3823.4	5202.1	5473.1	5570.0	5415.3	−1.77	1.06
Yan Jin	2426.0	3438.8	94.6	3272.9	4494.9	5220.3	5343.0	4804.8	−2.34	7.96
Qing Feng	2897.4	3551.5	106.9	3834.8	5498.1	5417.9	5557.9	5481.6	−2.59	−1.2
Chang Ge	3237.2	3642.4	130.2	4210.7	4855.7	5948.1	5612.9	5187.0	5.64	12.8
Fu Gou	2781.8	3549.3	97.7	3530.0	4764.6	5132.1	5296.7	4934.0	−3.21	3.86
Nan Zhao	1394.4	3772.0	46.2	2749.7	2698.0	3420.8	3394.8	2837.2	0.76	17.1

(Kawsar Akhand et.al (2018))

Remote Sensing for Crop Classification/Cropping

P Kumar et al(2016) have used ANN algorithm for classification of corn, pigeon pea, rice, green gram, corn, other crops and non-crop classes in Varanasi District, UP, India using RISAT-1 with medium resolution of C-band, dual polarimertic temporal satellite datasets. Ground truth data were collected using Global Positioning System (GPS) on the same day of satellite data acquisition. Jefferies Matusita (JM) and Transformed Divergence (TD) distance methods were compared for separability analysis. The comparison result shows that the transformed divergence method has shown the better separation between the classes.

ANN is a mathematical model which is used for classification consisting of three input layers of satellite bands as neurons, a single hidden layer contains 8 neurons and one output layer contains 6 neurons of crop classes which are used for classification. ENVI 5.1 is used for supervised learning which uses back propagation and reduces the RMSE between desired actual outputs with the expected output. The figure 14 shows the three layers of ANN structure.

Figure 14. Three layer of ANN structure of multiple crop classification using various polarizations
(*P Kumar et al(2016)*)

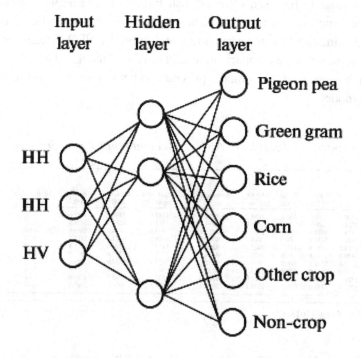

The result of classification shows the overall accuracy of 74.21 and 77.36 for the acquired satellite data on August 9th 2013 and Sept 28th 2013 respectively. The accuracy of September is better because of high reflection during crop maturity.

In this study Pradeep Kumar et.al (2015) have used Resourcesat-2, the Linear Imaging and Improved Self-Scanning (LISS IV) which is suitable satellite for crop classification which has a spatial resolution of 5.8 m was used for comparison of accuracies obtained by ANN, Support Vector Machine (SVM) and Spectral Angle Mapper (SAM) algorithms at UP, India. The overall accuracies of SVM, ANN and

SAM were 93.45%, 92.32% and 74.99% respectively. The results obtained were validated using error matrix and the results were compared with the ground truth.

Rajendra Prasad et.al(2015) are classified various crops such as wheat, barley, mustard, lentil, pigeon pea, sugar cane and other no-crops such as water, sand, fallow, built up, dense vegetation, sparse vegetation using the comparison of Landsat 8 OLI multispectral satellite data with LISS-IV to evaluate the performance of Artificial Neural Network algorithm using various learning parameters.

The comparison study reveals that, larger the learning rates, high fluctuation and lower the classification accuracy LISS-IV, while less but consistent results were found using Landsat 8 OLI.

Crop Mapping using satellite images is a challenging task due to complexities within field, and having the similar spectral properties with other crops in the same region. R. Saini & S.K. Ghosh(2018), have used Sentinel-2 satellite that 13 thirteen spectral bands, 5 days revisit time and resolution at three different level (10m, 20m, 60m), also the free availability of data, makes it a correct choice for vegetation mapping. The aim of this paper is to classify crop using single date Sentinel-2 imagery in the Roorkee, Uttarakhand, India.

Most efficient machine learning algorithms namely Support Vector Machine (SVM) and Random Forest (RF) are used for classification of crops by considering four spectral bands i.e., Near Infra-Red (NIR), Red, Blue, Green of sentinel-2 data are stacked for the classification. The comparison study of RF and SVM shows the overall accuracy achieved is 84.22% and 81.22% respectively, which states that the RF with sentinel-2 yields better results. Table 5 and figure 15 provides the brief description of the comparison study.

Table 5. Class specific accuracy by RF and SVM for crop images

Class Name	RF (%)	SVM (%)
High Density Forest	92.93	90.66
Low Density Forest	85.05	82.6
Orchard	75.37	74.46
Sandy area	84.47	81.76
Water	89.76	89.32
Built-up	86.47	83.53
Fallow land	90.48	87.99
Wheat	82.11	78.55
Sugarcane	84.76	81.77
Fodder	61.22	59.21
Other crops	83.24	80.99

(R. Saini & S.K. Ghosh(2018))

Figure 15. Classified crop images by RF and SVM
(R.& Saini, S.K. Ghosh(2018))

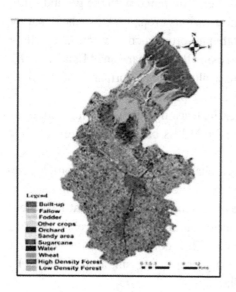 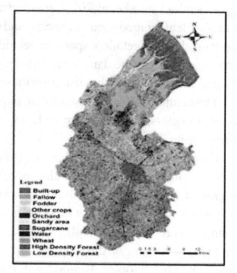

Contributions

The following are the contribution for the chapter.

- Provides an insight regarding various acquisition methods for remote sensed data.
- Introduction on ANN characteristics and functionalities
- Provide briefly an insight to various applications of ANN
- Provides applications of ANN for agriculture using remote sensed data in particular yield
- Prediction of crops and crop mapping/classification
- Future scope of research with other machine learning techniques deep learning and other domains for agriculture is covered

CHALLENGES AND FURTHER SCOPE

The existing challenges in this area will be presented. In addition future directions of research area for application agriculture using advance machine learning methods (deep learning) and suitable domains will be covered in this section.

Remote sensing plays an important role in future in agriculture. The different data can be taken in precise and high modeling of electromagnetic scattering and parameter extraction of crop and farm land images. In modern remote sensing application involves the implanting non-chips in plants and trees to monitor crop. The deep learning methodologies such as CNN, RNN and LSTM variants can be incorporated to extract and address spectral-spatial feature learning in various applications. Currently CNN is been used commonly for remote sensing. Further integration of CNN with other models like RNN, RBN might yield better temporal-spatial yields for remote image processing. Remote sensing future opportunities are listed below,

- Combination of deep learning methods for retrieval of images are structuring of part of images.
- Considering memory effects of climate and vegetation
- Classification of multi sensor data and any deep learning methods
- For damage estimation with high resolution UAV imagery
- RNN/LSTM for satellite imagery for reliable classification of land usage

CONCLUSION

Various ANN methods like Support Vector Machine, Random Forest algorithm, Decision tree, Back propagation method, K-means clustering in combination with various satellites images like optical or microwave data in agriculture can be efficiently used for crop classification, Yield prediction, effect of soil in yield prediction, calculating Leaf area Index, NDVI to obtain accurate results. Forecasting of crop yield is helpful in food management and growth of a nation, which has specially agriculture based economy. In the last few decades, Artificial Neural Networks have been used successfully in different fields of agricultural remote sensing especially in crop type classification and crop area yield estimation.

REFERENCES

Akhand, K., Nizamuddin, M., & Roytman, L. (2018). An Artificial Neural Network-Based Model for Predicting Boro Rice Yield in Bangladesh Using AVHRR-Based Satellite Data. *International Journal of Agriculture and Forestry*, 8(1), 16–25. doi:10.5923/j.ijaf.20180801.04

Akhand, K., Nizamuddin, M., & Roytman, L. (2018). Wheat Yield Prediction in Bangladesh using Artificial Neural Network and Satellite Remote Sensing Data. *Global Journal of Science Frontier Research: D Agriculture and Veterinary, 18*(2).

Ayoubi. (2011). Application of Artificial Neural Network (ANN) to Predict Soil Organic Matter Using Remote Sensing Data in Two Ecosystems. In *Biomass and Remote Sensing of Biomass*. InTech.

Chandra, A., Mitra, P. S. K., Dubey, & Ray. (2019). *Machine Learning Approach For Kharif Rice Yield Prediction Integrating Multi-Temporal Vegetation Indices And Weather And Non-Weather Variables.* The International Archives of the Photogrammetry, Remote Sensing and Spatial Information Sciences, New Delhi, India.

Dave, V. S., & Dutta, K. (2014). Neural network-based models for software effort estimation: A review. *Artificial Intelligence Review, 42*(2), 295–307.

Huang. (2017). Imitating the brain with neurocomputer a "new" way towards artificial general intelligence. *Int. J. Autom. Comput., 14*(5), 520-531.

Jiang, Yang, Clinton, & Wang. (2004). An artificial neural network model for estimating crop yields using remotely sensed information. *International Journal of Remote Sensing.* http://www.tandf.co.uk/journals

Kumar, Gupta, Mishra, & Prasad. (2015). Comparison of support vector machine, artificial neural network, and spectral angle mapper algorithms for crop classification using LISS IV data. *International Journal of Remote Sensing, 36*(6).

Kumar, P., Prasad, R., Prashant, K., & Srivasta. (2015). Artificial neural network with different learning parameters for crop classification using multispectral datasets. In *International Conference on Microwave, Optical and Communication Engineering (ICMOCE).* IEEE.

Kumara, P., Prasada, R., Mishraa, V. N., Guptaa, D. K., & Singhb, S. K. (2016). Artificial Neural Network for Crop Classification Using C-band RISAT-1 Satellite Datasets. *Russian Agricultural Sciences, 42*(3-4), 281–284.

Kuwataa, K. R., & Shibasakib. (2016), Estimating Corn Yield In The United States With Modis EVI And Machine Learning Methods. *ISPRS Annals Of The Photogrammetry, Remote Sensing And Spatial Information Sciences, 8.*

Manoj, Semwal, & Verma. (2019). *An Artificial Neural Network Model For Estimating Mentha Crop Biomass Yield Using Landsat 8 OLI.* Precision Agriculture. Https://Doi.Org/10.1007/S11119-019-09655-1

Mishra, S., Mishra, D., & Santra, G. H. (2016). Applications of Machine Learning Techniques in Agricultural Crop Production: A Review Paper. *Indian Journal of Science and Technology*, 9(38). doi:10.17485/ijst/2016/v9i38/95032

Mishra. (2016). Applications of Machine Learning Techniques in Agricultural Crop Production: A Review Paper. *Indian Journal of Science and Technology, 9*(38). www.indjst.org

Saini, R. S. K., & Ghosh. (2018). *Crop Classification On Single Date Sentinel-2 Imagery Using Random Forest And Suppor Vector Machine*. The International Archives of the Photogrammetry, Remote Sensing and Spatial Information Sciences, Dehradun, India.

Taşdemir & Wirnhardt. (2012). Neural network-based clustering for agriculture management. *EURASIP Journal on Advances in Signal Processing*, 200.

Yan, F., Gong, Y., & Feng, Z. (2015). Combination of Artificial Neural Network with Multispectral Remote Sensing Data as Applied in Site Quality Evaluation in Inner Mongolia. *Croatian Journal of Forest Engineering, 36*, 2.

Yao, C., Zhang, Y., Zhang, Y., & Liu, H. (2017). Application of convolutional Neural Network in classification of high resolution Agricultural Remote Sensing Images. The International archives of the photogrammetry, remote sensing and spatial information sciences, Wuhan, China.

Yao, C. (2017). *Application of convolutional Neural Network in classification of high resolution Agricultural Remote Sensing Images*. The International archives of the photogrammetry, remote sensing and spatial information sciences, Wuhan, China.

Chapter 5
Classification Approach for Sentiment Analysis Using Machine Learning

Satyen M. Parikh
Ganpat University, India

Mitali K. Shah
Ganpat University, India

ABSTRACT

A utilization of the computational semantics is known as natural language processing or NLP. Any opinion through attitude, feelings, and thoughts can be identified as sentiment. The overview of people against specific events, brand, things, or association can be recognized through sentiment analysis. Positive, negative, and neutral are each of the premises that can be grouped into three separate categories. Twitter, the most commonly used microblogging tool, is used to gather information for research. Tweepy is used to access Twitter's source of information. Python language is used to execute the classification algorithm on the information collected. Two measures are applied in sentiment analysis, namely feature extraction and classification. Using n-gram modeling methodology, the feature is extracted. Through a supervised machine learning algorithm, the sentiment is graded as positive, negative, and neutral. Support vector machine (SVM) and k-nearest neighbor (KNN) classification models are used and demonstrated both comparisons.

DOI: 10.4018/978-1-7998-4042-8.ch005

INTRODUCTION

Sentiment Analysis

The word opinion mining is utilized in many different applications for sentiment analysis. Its purpose is to check the opinion of the people on the product's benefits and product's characteristics (features). Essentially, an evaluation of opinion is a kind of common approach used to determine whether or not people are interested in the product. The emotions or feelings of people are expressed textually. These aspects are obtained from different sites or mobile applications. (Duygulu et al., 2002)

Analysis of sentiment is used to keep in touch or show the feelings of people. People give product's positive and negative opinion for the services of item. When making any choice for purchase the product, these opinions are very valuable for the customer (Zhang et al., 2013). It is very difficult to correctly interpret the right view in the sense of large textual data set and unstructured data sets. To identify the characteristics of an unstructured dataset, it is essential to structure a productive technique (Yu et al., 2010).

Preprocessing, feature extraction and classification are three main parts and analysis methods for sentiment analysis (Xu et al., 2013). Some association only works with positive and negative text. They skip the neutral text recognition. Such texts use the binary classification limits. Several researchers introduce polarity problems for perform three classes (Ren & Wu, 2013). For entropy and SVM classifiers, the neutral classes, presentation etc. are very essential. This improves the accuracy of overall classification. These principles ought to be considered by the neutral classes for the execution. The first algorithm understands the concept of neutral language and extracts people's remaining opinions. In simply single phase, this algorithm completes the three-level classification (Poria et al., 2013).

In every class, in the next methodology, the probability and distribution are calculated (Garcia-Moya et al., 2013). When the data is the most neutral with the variance between positive and negative outcomes, it becomes more difficult to implement this methodology (Cheng et al., 2013). Sentiment analysis is used in some various ways. It is useful for marketers to measure the credibility and accomplishment of some new product dispatch and to see what edition of the product is in demand and show the new product's famous highlights (Hai et al., 2013)

The below are some of the key features of tweets:

- Message Length
- Writing technique
- Availability
- Topics

- Real time

Benefits of Using Sentimental Analysis

Sentiment analysis has many benefits given to different business and organization. It helps and gives their business valuable insights that how people feel about their service and brand. It will allow user to identify potential of their products to create more influence on social media. Hence, it will be used to identify negative threads that are emerging online regarding your business, thereby allowing you to be practical in dealing with it more quickly. Some of the benefits are as follow:

- Marketing strategy
- Enlarge product quality
- Improve customer service
- Crisis management

Challenges of Sentimental Analysis

In case of sentiments analysis there are several challenges faced by user in order to tackle their issues, related to their daily life. Natural language processing and text analysis techniques are used to identify and extract the subjective information available in the applied in the practice of sentiment analysis. These challenges become obstacles in analyzing the accurate meaning of sentiments and detecting the suitable sentiment polarity.

Some challenges are as follow:

- Speaker's emotional state
- Multiple thoughts
- Fake Opinion
- Challenge in applying
- Language problem

SENTIMENT ANALYSIS TECHNIQUES

There are two main techniques for sentiment analysis: machine learning based, and lexicon based. Few research studies have also combined these two methods and gain relatively better performance.

1.   **Lexicon Based Approach:** opinion lexicon for sentiment classification is based on the insight that the polarity of a piece of text can be obtained on the grounds of the words which compose it. This approach is of two types: positive or negative opinions. Positive opinion is used to show the desired stage and negative stage is used to show undesired stage. Opinion lexicon is also known as opinion phrases or idioms.(Hussein, 2018)

   a.   **Dictionary Based Approach:** The resources used are lexicographical, initial method is to collect the seeds of the sentiment words and their orientation to find their antonyms and synonyms to expand their set. When no more words left this iteration stops. This approach is unable to extract opinions with domain specific orientations which are counted as its disadvantage.

   b.   **Corpus-Based Approach:** It can help to find domain specific opinion words and their orientation if a corpus from only the specific domain is used in the discovery process. It resolves the problem of dictionary-based approach and also explores the idea of intra-sentential and inter-sentential sentiment. Despite showing domain dependent words it showed the same word having different contexts even in the same domain.

2.   **Machine Learning Approach**: Machine learning approach has been used to solve the sentence classifications problems that totally based on the algorithms. It trains a text classifier on a human labeled training dataset. Two approaches were used that is supervised leaning approach and unsupervised learning approach. Bulk of labeled training document is known as supervised learning and further it is of two types: Naïve Baye's algorithm and Maximum Entropy Classifier. (Astya, 2017)

   a.   **Naïve Baye's Algorithm:** Naive Baye's provides good result in spite of having low Naïve Baye's Classification probability. It is a supervised machine learning approach. It is totally based on Baye's Theorem.

   b.   **Maximum Entropy Algorithm:** It is widely used in the field of computer vision for the prediction, using machine learning technique which is known as multinomial logic model. The advantage of using this algorithm is that, it will provide us with extra semantic, syntactic feature and very much flexible in use.

   c.   2. c. **SVM Classifier:** This classifier has enormous edge for classification. Hyper plane technique is used to separates the tweets using comparison difference between the tweet and hyper plane. The discriminative function used by SVM classifier is defined as:

$$g(X) = wT\varphi(X) + b \tag{1}$$

In the above given equation (1), feature vector is denoted by "X", weight vector denoted by "w" and bias vector is "b". Linear kernel is used for classification as it maintains the gap between two classes.

TYPES

Sentiment analysis is a new field of research born in Natural Language Processing (NLP), aiming at detecting subjectivity in text and/or extracting and classifying opinions and sentiments. Sentiment analysis studies people's sentiments, opinions, attitudes, evaluations, appraisals and emotions towards services, products, individuals, organizations, issues, topics events and their attributes. In sentiment analysis text is classified according to the following different criteria:

- the polarity of the sentiment expressed (into positive, negative, and neutral);
- the polarity of the outcome (e.g. improvement versus death in medical texts)
- agree or disagree with a topic (e.g. political debates)
- good or bad news;
- support or opposition;
- pros and cons

APPLICATION

When consumers have to make a decision or a choice regarding a product, important information is the reputation of that product, which is derived from the opinion of others. Sentiment analysis can reveal what other people think about a product. The first application of sentiment analysis is thus giving indication and recommendation in the choice of products according to the wisdom of the crowd. When you choose a product, you are generally attracted to certain specific aspects of the product. A single global rating could be deceiving. Sentiment analysis can regroup the opinions of the reviewers and estimate ratings on certain aspects of the product.

Another utility of sentiment analysis is for companies that want to know the opinion of customers on their products. They can then improve the aspects that the customers found unsatisfying. Sentiment analysis can also determine which aspects are more important for the customers.

Finally, sentiment analysis has been proposed as a component of other technologies. One idea is to improve information mining in text analysis by excluding the most subjective section of a document or to automatically propose internet ads for products that fit the viewer's opinion (and removing the others). Knowing what people think gives numerous possibilities in the Human/Machine interface domain. Sentiment analysis for determining the opinion of a customer on a product (and consequently the reputation of the product) is the main focus of this paper. In the following section, we will discuss solutions that allow determining the expressed opinion on products.

STEPS FOR THE SENTIMENT ANALYSIS

- Data Collection
- Data Preparation
- Develop Model
- Train and Update

VARIOUS FACES OF SENTIMENT ANALYSIS

- Data Extraction
- Data Pre-processing

Figure 1. Data Extraction
(Source: ICACSE-2019, p. 92)

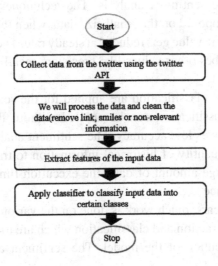

99

- Feature Extraction
- Sentiment Classification

WHY MACHING LEARNING NEEDS?

- Nearly 80% of the world's digital data is unstructured, and data obtained from social media sources is no exception to that. Since the information is not organized in any predefined way, it's difficult to sort and analyze. Fortunately, thanks to the developments in Machine Learning and NLP, it is now possible to create models that learn from examples and can be used to process and organize text data.
- Twitter sentiment analysis systems allow you to sort large sets of tweets and detect the polarity of each statement automatically. And the best part, it's fast and simple, saving times valuable hours and allowing them to focus on tasks where they can make a bigger impact. By training a machine learning model to perform sentiment analysis on Twitter, you can set the parameters to analyze all your data and obtain more consistent and accurate results.

RESEARCH GAP

Following are the various research gap of this study:-

- The sentiment analysis is the type of approach which is applied to analysis the sentiments. In the previous research, the technique of lexical analysis is applied for the sentiment analysis. The techniques which are designed previously are proposed on the small size data, when the size of the data gets increase parametric value gets reduced at steady rate. The accuracy parametric value also describes other values like precision, recall and f-measure which also get affected.
- The techniques of classification are applied for the sentiment analysis. The techniques of classification can be applied without the feature extraction due to which it gives less accuracy. The sentiment analysis approaches need to handle large quantity of historical information to train the model. While handling such large amount of data, the execution time is increased which affects performance
- In the previous years, much work is done on the various types of techniques for the feature extraction and classification which are too complex, it directly increase the execution of the model. The sentiment analysis can be done

using the lexical analysis phase; the technique of lexical analysis can be done using the priority phases. The threshold value can assign by taking average of the priority values which affect efficiency of the proposed model. The approach is required which have the both techniques of feature extraction and the classification when combined it improve accuracy of classification

PROBLEM STATEMENT

Sentiment analysis is a way to study the opinion of the users towards an entity, like products, services, brands, movies, events, and so on. Sentiment analysis is applied on the comments posted by users on micro blogging sites, social networking websites, online user review portals etc. In this method, the features of the input data are extracted using pattern matching algorithm and the extracted features are classified using classification techniques. In the existing method, N-gram technique is used for feature extraction and SVM classifier is used for feature classification. In this work two issues may arise. N-gram algorithm extracts the color features from the posts and to improve its efficiency textual features also need to be analyzed. The second issue is when classification is done using SVM classifier, the complexity increases which increase the execution time.

SIGNIFICANCE OF PURPOSE WORK

'Sentiment' literally means 'Emotions' of an individual. Sentiment analysis, also known as opinion mining, is a type of data mining that refers to the analysis of data obtained from micro blogging sites, social media updates, online news reports, user reviews etc., in order to study the sentiments of the people towards an event, organization, product, brand, person etc.

With the expansion of users posting their viewpoints in micro blogging sites, sentiment analysis of the posted texts has turned into a happening field of research, as it serves as a potential source for studying the opinions held by the users towards an entity.

In this work, sentiment classification is done into three categories, namely positive, negative and neutral. The data used for analysis has been taken from twitter, it being the most popular micro blogging site. The source data has been extracted from twitter using python's Tweepy. N-gram modeling technique is used for feature extraction and the supervised machine learning algorithm k-nearest neighbor is used for sentiment classification into positive, negative and neutral classes. The implementation of the proposed approach has been done in python language.

LITERATURE REVIEW

Endang wahyu pamungkas, et.Al (2016) performed lexicon-based sentiment analysis of Indonesian language (Pamungkas et al., 2016). The classification of sentiment data was carried out in three sentiments such as positive, negative, and neutral. The tested outcomes demonstrated that the recommended approach achieved classification accuracy of 0.68. In general, the recommended approach achieved good results in sentiment classification. This work detected some problems as well. It was possible to use these issues as a base to carry out more research work. Initially, a non-standard language was detected in the dataset. The next issue was related to the dissatisfaction of expectation event. The very last issue was related to vagueness.

Shahnawaz, et.Al, (2017) presented that sentiment analysis is the process to identify the opinion or feelings expressed in the opinioned data, in order to find the attitude of writer towards the particular topic whether it is positive, negative or neutral. It provides idea to the customer to identify the product or service is satisfactory or not before the customer buys it. Public opinions on different types of social media are the major concern of the scientific communities and business world to gather and extract public views. Inadequacy accuracy, inability to perform well in different domain and performance are the main issues in the current techniques. Author concluded, by using semi-supervised and unsupervised learning based models, it will be easy minimize lack of labeled data if sufficient amount of unlabeled data is available. (Astya, 2017)

Pulkit garg, et.Al, (2017) as surveyed that social media has becoming a medium for online sharing by the increase of more number of people coming online. In this paper, we study post- terror attack tweets by extracting it from twitter. The flow data posted on twitter is used to study factors like last retweet, number of retweets and number of favorites. Maximum number of retweets indicates maximum reach. It creates widespread reaction on the social media. Governments are concentrating on digitalizing the whole nation. Due to increase in number of people, huge data is generated. Author discussed the Uri terror attacks that show more negative tweets tend to survive as compare to positive tweets, although their amount is low. It will lead to public unrest if people start targeting a community and provide negative information. Misleading information, the trends of retweets and number of favorites are the future scope to study its flow and survival (Garg et al., 2017).

Ana valdivia et.Al, (2017) researchers working in the field of natural language processing and text mining received a lot of attention on sentiment analysis. To operate all domains there was lack of annotated data being used that hampered the accuracy of sentiment analysis. The issue is geared up after attempting many attempts. In this paper, authors' provided techniques and systematic literature review on cross-domain sentiment analysis. According to author there was no perfect solution hence to solve the problems of cross domain sentiment analysis different techniques, methods and approaches had been used in order to develop more accurate data in near future. The fuzzy majority based on aggregating polarity for several sentiment analyses the use of induced ordered weighted is proposed. Author's main focused on removing those neutral reviews labeled by accord of collections (Valdivia et al., 2017).

Wei zhao, ziyu guan et.Al, (2017) to ease new buyers in making good decisions products review are necessary. A new technique has been introduced for opinion mining which help us to determine the positive and negative of a post or review. For solving sentiment classification problems deep learning has effective means and without using human efforts a neutral network represents. Success of deep learning solely depends on the large-scale training data. In this paper, they had given a review on different sentiment classification using purposed deep learning framework that employs commonly existing rating. Adding a classification layer and learning a high level representation are the two steps consists in purposed framework. In order to achieve supervised fine tunings a level sentences are used and on the top of embedding layer a classification layer is added on the other hand in the first step rating information is used to capture the general sentiment distribution. The long short memory and conventional feature extractors are used for low level network structure that helps in modeling review sentences. The Amazon data sets have been used that contained 1.1 weakly review sentences and 11,754 labeled review sentences. To check the proposed framework different experiments have been performed that show its superiority over baselines (Zhao, 2017)

Kulkarni, D. S., Et.Al, (2018) presented sentiment analysis is broadly utilized in a large portion of real time applications. The exact recognizable proof of content features collected from the unstructured textual information is significant research challenge. A few strategies which present the extraction of sentiment-based component in dataset mining patterns are utilized by single survey corpus and avoid by the non-trivial uniqueness in the word of distributional attributes of sentiment feature. Such techniques are not comfortable to predict the people feedback effectively. Sentiment analysis is an alternate strategy directly from mining classification to advance sentiment analysis. To start with, traditional procedures were examined for taking care of the issue of sentiment analysis. At that point they examined the ongoing technique for sentiment features, classification and information recovery. They likewise examined the near investigation among every one of these methods. At last, they watched and saw the present research issues of interest based on expanded study of ongoing techniques. From their investigation, they can reason that sentiment analysis is an attraction in numerous researchers. (Kulkarni & Rodd, 2018).

Soonh Taj, et.al (2019) proposed a lexicon-based approach for sentiment analysis of news articles. It was observed that categories of business and sports had more positive articles, whereas entertainment and tech had a majority of negative articles.

The experiments have been performed on BBC news dataset, which expresses the applicability and validation of the adopted approach. Future work in this regard will be based on sentiment analysis of news using various machine learning approaches with the development of an online application from where users can read news of their interests. Also, based on sentiment analysis methods, readers can customize their news feed. (Taj et al., 2019)

Annet John, et.al (2019) studied that the lexicon based approaches plays an active role regarding the aforementioned aspects. Here handling of contextual polarity of text was the major focus wherein which the prior polarity of the term expressed in the lexicon may be different from the polarity expressed in the text. The hybrid lexicon eliminates such hurdles. Not all problems are handled by the usage of hybrid lexicon; certain other problems such as negation, emoticons and modifiers adversely affect the sentiment score of textual data. Experimental results give evidence in the performance improvement of the proposed system in terms of accuracy, recall and precision when compared with the existing systems. (John et al., 2019)

Farkhund Iqbal, et.al (2019) proposed a novel Genetic Algorithm (GA) based feature reduction technique. By using this hybrid approach, it was possible to reduce the feature-set size by up to 42% without compromising the accuracy. Furthermore, our sentiment analysis framework was evaluated on other metrics including precision, recall, F-measure, and feature size. In order to demonstrate the efficacy of GA based designs, a novel cross-disciplinary area of geopolitics was also proposed as a case study application for our sentiment analysis framework. The experiment results have shown to accurately measure public sentiments and views regarding various topics such as terrorism, global conflicts, social issues etc. The applicability of proposed work was evaluated in various areas including security and surveillance, law-and-order, and public administration.(Iqbal et al., 2019)

Korovkinas, et.al, (2019) submitted that ascent of social networks and spread of Internet-related smart gadgets contraptions was trailed by explosion in data available for assortment and making, offering certified mechanical and computational troubles together with new alluring results in research, appointment and utilization of new and existing data science and machine learning procedures. Author closed; by propose a hybrid procedure to enhance SVM characterization accuracy utilizing training data set and hyper parameter tuning. The proposed system uses clustering to select training data and tuning parameters to enhance the viability of the classifier. The paper reports that advance results have been achieved using this proposed method in all analysis compared to previous results showing the work of the technique (Korovkinas et al., 2019).

Priyanka tyagi, et.Al, (2019) presented that any sentiment of a people through which the emotions, attitude and thoughts can be communicated is known as opinion. The sorts of information examination which is accomplished from the news reports, client surveys, social media updates or micro blogging sites are called sentiment analysis which is otherwise called opinion mining. The surveys of people towards specific occasions, brands, item or organization can be known through sentiment analysis. The reactions of overall population are gathered and improvised by specialists to perform evaluation. The fame of sentiment analysis is developing today since the quantities of perspectives being shared by public on the micro blogging sites are additionally expanding. Every one of the opinions can be ordered into three distinct classifications called positive, negative and neutral. Twitter, being the most well-known micro blogging web page, is utilized to gather the information to perform examination. Tweepy is utilized to extract the source information from twitter. Python language is utilized in this exploration to execute the algorithm on the gathered information. Author concluded using n-gram modeling method the features are to be extracted. The opinion is ordered among positive, negative and neutral utilizing a supervised learning algorithm known as k-nearest neighbor. (Tyagi et al., 2019)

Mondher bouazizi et.Al,(2019) presented that most of the work related to sentiment analysis of texts focuses on the binary and ternary classification of these data, the task of multi-class classification has received less attention. Multi-class classification has always been a challenging task given the complexity of natural languages and the difficulty of understanding and mathematically "quantifying" how humans express their feelings. In that work, they study the task of multi-class classification of online posts of twitter users, and show how far it is possible to go with the classification, and the limitations and difficulties of that task. Nonetheless, they propose a novel model to represent the different sentiments and show how this model helps to understand how sentiments are related. The model is then used to analyze the challenges that multi-class classification presents and to highlight possible future enhancements to multi-class classification accuracy. (Bouazizi et al., 2019)

MeghaRathi, et.al (2018) studied that previously, researchers were using existing machine learning techniques for sentiment analysis but the results showed that existing machine learning techniques were not providing better results of sentiment classification. In order to improve classification results in the domain of sentiment analysis, this research used ensemble machine learning techniques for increasing the efficiency and reliability of proposed approach. For the same, Support Vector Machine was merged with Decision Tree and experimental results prove that our proposed approach is providing better classification results in terms of f-measure and accuracy in contrast to individual classifiers. (Rathi et al., 2018)

Mohammed H. Abd El-Jawad, et.al (2018) compared the performance of different machine learning and deep learning algorithms, in addition to introducing a new hybrid system that uses text mining and neural networks for sentiment classification. The dataset used in this work contains more than 1 million tweets collected in five domains. The system was trained using 75% of the dataset and was tested using the remaining 25%. The results show a maximum accuracy rate of 83.7%, which shows the efficiency of the hybrid learning approach used by the system over the standard supervised approaches. (El-Jawad et al., 2018)

PROPOSED METHODOLOGY

Twitter data sentiment analysis is the main purpose of this research work. In the existing framework, a classification model called SVM is used to classify input data into seven classes using the SANTA Tool. The research suggested substitutes the system of classification SVM with the model of classification KNN. This model of classification classifies seven classes of input data. On the basis of accuracy, the performance analysis of both approaches is carried out.

SVM Classifier for Sentiment Analysis

To achieve the prime objective of the classification, SVMs was introduced and it was utilized in that direction, down time use case of SVMs was extended for reference learning and regression. Mainly SVMs algorithm is working on the binary classifier style same as how computer interpret the data. SVMs classifier achieves learned function in terms of positive or negative output (Juneja & Ojha, 2017). Same way by making use of multiple binary classifiers and as core pair-wise coupling, multiclass classification can be implemented. The mapping is made from input space to feature space by SVM to support the constraints related to non-linear classification.

The kernel trick of the mapping function is utilized by preventing accurate formulation. This generates the curse of dimensionality. Such approach makes the linear classification in new space equal to the non-linear classification in original space. With Input vector of SVMs classifier mapping is done.

For instance, there are N training data points $\left\{ \left(x_1, y_1\right), \left(x_2, y_2\right) \dots \left(x_N, y_N\right) \right\}$. Here, $x_i \in R^d$ and $y_i \in \left\{+1, -1\right\}$. Equation (1) shows the issue of identifying a maximum margin that separates the hyperplane as:

$$\min_{w,b} \frac{1}{2} w^T w \; subject \; to \; y_i \left(w^T x_i - b\right) \geq i = 1, \dots N$$

In general, this is a convex quadratic programming problem. Lagrange multipliers α is introduced to achieve Wolfe dual in the given equation:

$$maximize_{\alpha} \mathcal{L}_D \equiv \sum_{i=1}^{N} \alpha_i - \frac{1}{2} \sum_{i,j} \alpha_i \alpha_j y_i y_j x_i . x_j \qquad (1)$$

Subject to

$$\alpha \geq 0, \sum_i \alpha_i y_i = 0 .$$

Following is the equation (2) of providing primary solution:

$$w = \sum_{i=1}^{N} \alpha_i y_i x_i \qquad (2)$$

KNN Classifier for Sentiment Analysis

K Nearest Neighbor (KNN) comes under a non-parametric classifier. In many aspects this algorithm seems quite simple and effectual. Because of its effectiveness and competent outcomes, KNN is one of most common neighborhood classifiers in pattern recognition. The feature of this classifier can be used easily. There are number of application where such algorithm is used. As example consider pattern recognition, machine learning, text categorization, data mining, object recognition etc. (Hassan et al., 2017). as each algorithm has its own advantages and limitation, KNN also has limitation when It comes to memory requirement and time complexity due to dependency on each instance in training set. One advance feature of using this algorithm is that it resolves the issue if clustering. With compare to another complex algorithm, KNN is bit easy to understand and simple to implement. It's kind of unsupervised learning algorithm. Fixed number of simple clusters is used and also same can be efficiently classified by given data earlier.

This technique can be considered as on the distance function as these algorithms can be implemented During the non-existence labeled data. In the same range this technique normalized the overall features. As this is the This is a conventional non-parametric classification model, K-nearest neighbor classification model computes the optimum performance of the best values of k. This technique assigns this pattern within the k nearest patterns (Astya, 2017). based on individual attribute by combining local distance functions, A global distance function can be computed. The easiest method is to add the values as described by the given equation:

$$dist\left(x,q\right) = \sum_{i=1}^{N} dist_{A_i}\left(x.A_i, q.A_i\right). \tag{3}$$

The global distance is identified as the weighted sum of local distances. For calculating the overall distance, there are different levels of importance provided by weight w_i. The values amongst zero and one are sometimes the weight of values. A completely irrelevant attribute might be generated by the weight of zero. Therefore, the modified form of equation (3) can be inscribed as:

$$dist\left(x,q\right) = \sum_{i=1}^{N} w_i \times dist_{A_i}\left(x.A_i, q.A_i\right). \tag{4}$$

There is a common weighted average which is given as in equation (5):

$$dist\left(x,q\right) = \frac{\sum_{i=1}^{N} w_i \times dist_{A_i}\left(x.A_i, q.A_i\right)}{\sum_{i=1}^{n} w_i}. \tag{5}$$

FACILITIES REQUIRED FOR PURPOSE WORK

Following are the various software and hardware requirements:-

1. Hardware Requirements
    a. Dual core Processor
    b. 2 GB RAM
2. Software Requirements
    a. Anaconda
    b. Microsoft Word

PROPOSED RESEARCH PLAN

This research aims at sentiment analysis of text, namely tweets, taken from Twitter. The complete approach for sentiment analysis consists of the following steps:

Step 1: Data Extraction: The input data set consists of real time tweets that have been extracted from Twitter using Tweepy.

Step 2: Data Pre-processing: In the pre-processing phase, the input data set is cleaned and transformed into a form suitable for feature extraction.

Step 3: Feature Extraction: The pre-processed data is fed as input to the feature extraction algorithm. In this step weights are assigned to the keywords thus preparing them for classification. In this paper N-Gram modeling technique has been used for designing the feature extraction algorithm.

Step 4: Sentiment Classification: In based on their polarity. In this work, machine learning technique k-nearest neighbor classifier has been used for classification into positive, negative and neutral classes.

Figure 2. Proposed research plan

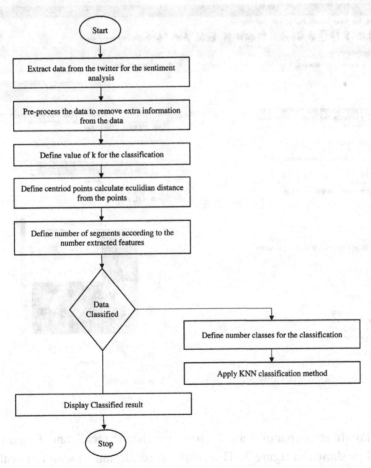

RESULT AND DISCUSSION

Python is a language of programming at the highest level. This tool includes semantics that are dynamic. Within the data structures, this language is created. Thanks to the incorporation of data structures and adaptive typing and linking, the Rapid Application Development can effectively use this tool. In this method, scripting interrelates the previously available components. Therefore, since this language is incredibly simple and easy to understand, it can easily be read. This also minimizes the program's maintenance cost.

Figure 3. Classification report plotting

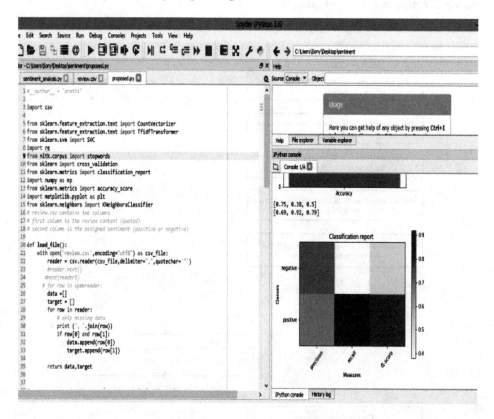

The classification parameters, such as precision, recall and f-measure, are calculated as shown in figure 3. The precision recall and f-measure is calculated as positive, negative for each class. That parameter's values are plotted as a figure.

The figure4 shows the examination of WDE-LSTM and KNN as far as accuracy. KNN classification model shows preferred accuracy over WDE-LSTM for sentiment examination.

Figure 4. Accuracy analysis

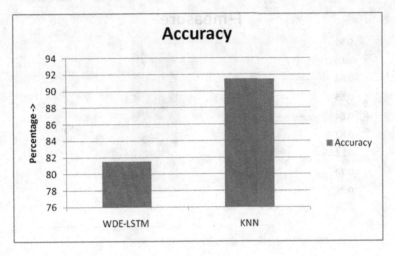

The figure 5 shows the examination of WDE-LSTM and KNN regarding precision, recall. The estimations of the precision and recall are appeared in the above figure.

Figure 5. Precision-recall analysis

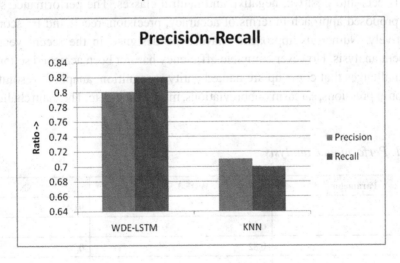

Figure 6 demonstrates the f-measure relation between WDE-LSTM and KNN. KNN classification system has a higher f scale of sentiment analysis than WDE-LSTM

Figure 6. F-measure analysis

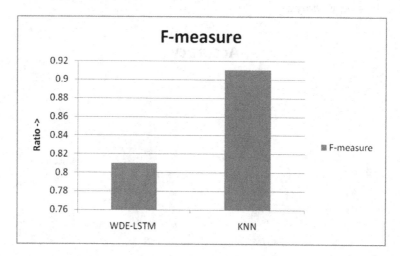

CONCLUSION

Prior of this work was done for twitter data to study the sentiments of users by considering mainly two algorithms named as one is N-Gram technique used for feature extraction and one another is K-Nearest Neighbor classifier used for classification of the tweets into positive, negative and neutral classes. The performance scores of the proposed approach in terms of accuracy, precision, recall and F1 score are respectively. Numerous approaches have been designed in the recent years for sentiment analysis. However complete efficiency has not been achieved so far. The main challenges that come up are named entity recognition, anaphora resolutions, negation expressions, sarcasms, abbreviations, misspellings, etc. The main challenges

Table 1. Performance analysis

Parameter	WDE-LSTM	KNN
Accuracy	81.51	91.45
Precision	0.80	0.71
Recall	0.82	0.70
F-measure	0.81	0.91

that come up are named entity recognition, anaphora resolutions, negation expressions, sarcasms, abbreviations, misspellings, etc. Using huge amount of labeled data for improving results.

REFERENCES

Astya, P. (2017, May). Sentiment analysis: approaches and open issues. In *2017 International Conference on Computing, Communication and Automation (ICCCA)* (pp. 154-158). IEEE.

Bouazizi, Mondher, & Ohtsuki. (2019). Multi-class sentiment analysis on twitter: classification performance and challenges. *Big Data Mining and Analytics, 2*(3), 181-194.

Cheng, V. C., Leung, C. H., Liu, J., & Milani, A. (2013). Probabilistic aspect mining model for drug reviews. *IEEE Transactions on Knowledge and Data Engineering, 26*(8), 2002–2013. doi:10.1109/TKDE.2013.175

Clavel, C., & Callejas, Z. (2015). Sentiment analysis: From opinion mining to human-agent interaction. *IEEE Transactions on Affective Computing, 7*(1), 74–93. doi:10.1109/TAFFC.2015.2444846

Duygulu, P., Barnard, K., de Freitas, J. F., & Forsyth, D. A. (2002, May). Object recognition as machine translation: Learning a lexicon for a fixed image vocabulary. In *European conference on computer vision* (pp. 97-112). Springer.

El-Jawad, M. H. A., Hodhod, R., & Omar, Y. M. (2018, December). Sentiment Analysis of Social Media Networks Using Machine Learning. In *2018 14th International Computer Engineering Conference (ICENCO)* (pp. 174-176). IEEE. 10.1109/ICENCO.2018.8636124

Garcia-Moya, L., Anaya-Sánchez, H., & Berlanga-Llavori, R. (2013). Retrieving product features and opinions from customer reviews. *IEEE Intelligent Systems, 28*(3), 19–27. doi:10.1109/MIS.2013.37

Garg, Pulkit, Garg, & Ranga. (2017). Sentiment analysis of the uri terror attack using twitter. In *2017 international conference on computing, communication and automation (ICCCA)*. IEEE.

Go, A., Bhayani, R., & Huang, L. (2009). Twitter sentiment classification using distant supervision. CS224N Project Report, Stanford, 1(12), 2009.

Hai, Z., Chang, K., Kim, J. J., & Yang, C. C. (2013). Identifying features in opinion mining via intrinsic and extrinsic domain relevance. *IEEE Transactions on Knowledge and Data Engineering*, *26*(3), 623–634. doi:10.1109/TKDE.2013.26

Hassan, A. U., Hussain, J., Hussain, M., Sadiq, M., & Lee, S. (2017, October). Sentiment analysis of social networking sites (SNS) data using machine learning approach for the measurement of depression. In *2017 International Conference on Information and Communication Technology Convergence (ICTC)* (pp. 138-140). IEEE. 10.1109/ICTC.2017.8190959

Hussein, D. M. E. D. M. (2018). A survey on sentiment analysis challenges. *Journal of King Saud University-Engineering Sciences*, *30*(4), 330–338. doi:10.1016/j.jksues.2016.04.002

Iqbal, F., Hashmi, J. M., Fung, B. C., Batool, R., Khattak, A. M., Aleem, S., & Hung, P. C. (2019). A Hybrid Framework for Sentiment Analysis Using Genetic Algorithm Based Feature Reduction. *IEEE Access: Practical Innovations, Open Solutions*, *7*, 14637–14652. doi:10.1109/ACCESS.2019.2892852

John, A., John, A., & Sheik, R. (2019, April). Context Deployed Sentiment Analysis Using Hybrid Lexicon. In *2019 1st International Conference on Innovations in Information and Communication Technology (ICIICT)* (pp. 1-5). IEEE. 10.1109/ICIICT1.2019.8741413

Juneja, P., & Ojha, U. (2017, July). Casting online votes: to predict offline results using sentiment analysis by machine learning classifiers. In *2017 8th International Conference on Computing, Communication and Networking Technologies (ICCCNT)* (pp. 1-6). IEEE. 10.1109/ICCCNT.2017.8203996

Kennedy, A., & Inkpen, D. (2006). Sentiment classification of movie reviews using contextual valence shifters. *Computational Intelligence*, *22*(2), 110–125. doi:10.1111/j.1467-8640.2006.00277.x

Korovkinas, K., Danėnas, P., & Garšva, G. (2019). SVM and k-Means Hybrid Method for Textual Data Sentiment Analysis. *Baltic Journal of Modern Computing*, *7*(1), 47–60. doi:10.22364/bjmc.2019.7.1.04

Kulkarni & Rodd. (2018). Extensive study of text based methods for opinion mining. In *2018 2nd international conference on inventive systems and control (ICISC)*. IEEE.

Pamungkas, Wahyu, & Putri. (2016). An experimental study of lexicon-based sentiment analysis on Bahasa Indonesia. In *2016 6th international annual engineering seminar (INAES)*. IEEE.

Poria, S., Gelbukh, A., Hussain, A., Howard, N., Das, D., & Bandyopadhyay, S. (2013). Enhanced SenticNet with affective labels for concept-based opinion mining. *IEEE Intelligent Systems, 28*(2), 31–38. doi:10.1109/MIS.2013.4

Rathi, M., Malik, A., Varshney, D., Sharma, R., & Mendiratta, S. (2018, August). Sentiment Analysis of Tweets Using Machine Learning Approach. In *2018 Eleventh International Conference on Contemporary Computing (IC3)* (pp. 1-3). IEEE. 10.1109/IC3.2018.8530517

Ren, F., & Wu, Y. (2013). Predicting user-topic opinions in twitter with social and topical context. *IEEE Transactions on Affective Computing, 4*(4), 412–424. doi:10.1109/T-AFFC.2013.22

Spencer, J., & Uchyigit, G. (2012, September). Sentimentor: Sentiment analysis of twitter data. In SDAD@ ECML/PKDD (pp. 56-66). Academic Press.

Taj, S., Shaikh, B. B., & Meghji, A. F. (2019, January). Sentiment Analysis of News Articles: A Lexicon based Approach. In *2019 2nd International Conference on Computing, Mathematics and Engineering Technologies (iCoMET)* (pp. 1-5). IEEE. 10.1109/ICOMET.2019.8673428

Tyagi, Priyanka, & Tripathi. (2019). A review towards the sentiment analysis techniques for the analysis of twitter data. Academic Press.

Valdivia, Luzión, & Herrera. (2017). Neutrality in the sentiment analysis problem based on fuzzy majority. In *2017 IEEE international conference on fuzzy systems (FUZZ-IEEE)*. IEEE.

Xu, X., Cheng, X., Tan, S., Liu, Y., & Shen, H. (2013). Aspect-level opinion mining of online customer reviews. *China Communications, 10*(3), 25–41. doi:10.1109/CC.2013.6488828

Yu, X., Liu, Y., Huang, X., & An, A. (2010). Mining online reviews for predicting sales performance: A case study in the movie domain. *IEEE Transactions on Knowledge and Data Engineering, 24*(4), 720–734. doi:10.1109/TKDE.2010.269

Zhang, X., Cui, L., & Wang, Y. (2013). Commtrust: Computing multi-dimensional trust by mining e-commerce feedback comments. *IEEE Transactions on Knowledge and Data Engineering, 26*(7), 1631–1643. doi:10.1109/TKDE.2013.177

Zhao. (2017). Weakly-supervised deep embedding for product review sentiment analysis. *IEEE Transactions on Knowledge and Data Engineering, 30*(1), 185-197.

Section 2
Applications and Analytics

Chapter 6
Predicting the Determinants of Mobile Payment Acceptance:
A Hybrid SEM–Neural Network Approach

Yakup Akgül
Alanya Alaaddin Keykubat University, Turkey

ABSTRACT

This chapter aims to determine the main factors of mobile payment adoption and the intention to recommend this technology. An innovative research model has been proposed with the advancement of the body of knowledge on this subject that combines the strengths of two well-known theories: the extended unified theory of acceptance and use of technology (UTAUT2) with the innovation characteristics of the diffusion of innovations (DOI) with perceived security and intention to recommend the technology constructs. The research model was empirically tested using 259 responses from an online survey conducted in Turkey. Two techniques were used: first, structural equation modeling (SEM) was used to determine which variables had significant influence on mobile payment adoption; in a second phase, the neural network model was used to rank the relative influence of significant predictors obtained by SEM. This study found that the most significant variables impacting the intention to use were perceived technology security and innovativeness variables.

INTRODUCTION

Digital payment using a mobile device has been recognized as one of the innovative technological changes in recent years. These devices provide consumers with an improved functionality, which makes the overall payment activity hassle-free

DOI: 10.4018/978-1-7998-4042-8.ch006

(Bauer, Reichardt, Barnes & Neumann, 2005; Dwivedi, Shareef, Simintiras, Lal, & Weerakkody, 2016; Hsu & Kulviwat, 2006; Liébana-Cabanillas, Marinkovic, de Luna, & Kalinic, 2018; Masamila et al., 2010 ; Varshney & Vetter, 2002; Veríssimo, 2016). According to the statistics published by Statista.com (2015), the total number of mobile phone users across the world is projected to surpass five billion users by 2019. On the other hand, Smartphone users worldwide are expected to reach almost 2.5 billion in 2019. Mobile technologies are presenting a large number of service innovations to the users. M-payment, as one of the major mobile innovations, became popular among the users across the World (Laukkanen, 2016).

New generation mobile devices (e.g., Smartphone), a strategic and profitable tool for delivering the products, services and information, equipped with distinctive and extraordinary features, have been widely accepted by consumers as an innovative method for digital payments (Slade et al., 2013; Yadav, Sharma, & Tarhini, 2016; Bauer, Reichardt, Barnes & Neumann, 2005; Hsu & Kulviwat, 2006; Varshney & Vetter, 2002).

Various definitions have been given to m-payment. Dewan and Chen (2005, p. 4) defined m-payment as ''making payments using mobile devices including wireless handsets, personal digital assistants (PDA), radio frequency (RF) devices, and NFC based devices''. M-payment also refer to as ''payments for goods, services, and bills with a mobile device such as mobile phone, smart-phone, or PDA by taking advantage of wireless and other communication technologies'' (Dahlberg, Mallat, Ondrus, & Zmijewska, 2008: 165). Besides that, m-payment may be referred to as ''using mobile devices to make transactions such as pay bills and perform banking transactions'' (Gerpott & Kornmeier, 2009: 1). Mobile payment or m-payment (MP) is referred to the transfer of money (in digital form) from one party (e.g., consumer) to another party (e.g., seller or merchant) using a mobile device (Chandra, Srivastava, & Theng, 2010; Pham & Ho, 2015). m-Payment enables users to make payment and fund transfer in comfortable and efficient manner (Mallat, Rossi & Tuunainen, 2004). m-Payment facilitates efficient and secure commercial transaction between service provider and consumers (Ondrus & Pigneur, 2006). m-Payment is initiation, authorization and completion of financial transaction through mobile devices (Mallat, 2007). Mobile payment can be grouped into three major forms – (a) in-person mobile payment or contactless payment. This type of m-payments works on near field communication (NFC) technology in which transaction is done by establishing a connection between mobile device and point of sale (POS) through radio waves, (b) payments through mobile app or website (remote MP), and (c) person-to-person payment using the dedicated mobile (Liébana-Cabanillas et al., 2017a). Business Insider (2015) expects that m-payment volume will reach $808 billion by 2019.

The present book chapter develops a new research model used to predict the most significant factors influencing the decision to use mobile payments. The originality of the model approached in this research revolves around the fact that combines the strengths of two well-known theories; the extended unified theory of acceptance and use of technology (UTAUT2) with the innovation characteristics of the diffusion of innovations (DOI), with perceived security and intention to recommend the technology constructs. In this sense, their influence on mobile payment adoption is examined in a rather limited number of studies in the literature. Usually, conventional statistical techniques used for the prediction of consumers' behavior only examine linear relationships among the different variables. In order to overcome this shortcoming, the relative importance of the most significant variables will be determined through artificial neural networks, a technique capable of modeling complex nonlinear relationships.

LITERATURE REVIEW

Even if research on mobile payment systems is scarce (Di Pietro et al., 2015; Liébana-Cabanillas et al., 2014). Intention to use was adopted as a dependent variable in the numerous studies in the area of mobile payment (Aslam et al, 2017; Chandrasekhar & Nandagopal, 2016; Fitriani et al, 2017; Guo, 2017; Hampshire, 2017;Hossain & Mahmud, 2016; Kaitawarn, 2015; Khalilzadeh et al, 2017; Kim et al., 2010; Kim et al, 2016; Koenig-Lewis et al, 2015; Leong et al., 2013; Li et al., 2014; Liébana-Cabanillas et al., 2014, 2015a, 2015b, 2017a, 2017b, 2017c; 2018; Lu et al., 2011; Martens et al, 2017; Meixin and Wei (2014); Morosan and DeFranco, 2016a; Morosan and DeFranco (2016b); Mun et al, 2017;Oliveira et al., 2016; Ooi and Tan, 2016; Pham and Ho, 2015; Phonthanukitithaworn et al, 2016;Ramos de Luna et al., 2016; Schierz et al., 2010; Shin, 2009; Slade et al., 2015a, 2015b; Su et al, 2018; Tan et al., 2014; Thakur and Srivastava, 2014; Yang et al., 2012; Zhou, 2011).

The adoption of mobile payments or m-payment services is seen not only as the innovative payment system for hassle-free transactions but also as the buttress for the economic growth worldwide (AlAlwan, Dwivedi, & Rana, 2017; Carton, Hedman, Damsgaard, Tan, & McCarthy, 2012; Dennehy & Sammon, 2015; Liébana-Cabanillas et al., 2017a; Shareef, Baabdullah, Dutta, Kumar, & Dwivedi, 2018; Shareef, Dwivedi, Kumar, & Kumar, 2017; Slade et al., 2013; Veríssimo, 2016).

Existing research suggested well-known technology acceptance models analyze and predict the most significant factors impacting consumers' perceptions of using mobile services. These models include diffusion of innovation (DOI) theory (Rogers, 1983), "addressed the significance of diffusion of a new idea or technology among the members of a social system over the time", and unified theory of acceptance and use of technology (UTAUT) model by Venkatesh, Ramesh, and Massey (2003) that suggested four key constructs to examine user's intention and system use. These models have been widely applied and extended by several researchers (Kapoor, Dwivedi, & Williams, 2015; Liébana-Cabanillas et al., 2017a; Liébana-Cabanillas, Marinković, & Kalinić, 2017b; Sharma, 2017; Dwivedi et al., 2017 A, 2017 B; Rana, Dwivedi, Lal, Williams, & Clement, 2017; Rana, Dwivedi, Williams, & Weerakkody, 2016; Slade, Williams, Dwivedi, & Piercy, 2015a; Slade, Dwivedi, Piercy, & Williams, 2015b; Chen & Tseng, 2012; Venkatesh & Davis, 2000) and determine the most significant factors influencing the user's intention.

Mallat (2007) explored relative advantage, compatibility, complexity, costs, network extension, trust and perceived security risks as determinants of m-payment through focus group analysis. The same year, Pousttchi and Wiedemann (2007) conducted a study on m-payment adoption in Germany in the light of TAM with some extended constructs. They argued that PU, PEOU and task-technology fit have significant impact on m-payment adoption intention. However, subjective security has insignificant impact on it. Through detailed literature review, Dahlberg et al. (2008) concluded that consumer and technical perspectives are well covered by existing research but impact of social and cultural factors on m-payment adoption is less explored. Kim et al. (2010) adopted TAM model with two consumer-centric and four systems that characterizes to explain the factors affecting m-payment adoption in Korea. They found that PI and m-payment knowledge, mobility, reachability and convenience have significant impact on m-payment adoption. However, compatibility has no role in m-payment adoption decision. Zhou (2011) conducted a study to measure the effect of trust on m-payment adoption intention in China. Findings of the study suggested that perceived security, perceived ubiquity and PEOU have significant impact on trust and trust has direct impact on usage intention. The same year, another research on mobile service acceptance, conducted by Zarmpou, Saprikis, Markos, and Vlachopoulou (2012), tested the influence of functionality, trust, innovativeness, and relationship drivers with mediating factors – PEOU and PU on behavioral intention of the consumers. The results indicated that trust and PEOU had no direct impact on consumers' intention, whereas both innovativeness and PU were found as the strongest factors. Keramati, Taeb, Larijani and Mojir (2012) examined the impact of technological and behavioural factors on m-payment adoption. Findings of the study suggested that ease of use, usefulness, trust, compatibility, cost, norm, payment habit, skills and convenience have significant impact on adoption intention. They have also examined impact of cultural and demographic characteristics on adoption behaviour. Arvidsson (2014) adopted TAM and DOI model to explore m-payment adoption intention in Sweden and explained that PEOU, PU, relative advantage, high trust, low perceived security risks, higher age and lower income have positive association with adoption. The TAM model has been used by Duane, O'Reilly and Andreev (2014) in Ireland to confirm the positive impact of PEOU, PU and trust on m-payment service adoption. Phonthanukitithaworn, Sellitto and

Fong (2015) also studied the factors affecting m-payment adoption behaviour of early adopters in Thailand through TAM and found that PEOU, PU, compatibility, SN, perceived trust and perceived cost have significant impact on adoption intention. In an empirical research of mobile payment acceptance on restaurant industry, researchers (Cobanoglu, Yang, Shatskikh, & Agarwal, 2015) found "compatibility with lifestyle" as the strongest factors that influence consumers' intention to adopt m-payment in restaurants followed by other significant predictors – usefulness, subjective norm, security, and previous experience with mobile payment. The same year, Ting, Yacob, Liew and Lau (2016) compared the consumer adoption behaviour in China and Malaysia with TPB model and argued that attitude, SN and perceived behaviour have significant impact on m-payment adoption in both the countries. The same year, de Sena Abrahão, Moriguchi and Andrade (2016) adopted UTAUT model to examine m-payment usage intention in Brazil. They described that social influence performance expectation and effort expectation have positive impact and perceived risk has negative impact on it. The same year, to explore stakeholders' expectation, Apanasevic, Markendahl and Arvidsson (2016) conducted a study in Sweden and concluded that technological feasibility, lower service cost, added value of a service and ease of use have significant impact on customer as well as stakeholders' expectation in m-payment service. Recently, Oliveira et al. (2016) used UTAUT2 and DOI models to examine adoption intention in Portugal and found innovativeness, compatibility, performance expectancy, effort expectancy and social influence have a significant association with m-payment usage intention. In comparison with internet banking and mobile banking, m-payment is relatively underexplored arena of research. The study still comments that m-payment adoption research is in its early stage (Slade et al., 2013).

There is significant increase in m-payment adoption studies in recent years (Dahlberg et al., 2008). In the last couple of years, the introduction of NFC embedded smartphones has supported m-payment adoption. However, there have been few studies published in top tier journals (de Sena Abrahao et al., 2016; Oliveira et al., 2016; Slade et al., 2013; Tan, Ooi, Chong & Hew, 2014). Previous studies have pointed out that there is a need for more exploration in the field of m-payment adoption. Most of the studies have been conducted in the early stage and rigorous research is required in the area of m-payment (Dahlberg et al., 2008).

In context of structural equation modeling–artificial neural networks (SEM–ANN) approach studies; Teo et al., (2015); Sharma et al. (2019); Shankar and Datta (2018); Khan and Ali (2018); Leong et al., (2013); Liébana-Cabanillas et al., (2018); Salloum et al.,(2019); Khan et al.,(2019); Gbongli et al., (2019).

RESEARCH METHODS

In this paper, two staged SEM and neural network modeling was used. The SEM is a commonly used statistical modeling to test linear relationship proposed in the hypotheses. Sometimes, relationship between decision variables may not be linear. To address this important issue, neural network modeling was employed. Neural network modeling helps in understanding linear as well as non-linear relations among associated decision variables. This is one of the commonly cited advantages of the neural network modeling. However, there are some disadvantages of using neural network modeling also; one of the commonly discussed concerns is of its "black box" approach. It is difficult to use neural network models to test hypotheses and understand causal relationships (Chong, 2013). In this research, an attempt is made to take advantages of these two advanced statistical tools. In the first stage, SEM is employed to test proposed research hypotheses whereas in the second stage statistically significant independent variables are used as input to the neural network model for the prediction of mobile payment acceptance.

Instrument Development/Data Collection

A convenient sampling method was adopted for data collection because the actual population size is not known for this research study (San Martín & Herrero, 2012). The quota sampling method was employed to match the target population structure in both age and gender (San Martín and Herrero, 2012).

STRUCTURAL EQUATION MODELLING

Analysis of the Measurement Model

The instrument was developed based on ten latent constructs mentioned in the research model. All the construct items were adopted from previous research works. There were four items for performance expectancy were adopted from (Venkatesh et al., 2012), and four items for effort expectancy were adopted from (Venkatesh et al., 2012), and three items for each for social influence, facilitating conditions, hedonic motivation, and price value were adopted from (Venkatesh et al., 2012), three items for innovativeness were adopted from (Yi et al., 2006), four items for compatibility were adopted from (Moore & Benbasat, 1991), four items for perceived technology security were adopted from (Cheng et al., 2006) Chandra et al. (2010), Featherman and Pavlou (2003), and Lu et al. (2011). Finally, six items for behavioral intention to adopt were adopted from (Belanger & Carter, 2008; Venkatesh et al., 2012).

Data Collection

In total, 259 respondents successfully completed the questionnaire, which can be considered an adequate sample for a research of this kind (Akgül et al., 2019a; Akgül et al., 2019b; Akgül and Tunca, 2019; Göktaş and Akgül, 2019). For this purpose, Hair et al. (2017:20) have suggested the use of 10 times rule, which was proposed by Barclay et al. (1995) for determining minimum sample size in a PLS-SEM analysis. This rule states that minimum sample should be "10 times the largest number of structural paths directed at a particular construct in structural model". Structural model of this study involves twelve constructs (i.e.ten independent and two dependent variable) and according to 10 times rule criterion, minimum sample size should be 120 respondents. However, author has adopted a more rigorous criterion proposed by Westland (2010).

These valid responses were analyzed to assess reliability, validity, and appropriateness for hypotheses testing. The final sample comprised 259 individuals, in which 40,4% are female and 59,6% are male. The percent of 80,4 was in the age group 20-30 years, 11,2 percent of respondents were above 30 years of age, 8,5 percent of respondents were below 20 years of age. In this context, younger generation prefers to use mobile payment services compared to older age groups (35 years old above). The majority of respondents were bachelor degree and represented 54,6%, followed by vocational school (20,8 percent), high school (12,7 percent) and other education levels 11,8% master and phd degree.

STRUCTURAL EQUATION MODELLING

Analysis of the Measurement Model

After checking the variable-to-sample ratio, the analysis followed Hair et al.'s (2014) and Fornell and Larcker's (1981) suggested procedure for assessing convergent and discriminate validity (Table 1). Convergent validity depends on 4 criteria: (1) all indicator loadings should exceed .7 and be significant; (2) composite reliabilities should be above the required threshold of .7; (3) Cronbach's alpha should exceed .7; (4) average variance extracted (AVE) for each construct should exceed .5. The results indicated that indicator loadings are above the recommended threshold, the composite reliability ranges from .850 to .950, Cronbach's alpha ranges from .736 to .928, and AVE ranges from .654 to .864. All four conditions for convergent validity thus hold. To test whether constructs differed sufficiently, two approaches were used: (1) Fornell and Larcker (1981) criterion, which requires a construct's AVE to be larger than the square of its biggest correlation with any construct (see

Table 2) and our constructs met this requirement. (2) Additionally, discriminant validity was also checked method suggested by Henseler, Ringle, and Sarstedt (2009) through multitrait and multimethod matrix, namely the Heterotrait-Monotrait Ratio (HTMT). HTMT values were lower than the required threshold value of HTMT.85 by Kline (2011) and HTMT 0.90 by Gold and Arvind Malhotra (2001); confirmed the discriminant validity of the measure (Table 4).

Table 1. Results of the measurement model

Constructs/Items	Loading	Cronbach's α	CR	(AVE)
Performance expectancy (PE)		0,881	0,918	0,737
PE1 - Mobile payment is useful to carry out my tasks.	0,822			
PE2 -1 think that using mobile payment would enable me to conduct tasks more quickly.	0,892			
PE3 - I think that using mobile payment would increase my productivity.	0,897			
PE4 - I think that using mobile payment would improve my performance.	0,818			
Effort expectancy (EE)		0,858	0,904	0,702
EE1 - My interaction with mobile payment would be clear and understandable.	0,839			
EE2 - It would be easy for me to become skillful at using mobile payment.	0,785			
EE3 -1 would find mobile payment easy to use.	0,878			
EE4 -1 think that learning to operate mobile payment would be easy for me.	0,847			
Social influence (SI)		0,888	0,931	0,818
SI1- People who influence my behavior think that I should use mobile payment.	0,863			
SI2-People who are important to me think that I should use mobile payment.	0,933			
SI3-People whose opinions that I value prefer that I use mobile payment.	0,916			
Facilitating conditions (FC)		0,861	0,916	0,783
FC1 - I have the resources necessary to use mobile payment.	0,902			
FC2 - I have the knowledge necessary to use mobile payment.	0,907			
FC3 - Mobile payment is compatible with other systems I use.	0,845			
Hedonic motivation (HM)		0,921	0,950	0,864
HM1 - Using mobile payment is fun.	0,930			
HM2 - Using mobile payment is enjoyable.	0,952			
HM3 - Using mobile payment is very entertaining.	0,905			
Price value (PV)		0,859	0,914	0,780
PV1 - Mobile payment is reasonably priced.	0,852			
PV2 - Mobile payment is a good value for the money.	0,893			
PV3 - At the current price, mobile payment provides a good value.	0,904			
Innovativeness (I)		0,736	0,850	0,654
I1- If I heard about a new information technology, I would look for ways to experiment with it.	0,841			
I2- Among my peers, I am usually the first to try out new information technologies.	0,788			
I4- I like to experiment with new information technologies.	0,798			
Compatibility (C)		0,816	0,916	0,845
C1 - Using mobile payment is compatible with all aspects of my life style.	0,911			
C2 - Using mobile payment is completely compatible with my current situation.	0,927			
C4 - Using mobile payment fits into my life style.				
Perceived technology security (PTS)		0,925	0,945	0,778
PTS1 - I would feel secure sending sensitive information across mobile payment.	0,702			
PTS2 - Mobile payment is a secure means through which to send sensitive information.	0,937			
PTS3 -1 would feel totally safe providing sensitive information about myself over mobile payment.	0,930			
PTS4 - Overall mobile payment is a safe place to send sensitive information	0,921			
Behavioral intention to adopt (BI)		0,928	0,947	0,782
BI1 -1 intend to use mobile payment in the next months.	0,912			
BI2 - I predict I would use mobile payment in the next months.	0,931			
BI3 - I plan to use mobile payment in the next months.	0,928			
BI4 - I will try to use mobile payment in my daily life.	0,893			
BI6 - I would not hesitate to provide personal information to mobile payment service.	0,744			

Table 2. Discriminant validity using Fornell and Larcker criterion

	BI	C	EE	FC	HM	I	PE	PTS	PV	SI
BI	0,884									
C	0,734	0,919								
EE	0,613	0,638	0,838							
FC	0,572	0,581	0,676	0,885						
HM	0,664	0,651	0,614	0,603	0,929					
I	0,699	0,702	0,622	0,619	0,611	0,809				
PE	0,585	0,599	0,754	0,559	0,616	0,550	0,858			
PTS	0,804	0,728	0,557	0,486	0,621	0,670	0,478	0,882		
PV	0,597	0,571	0,530	0,498	0,632	0,531	0,489	0,617	0,883	
SI	0,466	0,471	0,424	0,336	0,471	0,393	0,487	0,581	0,488	0,904

As for the evaluation of cross-loadings, an indicator's loadings with its associated latent construct (in bold and italic) should be higher than its loadings with all the remaining constructs (Hair et al., 2011; Ringle et al., 2018). All the indicators show a qualified discriminant validity via the cross-loadings evaluation (see Table 3).

STRUCTURAL MODEL

Hypotheses Testing

In order to assess the significance and relevance in the relationships presented in the structural model bootstrapping procedure (bootstrapping with 5000 sub-samples) was used. The values obtained for the loads between variables and the R^2 of the endogenous variables of the model can be seen in Fig. 1.

As demonstrated in Table 5, the findings further reveal that compatibility (β = 0,125, t-value= 1,755, significance at p<0,0079; f^2=0,02), innovativeness (β = 0,117, t-value= 1,983, significance at p<0,047; f^2=0,02), performance expectancy (β = 0,142, t-value= 1,997, significance at p<0,046; f^2=0,03) have significant and positive impact with a small effect size was found on mobile payment acceptance while perceived technology security (β = 0,512, t-value= 7,381, significance at p<0,000; f^2=0,34) have significant and positive impact on mobile payment acceptance with medium effect size. Therefore, H1, H5, H6, and H7 were supported. However, five of the nine hypothesized paths, from effort expectancy to mobile payment acceptance (H2), from facilitating conditions mobile payment acceptance (H3),

Table 3. Cross-loading evaluation results for discriminant validity evaluation

	BI	C	EE	FC	HM	I	PE	PTS	PV	SI
BI1	*0,912*	0,686	0,600	0,509	0,569	0,629	0,541	0,705	0,532	0,410
BI2	*0,931*	0,700	0,564	0,550	0,581	0,635	0,543	0,699	0,519	0,394
BI3	*0,928*	0,655	0,536	0,497	0,600	0,633	0,541	0,701	0,542	0,368
BI4	*0,893*	0,660	0,598	0,557	0,659	0,649	0,604	0,651	0,542	0,409
BI5	*0,744*	0,534	0,400	0,407	0,520	0,535	0,346	0,795	0,501	0,480
C1	0,642	*0,911*	0,542	0,503	0,602	0,619	0,511	0,671	0,562	0,472
C2	0,705	*0,927*	0,626	0,563	0,595	0,669	0,587	0,668	0,491	0,399
EE1	0,526	0,558	*0,839*	0,605	0,530	0,503	0,685	0,467	0,458	0,364
EE2	0,504	0,526	*0,785*	0,503	0,530	0,533	0,577	0,516	0,440	0,404
EE3	0,528	0,555	*0,878*	0,605	0,540	0,545	0,653	0,466	0,463	0,333
EE4	0,493	0,494	*0,847*	0,546	0,453	0,501	0,606	0,415	0,412	0,320
FC1	0,490	0,533	0,611	*0,902*	0,544	0,547	0,499	0,382	0,438	0,272
FC2	0,479	0,489	0,595	*0,907*	0,488	0,564	0,421	0,382	0,350	0,228
FC3	0,541	0,517	0,585	*0,845*	0,561	0,531	0,554	0,514	0,521	0,380
HM1	0,628	0,620	0,566	0,590	*0,930*	0,555	0,541	0,579	0,581	0,404
HM2	0,645	0,602	0,609	0,587	*0,952*	0,623	0,615	0,578	0,615	0,427
HM3	0,574	0,593	0,533	0,499	*0,905*	0,523	0,561	0,575	0,566	0,489
I1	0,623	0,603	0,604	0,574	0,619	*0,841*	0,571	0,541	0,549	0,324
I2	0,524	0,500	0,364	0,393	0,462	*0,788*	0,314	0,577	0,398	0,393
I4	0,542	0,596	0,523	0,523	0,385	*0,798*	0,428	0,512	0,325	0,241
PE1	0,433	0,432	0,598	0,462	0,480	0,462	*0,822*	0,286	0,345	0,267
PE2	0,532	0,532	0,696	0,538	0,539	0,465	*0,892*	0,400	0,438	0,356
PE3	0,504	0,495	0,682	0,445	0,552	0,467	*0,897*	0,424	0,427	0,458
PE4	0,528	0,583	0,606	0,471	0,538	0,493	*0,818*	0,512	0,457	0,568
PTS1	0,624	0,785	0,595	0,504	0,549	0,694	0,564	*0,702*	0,459	0,422
PTS2	0,744	0,641	0,469	0,450	0,579	0,598	0,389	*0,937*	0,550	0,528
PTS3	0,740	0,633	0,478	0,397	0,539	0,575	0,431	*0,930*	0,583	0,540
PTS4	0,711	0,606	0,444	0,404	0,520	0,555	0,351	*0,921*	0,553	0,580
PTS5	0,715	0,568	0,485	0,400	0,552	0,547	0,393	*0,896*	0,566	0,481
PV1	0,519	0,472	0,416	0,406	0,551	0,399	0,390	0,528	*0,852*	0,407
PV2	0,495	0,502	0,489	0,419	0,561	0,495	0,455	0,535	*0,893*	0,444
PV3	0,565	0,536	0,498	0,490	0,563	0,511	0,450	0,571	*0,904*	0,443
SI1	0,417	0,444	0,411	0,267	0,432	0,347	0,475	0,518	0,435	*0,863*
SI2	0,437	0,445	0,401	0,352	0,451	0,377	0,442	0,555	0,456	*0,933*
SI3	0,410	0,388	0,337	0,289	0,394	0,342	0,403	0,501	0,434	*0,916*

Table 4. Heterotrait-Monotrait ratio (HTMT)

	BI	C	EE	FC	HM	I	PE	PTS	PV	SI
BI										
C	0,841									
EE	0,686	0,759								
FC	0,636	0,690	0,784							
HM	0,717	0,751	0,689	0,672						
I	0,842	0,901	0,773	0,770	0,732					
PE	0,643	0,700	0,865	0,636	0,682	0,672				
PTS	0,871	0,848	0,632	0,545	0,677	0,822	0,531			
PV	0,668	0,683	0,616	0,572	0,711	0,658	0,558	0,692		
SI	0,515	0,556	0,486	0,378	0,523	0,488	0,543	0,641	0,559	

Hedonic motivation to mobile payment acceptance (H4), from price value to mobile payment acceptance (H8), from social influence to mobile payment acceptance (H9) were not supported by statistically significant path coefficients. A summarized overview of these findings is presented in Table 5.

Because PLS is predictive-oriented, the R^2 measure is the essential criterion for structural model assessment, which presents the amount of explained variance of the endogenous latent variable. Although no generalities exist with regard to what is a high or low level of R^2, Chin (1998) and Henseler, Ringle, and Sinkovics (2009) describe R^2 values of 0.67, 0.33 and 0.19 as substantial, moderate and weak, respectively. Thus, compatibility, effort expectancy, facilitating conditions, hedonic motivation, innovativeness, performance expectancy, perceived technology security, price value, and social influence variables %74 of the variance in mobile payment acceptance is high.

Predictive Relevance Q^2

Researchers used blindfolding procedure in order to assess the predictive relevance of the research model. This study picked an omission distance (OD)=8. Blindfolding procedure should only be applied to endogenous constructs that have a reflective measurement. According to Hair Jr et al. (2016) blindfolding procedure is applied on endogenous constructs. Table 6 presented the results of Q^2. As shown in Table 6 the Q^2 values for mobile payment acceptance (0.534) is greater than 0, indicating that the model has sufficient predictive relevance. The Stone-Geisser Q^2 has also been calculated to evaluate the model's predictive capacity (Gefen et al., 2011;

Table 5. Structural model results

Hypothesis	Relationship	β-Value	Effect Size [1]f^2	t-Statistic [a]	p-Value	R^2	Q^2 (=1-SSE/SSO) (OD=8)
H1	C -> BI	0,125	0,02	1,755*	0,079	0,740	0,534
H2	EE -> BI	-0,016	0,01	0,196	0,845		
H3	FC -> BI	0,062	0,01	1,018	0,309		
H4	HM -> BI	0,093	0,02	1,536	0,125		
H5	I -> BI	0,117	0,02	1,983**	0,047		
H6	PE -> BI	0,142	0,03	1,997**	0,046		
H7	PTS -> BI	0,512	0,34	7,381***	0,000		
H8	PV -> BI	0,037	0,01	0,787	0,431		
H9	SI -> BI	-0,081	0,02	1,627	0,104		

[a]t-values for two-tailed test:
* 1.65 (sig. level 10%).
** 1.96 (sig. level=5%).
*** t-value 2.58 (sig. level = 1%) (Hair et al., 2011).
Notes:***p<0.01, **p<0.05, *p<0.1
effective size: 0 – none, 0.02 – small, 0.15 - medium, 0.35 – large (Cohen, 1988).
Effect size calculated using the following formula
[1]f^2= R^2included - R^2excluded / 1- R^2included

Geisser, 1974) and it is concluded that the model has predictive relevance as all the Q^2 values of the table are greater than 0 (Roldán and Sánchez-Franco, 2012). The Q^2 values confirm the model's predictive relevance. Specifically, the Q^2 values are small (i.e., lower than 0.15); medium (i.e., 0.15–0.35) and high if higher than 0.35 (Fornell and Cha, 1994) as shown in Table 6.

Table 6 also shows the results of small (q^2) effect size. Compatibility, hedonic motivation, innovativeness, performance expectancy, and social influence have small effect size (q^2) on mobile payment acceptance. However, effort expectancy, facilitating conditions, price value exhibit none effect size (q^2) on mobile payment acceptance. Finally, perceived technology security has small effect size (q^2) on mobile payment acceptance.

The model finally shows a high explanatory power of 74% (see Fig. 1) above the minimum level recommended by Falk and Miller (1992) which is 10%. The Stone-Geisser Q^2 has also been calculated to evaluate the model's predictive capacity (Gefen et al., 2011) and it is concluded that the model has predictive relevance as all the Q^2 values of the table are greater than 0 (Roldán and Sánchez-Franco, 2012). The Q^2 values confirm the model's predictive relevance. Specifically, the Q^2 values

Table 6. Predictive relevance Q^2 and (q^2) analysis

Construct	Effect Size [1] q^2	Q^2 (=1-SSE/SSO) (OD=8)	Decision
C	0,01		None
EE	-0,01		None
FC	0		None
HM	0,01		None
I	0,01		None
PE	0,01		None
PTS	0,13		Small
PV	0		None
SI	0,01		None
Mobile payment acceptance		0,534	High

effective size: 0 – none, 0.02 – small, 0.15 - medium, 0.35 – large (Cohen, 1988).

Effect size calculated using the following formula

[1]q^2 = Q^2included - Q^2excluded / 1- Q^2included (2)

are small (i.e., lower than 0.15); medium (i.e., 0.15–0.35) and high if higher than 0.35 (Fornell and Cha, 1994) as shown in Table 6 and Table 7.

Importance-Performance Map Analysis (IPMA)

In our case, mobile payment acceptance is a target construct, which is predicted by nine predecessors (i.e. compatibility, effort expectancy, facilitating conditions, hedonic motivation, innovativeness, performance expectancy, perceived technology security, price value, and social influence); refer to Figure 1. We have performed IPMA for this study and result is presented in Figure 2. Based on Figure 2, it can be observed perceived technology security, performance expectancy, innovativeness, and compatibility are very important. For the ease of readers, a complete list of importance-performance values is provided in Table 7.

ASSESSMENT OF THE PREDICTIVE VALIDITY USING HOLDOUT SAMPLES

With the objective of producing valid predictions of Behavioral intention for mobile payment acceptance, we used PLS predict (Shmueli et al., 2016; Shmueli et al., 2019; Felipe et al., 2017). In general, if we compare the results of PLS (partial least

Figure 1. Findings of structural model

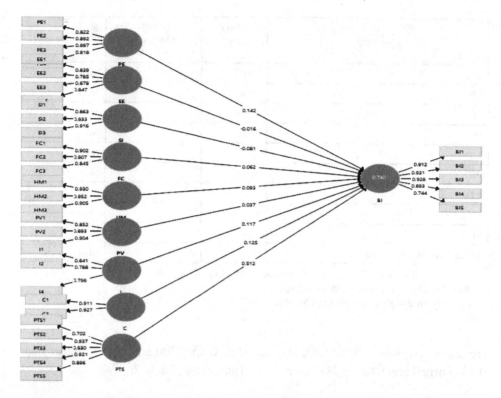

squares) with LM (linear model), PLS predict allows predictions very close to those obtained by using LM (Table 8).

GOODNESS OF FIT (GOF)

A large value for goodness of fit (GOF) is 0.36 or higher (Wetzels, Odekerken, & Van Oppen, 2009). In this study, GOF is exceptional with a value of 0.76. The proposed model adequately reflects the behavioral intention in mobile payment acceptance. GoF = Ö(0,78 × 0,74)=0,76

NEURAL NETWORK ANALYSIS

According to Haykin (1994), "neural network signifies "fundamentally parallel distributed processor constituted from simple processing units that have a natural ability to preserve experimental knowledge and pr esent it for being used". NN is

Figure 2. Importance-performance map analysis for customer satisfaction

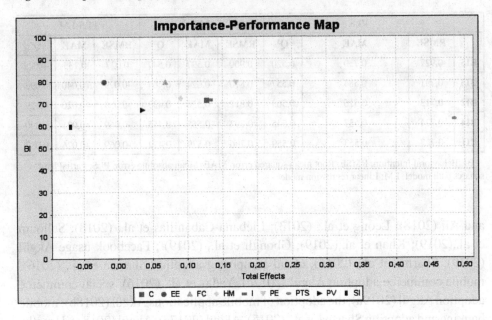

also perceived as a statistical learning model that works just like the human brain. SPSS 24.0 was used to develop the back propagation NN. There is widespread use of the NN model when the IS research is employed to determine the importance of influencing adoption factors in various situations, for example, a mobile payment system Khan and Ali (2018), Sharma et al. (2019); Shankar and Datta (2018); Khan

Table 7. Importance-performance map analysis for mobile payment acceptance.

Latent Variables	Total Effect of the Latent Variable for Behavioral Intention	Index Values (Performance)
C	0,127	71,418
EE	-0,019	**79,837**
FC	0,069	79,532
HM	0,090	72,365
I	0,133	71,313
PE	0,170	79,311
PTS	**0,484**	62,653
PV	0,036	66,967
SI	-0,069	59,563

Note: All total effects (importance) larger than 0.10 are significant at the α£0.10 level. The bold values indicate the highest importance (total effect) and highest performance value.

Table 8. Partial least square predict assessment.

	PLS			LM			PLS-LM		
	RMSE	MAE	Q^2	RMSE	MAE	Q^2	RMSE	MAE	Q^2
BI5	0,927	0,730	0,520	0,900	0,597	0,547	0,027	0,133	-0,027
BI3	0,791	0,584	0,557	0,870	0,624	0,464	-0,079	-0,040	0,093
BI2	0,713	0,516	0,563	0,812	0,536	0,433	-0,099	-0,020	0,129
BI4	0,724	0,537	0,545	0,793	0,558	0,455	-0,069	-0,021	0,090
BI1	0,727	0,553	0,559	0,796	0,579	0,472	-0,069	-0,026	0,087

BI: Behavioral Intention, RMSE: Root mean squared error. MAE: Mean absolute error. PLS: Partial least squares path model; LM: Linear regression model.

and Ali (2018); Leong et al., (2013); Liébana-Cabanillas et al., (2018); Salloum et al.,(2019); Khan et al.,(2019); Gbongli et al., (2019) ; Facebook usage Akgül (2019), Sharma et al., (2016); cloud computing adoption Sharma et al., (2016); mobile commerce adoption Akgül (2017c), Yadav et al., (2016); social commerce adoption Akgül (2019a); the adoption of mobile applications Akgül (2018b); mobile banking and adoption Sharma et al., (2015), Akgül (2017a), Akgül (2018c). Usually, the NN model has three layers, i.e. input layers, output layers and hidden layers. Weights (synaptic weight) are allocated to the nodes in every layer after zero, and for a layer ornode, there is a related linear or non-linear activation function Sharma et al., (2017). A synaptic weight is assigned to each input neuron, which is then disseminated to the hidden neurons in the hidden layers before they are changed to an output value using a non-linear activation function, such as sigmoid. The NN weights will be adjusted using an iterative training process, and the information obtained will be stored for being used in future projects.

Since only the linear relationship can be tested using the SEM, the issues in acceptance evaluation may at times be overgeneralized. Hence, to counter this possibility, an NN method that can recognize non-linear and linear relationship was employed. In contrast to causal-statistical models, ANN models have various advantages. These models are able to identify both non-linear and linear associations between independent and dependent variables. Improved performance is shown by the NN models as compared to the conventional statistical models like MLR and logistic regression (Sharma et al., 2015). Therefore, from the Smart PLS analysis significant and influential factors were used to advance the NN analysis. Five independent important factors which extracted from the SEM analysis were included in the input section, while the output section included a single output variable, i.e. the IRs adoption, as revealed in Figure 3.

Figure 3. The Proposed artificial neural network architect.

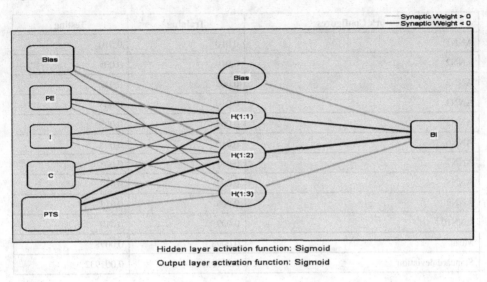

The Root Mean Square Error (RMSE) was used to assess the precision of the NN model that was developed. The 10 hidden nodes have been used for neural network analysis as it was quite complex for dataset design without generating additional errors in the neural network model (Sharma et al., 2017). The multi-layer perceptron training algorithm was used to develop the NN model. This study employed 10-fold cross-validations, where for the training of the network model 70% of the data points were used, while 30% of the data points were used for model testing. The input layer of the network model comprised of four covariates, i.e. PE, I, C, and PTS. The output layer of the NN model comprised of the dependent variable BI. It was found that the RMSE of the training model was 0.0093 and that of the testing model was 0.0098 (Table 9). The normalized significance in the sensitivity analysis was used to assess the relevant weights of the causal relationships (refer to Table 10). The results of the normalized variable importance computations showed that 'perceived technology security (PTS)' of the social commerce is the most significant factor that predicts the acceptance of social commerce, while the 'compatibility (C)' factor comes next.

DISCUSSION

On the basis of the summary of the results presented in the aforementioned sub-sections, it can be inferred that the research model proposed in this study was able to Show predictive power in terms of the coefficient of determination (R^2) at a substantial

Table 9. RMSE values of artificial neural networks

Network Configures	Training	Testing
ANN1	0,010	0,010
ANN2	0,010	0,008
ANN3	0,008	0,012
ANN4	0,010	0,008
ANN5	0,009	0,009
ANN6	0,010	0,008
ANN7	0,011	0,008
ANN8	0,008	0,012
ANN9	0,008	0,013
ANN10	0,009	0,010
Mean	0,0093	0,0098
Standard deviation	0,001059	0,001932

level as: intention to use (74%). The values of reliability indices, validity indices and other all fit indices were within the established range as recommended in Hair et al. (2010). In addition to SEM results, this study used neural network results to rank the constructs of intention to use, perceived usefulness, and perceived ease of use. Moreover, neural network modeling provided evidence to validate SEM results.

The results of our research are mostly in line with previous research. For instance, our study provides results from both SEM and ANN analysis, which found the Perceived technology security variable as the most significant determinant of intention to use for mobile payment, followed by the compatibility. Similar results were confirmed in previous research (Harris et al., 2016; Liébana-Cabanillas et al., 2017a).

Facilitating conditioning were not significant factor in this research which is consistent the findings of some previous studies Slade et al., 2015a Oliveira et al.

Table 10. Normalized variable importance

	Importance	Normalized Importance
PE	0,167	0,339%
I	0,135	0,273%
C	0,204	0,411%
PTS	0,497	100%

(2016) and Khan and Ali (2018), Thakur, 2013, however not consistent with (Ting et al., 2016; Morosan and DeFranco, 2016),

These findings imply that security in terms of m-payments play a major role in the adoption of mobile-based services. These results are found consistent with the previous information systems studies (Cheong et al., 2014; Oliveira et al., 2016; Ooi&Tan, 2016; Sharma, 2017; Szopiński, 2016; Sharma et al., 2019; Liébana-Cabanillas et al.,2017a; Alalwan et al., 2017; Sinha and Mukherjee, 2016; Yang et al., 2015; Rouibah et al., 2016). The effect of perceived risk, as a singular construct, on behavioural intention has been both supported in some studies (Chen, 2008; Lu et al., 2011; Shin, 2010; Yang et al., 2012), and rejected in others (Hongxia et al., 2011; Kapoor et al., 2014; Tan et al., 2014; Wang & Yi, 2012), in the MP context. Recently, Liébana Cabanillas et al. (2014) found the negative effect of perceived risk on behavioural intention to be significant for both non-users and existing users of MP. Results mentioned above are parallel to literature (Trachuk & Linder, 2017) (Cobanoglu, Yang, Shatskikh, & Agarwal, 2015) (Salloum et al., 2019). For the effect of security on ease of use results are similar to literature as well (Khalilzadeh et al, 2017).

The results given above can be supported with many other research from literature (Ooi & Tan, 2016) (Ramos-de-Luna, 2016) (Pham & Ho, 2015) (Pal et al., 2015), (de Sena Abraha~o et al., 2016), (Cobanoglu, Yang, Shatskikh, & Agarwal, 2015) and Khan and Ali (2018). Miltgen et al., 2013; Schierz et al., 2010. In the study, (Oliveira et al, 2016), compatibility has a positive effect on usefulness and ease of use. It is almost parallel with the findings reference study (Peng et al, 2012).

In SEM model the factor "innovativeness" is tested for its effect on behavioral intention to use of mobile payments. Findings of research model is parallel with several studies from literature (Liébana-Cabanillas et al, 2015; (Slade et al, 2015; Tan et al, 2014; Oliveira et al, 2016). However, they are conflicting with the research (Martens et al, 2017).

Hypothesis that suggests the effect of social influence on use of mobile payments is accepted in this study, and it is conflicting with the researches (Kim et al, 2016; Tian & Dong, 2013; Shin, 2009; Qasim and Abu-Shanab, 2016; Alshare et al. 2004; Peng et al. 2011; Yang et al. 2012; Koenig-Lewis et al, 2015; Slade et al., 2015a). Consequently, in the context of m-payment, a positive relationship between social influence and individual adoption behavior is expected. Social influence may also have an indirect effect via perceived usefulness on intention to adopt m-payment (Yang, Lu, Gupta, & Zhang, 2012).

Of the four original UTAUT constructs, social influence has been the most tested in the context of MP, and its effect on behavioural intention has acquired more support (Hongxia et al., 2011; Tan et al., 2014; Yang, Lu, Gupta, Cao, & Zhang, 2012) than rejection (e.g. Shin, 2010; Wang & Yi, 2012).

In the study, these results are found consistent with the previous studies (Koenig-Lewis et al, 2015), Slade et al., 2015a enjoyment is found to be affecting usefulness, ease of use and security. They found hedonic motivation to be the second strongest predictor of behavioural intention in UTAUT2. Although hedonic motivation has not been tested in the MP context, the effect of perceived enjoyment on behavioural intention has gained support in the m-commerce context (e.g. Ko, Kin, & Lee, 2009; Zhang, Zhu, & Liu, 2012).

In the study, these results are found consistent with the previous study (Slade et al., 2015a) price value. Although price value has not been tested in the MP context, perceived financial cost (Hongxia et al., 2011; Kapoor et al., 2014; Lu et al., 2011) has been found to negatively affect behavioural intention. Yang et al. (2012) found that perceived financial cost negatively affected behavioural intention for non users, but was not significant for actual users. Tan et al. (2014) found the effect of perceived financial cost to be insignificant.

Performance expectancy was found to be a significant factor in determining the behavioral intention to use e-payment systems Moodley and Govender (2016), Alalwan et al., 2017, Chaouali et al., 2016, Qasim and Abu-Shanab (2016), Martins et al., (2014), Salloum et al., 2019, Morosan and DeFranco, 2016, Cheng et al. (2006), Slade et al. (2013), Slade et al., 2014; and Zhou (2014); Alshare et al. 2004; Peng et al. 2011; Thakur 2013) Slade et al., 2015a. The effect of performance expectancy on behavioural intention has been supported in the MP context (Hongxia et al., 2011; Thakur, 2013; Wang & Yi, 2012).

While some researchers have found effort expectancy significant (Alshare et al., 2004; Thakur 2013), our finding is supported by previous researches (Wu et al. 2007, Hongxia et al., 2011, Qasim and Abu-Shanab (2016) Slade et al., 2015a. Effort expectancy is one of most significant predictors of intention to use MP in Wang and Yi's (2012) study.

On the other side, results from the neural network analysis confirmed many SEM findings, but also gave a slightly different order of influence for a variety of significant predictors. For example, perceived technology security was found to be the most influential factor on intention to use of mobile payment, which was the case in results from the SEM analysis. Also, innovativeness and performance expectancy got almost the same influence on intention to use. These and other minor differences between SEM and ANN results could be explained by the higher prediction accuracy of the neural network models with their nonlinear and non-compensatory nature.

LIMITATIONS AND FUTURE STUDIES

There are a number of limitations of this current study. First, this research was conducted in Turkey, a developing country in the boundary of one country. Hence, it is advised to use the proposed model in this research to conduct a cross-country and cross-cultural examination and to predict the preferences of different countries. Finally, it would be interesting to see the comparison of results of the proposed model in this research from different gender and different age groups in the future research studies. Apart from that, future research should extend our research model by including some other variables such as complexity, firm size, financial risk, government role and some external variables which has strong influence on adoption decision as mentioned in previous studies Liébana-Cabanillas et al., (2017a); Leong et al., (2013); Mallat and Tuunainen (2008).

CONCLUSION

To sum up, the objective of this research study was to explore key constructs influencing the decision of users' intention towards mobile payment services in a developing country, namely, Turkey. This study proposed and tested a new research model to understand and predict mobile payment services acceptance. It was observed that two well-known theories; the extended unified theory of acceptance and use of technology (UTAUT2) with the innovation characteristics of the diffusion of innovations (DOI), with perceived security and intention to recommend the technology constructs.

This book chapter adopted two staged research methodology to test and validate the proposed research model. The structural equation modeling was employed to test the research model, and neural network models were used to validate as well as rank the key constructs influence the mobile payment services acceptance. The results obtained imply that effort expectancy, facilitating conditions, hedonic motivation, social influence, and price value is not enough to motivate users to adopt mobile payment services.

REFERENCES

Akgül, Y. (2017). *A multi-analytical approach for predicting antecedents of m-commerce adoption. In Academic Studies about communication, business and economics. Strategic Researches Academy Strategic Researches Academic Publishing.*

Akgül, Y. (2017a). Integrating e-trust antecedents into TAM to explain mobile banking behavioral intention: A SEM-neural network modeling. *4th International Conference on Business and Economics Studies (Özet Bildiri/Sözlü Sunum).* (Yayın No:4406728)

Akgül, Y. (2018a). An Analysis of Customers' Acceptance of Internet Banking: An Integration of E-Trust and Service Quality to the TAM–The Case of Turkey. In *E-Manufacturing and E-Service Strategies in Contemporary Organizations* (pp. 154–198). IGI Global. doi:10.4018/978-1-5225-3628-4.ch007

Akgül, Y. (2018b). A SEM-Neural Network Approach for Predicting Antecedents of Factors Influencing Consumers' Intent to Install Mobile Applications. In *Mobile Technologies and Socio-Economic Development in Emerging Nations* (pp. 262–308). IGI Global. doi:10.4018/978-1-5225-4029-8.ch012

Akgül, Y. (2018c). Predicting determinants of Mobile banking adoption: A two-staged regression-neural network approach. *8th International Conference of Strategic Research on Scientific Studies and Education (ICoSReSSE) 2018 (Özet Bildiri/Sözlü Sunum).* (Yayın No:4405980)

Akgül, Y. (2019). Understanding and Predicting the Determinants of the Facebook Usage in Higher Education: A Two Staged Hybrid SEM-Neural Networks Approach. *11th International Conference of Strategic Research on Scientific Studies and Education (ICoSReSSE).*

Akgül, Y. (2019a). A social commerce investigation of the role of trust in a social networking site on purchase intentions: A Multi-Analytical Structural Equation Modeling and Neural Network Approach. *11th International Conference of Strategic Research on Scientific Studies and Education (ICoSReSSE) (Tam Metin Bildiri/Sözlü Sunum).* (Yayın No:5486037)

Akgül, Y., Öztürk, T., & Varol, Z. (2019). Investigation of Internet Banking Users' Perceptions and Factors Affecting Internet Banking Benchmarks: Expanded With Unified Theory of Acceptance and Use of Technology 2 (UTAUT2) Risk. In Structural Equation Modeling Approaches to E-Service Adoption (pp. 64-82). IGI Global.

Akgül, Y., & Tunca, M. Z. (2019). Strategic Orientation and Performance of Istanbul Stock Market Businesses: Empirical Studies Based on Business, Information Systems, and Knowledge Strategic Orientation. In Strategy and Superior Performance of Micro and Small Businesses in Volatile Economies (pp. 94-114). IGI Global.

Akgül, Y., Yaman, B., Geçgil, G., & Yavuz, G. (2019). The Influencing Factors for Purchasing Intentions in Social Media by Utaut Perspective. In *Structural Equation Modeling Approaches to E-Service Adoption* (pp. 254–267). IGI Global. doi:10.4018/978-1-5225-8015-7.ch013

AlAlwan, A., Dwivedi, Y. K., & Rana, N. P. (2017). Factors influencing adoption of mobile banking by jordanian bank customers: Extending UTAUT2 with trust. *International Journal of Information Management*, 37(3), 99–110. doi:10.1016/j.ijinfomgt.2017.01.002

Alshare, K., Grandon, E., & Miller, D. (2004). Antecedents of computer technology usage: Considerations of the technology acceptance model in the academic environment. *Journal of Computing Sciences in Colleges*, 19(4), 164–180.

Alshare, K. A., & Mousa, A. A. (2014). *The moderating effect of espoused cultural dimensions on consumer's intention to use mobile payment devices.* Paper presented at the 35th International Conference on Information Systems "Building a Better World through Information Systems", ICIS 2014, Auckland: Association for Information Systems.

Apanasevic, T., Markendahl, J., & Arvidsson, N. (2016). Stakeholders' expectations of mobile payment in retail: Lessons from Sweden. *International Journal of Bank Marketing*, 34(1), 37–61. doi:10.1108/IJBM-06-2014-0064

Arvidsson, N. (2014). Consumer attitudes on mobile payment services - results from aproof of concept test. *International Journal of Bank Marketing*, 32(2), 150–170. doi:10.1108/IJBM-05-2013-0048

Aslam, W., Ham, M., & Arif, I. (2017). Consumer Behavioral Intentions towards Mobile Payment Services: An Empirical Analysis in Pakistan. *Market-Trziste*, 29(2), 161–176. doi:10.22598/mt/2017.29.2.161

Bauer, H. H., Reichardt, T., Barnes, S. J., & Neumann, M. M. (2005). Driving consumer acceptance of mobile marketing: A theoretical framework and empirical study. *Journal of Electronic Commerce Research*, 6(3), 181.

Belanger, F., & Carter, L. (2008). Trust and risk in e-government adoption. *The Journal of Strategic Information Systems*, 17(2), 165–176. doi:10.1016/j.jsis.2007.12.002

Carton, F., Hedman, J., Damsgaard, J., Tan, K.-T., & McCarthy, J. (2012). Framework for mobile payments integration. *The Electronic Journal of Information Systems Evaluation, 15*(1), 14–25.

Chandra, S., Srivastava, S. C., & Theng, Y. L. (2010). Evaluating the role of trust in consumer adoption of mobile payment systems: An empirical analysis. *Communications of the Association for Information Systems, 27*(29), 561–588. doi:10.17705/1CAIS.02729

Chandrasekhar, U., & Nandagopal, R. (2016). Mobile payment usage intent in an Indian context: An exploratory study. *Asian Journal of Information Technology, 15*(3), 542–552.

Chaouali, W. I., Ben Yahia, I., & Souiden, N. (2016). The interplay of counter-conformity motivation, social influence, and trust in customers' intention to adopt Internet banking services: The case of an emerging country. *Journal of Retailing and Consumer Services, 28*, 209–218. doi:10.1016/j.jretconser.2015.10.007

Chen, H. R., & Tseng, H. F. (2012). Factors that influence acceptance of web-based e-learning systems for the in-service education of junior high school teachers in Taiwan. *Evaluation and Program Planning, 35*(3), 398–406. doi:10.1016/j.evalprogplan.2011.11.007 PMID:22321703

Chen, L.-D. (2008). A model of consumer acceptance of mobile payment. *International Journal of Mobile Communications, 6*(1), 32–52. doi:10.1504/IJMC.2008.015997

Cheng, T. C. E., Lam, D. Y. C., & Yeung, C. L. (2006). Adoption of internet banking: An empirical study in Hong Kong. *Decision Support Systems, 42*(3), 1558–1572. doi:10.1016/j.dss.2006.01.002

Cheong, S. N., Ling, H. C., & Teh, P. L. (2014). Secure encrypted steganography graphical password scheme for near field communication smartphone access control system. *Expert Systems with Applications, 41*(7), 3561–3568. doi:10.1016/j.eswa.2013.10.060

Chin, W. W. (1998). The Partial Least Squares Approach to Structural Equation Modeling. In G. A. Marcoulides (Ed.), *Modern Methods for Business Research* (pp. 295–358). Lawrence Erlbaum Associates.

Chong, A. Y. L. (2013). A two-staged SEM-neural network approach for understanding and predicting the determinants of m-commerce adoption. *Expert Systems with Applications, 40*(4), 1240–1247. doi:10.1016/j.eswa.2012.08.067

Cobanoglu, C., Yang, W., Shatskikh, A., & Agarwal, A. (2015). Are consumers ready for mobile payment? An examination of consumer acceptance of mobile payment technology in restaurant industry. *Hospitality Review, 31*(4), 6.

Cohen, J. (1988). *Statistical Power Analysis for the Behavioral Sciences*. Lawrence Erlbaum.

Dahlberg, T., Mallat, N., Ondrus, J., & Zmijewska, A. (2008). Past, present and future of mobile payments research: A literature review. *Electronic Commerce Research and Applications, 7*(2), 165–181. doi:10.1016/j.elerap.2007.02.001

de Sena Abrahão, R., Moriguchi, S. N., & Andrade, D. F. (2016). Intention of adoption of mobile payment: An analysis in the light of the Unified Theory of Acceptance and Use of Technology (UTAUT). *RAI Revista de Administração e Inovação, 13*(3), 221–230. doi:10.1016/j.rai.2016.06.003

Dennehy, D., & Sammon, D. (2015). Trends in mobile payments research: A literature review. *Journal of Innovation Management, 3*(1), 49–61. doi:10.24840/2183-0606_003.001_0006

Dewan, S. G., & Chen, L. D. (2005). Mobile payment adoption in the USA: A crossindustry, cross-platform solution. *Journal of Information Privacy & Security, 1*(2), 4–28. doi:10.1080/15536548.2005.10855765

Di Pietro, L., Guglielmetti Mugion, R., Mattia, G., Renzi, M. F., & Toni, M. (2015). The integrated model on mobile payment acceptance (IMMPA): An empirical application to public transport. *Transportation Research Part C, Emerging Technologies, 56*, 463–479. doi:10.1016/j.trc.2015.05.001

Duane, A., O'Reilly, P., & Andreev, P. (2014). Realising M-payments: Modelling consumers' willingness to M-pay using smart phones. *Behaviour & Information Technology, 33*(4), 318–334. doi:10.1080/0144929X.2012.745608

Dwivedi, Y. K., Rana, N. P., Janssen, M., Lal, B., Williams, M. D., & Clement, R. M. (2017). B). an empirical validation of a Unified Model of Electronic Government Adoption (UMEGA). *Government Information Quarterly, 34*(2), 211–230. doi:10.1016/j.giq.2017.03.001

Dwivedi, Y. K., Shareef, M. A., Simintiras, A. C., Lal, B., & Weerakkody, V. (2016). A generalised adoption model for services: A cross-country comparison of mobile health (mhealth). *Government Information Quarterly, 33*(1), 174–187. doi:10.1016/j.giq.2015.06.003

Featherman, M., & Pavlou, P. (2003). Predicting e-services adoption: A perceived risk facets perspective. *International Journal of Human-Computer Studies*, *59*(4), 451–474. doi:10.1016/S1071-5819(03)00111-3

Felipe, C. M., Roldán, J. L., & Leal-Rodríguez, A. L. (2017). Impact of organizational culture values on organizational agility. *Sustainability*, *9*(12), 2354. doi:10.3390u9122354

Fitriani, F., Suzianti, A., & Chairunnisa, A. (2017). Analysis of factors that affect nfc mobile payment technology adoption:(case study: telkomsel cash). *Proceedings of the 2017 International Conference on Telecommunications and Communication Engineering*, 103-109. 10.1145/3145777.3145778

Fornell, C., & Larcker, D. F. (1981). Evaluation Structural Equation Models with Unobservable Variables and Measurement Error. *JMR, Journal of Marketing Research*, *18*(1), 39–50. doi:10.1177/002224378101800104

Fornell, C. I. J. (1994). Partial Least Squares. *Advanced Methods of Marketing Research*, 52-78.

Gbongli, K., Xu, Y., & Amedjonekou, K. M. (2019). Extended Technology Acceptance Model to Predict Mobile-Based Money Acceptance and Sustainability: A Multi-Analytical Structural Equation Modeling and Neural Network Approach. *Sustainability*, *11*(13), 3639. doi:10.3390u11133639

Gefen, D., Ridgon, E. E., & Straub, D. W. (2011). Editor's Comments: An Updated and Extension to SEM Guidelines for Administrative and Social Science Research. *Management Information Systems Quarterly*, *35*(2), iii–xiv. doi:10.2307/23044042

Geisser, S. (1974). A predictive approach to the random effect model. *Biometrika*, *61*(1), 101–107. doi:10.1093/biomet/61.1.101

Gerpott, T., & Kornmeier, K. (2009). Determinants of customer acceptance of mobile payment systems. *International Journal of Electronic Finance*, *3*(1), 1–30. doi:10.1504/IJEF.2009.024267

Göktaş, P., & Akgül, Y. (2019). The Investigation of Employer Adoption of Human Resource Information Systems at University Using TAM. In *Structural Equation Modeling Approaches to E-Service Adoption* (pp. 1–27). IGI Global. doi:10.4018/978-1-5225-8015-7.ch001

Gold, A. H., Malhotra, A., & Segars, A. H. (2001). Knowledge management: An organizational capabilities perspective. *Journal of Management Information Systems*, *18*(1), 185–214. doi:10.1080/07421222.2001.11045669

Guo, K. (2017). An Empirical Examination of Initial Use Intention of Mobile Payment. *Boletrn Tecnico, 55*(10).

Hair, J. F., Ringle, C. M., & Sarstedt, M. (2011). PLS-SEM: Indeed a Silver Bullet. *Journal of Marketing Theory and Practice, 18*(2), 139–152. doi:10.2753/MTP1069-6679190202

Hampshire, C. (2017). A mixed methods empirical exploration of UK consumer perceptions of trust, risk and usefulness of mobile payments. *International Journal of Bank Marketing, 35*(3), 354–369. doi:10.1108/IJBM-08-2016-0105

Harris, M. A., Brookshire, R., & Chin, A. G. (2016). Identifying factors influencing consumers' intent to install mobile applications. *International Journal of Information Management, 36*(3), 441–450. doi:10.1016/j.ijinfomgt.2016.02.004

Henseler, J., Ringle, C., & Sinkovics, R. (2009). The Use Of Partial Least Squares Path Modeling In International Marketing. *Advances in International Marketing, 20*(1), 277–319. doi:10.1108/S1474-7979(2009)0000020014

Hongxia, P., Xianhao, X., & Weidan, L. (2011). Drivers and barriers in the acceptance of mobile payment in China. In *International conference on E-business and E-government*. 10.1109/ICEBEG.2011.5887081

Hossain, R., & Mahmud, I. (2016). *Influence of cognitive style on mobile payment system adoption: An extended technology acceptance model*. Paper presented at the 2016 International Conference on Computer Communication and Informatics, ICCCI 2016, 10.1109/ICCCI.2016.7479973

Hsu, H. S., & Kulviwat, S. (2006). An integrative framework of technology acceptance model and personalisation in mobile commerce. *International Journal of Technology Marketing, 1*(4), 393–410. doi:10.1504/IJTMKT.2006.010734

Insider, B. (2015). The mobile payments report: Forecasts, user trends, and the companies vying to dominate mobile payments. *BI Intelligence*. https://www.businessinsider.com/the-free-mobile-payments-report-2015-06

Jr, J. F., Hult, G. T. M., Ringle, C., & Sarstedt, M. (2016). *A primer on partial least squares structural equation modeling (PLS-SEM)*. Sage Publications.

Kaitawarn, C. (2015). Factor influencing the acceptance and use of M-payment in Thailand: A case study of AIS mPAY rabbit. *Rev. Integr. Bus. Econ. Res., 4*(3), 222.

Kapoor, K., Dwivedi, Y., & Williams, M. (2014). Examining the role of three sets of innovation attributes for determining adoption of the interbank mobile payment service. *Information Systems Frontiers*. Advance online publication. doi:10.100710796-014-9484-7

Kapoor, K. K., Dwivedi, Y. K., & Williams, M. D. (2015). Examining the role of three sets of innovation attributes for determining adoption of the interbank mobile payment service. *Information Systems Frontiers*, *17*(5), 1039–1056. doi:10.100710796-014-9484-7

Keramati, A., Taeb, R., Larijani, A. M., & Mojir, N. (2012). A combinative model of behavioural and technical factors affecting 'Mobile'-payment services adoption: An empirical study. *Service Industries Journal*, *32*(9), 1489–1504. doi:10.1080/0 2642069.2011.552716

Khalilzadeh, J., Ozturk, A. B., & Bilgihan, A. (2017). Security-related factors in extended UTAUT model for NFC based mobile payment in the restaurant industry. *Computers in Human Behavior*, *70*, 460–474. doi:10.1016/j.chb.2017.01.001

Khan, A. N., & Ali, A. (2018). Factors affecting Retailer's Adopti on of Mobile payment systems: A SEM-neural network modeling approach. *Wireless Personal Communications*, *103*(3), 2529–2551. doi:10.100711277-018-5945-5

Khan, A. N., Cao, X., & Pitafi, A. H. (2019). Personality Traits as Predictor of M-Payment Systems: A SEM-Neural Networks Approach. *Journal of Organizational and End User Computing*, *31*(4), 89–110. doi:10.4018/JOEUC.2019100105

Kim, C., Mirusmonov, M., & Lee, I. (2010). An empirical examination of factors influencing the intention to use mobile payment. *Computers in Human Behavior*, *26*(3), 310–322. doi:10.1016/j.chb.2009.10.013

Kim, Y., Choi, J., & Park, Y., & Yeon, J. (2016). The adoption of mobile payment services for "fintech". *International Journal of Applied Engineering Research*, *11*(2), 1058–1061.

Kline, R. (2011). *Principles and Practice of Structural Equation Modeling* (3rd ed.). Guilford Press.

Ko, E., Kim, E., & Lee, E. (2009). Modeling consumer adoption of mobile shopping for fashion products in Korea. *Psychology and Marketing*, *26*(7), 669–687. doi:10.1002/mar.20294

Koenig-Lewis, N., Marquet, M., Palmer, A., & Zhao, A. L. (2015). Enjoyment and social influence: Predicting mobile payment adoption. *Service Industries Journal*, *35*(10), 537–554. doi:10.1080/02642069.2015.1043278

Laukkanen, T. (2016). Consumer adoption versus rejection decisions in seemingly similar service innovations: The case of the Internet and mobile banking. *Journal of Business Research*, *69*(7), 2432–2439. doi:10.1016/j.jbusres.2016.01.013

Leong, L.-Y., Hew, T.-S., Tan, G. W.-H., & Ooi, K. B. (2013). Predicting the determinants of the NFC-enabled mobile credit card acceptance: A neural network approach. *Expert Systems with Applications*, *40*(14), 5604–5620. doi:10.1016/j.eswa.2013.04.018

Li, H., Liu, Y., & Heikkilä, J. (2014). Understanding the factors driving NFC-enabled mobile payment adoption: an empirical investigation. PACIS 2014 Proceedings, 231.

Liébana-Cabanillas, F., Marinkovic, V., de Luna, I. R., & Kalinic, Z. (2018). Predicting the determinants of mobile payment acceptance: A hybrid SEM-neural network approach. *Technological Forecasting and Social Change*, *129*, 117–130. doi:10.1016/j.techfore.2017.12.015

Liébana-Cabanillas, F., Marinković, V., & Kalinić, Z. (2017b). A SEM-neural network approach for predicting antecedents of m-commerce acceptance. *International Journal of Information Management*, *37*(2), 14–24. doi:10.1016/j.ijinfomgt.2016.10.008

Liébana-Cabanillas, F., Munoz-Leiva, F., & Sánchez-Fernandez, J. (2015b). Payment systems in new electronic environments: Consumer behavior in payment systems via SMS. *International Journal of Information Technology & Decision Making*, *14*(02), 421–449. doi:10.1142/S0219622015500078

Liébana-Cabanillas, F., Muñoz-Leiva, F., & Sánchez-Fernández, J. (2017a). A global approach to the analysis of user behavior in mobile payment systems in the new electronic environment. *Service Business*, 1–40.

Liébana-Cabanillas, F., Ramos de Luna, I., & Montoro-Ríos, F. (2017c). Intention to use new mobile payment systems: A comparative analysis of SMS and NFC payments. *Economic Research Journal*, *30*(1), 892–910. doi:10.1080/1331677X.2017.1305784

Liébana-Cabanillas, F., Ramos de Luna, I., & Montoro-Ríos, F. J. (2015a). User behaviour in QR mobile payment system: The QR payment acceptance model. *Technology Analysis and Strategic Management*, *27*(9), 1031–1049. doi:10.1080/09537325.2015.1047757

Liébana-Cabanillas, F., Sánchez-Fernández, J., & Muñoz-Leiva, F. (2014). Antecedents of the adoption of the new mobile payment systems: The moderating effect of age. *Computers in Human Behavior, 35*, 464–478. doi:10.1016/j.chb.2014.03.022

Lu, Y., Yang, S., Chau, P. Y. K., & Cao, Y. (2011). Dynamics between the trust transfer process and intention to use mobile payment services: A cross-environment perspective. *Information & Management, 48*(8), 393–403. doi:10.1016/j.im.2011.09.006

Mallat, N. (2007). Exploring consumer adoption of mobile payments–a qualitative study. *The Journal of Strategic Information Systems, 16*(4), 413–432. doi:10.1016/j.jsis.2007.08.001

Mallat, N., Rossi, M., & Tuunainen, V. K. (2004). Mobile banking services. *Communications of the ACM, 47*(5), 42–46. doi:10.1145/986213.986236

Mallat, N., & Tuunainen, V. K. (2008). Exploring merchant adoption of mobile payment systems: An empirical study. *e-Service Journal, 6*(2), 24–57. doi:10.2979/esj.2008.6.2.24

Martens, M., Roll, O., & Elliott, R. (2017). Testing the technology readiness and acceptance model for mobile payments across Germany and South Africa. *International Journal of Innovation and Technology Management, 14*(6), 1750033. Advance online publication. doi:10.1142/S021987701750033X

Martins, C. T. O., & Popovič, A. (2014). Understanding the internet banking adoption: A unified theory of acceptance and use of technology and perceived risk application. *International Journal of Information Management, 34*(1), 1–13. doi:10.1016/j.ijinfomgt.2013.06.002

Masamila, B., Mtenzi, F., Said, J., & Tinabo, R. (2010). A secured mobile payment model for developing markets. In *International Conference on Networked Digital Technologies*. Springer. 10.1007/978-3-642-14292-5_20

Meixin, X., & Wei, L. (2014). *A Study on the Intention to Use NFC Mobile Phone Payment and Strategies to Expand the NFC Market—Based on Users' Perspective.* Academic Press.

Miltgen, C. L., Popovič, A., & Oliveira, T. (2013). Determinants of end-user acceptance of biometrics: Integrating the "Big 3" of technology acceptance with privacy context. *Decision Support Systems, 56*, 103–114. doi:10.1016/j.dss.2013.05.010

Moodley, T., & Govender, I. (2016). Factors influencing academic use of internet banking services: An empirical study. *African Journal of Science, Technology, Innovation and Development*, 8(1), 43–51. doi:10.1080/20421338.2015.1128043

Moore, G. C., & Benbasat, I. (1991). Development of an instrument to measure the perceptions of adopting an information technology innovation. *Information Systems Research*, 2(3), 192–222. doi:10.1287/isre.2.3.192

Morosan, C., & DeFranco, A. (2016a). It's about time: Revisiting UTAUT2 to examine consumers' intentions to use NFC mobile payments in hotels. *International Journal of Hospitality Management*, 53, 17–29. doi:10.1016/j.ijhm.2015.11.003

Morosan, C., & DeFranco, A. (2016b). Investigating American iPhone users' intentions to use NFC mobile payments in hotels. In *Information and Communication Technologies in Tourism 2016* (pp. 427–440). Springer International Publishing. doi:10.1007/978-3-319-28231-2_31

Mun, Y. P., Khalid, H., & Nadarajah, D. (2017). Millennials' Perception on Mobile Payment Services in Malaysia. *Procedia Computer Science*, 124, 397–404. doi:10.1016/j.procs.2017.12.170

Oliveira, T., Thomas, M., Baptista, G., & Campos, F. (2016). Mobile payment: Understanding the determinants of customer adoption and intention to recommend the technology. *Computers in Human Behavior*, 61, 404–414. doi:10.1016/j.chb.2016.03.030

Ondrus, J., & Pigneur, Y. (2006). Towards a holistic analysis of mobile payments: A multiple perspectives approach. *Electronic Commerce Research and Applications*, 5(3), 246–257. doi:10.1016/j.elerap.2005.09.003

Ooi, K., & Tan, G. W.-H. (2016). Mobile technology acceptance model: An investigation using mobile users to explore smartphone credit card. *Expert Systems with Applications*, 59, 33–46. doi:10.1016/j.eswa.2016.04.015

Ozturk, A. B., Bilgihan, A., Salehi-Esfahani, S., & Hua, N. (2017). Understanding the mobile payment technology acceptance based on valence theory: A case of restaurant transactions. *International Journal of Contemporary Hospitality Management*, 29(8), 2027–2049. doi:10.1108/IJCHM-04-2016-0192

Pal, D., Vanijja, V., & Papasratorn, B. (2015). An empirical analysis towards the adoption of NFC mobile payment system by the end user. *Procedia Computer Science*, 69, 13–25. doi:10.1016/j.procs.2015.10.002

Peng, H., Xu, X., & Liu, W. (2011). Drivers and barriers in the acceptance of mobile payment in China. *Communications in Information Science and Management Engineering, 1*(5), 73–78.

Peng, R., Xiong, L., & Yang, Z. (2012). Exploring tourist adoption of tourism mobile payment: An empirical analysis. *Journal of Theoretical and Applied Electronic Commerce Research, 7*(1), 21–33. doi:10.4067/S0718-18762012000100003

Pham, T. T. T., & Ho, J. C. (2015). The effects of product-related, personal-related factors and attractiveness of alternatives on consumer adoption of NFC-based mobile payments. *Technology in Society, 43*, 159-172.doi: .techsoc.2015.05.004 doi:10.1016/j

Phonthanukitithaworn, C., Sellitto, C., & Fong, M. (2015). User intentions to adopt mobile payment services: A study of early adopters in Thailand. *Journal of Internet Banking and Commerce, 20*(1), 1–29.

Phonthanukitithaworn, C., Sellitto, C., & Fong, M. W. L. (2016). An investigation of mobile payment (m-payment) services in Thailand. *Asia-Pacific Journal of Business Administration, 8*(1), 37–54. doi:10.1108/APJBA-10-2014-0119

Pousttchi, K., & Wiedemann, D. G. (2007). What influences consumers' intention to use mobile payments. *Proceedings of the 6th Annual Global Mobility Roundtable.*

Qasim, H., & Abu-Shanab, E. (2016). Drivers of mobile payment acceptance: The impact of network externalities. *Information Systems Frontiers, 18*(5), 1021–1034. doi:10.100710796-015-9598-6

Ramos-de-Luna, I., Montoro-Rios, F., & Liebana-Cabanillas, F. (2016). Determinants of the intention to use NFC technology as a payment system: An acceptance modelapproach. *Information Systems and e-Business Management, 14*(2), 293–314. doi:10.100710257-015-0284-5

Rana, N. P., Dwivedi, Y. K., Lal, B., Williams, M. D., & Clement, M. (2017). Citizens' adoption of an electronic government system: Towards a unified view. *Information Systems Frontiers, 19*(3), 549–568. doi:10.100710796-015-9613-y

Rana, N. P., Dwivedi, Y. K., Williams, M. D., & Weerakkody, V. (2016). Adoption of online public grievance redressal system in India: Toward developing a unified view. *Computers in Human Behavior, 59*, 265–282. doi:10.1016/j.chb.2016.02.019

Ringle, C. M., Sarstedt, M., Mitchell, R., & Gudergan, S. P. (2018). Partial least squares structural equation modeling in HRM research. *International Journal of Human Resource Management,* 1–27.

Rogers, E. M. (1983). *Diffusion of innovations* (3rd ed.). Free Press of Glencoe.

Roldán, J. L., & Sánchez-Franco, M. J. (2012). Variance-based structural equation modeling: Guidelines for using partial least squares in information systems research. In *Research methodologies, innovations and philosophies in software systems engineering and information systems* (pp. 193–221). IGI Global. doi:10.4018/978-1-4666-0179-6.ch010

Rouibah, K. P. B. L., & Hwang, Y. (2016). The effects of perceived enjoyment and perceived risks on trust formation and intentions to use online payment systems: New perspectives from an Arab country. *Electronic Commerce Research and Applications*, *19*, 33–43. doi:10.1016/j.elerap.2016.07.001

Salloum, S. A., Al-Emran, M., Khalaf, R., Habes, M., & Shaalan, K. (2019). An Innovative Study of E-Payment Systems Adoption in Higher Education: Theoretical Constructs and Empirical Analysis. *International Journal of Interactive Mobile Technologies*, *13*(6), 68. doi:10.3991/ijim.v13i06.9875

San Martín, H., & Herrero, Á. (2012). Influence of the user's psychological factors on the online purchase intention in rural tourism: Integrating innovativeness to the UTAUT framework. *Tourism Management*, *33*(2), 341–350. doi:10.1016/j.tourman.2011.04.003

Schierz, P. G., Schilke, O., & Wirtz, B. W. (2010). Understanding consumer acceptance of mobile payment services: An empirical analysis. *Electronic Commerce Research and Applications*, *9*(3), 209–216. doi:10.1016/j.elerap.2009.07.005

Shareef, M. A., Baabdullah, A., Dutta, S., Kumar, V., & Dwivedi, Y. K. (2018). Consumer Adoption of Mobile Banking Services: An Empirical Examination of Factors According to Adoption Stages. *Journal of Retailing and Consumer Services*, *43*(July), 54–67. doi:10.1016/j.jretconser.2018.03.003

Shareef, M. A., Dwivedi, Y. K., Kumar, V., & Kumar, U. (2017). Content design of advertisement for consumer exposure: Mobile marketing through short messaging service. *International Journal of Information Management*, *37*(4), 257–268. doi:10.1016/j.ijinfomgt.2017.02.003

Sharma, S. K. (2017). Integrating cognitive antecedents into TAM to explain mobile banking behavioral intention: A SEM-neural network modeling. In *Information Systems Frontiers* (pp. 1–13). Springer Nature.

Sharma, S. K., Al-Badi, A. H., Govindaluri, S. M., & Al-Kharusi, M. H. (2016). Predicting motivators of cloud computing adoption: A developing country perspective. *Computers in Human Behavior*, *62*, 61–69. doi:10.1016/j.chb.2016.03.073

Sharma, S. K., Govindaluri, S. M., & Al Balushi, S. M. (2015). Predicting determinants of Internet banking adoption. *Management Research Review*, *38*(7), 750–766. doi:10.1108/MRR-06-2014-0139

Sharma, S. K., Joshi, A., & Sharma, H. (2016). A multi-analytical approach to predict the Facebook usage in higher education. *Computers in Human Behavior*, *55*, 340–353. doi:10.1016/j.chb.2015.09.020

Sharma, S. K., Sharma, H., & Dwivedi, Y. K. (2019). A Hybrid SEM-Neural Network Model for Predicting Determinants of Mobile Payment Services. *Information Systems Management*, *36*(3), 1–19. doi:10.1080/10580530.2019.1620504

Shin, D. (2009). Towards an understanding of the consumer acceptance of mobile wallet. *Computers in Human Behavior*, *25*(6), 1343–1354. doi:10.1016/j.chb.2009.06.001

Shin, D.-H. (2010). Modelling the interaction of users and mobile payment system: Conceptual framework. *International Journal of Human-Computer Interaction*, *26*(10), 917–940. doi:10.1080/10447318.2010.502098

Shin, D.-H. (2010). Modelling the interaction of users and mobile payment system: Conceptual framework. *International Journal of Human-Computer Interaction*, *26*(10), 917–940. doi:10.1080/10447318.2010.502098

Shmueli, G., Ray, S., Estrada, J. M. V., & Chatla, S. B. (2016). The elephant in the room: Predictive performance of PLS models. *Journal of Business Research*, *69*(10), 4552–4564. doi:10.1016/j.jbusres.2016.03.049

Shmueli, G., Sarstedt, M., Hair, J. F., Cheah, J. H., Ting, H., Vaithilingam, S., & Ringle, C. M. (2019). Predictive model assessment in PLS-SEM: Guidelines for using PLSpredict. *European Journal of Marketing*, *53*(11), 2322–2347. doi:10.1108/EJM-02-2019-0189

Sinha, I., & Mukherjee, S. (2016). Acceptance of technology, related factors in use of off branch e-banking: An Indian case study. *The Journal of High Technology Management Research*, *27*(1), 88–100. doi:10.1016/j.hitech.2016.04.008

Slade, E., Williams, M., Dwivedi, Y., & Piercy, N. (2014). Exploring consumer adoption of proximity mobile payments. *Journal of Strategic Marketing*, 1–15.

Slade, E., Williams, M., Dwivedi, Y., & Piercy, N. (2015a). Exploring consumer adoption of proximity mobile payments. *Journal of Strategic Marketing*, *23*(3), 209–223. doi:10.1080/0965254X.2014.914075

Slade, E. L., Dwivedi, Y. K., Piercy, N. C., & Williams, M. D. (2015b). Modeling consumers' adoption intentions of remote mobile payments in the united kingdom: Extending UTAUT with innovativeness, risk, and trust. *Psychology and Marketing, 32*(8), 860–873. doi:10.1002/mar.20823

Slade, E. L., Williams, M. D., & Dwivedi, Y. K. (2013). Mobile payment adoption: Classification and review of the extant literature. *The Marketing Review, 13*(2), 167–190. doi:10.1362/146934713X13699019904687

Statista.com. (2015). *Mobile phone users worldwide 2013-2019.* Retrieved from https://www.statista.com/statistics/274774/forecast-of-mobile-phone-users-worldwide/

Su, P., Wang, L., & Yan, J. (2018). How users' Internet experience affects the adoption of mobile payment: A mediation model. *Technology Analysis and Strategic Management, 30*(2), 186–197. doi:10.1080/09537325.2017.1297788

Szopiński, T. S. (2016). Factors affecting the adoption of online banking in Poland. *Journal of Business Research, 69*(11), 4763–4768. doi:10.1016/j.jbusres.2016.04.027

Tan, G. W., Ooi, K.-B., Chong, S.-C., & Hew, T.-S. (2014). NFC mobile credit card: The next frontier of mobile payment? *Telematics and Informatics, 31*(2), 292307. doi:10.1016/j.tele.2013.06.002

Teo, A. C., Tan, G. W. H., Ooi, K. B., Hew, T. S., & Yew, K. T. (2015). The effects of convenience and speed in m-payment. *Industrial Management & Data Systems, 115*(2), 311–331. doi:10.1108/IMDS-08-2014-0231

Thakur, R. (2013). Customer adoption of mobile payment services by professionals across two cities in India: An empirical study using modified technology acceptance model. *Business Perspectives and Research, 1*(2), 17–30. doi:10.1177/2278533720130203

Thakur, R., & Srivastava, M. (2014). Adoption readiness, personal innovativeness, perceived risk and usage intention across customer groups for mobile payment services in India. *Internet Research, 24*(3), 369–392. doi:10.1108/IntR-12-2012-0244

Tian, Y., & Dong, H. (2013). *An analysis of key factors affecting user acceptance of mobile payment.* Paper presented at the 2013 2nd International Conference on Informatics and Applications, ICIA 2013. 10.1109/ICoIA.2013.6650263

Ting, H., Yacob, Y., Liew, L., & Lau, W. M. (2016). Intention to use mobile payment system: A case of developing market by ethnicity. *Procedia: Social and Behavioral Sciences, 224*, 368–375. doi:10.1016/j.sbspro.2016.05.390

Trachuk, A., & Linder, N. (2017). The adoption of mobile payment services by consumers: An empirical analysis results. *Business and Economic Horizons, 13*(3), 383–408. doi:10.15208/beh.2017.28

Varshney, U., & Vetter, R. (2002). Mobile commerce: Framework, applications and networking support. *Mobile Networks and Applications, 7*(3), 185–198. doi:10.1023/A:1014570512129

Venkatesh, V., & Davis, F. D. (2000). A theoretical extension of the technology acceptance model: Four longitudinal field studies. *Management Science, 46*(2), 186–204. doi:10.1287/mnsc.46.2.186.11926

Venkatesh, V., Ramesh, V., & Massey, A. P. (2003). Understanding usability in mobile commerce. *Communications of the ACM, 46*(12), 53–56. doi:10.1145/953460.953488

Venkatesh, V., Thong, J. Y., & Xu, X. (2012). Consumer acceptance and use of information technology: Extending the unified theory of acceptance and use of technology. *MIS Quartely, 36*(1), 157–178. doi:10.2307/41410412

Veríssimo, J. M. C. (2016). Enablers and restrictors of mobile banking app use: A fuzzy set qualitative comparative analysis (fsQCA). *Journal of Business Research, 69*(11), 5456–5460. doi:10.1016/j.jbusres.2016.04.155

Wang, L., & Yi, Y. (2012). The impact of use context on mobile payment acceptance: An empirical study in China. In A. Xie & X. Huang (Eds.), *Advances in computer science and education* (pp. 293–300). Springer. doi:10.1007/978-3-642-27945-4_47

Westland, J. C. (2010). Lower bounds on sample size in structural equation modeling. *Electronic Commerce Research and Applications, 9*(6), 476–487. doi:10.1016/j.elerap.2010.07.003

Wetzels, M., Odekerken-Schroder, G., & Van Oppen, C. (2009). Using PLS path modeling for assessing hierarchical construct models: Guidelines and empirical illustration. *Management Information Systems Quarterly, 33*(1), 33177–33195. doi:10.2307/20650284

Wu, U., & Kaohsiung, T., & Yang. (2007). Using UTAUT to explore the behavior of 3G mobile communication users. *2007 IEEE International Conference on Industrial Engineering and Engineering Management,* 199–203. 10.1109/IEEM.2007.4419179

Yadav, R., Sharma, S. K., & Tarhini, A. (2016). A multi-analytical approach to understand and predict the mobile commerce adoption. *Journal of Enterprise Information Management, 29*(2), 222–237. doi:10.1108/JEIM-04-2015-0034

Yang, Q. C., Pang, C., Liu, L., Yen, D. C., & Michael Tarn, J. (2015). Exploring consumer perceived risk and trust for online payments: An empirical study in China's younger generation. *Computers in Human Behavior, 50*, 9–24. doi:10.1016/j. chb.2015.03.058

Yang, S., Lu, Y., Gupta, S., Cao, Y., & Zhang, R. (2012). Mobile payment services adoption across time: An empirical study of the effects of behavioral beliefs, social influences, and personal traits. *Computers in Human Behavior, 28*(1), 129–142. doi:10.1016/j.chb.2011.08.019

Yi, M. Y., Jackson, J. D., Park, J. S., & Probst, J. C. (2006). Understanding information technology acceptance by individual professionals: Toward an integrative view. *Information & Management, 43*(3), 350–363. doi:10.1016/j.im.2005.08.006

Zarmpou, T., Saprikis, V., Markos, A., & Vlachopoulou, M. (2012). Modeling users' acceptance of mobile services. *Electronic Commerce Research, 12*(2), 225–248. doi:10.100710660-012-9092-x

Zhou, T. (2011). The effect of initial trust on user adoption of mobile payment. *Information Development, 27*(4), 290–300. doi:10.1177/0266666911424075

Zhou, T. (2014). Understanding the determinants of mobile payment continuance usage. *Industrial Management & Data Systems, 114*(6), 936–948. doi:10.1108/IMDS-02-2014-0068

Chapter 7
An Integrated SEM–Neural Network Approach for Predicting Mobile Banking Determinants of Adoption in Turkey

Yakup Akgül
Alanya Alaaddin Keykubat University, Turkey

ABSTRACT

Higher penetration of the most widely used mobile technology applications and 3G and 4G mobile networks have led to the higher usage of smartphones for mobile banking activities in recent times. Data were collected from 395 mobile banking users and analyzed using an innovative two-staged regression and neural network (NN) model. In the first stage, structural equation modeling was employed to test the research hypotheses and identify significant antecedents influencing mobile banking acceptance. In the second stage, the significant antecedents obtained from the first stage were input to a neural network model for ranking. The results revealed that autonomous motivation and perceived ease of use are the two main predictors influencing mobile banking acceptance. Theoretical and practical implications of findings are discussed. Policy makers can find significant results in this chapter for implementing future service design. Limitations and future research scope are also discussed.

DOI: 10.4018/978-1-7998-4042-8.ch007

INTRODUCTION

With the accelerate speed of Information and Communication Technology and the emergence and the higher penetration of the 3G and the 4G services by telecom companies, mobile technology has become an integral part of our day-to-day life. Mobile services have been introduced in many different sectors including government, banking, healthcare, and commerce (Alalwan et al. 2016; Alalwan et al. 2017; Baptista & Oliveira, 2016; Chong, 2013; Ha, Canedoli, Baur, & Bick, 2012; Hanafizadeh et al. 2014; Kapoor et al. 2015; Laukkanen and Kiviniemi 2010; Luarn and Lin, 2005; O'Connor and O'Reilly 2016). These technologies are increasingly being implemented for achieving competitive advantage through economies of scale resulting from larger customer base, personalization of banking services and reductions in operational cost (Laukkanen, 2016; Sharma et al., 2015). Mobile banking (Mbanking) supports customers to perform various banking activities using mobile devices. The term Mbanking refers to the banking activities conducted through mobile internet technologies (Chong, 2013).

Mobile banking is one of the key latest technological innovations of mobile communication technology. Mobile Banking (or M-Banking) refers to a service provided by banks or other financial institutions that allow its customers to conduct a range of financial (Bill Payments, Peer-to-peer payments, Fund Transfers, Remittance, Shopping and donations, Mobile balance recharge, Dish TV Recharge & Top-up, and M-Commerce) and non-financial transactions (Balance Enquiry, Mini-bank Statement, PIN Change, Cheque book request, Due alerts for payments, Locate ATMs, Enquire Deposit Rates, and Loan calculator). These transactions can be realized remotely using a mobile device such as a mobile phone or tablet on dedicated mobile applications (apps), provided by the financial institutions (Shaikh and Karjaluoto, 2015).

A review of the recent literature on mBanking showed that the majority of the existing researches have generally focused on the technological aspects of mBanking (Aboelmaged and Gebba, 2013; Gu et al., 2009; Hanafizadeh et al., 2014; Hsu et al., 2011; Luarn and Lin, 2005; Wessels and Drennan, 2010). Despite various benefits offered by the banking sector and widespread adoption of mobile devices in the developing countries, the adoption rate of M-Banking across the World is still low (Alalwan et al. 2017; Alalwan et al. 2016; Akturan and Tezcan 2012; Malaquias and Hwang 2016). Examining the latest literature on m-banking, it is revealed that technological aspects are the focus of most of research works (Baptista & Oliveira, 2016; Ha et al., 2012; Hsu, Wang, & Lin, 2011). Majority of m-banking research have adopted technology acceptance model (TAM) as the key to establish causal theories of m-banking adoption (Baptista & Oliveira, 2016). Among others, Chong (2013), Hew, Leong, Ooi, and Chong (2016) and Sharma, Govindaluri, Al-Muharrami, and

Tarhini (2016) criticized using exploratory models for technology adoption purpose. They stressed on using nonlinear statistical model such as artificial neural network (ANN). Their findings revealed better prediction ability through ANN model.

This book chapter has three objectives. First, the study intends to investigate the key factors that predict the use of Mbanking adoption by extending the TAM proposed by Davis (1989) from a developing country perspective. The TAM is extended by integrating additional variables, namely, trust, social influence, compatibility, and demographic variables. Second, this study investigates the relationship between the dependent variable, adoption and other variables using two methods, regression and neural networks (NNs), and compares these explanatory and predictive modelling methods (Chong, 2013; Shmueli, 2010). A large majority of empirical studies in information systems use explanatory methods, for example, multiple linear regression (MLR) model and structural equation modelling. The research study compares the performance of the non-linear NN model with an MLR in understanding and predicting mBanking adoption. Finally, this study examines the Mbanking adoption from a developing country perspective. Furthermore, the primary focus of this study is to use predictive modelling for Mbanking adoption, so there is no need to develop and test research hypotheses.

LITERATURE REVIEW

The impact of the individual's acceptance on the success of any technology implementation motivated research in the area of technology acceptance. The development of the intention-based models, namely theory of reasoned action model has the role, which is the foundations for understanding the nature of technology acceptance recognized behavioral intention as the key determinant of technology acceptance (Ajzen and Fishbein, 1980). Theory of planned behavior model (Ajzen and Madden, 1986) and TAM (Davis, 1989). These models were followed by the Unified theory for acceptance and use of technology (Venkatesh et al., 2003), also referred to as UTAUT, which combined elements of earlier intention-based models and expectancy theory (Vroom, 1964). Among the models proposed for understanding user acceptance behaviors, TAM was widely used for understanding the factors influencing user acceptance with respect to Internet banking in various countries. Davis (1989) as part of TAM proposed two constructs perceived ease of use (PEOU) and perceived usefulness (PU). These constructs are defined as follows "PU is the degree to which a person believes that using a particular system would enhance his or her job performance"; and "PEOU refers to the degree to which a person believes that using a particular system would be free of effort".

Moreover, TAM allows extension of its core model and thus become popular among the practitioners and researchers. In this book chapter, an extension of original TAM model (E-TAM) has been initiated by incorporating social influence (SI), Compatibility (COM), trust (TRU), Controlled motivation (CM), and autonomous motivation with the original model, which includes perceived ease of use (PEOU) and perceived usefulness (PU) as proposed in (Davis, 1989). Social influence is the degree to which an individual get influenced by his social environments. The subjects of SI can be friends, family members, colleagues, neighbours or the society who belongs as a whole. SI has been revealed as the most influencing factor for adoption of technology in earlier studies by Venkatesh and Davis (2000) and Venkatesh et al. (2003). Second extended construct in this paper is trust defining important factors that can affect user behavior with respect to adoption of banking technology and it relates to the security aspects of the technology. Pavlou (2003) had defined trust as "a belief that customers entrust upon online retailers after careful consideration of the characteristics of retailers". Third extended construct in this book chapter is compatibility defining the ability of a technology by adopting customers need, want, values and dimensions to present correctly in front of a potential technology user. For banking environment, whether m-banking technology fits well with the different aspects of individual's personal life style. Compatibility is the degree to which the Mbanking technology is consistent with existing values, needs and past experiences of potential adopters (Rogers, 1995). Among the earlier studies, Koenig-Lewis, Palmer, and Moll (2010) and Wu and Wang (2005) found compatibility as the most significant factor in terms of predicting the intention to use mobile commerce for technology adoption. Fourth extended construct in this book chapter is Controlled motivation relies on two approaches, creating purchase pressure and creating fear of not using the technology (Michou et al. 2014; Ryan and Deci, 2000). Hagger et al. (2002) and Zhou (2016) argued that controlled motivation, which is considered as opposite of autonomous motivation will have a significant impact on the behavioral intention of users. Last extended construct in this book chapter is Autonomous motivation is defining to create a need for the supportive environment will help to achieve autonomous motivation (Vansteenkiste et al. 2007). Hagger et al. (2002) and Zhou (2016) argued that autonomous motivation plays a significant role in the user's behavioral intention.

RESEARCH METHODS

The methodology adopted in this book chapter is similar to the previous studies (Akgül, 2017; Akgül, 2017a; Akgül, 2018b; Chong, 2013a; Chong et al., 2015; Liébana-Cabanillas et al., 2017; Shmueli and Koppius, 2011) to validate the research model and test the proposed research hypotheses. There are two stages in the data analysis of this study. In the first stage, structural equation model (SEM) was employed to understand the significant influence of predictors on the M-Banking acceptance. The second stage employed neural network model to identify the importance of the predictors.

Instrument Development

The instrument was developed based on seven latent constructs mentioned in the research model. All the construct items adapted from the literature include perceived ease of use (PEOU) (Venkatesh et al., 2012; Wei et al., 2009) Wang et al. (2009); Davis (1989) Mansour et al., 2016), perceived usefulness (PU) (Hew et al., 2016; Venkatesh et al., 2012) Liebana-Cabanillas et al. (2017); Davis (1989) Sharma et al., 2015; Mansour et al., 2016), Compatibility (COM) (Hew et al., 2016; Wei et al., 2009) Wu and Wang, 2005); social influence (SI) (Hew et al., 2016; Park & Kim, 2013; Sharma et al., 2016; Wei et al., 2009; Venkatesh and Davis, 2000), Trust (Hew et al., 2016; Wei et al., 2009) Alalwan et al. (2017); Liebana-Cabanillas et al. (2017), Lin (2011); Kim et al., 2009), Autonomous Motivation Zhou (2016), Controlled Motivation Zhou (2016). Finally, five items of adoption adopted from (Sharma et al., 2016; Wei et al., 2009; Liebana-Cabanillas et al. (2017).

Data Collection

In total, 395 respondents successfully completed the questionnaire, which can be considered an adequate sample for a research of this kind (Akgül et al., 2019a; 2019b; 2019c; Akgül and Tunca, 2019; Göktaş and Akgül, 2019). For this purpose, Hair et al. (2017:20) have suggested the use of 10 times rule, which was proposed by Barclay et al. (1995) for determining minimum sample size in a PLS-SEM analysis. This rule states that minimum sample should be "10 times the largest number of structural paths directed at a particular construct in structural model". Structural model of this study involves twelve constructs (i.e. seven independent and one dependent variable) and according to 10 times rule criterion, our minimum sample size should be 80 respondents. However, author has adopted a more rigorous criterion proposed by Westland (2010).

These valid responses were analyzed to assess reliability, validity, and appropriateness for hypotheses testing. The final sample comprised 263 individuals, in which 55,9% are male and 44,1% are female. The average age is 30, the youngest respondent being 20 and the oldest 50. The majority of respondents were bachelor and vocational school degree and represented (%40,6), followed by master degree (6.5 percent), Phd degree (5.5 percent) and other education levels.

STRUCTURAL EQUATION MODELLING-NEURAL NETWORK APPROACHES

Analysis of the Measurement Model

The analyses were carried out in two stages. Confirmatory factor analysis (CFA) was first conducted to assess the measurement model's suitability, and then the constructs' validity was evaluated by means of reliability analysis, followed by convergent and discriminant validity assessments.

Subsequently, an assessment was conducted of the reliability and validity of the instrument used to measure the reflective constructs. This evaluation was necessary to check that the results are shown in Table 1 comply with simple reliability criteria, including Cronbach's alpha (CA), which must be superior to 0.70, according to Nunnally and Bernstein (1994). In addition, the assessment checked composite reliability (CR), which must be higher than 0.6, according to Bagozzi (1988), and convergent validity based on the average variance extracted (AVE), which must be over 0.5, according to Fornell and Larcker (1981) (Table 2). To evaluate the size of the factor loadings, Hair et al.'s criteria (2014) were used, thus ensuring that all loadings in Table 2 are greater than 0.70.

To evaluate the model's discriminant validity, Fornell and Larcker's criteria (1981) were applied in order to estimate the correlation matrix between latent variables and the heterotrait-monotrait (HTMT) ratio of correlations (Henseler et al., 2014). Inadequate discriminant validity exists if the HTMT ratio is over 0.85, according to Clark and Watson (1995) and Kline (2011), or 0.90, according to Gold et al., (2001) and Teo et al., (2008). The present analysis found an HT/MT ratio below these values, as shown in Table 4, so the model's discriminant validity was confirmed.

As for the evaluation of cross-loadings, an indicator's loadings with its associated latent construct (in bold) should be higher than its loadings with all the remaining constructs (Hair et al., 2011; Ringle et al., 2018). All the indicators show a qualified discriminant validity via the cross-loadings evaluation (see Table 3).

STRUCTURAL MODEL

Hypotheses Testing

Finally, the bootstrapping technique was used to estimate these parameters' significance, and the Student's t and p-value were determined. A series of random samples were obtained from the original sample in order to replace it. The new samples' average values were estimated and compared with those of the original

Table 1. Results of the measurement model

Constructs/Items	Loading	Cronbach's Alpha	Composite Reliability	Average Variance Extracted (AVE)
Adoption (ADOP)		0,873	0,940	0,887
ADOP1- I plan to use mobile banking in future	0,937			
ADOP2- I am using mobile banking	0,946			
Autonomous Motivation (AM)		0,949	0,967	0,908
AM1- I enjoy M-Banking usage.	0,965			
AM2- M-Banking is a pleasurable activity.	0,948			
AM3- M-Banking is beneficial to me.	0,946			
Controlled Motivation (CM)		0,801	0,825	0,617
CM1-I use M-Banking because others are using.	0,748			
CM2-I feel pressure to use M-Banking from my family.	0,639			
CM3- Not using M-Banking makes me uncomfortable.	0,940			
Compatibility (COM)		0,956	0,971	0,918
COM1-Compatibility (COM) Mobile banking is compatible with my work style	0,954			
COM2- Mobile banking is compatible with the way I manage transactions	0,960			
COM3- Mobile banking is close to my life style	0,960			
Perceived Ease of Use (PEOU)		0,978	0,986	0,958
PEOU1- It is/might be easy to learn or use m-banking.	0,977			
PEOU2- M-banking is understandable and clear.	0,977			
PEOU3- M-banking is/might be easy to use.	0,982			
Perceived Usefulness (PU)		0,963	0,971	0,871
PU1- Using m-banking would enhance my effectiveness in my daily work	0,928			
PU2- Using m-banking would improve the performance of my task.	0,945			
PU3- Using m-banking would increase my task productivity	0,944			
PU4- Using m-banking would improve my task quality.	0,919			
PU5- In general, I believe that m-banking will be useful.	0,929			
Social Influence (SI)		0,860	0,901	0,696
SI1- I use mobile banking on the recommendation of my relatives.	0,802			
SI2- I use mobile banking on the recommendation of my peers.	0,824			
SI3- Most people influence my decisions thinks I should use m-banking	0,888			
SI4- The use of mobile banking improve my status in society	0,820			
Trust (TRU)		0,956	0,972	0,920
TRU1- Payment made through m-banking will be processed securely	0,960			
TRU2- Transaction conducted through m-banking will be secure.	0,974			
TRU3- My personal information will be kept confidential.	0,943			

sample to assess whether the estimates of the original parameters were statistically significant. The analysis was carried out based on the following premises:

- Individual sign change is permissible, according to Hair et al., (2014) and Henseler et al.'s (2009) criteria.

Table 2. Discriminant validity using Fornell and Larcker criterion

	ADOP	AM	CM	COM	PEOU	PU	SI	TRU
ADOP	0,942							
AM	0,848	0,953						
CM	0,302	0,356	0,786					
COM	0,804	0,810	0,328	0,958				
PEOU	0,808	0,816	0,281	0,797	0,979			
PU	0,817	0,850	0,339	0,875	0,805	0,933		
SI	0,404	0,528	0,558	0,458	0,450	0,513	0,834	
TRU	0,798	0,826	0,348	0,806	0,795	0,810	0,487	0,959

- A total of 5000 subsamples must be used, that is, a larger quantity than the original sample of 4500, to comply with Hair et al.'s (2014) criteria.
- Each subsample's size is always that of the original sample, in accordance with Hair et al.'s (2011), Hair et al.'s (2014) criteria.

Once the measurement instrument had been refined and the structural model's evaluation was complete, the model was estimated once again, and the significance of the relationships between structures was evaluated a second time using bootstrapping. In this way, the latent dependent variables' variance explained by their predicting construct (i.e., R-squared R^2) could be examined. The results in Table 5 reveal that in no case is R^2 inferior to 0.1. In other words, the constructs' variance explained by the model is always above 0.1, thereby complying with Falk and Miller's criteria (1992).

Given that the size of R^2 has been acknowledged to be relevant predictive criteria on numerous occasions, this study applied the blindfolding technique developed by Geisser (1975) and Stone (1974) to evaluate the model's predictive validity. The technique required the omission of some data during estimations in the present research. This included profitability, operations, and asset quality from the latent dependent variables, as well as capital adequacy, size, and country profile from the latent independent variables. Thus, attempts were made to adjust these data using the information obtained previously. In this study, the omission distance was fixed at 7, which is a prime number between 5 and 10 that is not an exact divisor of the sample size, as required by Wold's (1982) criteria. The results support the conclusion that the proposed model has predictive validity since, in all cases, Q^2 is superior to 0 (see Table 5), which fits the criteria described by Geisser (1975) and Stone (1974).

Table 3. Cross-loading evaluation results for discriminant validity evaluation

	ADOP	AM	CM	COM	PEOU	PU	SI	TRU
ADOP1	0,937	0,769	0,296	0,710	0,714	0,727	0,386	0,718
ADOP2	0,946	0,827	0,274	0,802	0,804	0,808	0,376	0,783
AM1	0,800	0,965	0,342	0,760	0,757	0,798	0,506	0,790
AM2	0,753	0,948	0,382	0,724	0,716	0,759	0,540	0,748
AM3	0,864	0,946	0,299	0,825	0,850	0,866	0,469	0,819
CM1	0,165	0,199	0,748	0,141	0,128	0,212	0,534	0,225
CM2	-0,025	0,018	0,639	-0,025	-0,054	0,009	0,439	0,069
CM3	0,299	0,354	0,940	0,346	0,290	0,324	0,467	0,333
COM1	0,721	0,740	0,339	0,954	0,727	0,832	0,440	0,730
COM2	0,796	0,780	0,297	0,960	0,780	0,828	0,431	0,778
COM3	0,791	0,805	0,309	0,960	0,781	0,856	0,447	0,804
PEOU1	0,795	0,795	0,274	0,780	0,977	0,782	0,421	0,780
PEOU2	0,783	0,792	0,283	0,779	0,977	0,784	0,458	0,773
PEOU3	0,794	0,810	0,269	0,780	0,982	0,797	0,442	0,780
PU1	0,798	0,820	0,272	0,822	0,795	0,928	0,397	0,771
PU2	0,728	0,769	0,312	0,812	0,710	0,945	0,486	0,723
PU3	0,732	0,780	0,335	0,803	0,723	0,944	0,519	0,743
PU4	0,700	0,752	0,389	0,774	0,686	0,919	0,553	0,719
PU5	0,836	0,836	0,285	0,865	0,822	0,929	0,452	0,810
SI1	0,182	0,294	0,483	0,224	0,227	0,299	0,802	0,256
SI2	0,291	0,359	0,459	0,327	0,328	0,356	0,824	0,311
SI3	0,369	0,477	0,480	0,402	0,417	0,444	0,888	0,457
SI4	0,415	0,537	0,458	0,479	0,442	0,526	0,820	0,499
TRU1	0,780	0,794	0,306	0,791	0,764	0,809	0,434	0,960
TRU2	0,790	0,809	0,332	0,784	0,780	0,791	0,461	0,974
TRU3	0,724	0,774	0,365	0,742	0,742	0,727	0,509	0,943

Evaluating Effect Sizes

The effect size used to assess the relative impact of a predictor construct on an endogenous construct. It is said that p value can show you that effect exist however, it does not disclose the size of the effect.

Thus, researcher assessed the effect size. According to Cohen (1988) the acceptable effect sizes values of 0.35, 0.15 and 0.02 are considered substantial, medium and

Table 4. Heterotrait-Monotrait ratio (HTMT)

	ADOP	AM	CM	COM	PEOU	PU	SI	TRU
ADOP								
AM	0,928							
CM	0,244	0,274						
COM	0,877	0,847	0,232					
PEOU	0,872	0,843	0,210	0,823				
PU	0,885	0,884	0,274	0,910	0,825			
SI	0,432	0,551	0,699	0,471	0,459	0,535		
TRU	0,871	0,865	0,284	0,841	0,821	0,840	0,501	

small effect sizes respectively. Table 5 depicted, there is a difference for the effect size analysis results for intention to adopt mobile banking.

Table 5. Structural model results

Hypothesis	Relationship	β-value	Effect Size [1] f^2	Effect Size [2] q^2	t-Statistic [a]	p-Value	R[2]	Q[2] (=1- SSE/SSO) (OD=8)
H1	AM -> ADOP	0,388	0,14	0,08	6,192***	0,000	0,790	0,668
H2	CM -> ADOP	0,027	0,01	-0,01	0,905	0,366		
H3	COM -> ADOP	0,139	0,02	-0,01	1,881*	0,060		
H4	PEOU -> ADOP	0,201	0,05	0,03	3,293***	0,001		
H5	PU -> ADOP	0,139	0,02	0,01	1,724*	0,085		
H6	SI -> ADOP	-0,107	0,03	0,02	3,050***	0,002		
H7	TRU -> ADOP	0,136	0,02	0,01	2,336**	0,020		

[a]t-values for two-tailed test:
* 1.65 (sig. level 10%).
** 1.96 (sig. level=5%).
*** t-value 2.58 (sig. level = 1%) (Hair et al., 2011).
Notes:***p<0.01, **p<0.05, *p<0.1
effective size: 0 – none, 0.02 – small, 0.15 - medium, 0.35 – large (Cohen, 1988).
Effect sizes calculated using the following formulas
[1]f^2= R[2]included - R[2]excluded / 1- R[2]included (1)
[2]q^2 = Q[2]included - Q[2]excluded / 1- Q[2]included (2)

Figure 1. Findings of structural model

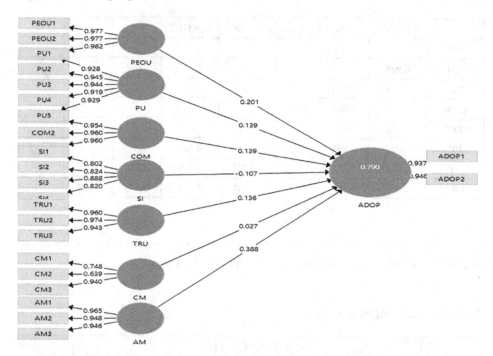

Importance-Performance Map Analysis (IPMA)

IPMA was further performed to breakdown the importance and performance of latent variables, in our case, adoption is a target construct, which is predicted by seven predecessors (i.e. perceived ease of use, perceived usefulness, compatibility, social influence, trust, controlled motivation, and autonomous motivation etc.); refer to Fig. 1. IPMA methodology has been performed for this study and the results are presented in Fig.2. Based on Figure 2, it can be observed autonomous motivation is very important. The other six constructs, perceived ease of use, perceived usefulness, compatibility, trust, controlled motivation, and social influence have relatively little relevance. For the ease of readers, a complete list of importance-performance values is provided in Table 6.

Assessment of the Predictive Validity Using Holdout Samples

With the objective of producing valid predictions of mobile banking adoption, PLS predict used (Shmueli et al., 2016; Shmueli et al., 2019; Felipe et al., 2017). In general, if author compares the results of PLS (partial least squares) with LM (linear model), PLS predict allows predictions very close to those obtained by using LM (Table 7).

Figure 2. Importance-performance map analysis for adoption

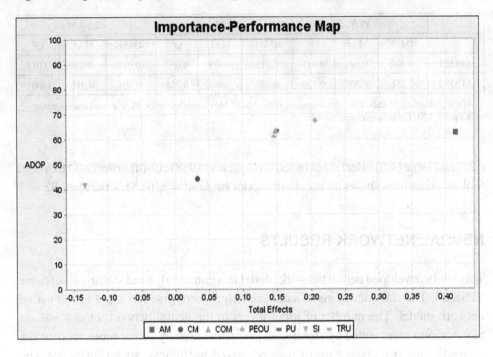

GOODNESS OF FIT (GOF)

Goodness of fit (GoF) index was also calculated using the procedure from Wetzels et al. (2009). The index is judged against the GoF criterion for small (.10), medium

Table 6. Importance-performance map analysis for adoption

Latent Variables	Total Effect of the Latent Variable for Adoption	Index Values (Performance)
AM	**0,414**	62,545
CM	0,033	44,164
COM	0,147	63,291
PEOU	0,205	**67,384**
PU	0,150	63,420
SI	-0,134	41,507
TRU	0,145	61,023

Note: All total effects (importance) larger than 0.10 are significant at the α≤0.10 level. The bold values indicate the highest importance (total effect) and highest performance value.

Table 7. Partial least square predict assessment

	PLS			LM			PLS-LM		
	RMSE	MAE	Q^2	RMSE	MAE	Q^2	RMSE	MAE	Q^2
ADOP1	0,903	0,591	0,617	0,915	0,621	0,607	-0,012	-0,030	0,011
ADOP2	0,732	0,502	0,756	0,733	0,486	0,755	-0,001	0,016	0,001

ADOP:Adoption, RMSE: Root mean squared error. MAE: Mean absolute error. PLS: Partial least squares path model; LM: Linear regression model.

(.25) and large (.36) effect sizes based on Cohen's (1988) cut-off criteria. The overall GoF is .82, which shows an excellent model fit. GoF = $\sqrt{(0,85 \times 0,79)}=0,82$

NEURAL NETWORK RESULTS

This study developed neural network model in a commonly used statistical software SPSS 24. The statistically significant predictors were given as input to the neural network model. The number of input layers in the neural network model was six as covariates represented by significant predictors namely autonomous motivation, compatibility, perceived ease of use, perceived usefulness, social influence, and trust (see Fig. 2). The output layer of the network model was represented by the dependent variable namely adoption towards mobile banking adoption.

Nevertheless, these simple linear models may not be sufficient in capturing the complexity of the actual world problems in decision making (Wong et al., 2011). A nonlinear model is able to provide high predictive power than linear model (Pant and Srinivasan, 2010: 356). The multilayer perceptron training algorithm was employed to train the neural network model. Over-fitting is a major concern in the predictive modeling approach? In order to overcome the over-fitting of the model, cross-validation is considered a suitable approach (Chong 2013a). The determination of exactly hidden nodes is considered one of the most difficult challenges in the literature. Wang and Elhag (2007) recommended a range of one to 10 hidden nodes in the neural network model. The 70% of data points were used to train the neural network model and 30% data points were used to test the model. The main objective of testing the model is to assess the accuracy of the model (Chong 2013a; Sharma et al., 2016; Chong et al. 2015; Liébana-Cabanillas et al. 2017). In the neural network applications, it is recommended to use accuracy using the root mean squared error (RMSE). The RMSE for both training and testing of the neural network model is summarized in Table 8 along with the mean and standard deviations. The average RMSE values (for training data points was 0.109 and for testing data points was 0.100) were relatively small with very small standard deviations justifying the higher order of accuracy in the results predicted by the neural network model (Akgül, 2017; Akgül, 2017a; Akgül, 2018; Liébana-Cabanillas et al. 2017). The standard deviation for training and testing all hidden nodes was 0.011 and 0.022, supports the relatively lesser error in the neural network model.

The sensitivity analysis of the performance computed using the average importance of predictors in predicting outcome variable (Chong, 2013). The normalized importance of predictors can be computed by dividing the importance of predictors by the highest value of the predictor (Akgül, 2017; 2017a; 2018a; 2018b; Liébana-Cabanillas et al. 2017). The importance of the predictors is summarized in Table 9. The results obtained from the neural network model shows that autonomous motivation is the key predictor of the mobile banking acceptance followed by perceived ease of use, perceived usefulness, trust, controlled motivation, and social influence.

Figure 3. Neural network models

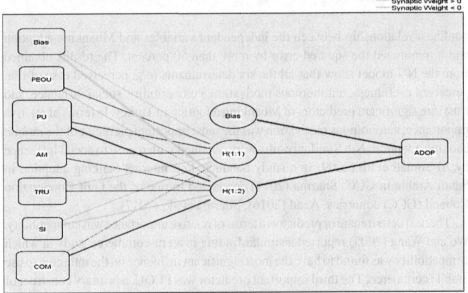

Hidden layer activation function: Hyperbolic tangent
Output layer activation function: Identity

DISCUSSION

The major aim of this book chapter was to investigate the factors influencing Mbanking adoption and predict adoption using the key determinants based on an extended TAM proposed in the proposed book chapter. The NN model was able to capture the

Table 8. RMSE for neural network model

Hidden Nodes	Training	Testing
1	0,112	0,082
2	0,118	0,086
3	0,105	0,079
4	0,112	0,088
5	0,102	0,125
6	0,133	0,065
7	0,098	0,120
8	0,107	0,119
9	0,100	0,108
10	0,098	0,121
Mean	0,109	0,100
Standard deviation	0,011	0,022

nonlinear relationship between the independent variables and Mbanking adoption and it minimized the squared error by more than 50 percent. The results obtained from the NN model show that all the six determinants (e.g. perceived ease of use, perceived usefulness, autonomous motivation, compatibility, social influence, and trust) are significant predictors of Mbanking adoption in Turkey. In terms of relative importance, autonomous motivation was the most important predictor of the mobile banking adoption. Not Similar results were obtained with regard to social influence by Al-Somali et al. (2009) in a study conducted on internet banking adoption in Saudi Arabia in GCC. Sharma (2019) conducted in one of the Gulf Cooperation Council (GCC) countries. Azad (2016); Sharma et al., (2017).

The next determinant or predictor in terms of relative importance was compatibility. Wu and Wang (2005) reported a similar finding in an m-commerce study in which compatibility was found to have the most significant influence on the intention to use mobile commerce. The third important predictor was PEOU, a primary construct of TAM. This is consistent with the findings of the study by Hanafizadeh et al. (2014) which established that PEOU significantly influences the adoption of Mbanking. Independent variables Trust and PU are also significant predictors of adoption of Mbanking. Therefore, individuals in Turkey adopt Mbanking to reduce uncertainty and risk. They are looking for technology that fits well with different individuals' needs and fits well with other technology. Also, they are selecting technology that is ease to use and perceived to be useful. These predictors are important in the studies related to information systems research (Al-Somali et al., 2009; Chong et al., 2012).

Table 9. Predictor importance

Predictors	Importance	Normalized Importance (%)
AM	0,302	100
PEOU	0,166	55
PU	0,157	53,4
TRU	0,156	51,4
COM	0,156	51,4
SI	0,066	35,3

MANAGERIAL IMPLICATIONS, LIMITATIONS AND FUTURE WORK

The testing of the proposed model suggested that social influence, compatibility, trust, PEOU and PU are significant predictors of the intention to adopt by Turkish mobile banking users. The study has several implications from a managerial perspective. First, the study is conducted in a developing country, Turkey, where service providers have implemented mobile banking technologies anticipating the user penetration to grow at an accelerated rate in the coming years. Currently, the findings can prove to be useful to Turkish banks seeking to exploit these technologies as the primary driver of competitive advantage. Overall, this study can be helpful for mobile banking professionals to enhance adoption of mobile banking in Turkey. From a technical standpoint, the application of NN models enables prediction of adoption instead of merely establishing a causal relationship. Common methods such as regression are useful merely to explain the causal relationship. The application of two-staged NN regression approach is a relatively new approach and can serve as a useful tool for future research in the area of mobile banking adoption.

LIMITATIONS AND FUTURE WORK

The study has a few limitations. One of the main limitations is associated with the sample size used in the study. Therefore, the results of the study may not be generalized to the entire country. This study was conducted in a developing country in Turkey. Therefore, it is recommended to conduct a comparative study between one developing and one developed country. This study was cross-sectional, future research could be done to understand the behavioral intention in the longitudinal settings. Third, the research model in this study does not include the moderating effect of any variable. It is recommended to study the moderating effect of demographic variables as a future study for better understanding of mobile banking behavioral intention from a different segment of the population. Finally, the variance explained in the behavioral intention towards MBanking by predictors was 79%, it suggests including additional variables such as mobility, involvement, and customization in the future research models.

CONCLUSION

Mobile banking is one of the latest innovative applications of mobile technologies in the recent times. Owing to the higher acceptance of mobile banking in Turkey, this study realized the importance of understanding and examining key antecedents influencing mobile banking acceptance. Thus, a well-known technology acceptance model (TAM) developed by Davis (1989), was selected as the theoretical base to develop research model in this study. This study presented and tested a new research model with seven potential independent variables namely perceived ease of use, perceived usefulness, autonomous motivation, controlled motivation, trust, compatibility, and social influence to understand the users' behavioral intention towards the acceptance of mobile banking from a developing country perspective.

A two stage innovative methodology was employed, which is one of the many unique features of this study. In the first stage, structural equation modeling was employed to test the research hypotheses and in the second stage, neural network modeling was employed to rank the predictors influencing the behavioral intention of users towards M-Banking acceptance.

REFERENCES

Aboelmaged, M., & Gebba, T. R. (2013). Mobile banking adoption: An examination of technology acceptance model and theory of planned behavior. *International Journal of Business Research and Development*, 2(1), 35–50. doi:10.24102/ijbrd.v2i1.263

Ajzen, I., & Fishbein, M. (1980). *Understanding attitudes and predicting social behaviour*. Prentice Hall.

Ajzen, I., & Madden, T. J. (1986). Prediction of goal-directed behavior: Attitudes, intentions, and perceived behavioral control. *Journal of Experimental Social Psychology*, 22(5), 453–474. doi:10.1016/0022-1031(86)90045-4

Akgül, Y. (2017). *A multi-analytical approach for predicting antecedents of m-commerce adoption. In Academic Studies about communication, business and economics. Strategic Researches Academy Strategic Researches Academic Publishing.*

Akgül, Y. (2017a). Integrating e-trust antecedents into TAM to explain mobile banking behavioral intention: A SEM-neural network modeling. *4th International Conference on Business and Economics Studies (Özet Bildiri/Sözlü Sunum).* (Yayın No:4406728)

Akgül, Y. (2018a). An Analysis of Customers' Acceptance of Internet Banking: An Integration of E-Trust and Service Quality to the TAM–The Case of Turkey. In *E-Manufacturing and E-Service Strategies in Contemporary Organizations* (pp. 154–198). IGI Global., doi:10.4018/978-1-5225-3628-4.ch007

Akgül, Y. (2018b). A SEM-Neural Network Approach for Predicting Antecedents of Factors Influencing Consumers' Intent to Install Mobile Applications. In Mobile Technologies and Socio-Economic Development in Emerging Nations (pp. 262–308). IGI Global. doi:10.4018/978-1-5225-4029-8.ch012

Akgül, Y. (2018c). Predicting determinants of Mobile banking adoption: A two-staged regression-neural network approach. 8th International Conference of Strategic Research on Scientific Studies and Education (ICoSReSSE) 2018 (Özet Bildiri/ Sözlü Sunum). (Yayın No:4405980)

Akgül, Y. (2019). Understanding and Predicting the Determinants of the Facebook Usage in Higher Education: A Two Staged Hybrid SEM-Neural Networks Approach. 11th International Conference of Strategic Research on Scientific Studies and Education (ICoSReSSE).

Akgül, Y. (2019a). A social commerce investigation of the role of trust in a social networking site on purchase intentions: A Multi-Analytical Structural Equation Modeling and Neural Network Approach. 11th International Conference of Strategic Research on Scientific Studies and Education (ICoSReSSE) (Tam Metin Bildiri/ Sözlü Sunum). (Yayın No:5486037)

Akgül, Y., Öztürk, T., & Varol, Z. (2019). Investigation of Internet Banking Users' Perceptions and Factors Affecting Internet Banking Benchmarks: Expanded With Unified Theory of Acceptance and Use of Technology 2 (UTAUT2) Risk. In Structural Equation Modeling Approaches to E-Service Adoption (pp. 64-82). IGI Global.

Akgül, Y., & Tunca, M. Z. (2019). Strategic Orientation and Performance of Istanbul Stock Market Businesses: Empirical Studies Based on Business, Information Systems, and Knowledge Strategic Orientation. In Strategy and Superior Performance of Micro and Small Businesses in Volatile Economies (pp. 94-114). IGI Global.

Akgül, Y., Yaman, B., Geçgil, G., & Yavuz, G. (2019). The Influencing Factors for Purchasing Intentions in Social Media by Utaut Perspective. In Structural Equation Modeling Approaches to E-Service Adoption (pp. 254–267). IGI Global. doi:10.4018/978-1-5225-8015-7.ch013

Akturan, U., & Tezcan, N. (2012). Mobile banking adoption of the youth market. *Marketing Intelligence & Planning, 30*(4), 444–459. doi:10.1108/02634501211231928

Al-Somali, S., Gholami, R., & Clegg, B. (2009). An investigation into the acceptance of online banking in Saudi Arabia. *Technovation, 29*(2), 130–141. doi:10.1016/j.technovation.2008.07.004

Alalwan, A. A., Dwivedi, Y. K., & Rana, N. P. (2017). Factors influencing adoption of mobile banking by Jordanian bank customers: Extending UTAUT2 with trust. *International Journal of Information Management, 37*(3), 99–110. doi:10.1016/j.ijinfomgt.2017.01.002

Alalwan, A. A., Dwivedi, Y. K., Rana, N. P., & Simintiras, A. C. (2016). Jordanian consumers' adoption of telebanking: Influence of perceived usefulness, trust, and self-efficacy. *International Journal of Bank Marketing, 34*(5), 690–709. doi:10.1108/IJBM-06-2015-0093

Azad, M. A. K. (2016). Predicting mobile banking adoption in Bangladesh: A neural network approach. *Transnational Corporations Review, 8*(3), 207–214. doi:10.10 80/19186444.2016.1233726

Bagozzi, R. Y., & Yi, Y. (1988). On the evaluation of structural equation models. *Journal of the Academy of Marketing Science, 16*(1), 74–94. doi:10.1007/BF02723327

Baptista, G., & Oliveira, T. (2016). A weight and a meta-analysis on mobile banking acceptance research. *Computers in Human Behavior, 63*, 480–489. doi:10.1016/j.chb.2016.05.074

Barclay, D., Higgins, C., & Thompson, R. (1995). The partial least squares (PLS) approach to causal modeling: Personal computer adoption and use as an illustration (with commentaries). *Technology Studies, 2*(2), 285–324.

Chong, A. Y. L. (2013). Predicting m-commerce adoption determinants: A neural network approach. *Expert Systems with Applications, 40*(2), 523–530. doi:10.1016/j.eswa.2012.07.068

Chong, A. Y. L., Liu, M. J., Luo, J., & Keng-Boon, O. (2015). Predicting RFID adoption in healthcare supply chain from the perspectives of users. *International Journal of Production Economics, 159*, 66–75. doi:10.1016/j.ijpe.2014.09.034

Chong, A. Y. L., Ooi, K. B., Lin, B., & Bao, H. (2012). An empirical analysis of the determinants of 3G adoption in China. *Computers in Human Behavior*, 28(2), 360–369. doi:10.1016/j.chb.2011.10.005

Chong, L.-Y. A. (2013a). A two staged SEM-neural network approach for understanding and predicting the determinants of m-commerce adoption. *Expert Systems with Applications*, 40(4), 1240–1247. doi:10.1016/j.eswa.2012.08.067

Clark, L., & Watson, D. (1995). Constructing validity: Basic issues in objective scale development. *Psychological Assessment*, 7(3), 309–319. doi:10.1037/1040-3590.7.3.309

Cohen, J. (1988). *Statistical Power Analysis for the Behavioral Sciences*. Lawrence Erlbaum.

Davis, F. D. (1989). Perceived usefulness, perceived ease of use, and user acceptance of information technology. *Management Information Systems Quarterly*, 13(3), 319–340. doi:10.2307/249008

Falk, R. F., & Miller, N. B. (1992). *A primer for soft modeling*. University of Akron Press.

Felipe, C. M., Roldán, J. L., & Leal-Rodríguez, A. L. (2017). Impact of organizational culture values on organizational agility. *Sustainability*, 9(12), 2354. doi:10.3390u9122354

Fornell, C., & Larcker, D. (1981). Evaluating structural equation models with unobservable variables and measurement error. *JMR, Journal of Marketing Research*, 18(1), 39–50. doi:10.1177/002224378101800104

Geisser, S. (1975). The predictive sample reuse method with applications. *Journal of the American Statistical Association*, 70(350), 320–328. doi:10.1080/0162145 9.1975.10479865

Göktaş, P., & Akgül, Y. (2019). The Investigation of Employer Adoption of Human Resource Information Systems at University Using TAM. In *Structural Equation Modeling Approaches to E-Service Adoption* (pp. 1–27). IGI Global. doi:10.4018/978-1-5225-8015-7.ch001

Gold, A., Malhotra, A., & Segars, A. (2001). Knowledge management: An organizational capabilities perspective. *Journal of Management Information Systems*, 18(1), 185–214. doi:10.1080/07421222.2001.11045669

Gu, J., Lee, S., & Suh, Y. (2009). Determinants of behavioral intention to mobile banking. *Expert Systems with Applications, 36*(9), 11605–11616. doi:10.1016/j. eswa.2009.03.024

Ha, K. H., Canedoli, A., Baur, A. W., & Bick, M. (2012). Mobile banking: Insights on its increasing relevance and most common drivers of adoption. *Electronic Markets, 22*(4), 217–227. doi:10.100712525-012-0107-1

Hagger, M. S., Chatzisarantis, N. L., & Biddle, S. J. (2002). A metaanalytic review of the theories of reasoned action and planned behavior in physical activity: Predictive validity and the contribution of additional variables. *Journal of Sport & Exercise Psychology, 24*(1), 3–32. doi:10.1123/jsep.24.1.3

Hair, J. F. Jr, Hult, G. T. M., Ringle, C., & Sarstedt, M. (2014). *A primer on partial least squares structural equation modeling (PLS-SEM)*. Sage publications.

Hair, J. F. Jr, Hult, G. T. M., Ringle, C., & Sarstedt, M. (2017). *A primer on partial least squares structural equation modeling (PLS-SEM)* (2nd ed.). Sage Publications Limited Inc.

Hair, J. F., Ringle, C. M., & Sarstedt, M. (2011). PLS-SEM: Indeed a silver bullet. *Journal of Marketing Theory and Practice, 19*(2), 139–152. doi:10.2753/MTP1069-6679190202

Hanafizadeh, P., Behboudi, M., Koshksaray, A. A., & Tabar, S. J. M. (2014). Mobile banking adoption by Iranian bank clients. *Telematics and Informatics, 31*(1), 62–78. doi:10.1016/j.tele.2012.11.001

Henseler, J., Ringle, C., & Sarsted, M. (2014). A new criterion for assessing discriminant validity in variance-based structural equation modeling. *Journal of the Academy of Marketing Science, 43*(1), 115–135. doi:10.100711747-014-0403-8

Henseler, J., Ringle, C. M., & Sinkovics, R. R. (2009). The use of partial least squares path modeling in international marketing. In *New challenges to international marketing* (pp. 277–319). Emerald Group Publishing Limited. doi:10.1108/S1474-7979(2009)0000020014

Hew, T. S., Leong, L. Y., Ooi, K. B., & Chong, A. Y. L. (2016). Predicting drivers of mobile entertainment adoption: A two-stage SEM artificial-neural-network analysis. *Journal of Computer Information Systems, 56*(4), 352–370. doi:10.1080 /08874417.2016.1164497

Hsu, C., Wang, C., & Lin, J. C. (2011). Investigating customer adoption behaviors in mobile financial services. *International Journal of Mobile Communications, 9*(5), 477–494. doi:10.1504/IJMC.2011.042455

Kapoor, K. K., Dwivedi, Y. K., & Williams, M. D. (2015). Examining the role of three sets of innovation attributes for determining adoption of the interbank mobile payment service. *Information Systems Frontiers, 17*(5), 1039–1056. doi:10.100710796-014-9484-7

Kim, G., Shin, B., & Lee, H. G. (2009). Understanding dynamics between initial trust and usage intentions of mobile banking. *Information Systems Journal, 19*(3), 283–311. doi:10.1111/j.1365-2575.2007.00269.x

Kline, R. (2011). *Principles and Practice of Structural Equation Modeling*. Guildford Press.

Koeni-Lewis, N., Palmer, A., & Moll, A. (2010). Predicting young consumers' take up of mobile banking services. *International Journal of Bank Marketing, 28*(5), 410–432. doi:10.1108/02652321011064917

Laukkanen, T. (2016). Consumer adoption versus rejection decisions in seemingly similar service innovations: The case of the Internet and mobile banking. *Journal of Business Research, 69*(7), 2432–2439. doi:10.1016/j.jbusres.2016.01.013

Laukkanen, T., & Kiviniemi, V. (2010). The role of information in mobile banking resistance. *International Journal of Bank Marketing, 28*(5), 372–388. doi:10.1108/02652321011064890

Liébana-Cabanillas, F., Marinković, V., & Kalinić, Z. (2017). A SEM neural network approach for predicting antecedents of m-commerce acceptance. *International Journal of Information Management, 37*(2), 14–24. doi:10.1016/j.ijinfomgt.2016.10.008

Lin, F. H. (2011). An empirical investigation of mobile banking adoption: The effect of innovation attributes and knowledge based trust. *International Journal of Information Management, 31*(3), 252–260. doi:10.1016/j.ijinfomgt.2010.07.006

Luarn, P., & Lin, H. H. (2005). Toward an understanding of the behavioral intention to use mobile banking. *Computers in Human Behavior, 21*(6), 873–891. doi:10.1016/j.chb.2004.03.003

Malaquias, F. R., & Hwang, Y. (2016). An empirical study on trust in mobile banking: A developing country perspective. *Computers in Human Behavior, 54*, 453–461. doi:10.1016/j.chb.2015.08.039

Mansour, I. H. F., Eljelly, A. M., & Abdullah, A. M. (2016). Consumers' attitude towards e-banking services in Islamic banks: The case of Sudan. *Review of International Business and Strategy, 26*(2), 244–260. doi:10.1108/RIBS-02-2014-0024

Michou, A., Matsagouras, E., & Lens, W. (2014). Dispositional achievement motives matter for autonomous versus controlled motivation and behavioral or affective educational outcomes. *Personality and Individual Differences, 69*, 205–211. doi:10.1016/j.paid.2014.06.004

Nunnally, J., & Bernstein, I. (1994). *Psychometric Theory* (3rd ed.). McGraw Hill.

O'Connor, Y., & O'Reilly, P. (2016). Examining the infusion of mobile technology by healthcare practitioners in a hospital setting. *Information Systems Frontiers*, 1–21.

Pant, G., & Srinivasan, P. (2010). Predicting web page status. *Information Systems Research, 21*(2), 345–364. doi:10.1287/isre.1080.0231

Park, E., & Kim, K. J. (2013). User acceptance of long-term evolution (LTE) services: An application of extended technology acceptance model. *Program, 47*(2), 188–205. doi:10.1108/00330331311313762

Pavlou, P. A. (2003). Consumer acceptance of electronic commerce: Integrating trust and risk with the technology acceptance model. *International Journal of Electronic Commerce, 7*(3), 101–131. doi:10.1080/10864415.2003.11044275

Ringle, C. M., Sarstedt, M., Mitchell, R., & Gudergan, S. P. (2018). Partial least squares structural equation modeling in HRM research. *International Journal of Human Resource Management, 5192*, 1–27. doi:10.1080/09585192.2017.1416655

Rogers, E. M. (1995). Diffusion of Innovations. Academic Press.

Ryan, R. M., & Deci, E. L. (2000). Intrinsic and extrinsic motivations: Classic definitions and new directions. *Contemporary Educational Psychology, 25*(1), 54–67. doi:10.1006/ceps.1999.1020 PMID:10620381

Shaikh, A. A., & Karjaluoto, H. (2015). Mobile Banking adoption: A literature review. *Telematics and Informatics, 32*(1), 129–142. doi:10.1016/j.tele.2014.05.003

Sharma, S. K. (2015). Adoption of e-Government services: The role of service quality dimensions and demographic variables. *Transforming Government: People, Process and Policy, 9*(2), 207–222. doi:10.1108/TG-10-2014-0046

Sharma, S. K. (2019). Integrating cognitive antecedents into TAM to explain mobile banking behavioral intention: A SEM-neural network modeling. *Information Systems Frontiers, 21*(4), 815–827. doi:10.100710796-017-9775-x

Sharma, S. K., Govindaluri, S. M., & Al-Balushi, S. M. (2015). Predicting determinants of internet banking adoption: A two-staged regression-neural network approach. *Management Research Review, 38*(11), 750–766. doi:10.1108/MRR-06-2014-0139

Sharma, S. K., Govindaluri, S. M., Al-Muharrami, S., & Tarhini, A. (2016). Predicting mobile banking adoption: A neural network approach. *Journal of Enterprise Information Management, 29*, 222–237.

Sharma, S. K., Govindaluri, S. M., Al-Muharrami, S., & Tarhini, A. (2017). A multi-analytical model for mobile banking adoption: A developing country perspective. *Review of International Business and Strategy, 27*(1), 133–148. doi:10.1108/RIBS-11-2016-0074

Sharma, S. K., Joshi, A., & Sharma, H. (2016). A multi-analytical approach to predict the Facebook usage in higher education. *Computers in Human Behavior, 55*, 340–353. doi:10.1016/j.chb.2015.09.020

Shmueli, G. (2010). To explain or to predict? *Statistical Science, 25*(3), 289–310. doi:10.1214/10-STS330

Shmueli, G., & Koppius, O. R. (2011). Predictive analytics in information systems research. *Management Information Systems Quarterly, 35*(3), 553–572. doi:10.2307/23042796

Shmueli, G., Ray, S., Estrada, J. M. V., & Chatla, S. B. (2016). The elephant in the room: Predictive performance of PLS models. *Journal of Business Research, 69*(10), 4552–4564. doi:10.1016/j.jbusres.2016.03.049

Shmueli, G., Sarstedt, M., Hair, J. F., Cheah, J. H., Ting, H., Vaithilingam, S., & Ringle, C. M. (2019). Predictive model assessment in PLS-SEM: Guidelines for using PLSpredict. *European Journal of Marketing, 53*(11), 2322–2347. doi:10.1108/EJM-02-2019-0189

Stone, M. (1974). Cross-validatory choice and assessment of statistical predictions. *Journal of the Royal Statistical Society. Series B. Methodological, 36*(2), 111–133. doi:10.1111/j.2517-6161.1974.tb00994.x

Teo, T., Srivastava, S., & Jiang, L. (2008). Trust and electronic government success: An empirical study. *Journal of Management Information Systems, 25*(3), 99–132. doi:10.2753/MIS0742-1222250303

Vansteenkiste, M., Neyrinck, B., Niemiec, C. P., Soenens, B., Witte, H., & Broeck, A. (2007). On the relations among work value orientations, psychological need satisfaction and job outcomes: A selfdetermination theory approach. *Journal of Occupational and Organizational Psychology*, *80*(2), 251–277. doi:10.1348/096317906X111024

Venkatesh, V., & Davis, F. D. (2000). A theoretical extension of the technology acceptance model: Four longitudinal field studies. *Management Science*, *46*(2), 186–204. doi:10.1287/mnsc.46.2.186.11926

Venkatesh, V., Morris, M. G., Davis, G. B., & Davis, F. D. (2003). User acceptance of information technology: Toward a unified view. *Management Information Systems Quarterly*, *27*(3), 425–478. doi:10.2307/30036540

Venkatesh, V., Thong, J. Y., & Xu, X. (2012). Consumer acceptance and use of information technology: Extending the unified theory of acceptance and use of technology. *Management Information Systems Quarterly*, *36*(1), 157–178. doi:10.2307/41410412

Vroom, V. H. (1964). *Work and Motivation*. Jossey-Bass.

Wang, Y. M., & Elhag, T. M. (2007). A comparison of neural network, evidential reasoning and multiple regression analysis in modelling bridge risks. *Expert Systems with Applications*, *32*(2), 336–348. doi:10.1016/j.eswa.2005.11.029

Wang, Y. S., Wu, M. C., & Wang, H. Y. (2009). Investigating the determinants and age and gender differences in the acceptance of mobile learning. *British Journal of Educational Technology*, *40*(1), 92–118. doi:10.1111/j.1467-8535.2007.00809.x

Wei, T. T., Marthandan, G., Chong, A. Y. L., Ooi, K. B., & Arumugam, S. (2009). What drives Malaysian m-commerce adoption? An empirical analysis. *Industrial Management & Data Systems*, *109*(3), 370–388. doi:10.1108/02635570910939399

Wessels, L., & Drennan, J. (2010). An investigation of consumer acceptance of m-banking. *International Journal of Bank Marketing*, *28*(7), 547–568. doi:10.1108/02652321011085194

Westland, J. C. (2010). Lower bounds on sample size in structural equation modeling. *Electronic Commerce Research and Applications*, *9*(6), 476–487. doi:10.1016/j.elerap.2010.07.003

Wetzels, M., Odekerken-Schroder, G., & Van Oppen, C. (2009). Using PLS path modeling for assessing hierarchical construct models: Guidelines and empirical illustration. *Management Information Systems Quarterly*, *33*(1), 33177–33195. doi:10.2307/20650284

Wold, H. (1982). Soft modeling: the basic design and some extensions. *Systems Under Indirect Observation, 2*, 343.

Wong, T. C., Wong, S. Y., & Chin, K. S. (2011). A neural network-based approach of quantifying relative importance among various determinants toward organizational innovation. *Expert Systems with Applications, 38*(10), 13064–13072. doi:10.1016/j. eswa.2011.04.113

Wu, J. H., & Wang, S. C. (2005). What drives mobile commerce?: An empirical evaluation of the revised technology acceptance model. *Information & Management, 42*(5), 719–729. doi:10.1016/j.im.2004.07.001

Zhou, M. (2016). Chinese university students' acceptance of MOOCs: A self-determination perspective. *Computers & Education, 92*, 194–203. doi:10.1016/j. compedu.2015.10.012

Chapter 8
Fault Severity Sensing for Intelligent Remote Diagnosis in Electrical Induction Machines:
An Application for Wind Turbine Monitoring

Saad Chakkor

(iD) https://orcid.org/0000-0002-9609-7040

LabTIC, National School of Applied Sciences of Tangier, University of Abdelmalek Essaâdi, Morocco

Mostafa Baghouri

Faculty of Sciences of Tetouan, Communication and Detection Laboratory, University of Abdelmalek Essaâdi, Morocco

Abderrahmane Hajraoui

Faculty of Sciences of Tetouan, Communication and Detection Laboratory, University of Abdelmalek Essaâdi, Morocco

ABSTRACT

Electrical induction machines are widely used in the modern wind power production. As their repair cost is important and since their down-time leads to significant income loss, increasing their reliability and optimizing their proactive maintenance process are critical tasks. Many diagnosis systems have been proposed to resolve this issue. However, these systems are failing to recognize accurately the type and the severity level of detected faults in real time. In this chapter, a remote automated

DOI: 10.4018/978-1-7998-4042-8.ch008

control approach applied for electrical induction machines has been suggested as an appropriate solution. It combines developed Fast-ESPRIT method, fault classification algorithm, and fuzzy inference system interconnected with vibration sensors, which are located on various wind turbine components. Furthermore, a new fault severity indicator has been formulated and evaluated to avoid false alarms. Study findings with computer simulation in Matlab prove the satisfactory robustness and performance of the proposed technique in fault classification and diagnosis.

INTRODUCTION

Intelligent sensors are commonly used as condition monitoring tools in several areas. Using these electronic devices, many methods are proposed and developed to detect and to diagnose incipient failures, shutdown and abnormal conditions in certain applications using electrical induction machines (S. Sheng et al., 2015). To accomplish this mission, these techniques are founded on the model approach, on the signal measurements and on the intelligent computing as machine learning. They provides embedded processing for systems that have calculation capacity built referring to expertise knowledge (J. C. Trigeassou, 2011). In fact, any fault diagnosis process should be supposed to apply an effective and a timely decision procedure to determine the cause, the nature and the location of each fault. This task should be done with a minimum of collected informations in order to reduce detection cost, to avoid the sudden machine process stoppage at any time if it is necessary, to indicate and to prevent catastrophic defects and their subsequent consequences such unsafe operation and expensive repair cost (Shawn Sheng, 2015). It main goals is to evade production loss and to maintain machines functionality (M. Blödt, et al., 2010), (Toliyat et al, 2013), (Mohanty, 2015).

BACKGROUND

In the literature, numerous recent works are available treating fault detection and recognition in induction machines. These researches can be classified into four kinds: time-domain, frequency-domain, time-frequency-domain, and artificial-intelligence-based methods (Peter Tavner et al., 2008). Each method of the previously mentioned categories usually have advantages of simple implementation, nevertheless they generally suffer from some difficulties in terms of fault recognition accuracy. Besides, the traditional method using vibration measurement may have several disadvantages, for example: technical difficulties of access to the machine, influence of the transmission path, environment noise and sensitivity to the sensor position. Consequently, the most logical implementing of the diagnosis procedure is to compare constantly the outputs of the system with its inputs. The most popular technique used by frequency-domain methods is MCSA which is based on signal spectral analysis (S. Chakkor et al., 2014a). It has been widely applied in the fault discrimination of induction machines (René Husson, 2009), (Vedreño Santos, 2013). Indeed, it has provided good results in many industrial applications. However, this technique can lead sometimes to erroneous diagnostic conclusion because it presents diverse practical limitations due mainly to the following reasons (Bonaldi, et al., 2012), (S. Chakkor, 2014a, 2014b): the spectral leakage, the need for a high frequency resolution, the variation in load conditions during the sampling period, the confusion between the electromechanical frequencies which are similar to others caused by real faults, long measurement period. For these reasons, several signal-processing techniques have been recently applied to facilitate the identification of faults and to enhance MCSA (F. Giri, 2013). All these drawbacks have prompted our motivation to develop and to integrate new diagnosis tool issued of advanced artificial intelligence. In fact, it seems necessary to implement robust detection and classification technique in the objective to ensure an operative monitoring and control of electrical induction machines. Actually, many researches studies have been realized to employ ANN (Z. Chen et al., 2008), fuzzy logic, soft computing algorithms, classification methods and machine learning to avert false alarms (R. E. Bourguet et al., 1994), (Tom M. Mitchell, 1997), (Peter Vas, 1999), (B. K. Bose, 2007), (B. M. Wilamowski et al., 2011). In this framework is sited the contribution of this paper. It consists to develop an approach allowing four tasks: increasing fault detectability, improving fault classification, fault localization and making decision taking into consideration the true quantification of its severity degree.

MAIN FOCUS OF THE CHAPTER

Problem Formulation

Despite its good performance provided in the diagnosis of certain wind turbine mechanical faults, Fast-ESPRIT method does not allow determination and recognition of several relevant aspects such as (S. Chakkor et al., 2014a, 2014b):

- The quantification of the detected fault severity to many levels or into degrees;
- The relationship of this severity with the fault harmonics number;

- The relationship of this severity with the fault harmonics amplitudes;
- The fault classification according to its types in the case of the occurrence of various failure types simultaneously;

In this situation, the discrimination of divers' anomalies becomes a difficult task especially when there is an overlapping between frequency values of the side harmonics characterizing the signature of each fault type apart. In (E. H. El Bouchikhi et al., 2012, 2013, 2015), the authors have proposed one parameter C without unity as a metric measuring the severity degree of a fault. It is based on its harmonics amplitudes only. This criterion has been expressed by the following formula:

$$C = \sum_{k=1}^{N_h} \left(\frac{\hat{a}_k^2}{\hat{a}_0^2} \right) \tag{1}$$

Where N_h is the harmonics number of the detected fault. $\hat{a}_k$ are theirs estimated amplitudes. $\hat{a}_0$ is the estimated amplitude of the fundamental frequency $f_0 = 50Hz$. However, this indicator C influence on the machine setting function. It have one major drawback. It does not allow measuring the real severity of a detected fault, especially when:

- The number of the fault harmonics increases: this means that the fault is more serious and it requires an immediate machine stopping with an urgent repair intervention;
- The simple faults generates harmonics having small amplitudes do not have a great influence;
- The increase of the ambient noise lead sometimes to the appearance of certain small harmonics which are interpreted as real fault signatures;
- Triggering a false alarm can lead to production loss and to a higher maintenance cost;

To highlight the restriction of the parameter C which is formulated in equation (1), some against examples are taken for misalignment and broken rotor bars fault detection as illustrated in the following comparative Table 1.

Where f_h are the fault harmonic signature sides and I_h are their corresponding amplitudes. The parameters used in this simulation are referenced in Table 2. Each fault harmonics frequencies are calculated from theirs mathematical model formulas as showed in Table 2. Thus, they are used neatly to classify the detected

Table 1. Indicator C values comparison for different fault types

Fault Type	f_0(Hz)	N_h	f_h(Hz)	I_h(A)	C
Misalignment 1	50	6	21 37.03 79 95.05 137.03 195.05	0.2220 0.3256 0.2748 0.3731 0.1813 0.1524	43.10^{-4}
Misalignment 2	50	4	21 37.03 79 137.03	0.275 0.385 0.39 0.23	43.10^{-4}
Broken rotor bars 1	50	4	22.525 25.825 70.875 74.175	0.302 0.4569 0.3583 0.3958	58.10^{-4}
Broken rotor bars 2	50	2	22.525 25.825	0.525 0.55	58.10^{-4}

faults according to theirs types via a proposed CAFH algorithm that is detailed in the proposed approach section.

Table 2. Wind turbine faults signatures

Fault Type	Harmonic Frequencies	Parameters
Broken rotor bars	$f_{brb} = f_0 \left[k\left(\dfrac{1-s}{q}\right) \pm s \right]$	$k= 1,3,5,...$
Bearing damage	$f_{bng} = \left\| f_0 \pm k f_{i,o} \right\|$	$k= 1,3,5,...$ $f_{i,o} = \begin{cases} 0.4\ n_b\ f_r \\ 0.6\ n_b\ f_r \end{cases}$
Misalignment	$f_{mis} = \left\| f_0 \pm k f_r \right\|$	$k= 1,3,5,...$
Air gap eccentricity	$f_{ecc} = f_0 \left[1 \pm m\left(\dfrac{1-s}{q}\right) \right]$	$m= 1,2,3,...$

With f_0 is the electrical supply frequency, s is the per-unit slip, q is the number of poles, f_r is the rotor frequency, n_b is the bearing balls number, $f_{i,o}$ is the inner and the outer frequencies depending on the bearing characteristics, and m, $k \in \mathbb{N}$ are the harmonics frequency index (E. Al-Ahmar et al., 2008, 2010). Slip s is defined as:

$$s = \frac{\omega_s - \omega_r}{\omega_s} \qquad (2)$$

$$\omega_s = \frac{120 f_0}{q} \qquad (3)$$

Where:

ω_s is the generator synchronous speed;
ω_r is the relative mechanical speed of the generator.

These harmonics are extensively used as diagnosis measures in the CSA (Current Stator Analysis) technique. From the analysis of Table 1, it is noticed that the severity indicator C was unable to measure correctly the severity degree for the same type of studied faults. In fact, the parameter C maintains the same value for both considered cases despite the remarkable change in the values of their harmonics number and of their amplitude values from one fault case to another. This means that the diagnosis algorithm using this parameter takes the same decision in the case of the manifestation of misalignment fault 1 and 2 since their severity indicator $C = 43.10^{-4}$. The same observation is noticed for broken rotor bars fault 1 and 2 with a value of $C = 58.10^{-4}$. Furthermore, in the case of a healthy machine this indicator C is set to zero so that to reflect the absence of any defects. Whereas, for a faulty machine, this indicator takes very small values which are more closely to zero in some cases. These values cause many calculation problems in the diagnosis algorithm employed to make an appropriate decision following the machine condition during its operation. This means that there is a confusion between the indicator C values which specifies a fault condition and the others which revealing a healthy state of a monitored machine. This occurs mainly when the C values are misinterpreted by the diagnosis system since they are enough small and even closest to zero. Certainly, when the harmonics number of a fault increase or when its amplitudes values increase likewise, this implies that the fault evolves and it gets worse progressively. We conclude that this metric C is remarkably limited in quantifying the severity levels of a particular fault. So, to solve this problem, we must describe a potential solution to achieve an accurate detection and an automatic diagnosis task with more rigor, precision and satisfaction.

SOLUTIONS AND RECOMMENDATIONS

Fault Severity Indicator

Since a rotating induction electric machine is driving a mechanical system, the input shaft of this system is rigidly coupled to its rotor. In such case, the load torque exerted on its rotor is a function of the input shaft speed and its modulated frequencies. This affects the electromagnetic field in the stator. Accordingly, the stator generates a current dependent on the variation of said field. Any fault will be translated by the appearance of an additive induced current with particular characteristics of frequency and amplitude. These are gainful in identifying the nature and the severity level of an incidental fault. To measure accurately the severity intensity of any fault, we have proposed an improvement in the calculation of the indicator C by introduction of the following formula:

$$C = -N_h \sum_{k=0}^{N_h} \log_{10} \left(\frac{\hat{a}_k^2}{\hat{a}_0^2} \right) \tag{4}$$

In fact, the new proposed coefficient C is entitled severity indicator. It allows quantifying accurately the gravity class of all defects relatives to electromechanical systems having spectral parameters. Indeed, in the case of the existence of a failure, this indicator takes a high value, which is divergent of zero. This confirms and ensures that the monitored machine is faulty. In the opposite case, when $N_h = 0$ and $\hat{a}_k = 0$, this value is equal to zero. In addition, the new indicator overcomes the duplication problem of the severity level values happening between different fault types. In reality, we are perfecting the indicator C according to formula (4) taking in our consideration the proportionality between N_h the number of the fault harmonics and their estimated amplitudes $\hat{a}_k$. Indeed, to obtain significant values of C which maintains the difference to Zero value, an amplification by the operator $\log_{10}(.)$ is realized. Thus, this improved parameter allows automatic recognition of severity degree of such mentioned faults shown in table 2. It helps also to establish an early and a preventative remote maintenance plan in real time. With this reformed indicator, the measurement of the severity level becomes adequate and satisfactory as given in the comparison illustrated in table 3. It is remarked from study findings of table 3, that the severity level of each studied fault is properly quantified. Each value of C is proportional to the harmonics number of each detected fault and to theirs amplitudes. We notice likewise that any value of C differs sharply with an acceptable gap from a fault type to another. This permit avoiding any confusion in taking tolerable action relative to the value of C of an identified fault.

Table 3. Fault severity indicators comparison

Fault Type	N_h	C	New C
Misalignment 1	6	43.10^{-4}	116.2649
Misalignment 2	4	43.10^{-4}	48.1793
Broken rotor bars 1	4	58.10^{-4}	45.6676
Broken rotor bars 2	2	58.10^{-4}	10.1579

New Fuzzy Approach for Fault Diagnosis

In condition monitoring of an electrical induction machine, we must consider the relationship between its input signals and its status indications. In most faults, which have predictable symptoms during their development, detection and interpretation, only simple sensors are required (S. Sheng et al., 2015). Contrariwise, the classification of the state of such machine and the determination of the severity of its possible faults from its input signals are not an easy task, because they are affected by many factors. In front of this situation, the recourse to the computerized systems using artificial intelligence that mimicking human intelligence is necessary (D. Dubois et al., 1980), (J. C. Bezdek et al., 1992), (B. Bouchon-Meunier, 1995), (J. Yen et al., 1999). They can indicate the precise state of the machine by putting different probabilities of radical causes resulting observed faults. They allowing also making diagnoses and taking swift and consistent decisions. However, this requires a certain amount of knowledge and expertise on the relationship between the machine condition and its fault symptoms. The application of fuzzy logic offers a very significant flexibility in making decision compared to other methods (M. Sugeno, 1985), (C. Lee, 1990), (Timothy J. Ross, 2010). This logic allows reasoning from inaccurate input data to generate output results approximately or gradually uncertain (George J. Klir et al., 1996). The use of this technique in our proposed diagnosis approach decision-making of wind turbine faults is justified by the difficulty to make an explicit mathematical model or an analytical formulation of the decision especially when a large number of inputs are used. So, it is possible to use an empirical model based on rules derived from human expertise in electrical induction machines which can be incorporated. Determinant informations can be exploited using fuzzy inference systems FIS to increase confidence and accuracy of diagnosis results. The proposed resolution, in (S. Chakkor et al., 2014a, 2014b, 2014c), of the automated remote control problem of wind turbine machines, which is described and detailed in problem formulation section, is based on three important units as illustrated in figure 1:

1. Development of a stator current sensor which has two roles: fault detection with a high-resolution spectral analysis method and taking a corrective decision following any detection ;
2. Use of a data collection module from various sensors installed on each wind turbine engine ;
3. Use of a communication network for an optimal routing of data and queries between wind turbines and supervision center ;

Figure 1. Automated remote control and diagnosis architecture

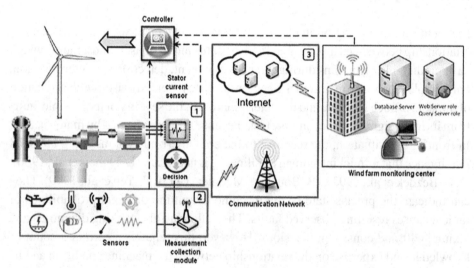

Fuzzy Diagnosis Steps

The surveillance suggested to be applied in this work, based on fuzzy logic, proves to be more effective than traditional methods for several reasons: the systems studied are complex having numerous continuous or discontinuous Inputs/Outputs and nonlinear responses which makes their modeling difficult or even impossible. Furthermore, for such systems, there are classes with poorly defined boundaries, whose confines cannot be specified precisely, or poorly separated categories that partially overlap. It is therefore possible to use fuzzy logic for classification, regression and even extrapolation.

The fuzzy rules and the functional steps of the proposed approach are applied under the following assumptions:

- The physical process is controllable;
- The existence of a human expertise, qualitative and gradual;
- The inputs and outputs are measurable or observable quantities;

Figure 2 summarizes the fuzzy rules used in our approach. The fuzzfication operation associates to each scalar value of real domain, one or more linguistic variables of the fuzzy area. This step involves evaluating the membership functions used in predicate rules. Whereas, the defuzzification combines the conclusion results of aggregation rules to infer the actual output value.

Proposed Approach

In the diagnosis mode, the input signal, which is the stator current in our case, is analyzed against any suspected signature. This later is previously obtained in the learning mode. The proposed algorithm generates decisions about machine condition in taking into account various fuzzy criteria and assumptions. We have suggested improving the diagnosis system by integration of a FIS because it seem necessary in order to make decision without excessive loss of accuracy. This is justified by the benefits and capabilities that provide a FIS. The proposed diagnosis approach

Figure 2. Fuzzy classification block diagram

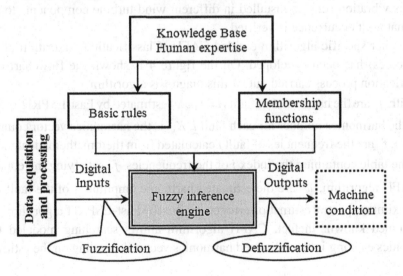

combines two techniques. It contains multiple steps that must be executed to arrive at the final decision of diagnosis as shown in figure 3.

Initially, acquisition of the stator current signal is carried out. Afterward, MDL criterion of Rissanen is applied to determine the number of sine waves (which include fundamental and harmonics) contained in the acquired stator current (S. Chakkor et al., 2014a, 2014b). From this number, our algorithm proceeds to calculate the different frequencies characterizing any prospective faults from their mathematical models as illustrated in table 2. These faults are recognized through theirs index number i as shown in table 4, then they have classified according to theirs types.

Table 4. Different faults types with their index

Fault Type	Index i
Broken rotor bars	1
Bearing damage	2
Misalignment	3
Air gap eccentricity	4

Based on the frequencies thus calculated, bounded intervals characterizing the frequency margin and the type of each fault are defined. This stage was necessary to facilitate the discrimination task. Thereafter, in each of these frequency intervals, detecting of any fault harmonic signature f_k and their amplitude a_k is examined using Fast-ESPRIT algorithm (S. Chakkor et al., 2014b). On other hand, the proposed diagnosis algorithm uses likewise the measurements collected in real time from the various vibration sensors installed in different wind turbine components to make sure that fault occurrence is verified.

Another specific algorithm entitled CAFH (Classification Algorithm of Fault Harmonics) has been developed. On the figure 4 is shown the flowchart of the classification process carried out by this diagnosis algorithm.

With $\hat{f}_j$ are the harmonics of faults $i = 1, \ldots, 4$ estimated by Fast-ESPRIT method. N_h is the harmonics number for each fault i. $K_{h,i}$ is the harmonics vector counter of a fault i. $f_{i,j}$ are the frequencies of fault i calculated from their mathematical models. T_i is the table containing the index j of the frequencies $\hat{f}_j$ satisfying the condition of CAFH algorithm. $\hat{a}_j$ are the estimated harmonic amplitudes of the fault i. ε is the maximum spectral estimation error committed by Fast-ESPRIT algorithm which is assumed known. In fact, CAFH algorithm allows searching modeled faults harmonics existing in the estimated harmonics vector depending on the estimation

Figure 3. Stages of the proposed diagnosis approach

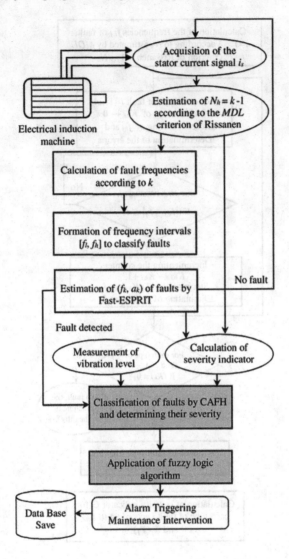

error ε of Fast-ESPRIT method. It makes a comparison between the fault frequencies and those estimated. In fact, the estimated harmonics satisfying CAFH criterion are counted and their indexes are stored in a specific vector in order to extract easily their corresponding amplitudes from the estimated ones by Fast-ESPRIT. This task is realized in the objective to calculate the severity level of each recognized fault. In the final phase, a decision algorithm based on fuzzy logic is applied. Consequently, this method allows an intelligent quantification of alarm level depending on the

Figure 4. Flowchart of the CAFH algorithm

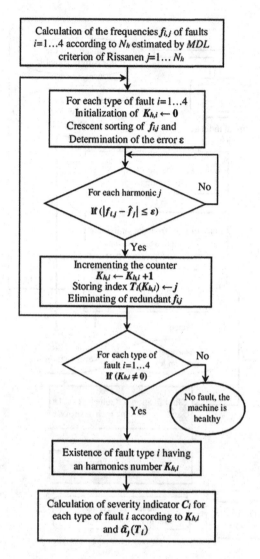

severity degree of an incident fault (F. Van der Heijden et al., 2004), (M. Emre Celebi, 2015).

Our proposed fuzzy algorithm uses as inputs, the vibration levels and the severity indicator C of the detected faults. As output, it generates a decision considered as an alarm signal. This decision indicates the nature and the adequate time of maintenance intervention (urgent or normal). This diagnosis system offers several advantages:

- Maximizing the performance of the monitoring and detection system since it limits the worsening of the incident failures;
- Knowing in the right time, the type and the nature of occurring failure to planning effectively an appropriate action for intervention;
- Take care to do not degrade the wind machine lifetime and to avoid unexpected accident;

SIMULATION AND RESULTS ANALYSIS

To evaluate the performance satisfaction of the proposed diagnosis system, its algorithm has been simulated with Matlab software tool. The most frequent faults that can occur in a wind turbine machine have been taken into account. These faults are described in table 2. The mathematical model of the stator current denoted x, which is adopted in this simulation, is defined by the following equation (E. H. El Bouchikhi et al., 2012, 2013, 2015):

$$x[n] = \sum_{k=0}^{N_h} a_k \cos\left[2\pi f_k \omega(n) \times \left(\frac{n}{F_s}\right) + \varphi_k\right] + b[n] \tag{5}$$

Where F_s is the sampling frequency, $x[n]$ corresponds to n^{th} sample of the stator current $n=0,...,N_s-1$, the vector $b[n]$ is the noise samples. This later is chosen Gaussian with zero mean and it have a variance equal to $\sigma^2 = 10^{-4}$. The quantities f_k, a_k, φ_k corresponding to the frequency, amplitude and phase respectively. The parameter $f_k(n)$ is to be estimated at every time n. It depends on the studied fault. The time and

Table 5. Simulation parameters

Parameters	Value
s	0,033
q	2
f_0	50 Hz
f_r	29,01 Hz
n_b	12
N_s	1024
F_s	1000 Hz
Stator Current Amplitude	10 A
Computing Processor	Intel Core2 Duo T6570 2,1 GHz

the space harmonics are assumed not considered. The others simulation parameters and the nominal values of the generator are summarized in table 5. Whereas, in table 6, the parameters and the methods used in this fuzzy inference system are shown.

The fuzzy inference system FIS that was used in our approach consists of four essential elements: fuzzifier, the inference engine, rules base and defuzzifier. On figure 5, a detailed architecture description of this system is presented with Matlab software. The use of the trapezoidal and the triangular membership functions for the fuzzy input variables (vibration and severity indicator C) are chosen arbitrarily by respecting the expert instructions or by statistical studies realized practically. This choice is also justified by their adaptation to the real numerical values needed

Table 6. FIS parameters

Parameter	Value
Fuzzy rules type	Mamdani
Input number	2
Output number	1
Rules number	9
AND Method	Min
Implication Method	Min
Aggregation Method	Max
Defuzzification Method	Centroïde

Figure 5. Fuzzy inference system architecture

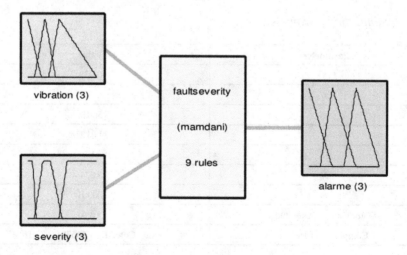

in diagnosis, in addition to their simplicity and their rapidity in the calculation of the membership value.

The selection of these membership functions positions and theirs overlaps must follow certain rules to avoid indeterminate or dead zones and to avert problems of the controller instability or the flattening of the decision surface. In the figures 6 and 7 the input fuzzy sets and theirs membership functions are illustrated.

Figure 6. Membership functions of the input1 fuzzy set

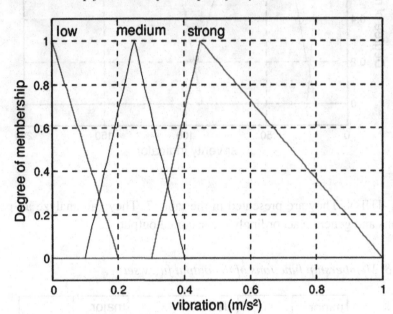

These sets thus constructed by human expertise are used in our fuzzy inference system FIS. This intelligent system is incorporated into the proposed diagnosis algorithm. Moreover, the vibration can be measured as a function of displacement, velocity or acceleration. In fact, accelerometers are used to measure vibration. They send data to the central controller of the wind turbine ("Detection and Classification", 2014), (Shawn Sheng, 2015), (Yiqi Liu et al., 2017). In wider or inaccessible wind park areas, wireless data transmission is an efficient solution for remote monitoring. The employed FIS uses two inputs having three different levels.

To simplify the reading of the output levels with an accurate manner, an alarm output having three possible levels is considered in the proposed approach as illustrated in figure 8. This graph shows the geometric shape of the output fuzzy set and its membership functions. Furthermore, this system allows exploiting nine

Figure 7. Membership functions of the input 2 fuzzy set

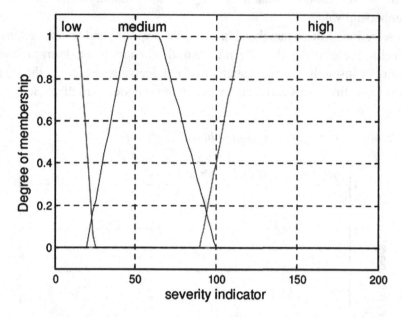

rules IF-THEN. They are presented in the table 7. They can analyze all possible situations and generate accordingly the accurate output.

Figure 8. Membership functions of the output fuzzy set

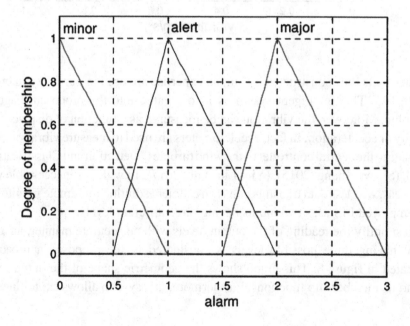

Table 7. IF-THEN rules of the FIS

Inputs		Output
Vibration	**Severity Indicator *C***	**Alarm Level**
Low	Low	Minor
Low	Medium	Minor
Low	High	Medium
Medium	Low	Medium
Medium	Medium	Medium
Medium	High	Major
Strong	Low	Medium
Strong	Medium	Major
Strong	High	Major

To produce the alarm, the FIS system pass through defuzzification phase using fuzzy centroid or gravity center technique developed by Sugeno (M. Sugeno, 1985). It can be expressed as follows:

Figure 9. Fuzzy inference system architecture

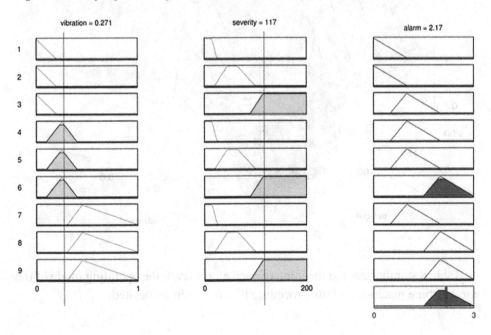

197

$$x^* = \frac{\int_{-\infty}^{+\infty} \mu_i(x)\, x\, dx}{\int_{-\infty}^{+\infty} \mu_i(x)\, dx} \tag{6}$$

Where x^* is the defuzzified output, $\mu_i(x)$ is the aggregated membership function and x is the output. With this procedure, the final decision which is the FIS output, is equal to the gravity center abscissa of the resulting membership function surface. This later characterizes the fuzzy set formed after the aggregation of all conclusions. Figure 9 shows an example of the resulting membership function for the output variable and its conversion into digital quantity.

In figure 10, the surface decisions is illustrated. It depends on each variable used in the employed FIS. It is observed that these decisions are in discontinuities, non-linear, flexible and are closer to human intelligence.

Figure 10. Output surface of the used FIS

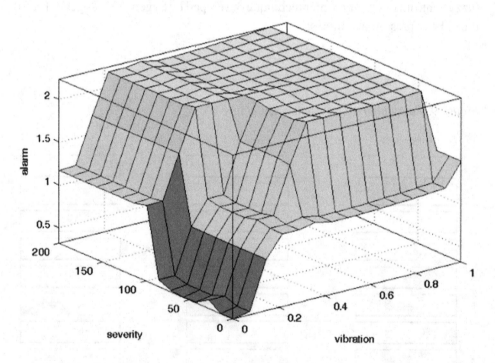

Table 8 summarizes the meaning of each alarm level, the operating mode of the wind turbine machine and the procedure that has been associated.

Table 8. Actions and procedures according to the alert level

Alarm Level	Associated Action
Minor	- The operational mode of wind turbine is into RUN - No alarm is activated
Medium	- Notification of occurrence of an event that exceeds the tolerance limits - Setting in DEGRADED mode to reduce the impact of the detected failure - Triggering a warning alarm - Requirement of consultation and revision
Major	- Evolution of a fault into fatal status - Setting the wind machine in STOP mode - Information of the maintenance staff for an immediate and an urgent repair intervention

The localization of the faulty wind machine at a park is very simple. Theirs positions are determined according to theirs IP addresses using GPS technology. In our diagnosis scheme, three systems are interconnected: proposed diagnosis algorithm, the control and classification system with an IESRCM remote monitoring module (S. Chakkor et al., 2014b, 2014c). This assembly is installed on each wind turbine machine. By this technique, through a supervision center, remote maintenance and control of the entire wind park become an easy task through the collaboration of all specified systems. In order to evaluate the proposed diagnosis approach in term of detection performance, computer simulation has been realized under the existence of various faults types.

Table 9. Simulation parameters of different types of faults

Fault Type	$f_{i,j}$ (Hz)	$a_{i,j}$ (A)	f_0 (Hz)	a_0 (A)	Vibration (m/s²)	SNR (dB)
Broken rotor bars	22.525 25.825 70.875 74.175 119.225 122.525	0.2220 0.2356 0.1748 0.1831 0.1813 0.1934				
Bearing damage	89.248 158.9 189.2 258.9	0.275 0.231 0.175 0.132	50	10	0.271	20
Misalignment	20.99 37.03 79.01 137.03	0.1022 0.2169 0.1158 0.2283				
Air gap eccentricity	1.65 98.35	0.325 0.311				

The faults parameters used in this simulation are listed in the table 9. The added value of our contribution is: the accurate recognition of anomalies and their rapid classification before they induce a severe degradation in the wind machine. This is in the objective to make appropriate actions and procedures in due time. These measures allow a correct feedback according to the triggered alarm level. In fact, the control system of wind turbine isolates and reconfigures the faulty components having a medium level of severity. Following this case, the wind machine operates in degraded mode. In the case of a serious fault, this system activates the emergency stop circuit and disconnects the wind machine from the electrical grid without any damages. This allows therefore a repair setting of this machine safely.

Simulation results are summarized in table 10. It is noteworthy from the showed results that the proposed approach is satisfactory. It has a good accuracy in detection and diagnosis despite the simultaneous occurrence of several faults having various types and despite the noisy environment.

Moreover, according to table 10, we observe a significant difference between the severity indicator values characterizing each type of defect. This reflects the robustness of the severity parameter which we have remedied because it allows avoiding overlap and diagnosis confusion. Another remark concerns the exact values of the counters $K_{h,i}$ which has been computed quantitatively and precisely.

Table 10. Diagnosis and classification simulation results

$\hat{f}_j\,(Hz)$	$\hat{a}_j$	ε	$N_{h,i}$	$K_{h,i}$	C_i	Alarm A_i	Decision	Detected Fault Type
258.8847	0.1340		16	6	122.3749	2.17	major	Broken rotor bars (i=1)
189.1870	0.1781							
158.9021	0.2301		16	4	54.5028	1.17	alert	Bearing damage (i=2)
137.0332	0.2295							
122.5209	0.1957		16	4	57.6619	1.17	alert	Misalignment (i=3)
119.2175	0.1872							
1.6520	0.3192							
98.3493	0.3191							
49.9999	9.9833	0.08						
89.2451	0.2802							
37.0317	0.2197		16	2	11.9680	1.17	alert	Air gap eccentricity (i=4)
79.0304	0.1182							
70.8679	0.1822							
25.8290	0.2430							
20.9691	0.1040							
74.1792	0.1784							
22.5162	0.2191							

FUTURE RESEARCH DIRECTIONS

To improving fault severity detection and as future research trends of this study, we proposed to investigate, with a comparative study, the robustness and efficiency of the proposed approach with others methods using advanced algorithms of artificial intelligence such as: ANN, Neuro-Fuzzy, CNN, DEEP and Machine Learning, etc. and advanced signal processing techniques as well as the study of their application to design an intelligent detection device or a virtual fault detection sensor.

CONCLUSION

This research deals with the problem of the false alarms and the severity quantification of a detected fault in induction machines. The fault classification has been also studied to avoid this issue. The proposed solution approach is based on the stator current spectrum analysis computed by Fast-ESPRIT method, a fuzzy inference system and an intelligent classification algorithm interconnected with vibration sensors. Effectively, the suggested diagnosis approach treat correctly the problem of fault detection despite the existence of a disturbing noise. Simulation results proves the fault detection accuracy and the knowledge extraction feasibility. Furthermore, it is concluded from the obtained outcomes that the proposed control, diagnosis and the classification tasks has been accomplished successfully in real-time. This promotes the implementation of this approach in the automated control and monitoring system of a wind turbine. As perspective, we proposed to extend this work to study the detection towards other types of failures affecting the mechanical components of wind machine using vibration analysis.

REFERENCES

Al-Ahmar, E. (2008). Wind Energy Conversion Systems Fault Diagnosis Using Wavelet Analysis. *International Review of Electrical Engineering*, *3*(4), 646–652.

Al Ahmar, E. (2010). *Advanced Signal Processing Techniques for Fault Detection and Diagnosis in a Wind Turbine Induction Generator Drive Train: A Comparative Study. IEEE Energy Conversion Congress and Exposition*. ECCE.

Bezdek, J. C., & Pal. (1992). Fuzzy Models for Pattern Recognition. IEEE Press.

Blödt, M. (2010). Mechanical Fault Detection. In F. Detection & W. Zhang (Eds.), Induction Motor Drives Through Stator Current Monitoring-Theory and Application Examples. Academic Press.

Bonaldi. (2012). *Predictive Maintenance by Electrical Signature Analysis to Induction Motors*. InTech.

Bouchon-Meunier, B. (1995). *La Logique Floue et ses Applications*. Addison-Wesley.

Bourguet & Antsaklis. (1994). *Artificial Neural Networks In Electric Power Industry*. Technical Report of the ISIS Group at the University of Notre Dame ISIS-94-007.

Chakkor, Mostafa, & Hajraoui. (2014). ESPRIT Method Enhancement for Real-time Wind Turbine Fault Recognition. *International Journal of Power Electronics and Drive System, 5*(4).

Chakkor, S., Mostafa, B., & Hajraoui, A. (2014). Performance Analysis of Faults Detection in Wind Turbine Generator Based on High-Resolution Frequency Estimation Methods. International Journal of Advanced Computer Science and Applications. *SAI Publisher, 5*(4), 139–148.

Chakkor, S., Mostafa, B., & Hajraoui, A. (2014). Wind Turbine Fault Detection System in Real Time Remote Monitoring. *Iranian Journal of Electrical and Computer Engineering, 4*(6), 1495–1502.

Chen. (2008). Neural Network Electrical Machine Faults Diagnosis Based On Multi-Population GA. *IEEE International Joint Conference on Neural Networks*.

Detection and Classification of Induction Motor Faults Using Motor Current Signature Analysis and Multilayer Perceptron. (2014). *IEEE 8th International Power Engineering and Optimization Conference (PEOCO2014)*.

Dubois, D., & Prade, H. (1980). Fuzzy Sets and Systems: Theory and Applications. Academic Press.

El Bouchikhi, E. H. (2012). Induction Machine Fault Detection Enhancement Using a Stator Current High Resolution Spectrum. *IECON - IEEE 38th Annual Conference on Industrial Electronics Society*, 3913-3918 10.1109/IECON.2012.6389267

El Bouchikhi, E. H. (2013). A Parametric Spectral Estimator for Faults Detection in Induction Machines. *The IEEE 39th Annual Conference on Industrial Electronics Society*. 10.1109/IECON.2013.6700357

El Bouchikhi, E. H., Choqueuse, V., & Benbouzid, M. (2015). Induction Machine Faults Detection Using Stator Current Parametric Spectral Estimation. Original Research Article, Elsevier. *Journal of Mechanical Systems and Signal Processing, 52–53*, 447–464. doi:10.1016/j.ymssp.2014.06.015

Emre Celebi, M. (2015). *Partitional Clustering Algorithms*. Springer International Publishing Switzerland.

Francisco, J. V. S. (2013). *Diagnosis of Electric Induction Machines in Non-Stationary Regimes Working in Randomnly Changing Conditions* (Thesis Report). Universitat Politècnica de València.

Giri, F. (2013). *AC Electric Motors Control: Advanced Design Techniques and Applications*. John Wiley & Sons. doi:10.1002/9781118574263

Husson, R. (2009). *Control Methods for Electrical Machines*. ISTE Ltd and John Wiley & Sons, Inc. doi:10.1002/9780470611760

Klir, G. J., & Yuan, B. (1996). Fuzzy Sets, Fuzzy Logic, and Fuzzy Systems: Selected Papers by Lotfi Asker Zadeh. World Scientific Publishing Co. Pte. Ltd.

Lee, C. (1990). Fuzzy Logic in Control Systems: Fuzzy Logic Controller. *IEEE Transactions on Systems, Man, and Cybernetics, 20*, 404–435.

Liu, Y., & Bazzi, A. M. (2017). A review and comparison of fault detection and diagnosis methods for squirrel-cage induction motors: State of the art. *ISA Transactions*.

Mitchell, T. M. (1997). *Machine Learning* (International Edition). McGraw-Hill.

Mohanty, A. R. (2015). *Machinery Condition Monitoring Principles and Practices*. CRC Press Taylor& Francis.

Ross, T. J. (2010). *Fuzzy Logic with Engineering Applications* (3rd ed.). John Wiley & Sons. doi:10.1002/9781119994374

Sheng, S. (2015). *Improving Component Reliability Through Performance and Condition Monitoring Data Analysis*. NREL-Wind Farm Data Management & Analysis North America.

Sheng, S., & Guo, Y. (2015). An Integrated Approach Using Condition Monitoring and Modeling to Investigate Wind Turbine Gearbox Design. In *ASME Turbo Expo: Turbine Technical Conference and Exposition Montréal, Canada, 2015*. National Renewable Energy Laboratory (NREL) Publications. 10.1115/GT2015-43888

Sugeno, M. (1985). An Introductory Survey of Fuzzy Control. *Information Sciences, Prentice-Hall, 36*(1-2), 59–83. doi:10.1016/0020-0255(85)90026-X

Tavner, P. (2008). Condition Monitoring of Rotating Electrical Machines. The Institution of Engineering and Technology IET.

Toliyat, H. A. (2013). *Electric Machines Modeling, Condition Monitoring, and Fault Diagnosis*. CRC Press Taylor & Francis Group NW.

Trigeassou, J.-C. (2011). *Electrical Machines Diagnosis*. ISTE Ltd and John Wiley & Sons, Inc. doi:10.1002/9781118601662

Van der Heijden, F. (2004). *Classification, Parameter Estimation and State Estimation an Engineering Approach using MATLAB*. John Wiley & Sons Ltd. doi:10.1002/0470090154

Vas. (1999). *Artificial-Intelligence-Based Electrical Machines and Drives Application of Fuzzy, Neural, Fuzzy-Neural, and Genetic-Algorithm-Based Techniques*. Oxford University Press. doi:10.1049/PBPO056E

Wilamowski, B. M., & David Irwin, J. (2011). *The Industrial Electronics Handbook Intelligent systems* (2nd ed.). CRC Press Taylor & Francis Group.

Yen, J., & Langari, R. (1999). *Fuzzy Logic: Intelligence, Control, and Information*. Prentice Hall, Inc.

ADDITIONAL READING

Baghouri, M., Chakkor, S., & Hajraoui, A. (2017). *Amélioration de l'efficacité énergétique pour les RCSF hétérogènes*. Editions Universitaires Européennes.

Chakkor, S. (2015). *E-diagnostic à base des capteurs intelligents Application sur les machines éoliennes*. Editions Universitaires Européennes.

Chakkor, S., Mostafa, B., & Hajraoui, A. (2014). On-line Intelligent Embedded System for Remote Monitoring and Fault Diagnosis of Wind Turbine. Recent Advances in Electrical and Electronic Engineering Series 41. Proceedings of the 3rd International Conference on Circuits, Systems, Communications, Computers and Applications (CSCCA '14). Florence, Italy. pp. 226-234

Chakkor, S., Mostafa, B., & Hajraoui, A. (2015). Improved ESPRIT-TLS Algorithm for Wind Turbine Fault Discrimination. *Recent Advances on Electro Science and Computers, Proceedings of the International Conference on Systems, Control, Signal Processing and Informatics (SCSI 2015)*, Barcelona, Spain

KEY TERMS AND DEFINITIONS

ANN: Artificial neural networks. Are one of the main tools used in machine learning. They are brain-inspired systems which are intended to replicate the way that we humans learn. Neural networks consist of input and output layers, as well as (in most cases) a hidden layer consisting of units that transform the input into something that the output layer can use. They are excellent tools for finding patterns which are far too complex or numerous for a human programmer to extract and teach the machine to recognize.

CAFH: Classification algorithm of fault harmonics. A classification method of Fault Harmonics for induction machines based on advanced signal-processing technique proposed by S. Chakkor et al.

ESPRIT: Estimation of signal parameters via rotation invariance techniques. A technique to determine parameters of a mixture of sinusoids in a background noise. This technique is first proposed for frequency estimation. However, with the introduction of phased-array systems in daily use technology, it is also used for Angle of arrival estimations as well.

FIS: Fuzzy inference system. Is defined as a system that uses fuzzy membership functions to make a decision. It uses the "IF…THEN" rules along with connectors "OR" or "AND" for drawing essential decision rules.

GPS: Global positioning system. A space-based radio-positioning and time-transfer system. GPS satellites transmit signals to proper equipment on the ground. These signals provide accurate position, velocity, and time (PVT) information to an unlimited number of users on ground, sea, air, and space.

IESRCM: Intelligent embedded system for control and remote monitoring. It is an intelligent electronic embedded device for remote monitoring of wind turbine components in wind parks. It was been proposed by S. Chakkor et al. in 2014.

MCSA: Motor current signature analysis. A condition monitoring technique used to diagnose problems in induction motors. It was first proposed for use in nuclear power parks for inaccessible motors and motors placed in hazardous areas. It is rapidly applied in industry today. Tests are performed online without interrupting production with motor running under the load at normal operating conditions. It can be used as predictive maintenance tool for detecting common motor faults at early stage and as such prevent expensive catastrophic failures, production outages and extend motor lifetime

MDL: Minimum description length. Is a principle in which the best hypothesis (a model and its parameters) for a given set of data is the one that leads to the best compression of the data. MDL was introduced by Jorma Rissanen in 1978. It is an important concept in information theory and computational learning theory.

TLS: Total least squares. In applied statistics, it is a type of errors-in-variables regression, a least squares data modeling technique in which observational errors on both dependent and independent variables are taken into account. It is a generalization of Deming regression and also of orthogonal regression, and can be applied to both linear and non-linear models.

Chapter 9
Wavelet Neural Networks and Equalization of Nonlinear Satellite Communication Channel

Saikat Majumder

ⓘ https://orcid.org/0000-0001-8230-9877
National Institute of Technology, Raipur, India

ABSTRACT

Wavelet neural networks are a class of single hidden layer neural networks consisting of wavelets as activation functions. Wavelet neural networks (WNN) are an alternative to the classical multilayer perceptron neural networks for arbitrary nonlinear function approximation and can provide compact network representation. In this chapter, a tutorial introduction to different types of WNNs and their architecture is given, along with its training algorithm. Subsequently, a novel application of WNN for equalization of nonlinear satellite communication channel is presented. Nonlinearity in a satellite communication channel is mainly caused due to use of transmitter power amplifiers near its saturation region to improve efficiency. Two models describing amplitude and phase distortion caused in a power amplifier are explained. Performance of the proposed equalizer is evaluated and compared to an existing equalizer in literature.

DOI: 10.4018/978-1-7998-4042-8.ch009

INTRODUCTION

Wavelet networks are a class of neural networks which have wavelets as activation function instead of conventional sigmoid function. Wavelets are a special kind of short duration oscillatory functions satisfying certain criteria. In contrast to Fourier transform, wavelet analysis represents a function by the combination of translations and dilations of a single basis function called mother wavelet. Wavelet analysis is especially efficient in decomposition and reconstruction of signals with abrupt changes in components of time or frequency. Although wavelet theory has found application in many fields, the implementations are usually limited to wavelets of small dimensions. Construction and application of wavelets of larger dimensions is complex and prohibitive in cost. Wavelets neural network has been proven to be a powerful tool for handling problems with large number of dimensions (Zhang, Q., 1997).

Artificial neural network are a potent tool for handling large dimensional and ill-defined problems. Neural networks can recover underlying dependencies between the given inputs and outputs by using training data. Training enables neural network to represent high-dimensional nonlinear functions. Neural networks can solve regression and classification problems by changing parameters that control how they learn as they go through training data. These parameters are called weights and influence the quality of classification or regression. Approximation of a function by conventional neural network is not efficient one because at a fundamental level such functions are constructed using weighted sum of sigmoid functions. Sigmoid function has a large support compared to wavelets which are more efficient in representing localized functions. Therefore, because of compact representation provided by wavelets, WNN are expected to be smaller compared to other neural networks.

This chapter explains different architecture of WNN, their specific capabilities and learning algorithm. Static and dynamic modeling of nonlinear system using WNN will be explained in subsequent sections. Similar to multilayer perceptron (MLP), WNN can be trained using backpropagation algorithm. In addition to training network weights, the training algorithm must also adapts the translation and dilation parameters of wavelet. A novel application of WNN, in the form of equalization of nonlinear satellite communication, is given which demonstrates the capability of WNN as nonlinear function approximation tool. Nonlinearity in satellite communication arises because of transmitter power amplifiers operating near saturation region for power efficiency considerations. This nonlinearity in satellite power amplifier causes distortion in the received signal and results in significant increase in bit error rate (BER). Channel with larger BER results in packet loss and delay in case of data transmission, audio distortion and video frame loss in case of multimedia transmission. Compensation of channel and power amplifier nonlinearity requires adaptive equalizer implementation at the front end of the communication receiver. Other techniques of reducing nonlinearity due to on-board amplifier, like cascading another nonlinear device to the amplifier, had been proposed but were not too successful.

Besides countering of the effects of channel nonlinearity, equalizers are also applied for compensating the effects of inter-symbol interference (ISI) and noise over dispersive channel. Conventional linear equalizers employ a linear filter with finite impulse response (FIR) or lattice filter structure and using a least mean square (LMS) or recursive least-squares (RLS) algorithm for training the equalizer which adaptively change the filter coefficients. Once the training is complete, the equalizer characteristic is exactly opposite to the effects of the channel. Thus an adaptive equalizer is an iterative optimization program with mean square error (MSE) as objective function which tries to approximate inverse of channel characteristics (Swayamsiddha, S. et al., 2018).

Performance of linear equalizer is limited especially in case of nonlinear channel, which require nonlinear mapping between equalizer input and output to compensate for the distortion. Various techniques of nonlinear equalization have been proposed in literature. These can be generally classified into two categories, namely Volterra filter-based methods and neural network based approaches (Park, D. C., et al., 2002). Problem with Volterra filter approach is its complexity and its practical implementation is limited to low order nonlinearities. Artificial neural network (ANN) approach is one of the successful methods for modeling complex nonlinear systems and forecasting time-series with relatively simple architecture. ANNs are capable of forming complex decision regions with nonlinear decision boundaries which enable its application as decision device in digital communication. The most distinguishing feature of neural network is its ability to learn from provided data. With proper training, ANN can correct classify the transmitted symbols even though the input to the system is contaminated by various noises.

In one of the first application of ANN to equalization, Siu et al. applied multilayer perceptron with decision feedback structure (Siu, S. et al., 1990). They have shown that the proposed network performs superior to conventional linear equalizer with LMS algorithm. Several research in the past have proven the effectiveness of multilayer perceptron (MLP) in the problem of channel equalization (Chen, S. et al., 1990; Pandey, R., 2005). Early development in ANN equalizer apply back propagation algorithm for training of neural network. However, back propagation algorithm is limited by its slow convergence and may get struck in suboptimal solution in case of nonlinear objective functions (Wang, X. et al., 2011). To avoid the limitations of backpropagation algorithm, some of the training methods proposed are natural gradient descent method (Ibnkahla, M. et al., 2004), information theory training (Ludwig, O. et al., 2010), and conjugate gradient training (Tivive, F. H. C. et al., 2005). In recent times, these limitations have been further overcome by application of nature inspired algorithms for training of neural networks. Nonlinear channel equalizers based on MLP and optimized by frog-leaping algorithm (Panda, S. et al., 2014), particle swarm optimization (Iqbal, N. et al., 2014), directed search optimization (Panda, S. et al., 2015), symbiotic search optimization (Nanda, S. J. et al, 2017), moth-flame optimization (Nanda, S. J. et al., 2019) have been proposed in literature.

MLP neural networks are typically more complex due to their requirement of multiple layers. Single layer neural networks were proposed to minimize the disadvantages associated with MLP equalizers. Polynomial perceptron network (PPN) is one such ANN consisting of only one hidden layer. A PPN based channel equalizer was proposed in which input pattern space is expanded nonlinear space by using polynomials (Chen, S. et al., 1990). Similarly, other single hidden layer equalizer architectures were proposed, namely Legendre neural networks (Patra, J. C. et al., 2009), functional link neural network (Zhao, H. et al., 2011), and exponential functional link neural network (Patel, V. et al., 2016). WNN is also one such neural network with single hidden layer which has its own distinct advantages and challenges compared to other networks (Oussar, Y. et al., 1998; Alexandridis, A. K. et al., 2013). Some recent works on the application of WNN are in channel equalization (Nanda, S. J. et al., 2017; Pradhan, A. K. et al., 2006), time-series prediction (Doucoure, B. et al., 2016), engine performance evaluation (Jafarmadar, S. et al., 2018) and characterization of lubricating oil (Wang, G. et al., 2019).

WAVELET NETWORK ARCHITECTURES

In multiresolution analysis (MRA), a function can be approximated at different levels of resolution. MRA allows a complicated function to be divided into simpler ones, called basis functions, and they can be studies separately. On similar argument, a complicated function can be constructed from simpler ones using MRA. Function space in MRA consists of two complimentary space, namely approximation subspace A_s and detail subspace W_s, where s represents the resolution scale. A_s is generated by basis function called scaling function

$$\{\phi_{k,s} : 2^{s/2}\phi(2^s t - k); k \in \mathbb{Z}\}$$

and W_s is constructed from wavelet function

$$\{\psi_{k,s} : 2^{s/2}\psi(2^s t - k); k \in \mathbb{Z}\} \text{ (Goswami, J. C. et al., 2011).}$$

Scaling functions are finite energy functions $\phi(t) \in L^2(\mathcal{R})$ that generates nested subspaces $\{A_i\}$, namely

$$\{0\} \subset \dots \subset A_0 \subset \dots \subset A_i \subset A_{i+1} \subset \dots \to L^2 \tag{1}$$

Thus, each space A_{i+1} consists of subspace A_i and some 'leftover' space called W_i. This remaining space W_i is called wavelet subspace and is complimentary to A_i in A_{i+1}.

$$A_i \cap W_i = \{0\}, \tag{2}$$
$$A_i \cup W_i = A_{i+1}.$$

Thus, any function $x_s(t) \in A_s$ and $y_s(t) \in W_s$ can be constructed from linear combination of scaling function ϕ and wavelet function ψ, respectively, as given below.

$$x_s(t) = \sum_k a_{k,s} \phi(2^s t - k), \tag{3}$$

$$y_s(t) = \sum_k w_{k,s} \psi(2^s t - k), \tag{4}$$

where $a_{k,s}$ are approximation coefficients and $w_{k,s}$ are detail or wavelet coefficients. Equation (3) and (4) forms the basis for wavenet and wavelet network, respectively.

Wavenet

Wavelet derives its existence from equation (3), which uses scaling function at sufficiently large resolution level S.

$$f(t) = \sum_k a_{k,S} \phi_{k,S} \tag{5}$$

where the coefficient $a_{k,S}$ is obtained by the inner product $\langle f, \phi_{k,S} \rangle$. Translation and dilation parameters in wavenet are fixed at initialization and are not modified during training. Therefore, the output of a wavenet is linear combination of M different scaling functions.

$$y(t) = \sum_{i=1}^{M} w_i \phi_{\tau_i, \lambda_i} \tag{6}$$

Wavelet Networks

A simple wavelet network consists of one dimensional (1-D) input applied to hidden layer consisting of M wavelons is shown in Figure 1. Each translated, dilated wavelet function $\psi_{\lambda, \tau}(t)$ is called wavelon and is the fundamental unit in a wavelet network. Output of the wavelet network is weighted sum of hidden layer outputs given as

$$y(t) = \sum_{i=1}^{M} w_i \psi_{\tau_i, \lambda_i}(t) + \tilde{y} \tag{7}$$

where $\tilde{y}$ is approximation error. This error is encountered in functions whose mean value is non-zero. Objective of wavelet network, similar to other ANN, is to adaptively learn the parameters λ_i, τ_i, w_i, and $\tilde{y}$ using suitable training algorithm.

Figure 1. One dimensional (1-D) wavelet neural network

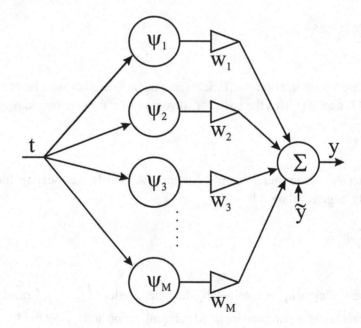

Multidimensional Wavelet Networks

A multidimensional wavelet networks consists of a vector **x** of N_I elements, where $\boldsymbol{x} = [x_1, \ldots, x_{N_I}]$. It consists of dense interconnection between N_I inputs and M wavelons. Output of wavelons are linearly combined at the output. In addition, direct connections between inputs and output is also provided to accommodate for linear systems (Alexandridis, A. K. et al., 2013). The output of such a neural network is given by the following expression:

$$\hat{y}(\boldsymbol{x}) = b_0 + \sum_{j=1}^{N_I} b_j x_j + \sum_{k=1}^{M} w_k \Psi_k(\boldsymbol{x}) \tag{8}$$

Such a network is shown in Figure 2. In this expression, b_0 is bias applied at the output, $b_j, j = 1, \ldots, N_I$ is weight of direct connection from input to output. Interconnection from inputs to the hidden node or wavelons is controlled by weights $w_k, k = 1, \ldots, M$. $\Psi_k(\boldsymbol{x})$ is a multidimensional wavelet constructed by the product of N_I monodimensional wavelets of each input:

$$\Psi_k(\boldsymbol{x}) = \prod_{j=1}^{N_I} \psi(v_{jk}) \tag{9}$$

where, $v_{jk} = (x_j - \tau_{jk}) / \lambda_{jk}$ and ψ is mother wavelet.

From the above discussion it can be concluded that a wavelet network or WNN consists of the following unknown parameters: $b_0, b_j, \tau_{jk}, \lambda_{jk}, w_k$ for $k = 1, \ldots, M$ and $j = 1, \ldots, N_I$. A WNN learns these parameters with objective to minimize squared error $|e(n)|^2$ at the output using already available data during training phase. As shown in Figure 2, WNN learns weights and wavelet parameters using a suitable learning algorithm like backpropagation training or particle swarm optimization.

TRAINING WAVELET NEURAL NETWORKS

This section will elaborate gradient based training algorithm for static modeling of wavelet neural networks (Oussar, Y. et al., 1998). Choices of initial parameters are critically important in WNN and will be discussed briefly in the later part of the section.

Figure 2. Multidimensional wavelet network

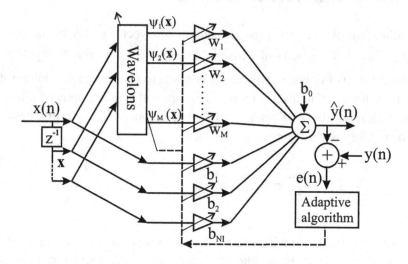

Backpropagation Training of Wavelet Network

A multidimensional WNN with N_I input is considered, as shown in Figure 2. Training set consists of N samples of input/output pairs $\{\mathbf{x}(n), y(n)\}, n = 1, ..., N$ which is used by the backpropagation algorithm for modifying the network parameters. Training input applied at time n is $\mathbf{x}(n) = [x_1(n), ..., x_N(n)]^T$ and $y(n)$ is the desired output in response to $\mathbf{x}(n)$. Let us assume that the ANN is trying to learn the static behavior of a system defined by the equation:

$$y(n) = f(\boldsymbol{x}(n)) + w(n), \tag{10}$$

for $n = 1, ..., N$. In (11), $f(.)$ is an unknown nonlinear function and $w(n)$ is independent identically distributed random noise with zero mean and variance σ_w^2. A neural network system which tries to emulate this function can be modeled as

$$\hat{y}(n) = \Psi(\boldsymbol{x}(n), \Theta) \tag{11}$$

The model in (12) shows that output of the WNN is function of present input $\mathbf{x}(n)$ and set of adjustable parameters $\Theta = \{b_0, b_j, w_k, \tau_{jk}, \lambda_{jk}\}$ for $j = 1, ..., N_I$ and $k = 1, ..., M$. Objective to the training algorithm is to estimate Θ so as to minimize the error between desired and actual output.

During training weights of the network are adjusted to minimize the mean quadratic cost function

$$J(\Theta) = E\left[|e|^2\right] = \frac{1}{2}\sum_{n=1}^{N} |y(n) - \hat{y}(n)|^2 \tag{12}$$

Computing of the weight vector Θ is done by iterative gradient descent based method. At each iteration t, each weight or element $\theta \in \Theta$ is updated according to delta learning rule:

$$\theta_{t+1} = \theta_t - \delta \frac{\partial J}{\partial \theta_t} + \varpi(\theta_t - \theta_{t-1}) \tag{13}$$

where δ is the learning rate and ϖ is a constant momentum term which increases training speed and prevents algorithm from getting stuck in oscillations. Both these control parameters are kept between 0 and 1. The partial derivative $\partial J/\partial \theta_t$ must be calculated individually for each of the weights as shown below:

$$\frac{\partial J}{\partial \theta} = -\sum_{n=1}^{N} e(n) \frac{\partial \hat{y}(n)}{\partial \theta} \tag{14}$$

Partial derivative with respect to each of the wavelet parameters and network weight is given next.

1. Partial derivative with respect to bias at the output node:

$$\frac{\partial \hat{y}(n)}{\partial b_0} = 1. \tag{15}$$

2. Partial derivative with respect to direct connection weights:

$$\frac{\partial \hat{y}(n)}{\partial b_j} = x_j, j = 1,...,N_I. \tag{16}$$

3. Partial derivative with respect to weights from wavelons to output node:

215

$$\frac{\partial \hat{y}(n)}{\partial w_k} = \Psi_k(x), k = 1, ..., M. \tag{17}$$

4. Partial derivative with respect to translation parameters:

$$\frac{\partial \hat{y}(n)}{\partial \tau_{jk}} = \frac{\partial \hat{y}(n)}{\partial \Psi_k(x)} \frac{\partial \Psi_k(x)}{\partial \psi(v_{jk})} \frac{\partial \psi(v_{jk})}{\partial v_{jk}} \frac{\partial v_{jk}}{\partial \tau_{jk}} = w_k \psi(v_{1k})...\,\psi\,'(v_{jk})...\psi(v_{N_I k})\frac{-1}{\lambda_{jk}} \tag{18}$$

where $\psi\,'(v_{jk})$ is the derivative of $\psi(v_{jk})$.

5. 5. Partial derivative with respect to dilation parameters:

$$\frac{\partial \hat{y}(n)}{\partial \lambda_{jk}} = \frac{\partial \hat{y}(n)}{\partial \Psi_k(x)} \frac{\partial \Psi_k(x)}{\partial \psi(v_{jk})} \frac{\partial \psi(v_{jk})}{\partial v_{jk}} \frac{\partial v_{jk}}{\partial \lambda_{jk}} = w_k \psi(v_{1k})...\,\psi\,'(v_{jk})...\psi(v_{N_I k})\frac{x_j - \tau_{jk}}{\lambda^2_{jk}} = v_{jk}\frac{\partial \hat{y}(n)}{\partial \tau_{jk}} \tag{19}$$

In this work, Mexican hat wavelet is chosen as mother wavelet. Mexican hat wavelet is itself the second derivative of Gaussian function and is given as

$$\psi(v) = \frac{2}{\sqrt{3}}\pi^{-1/4}(1-v^2)e^{-v^2/2} \tag{20}$$

From the equations (19)-(20) it is evident that the derivative of the wavelet needs to be calculated. First derivative of Mexican hat wavelet is

$$\psi(v) = \frac{2}{\sqrt{3}}\pi^{-1/4}e^{-v^2/2}(v^3 - 3v) \tag{21}$$

Initialization and Stopping Criteria

Training of WNN involves adaptation of translation and dilation parameters, besides other network weights. Translation and dilation parameters cannot be arbitrary random values and need to be initialized judiciously. For example, weighted sum of randomly initialized wavelets may lead to wavelons with a value of zero (Alexandridis, A. K. et al., 2013). Different techniques of initialization in WNN have been proposed in literature. Zhang and Benveniste (Zhang, Q. et al., 1992) gave constraints for the translation and dilation parameters so as to prevent the gradient descent algorithm from diverging:

$$\tau_{jk} = \frac{x_j^{(max)} + x_j^{(min)}}{2}$$
$$\lambda_{jk} = \frac{x_j^{(max)} - x_j^{(min)}}{5}$$

(22)

where $x_j^{(min)}$ and $x_j^{(max)}$ are the minimum and maximum of input x_j. The wavelet network parameters in case of multidimensional WNN can be initialized as follows (Veitch, D., 2005; Zhang, Q. et al., 1992):

1. Output bias b_0 can be initialized to the mean value of the observations.
2. Other multiplicative weights are initialized to zero.
3. 3. Let $\mathcal{D} = [a, b]$ be the domain of the function $f(t)$ to be approximated. If a point $p=(a+b)/2$ is selected, then following (23), the initial value of translation and dilation parameter for $k = 1$ is given as

$$\tau_{j1} = p, \lambda_{j1} = (b - a) / 5.$$

(23)

Next, initialization of $(\tau_{j2}, \lambda_{j2})$ and $(\tau_{j3}, \lambda_{j3})$ are made based on the interval $[a, p]$ and $[p, b]$, respectively. Subsequent initializations are done recursively in a similar manner till desired number of wavelons are obtained.

The training algorithm is stopped when it reaches given maximum number of iterations. In addition, the algorithm is stopped when variation of the parameters or error at the output reaches a lower bound.

SYSTEM MODEL AND NONLINEAR CHANNEL

Nonlinearity present in signal received from a satellite will be modeled mathematically and WNN architecture for its equalization will be proposed in this section. Figure 3 shows the schematic of satellite digital communication downlink with an equalizer at the front end of the receiver. Transmitted data is given by modulated symbols

$u(n)$, which pass through a nonlinear device $g(.)$ and its noisy version $x(n)$ is received at the ground station. Zero-mean additive white Gaussian noise (AWGN) at the receiver front end is represented as $w(n)$. In this work, binary phase shift keying (BPSK) modulation is considered for transmission where symbols in $u(n)$ belong to the set $\{+1, -1\}$. The equalizer consists of a multidimensional WNN trained by back propagation algorithm. Objective of the WNN equalizer is to adapt the weights of the network so that network output $\hat{y}(n)$ is as close as possible to desired symbol $y(n)$, where $y(n) = u(n-d)$ is delayed version of the transmitted symbol $u(n)$. Finally, hard decision is applied on continuous valued estimated signal to get discrete valued symbol estimate $\hat{u}(n)$.

Downlink communication from a satellite to the earth station consists of the cascade of travelling wave tube (TWT) amplifier and receive filter. Combined effect of both these is shown in the form of nonlinearity block $g(.)$ in Figure 3. Power limitations in satellites require TWT amplifiers to be operated very close to the saturation region to obtain maximum efficiency. Because of this satellite communication downlink suffer from nonlinearity and need to be equalized for improving the quality of detection. Typically, nonlinearity causes both amplitude and phase distortion which can be described using Saleh model (Jantunen, P., 2004; Saleh, A. A., 1981):

$$A(v) = \frac{\alpha_A v}{1 + \beta_A v^2} \tag{24}$$

$$\phi(v) = \frac{\alpha_\phi v^2}{1 + \beta_\phi v^2} \tag{25}$$

where v is the amplitude of input to the amplifier, $A(v)$ is amplitude conversion function and $\phi(v)$ is phase conversion function. Amount of nonlinearity introduced by the TWT is determined by the parameters $\alpha_A, \beta_A, \alpha_\phi$ and β_ϕ. For example, for a complex baseband input $\tilde{x}(t) = v e^{j\theta(t)}$, output of nonlinear device is $y(t) = A(v)e^{j[\theta(t)+\phi(v)]}$. Figure 4 shows the amplitude and phase conversion characteristics of this model along with parameters $a_0 = 1.9638$, $a_1 = 0.9945$, $b_0 = 2.5293$, $b_1 = 2.8168$.

TWT amplifiers are vacuum tube devices and are now being replaced by solid state power amplifiers (SSPA) in many applications. Saleh model of nonlinearity is suitable for TWT amplifiers, but is not sufficient for modelling nonlinearity introduced

Figure 3. Schematic diagram of satellite communication downlink with a channel equalizer

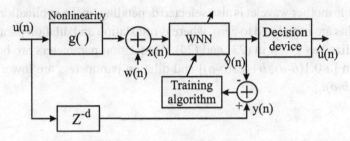

by solid state power amplifiers. To accommodate for low roll-off at saturation and smaller phase distortion, Ghorbani proposed a model similar to Saleh (Ghorbani, A. et al, 1991). Amplitude and phase conversion equations for this model are

$$A(v) = \frac{a_0 v^{a_1}}{1 + a_2 v^{a_1}} + a_3 v \tag{26}$$

$$\phi(v) = \frac{b_0 v^{b_1}}{1 + b_2 v^{b_1}} + b_3 v \tag{27}$$

where $a_0, a_1, a_2, a_3, b_0, b_1, b_2$, and b_3 are parameters of the model. The characteristics of this model for with parameters $a_0 = 8.1081$, $a_1 = 1.5413$, $a_2 = 6.5202$, $a_3 = -0.0718$, $b_0 = 4.6645$, $b_1 = 2.0965$, $b_2 = 10.88$, $b_3 = -0.003$ is shown in Figure 5.

TRAINING ALGORITHM FOR WNN CHANNEL EQUALIZER

Neural networks are trained using training input and target data. In case of an equalizer, training input are distorted and noisy samples $x(n)$, $n=1,…,N$ recorded at the input of the equalizer, where N is the length of training input. Target output is the signal or value which is desired at the output of the equalizer and is obtained by delaying the transmitter input symbols by d samples. The delay d is to accommodate for the propagation and processing delay from transmitter to the receiver. The algorithm for nonlinear satellite channel equalization and step-by-step procedure is explained below:

Step 1: Suitable value of number of number of hidden neurons M, length of input vector N_I, maximum number of iterations, learning rate δ are selected. A suitable mother wavelet is also selected depending on the application. Network weights are initialized to zero, whereas translation and dilation parameters are initialized as given in (23) and (24). Translation parameters are bound to be within $[a-0.1(b-a), b+0.1(b-a)]$ and dilation parameters are lower bound by $0.01(b-a)$.

Figure 4. Amplitude and phase conversion characteristics of Saleh model

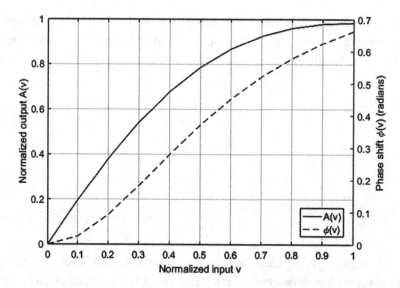

Step 2: At each iteration, training data set $\{x(n), y(n)\}$, $n = 1,\ldots, N$, is applied on the network to obtain the output $\hat{y}(n)$. Output error $e(n) = y(n) - \hat{y}(n)$ is calculated and is utilized for updating the weights and parameters of the wavelons using (13)-(20).

Step 3: Training is stopped when maximum number of iterations is reached or when there is no significant change in |e(n)| for 50 iterations.

Once training is completed, network weights b_0, b_p, w_k and parameters τ_{jk}, λ_{jk} for $k = 1,\ldots, M$ and $j = 1,\ldots, N_I$ are frozen. The network can then be used for equalizing the nonlinearity introduced by the transmitter power amplifier.

Figure 5. Amplitude and phase transfer characteristics of Ghorbani model

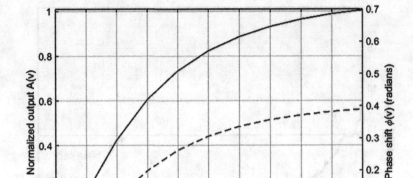

SIMULATION RESULTS

Simulations were carried out to evaluate the effectiveness of WNN equalizer for equalization of nonlinearity introduced by the satellite communication channel. The transmitted message $u(n)$ is BPSK modulated of the form ± 1. Each symbol was drawn from a uniform distribution and passed through nonlinear channel described earlier. A zero mean white Gaussian noise was added to the nonlinearly distorted output. The parameters of Saleh model are $a_0 = 1.9638$, $a_1 = 0.9945$, $b_0 = 2.5293$, $b_1 = 2.8168$ and that of Ghorbani model are $a_0 = 8.1081$, $a_1 = 1.5413$, $a_2 = 6.5202$, $a_3 = -0.0718$, $b_0 = 4.6645$, $b_1 = 2.0965$, $b_2 = 10.88$, $b_3 = -0.003$. The parameters of WNN are as follows: $N_1 = 4$, $N = 1000$, $\delta = 0.05$, $M = 35$ and maximum number of iterations is 1000. WNN based equalizer is compared with PSO optimized finite impulse response (FIR) filter based equalizer proposed in (Al-Shaikhi, A. A. et al., 2019).

Figure 6 plots mean value of MSE $E[|e|^2]$ for both the equalizers as function of number of training iterations. The simulation was performed for Saleh channel and signal to noise (SNR) of 15 dB. It can be seen that though FIR PSO algorithm quickly converges after 40 iterations, the final MSE obtained is much higher compared to that obtained by WNN. This can be attributed to the inherent nonlinear function approximation capabilities of WNN in contrast to linear FIR equalizer.

To further investigate the consistency in performance of WNN equalizer, both the equalizer models are trained and tested at four different values of SNR. Table 1

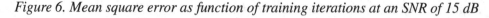

Figure 6. Mean square error as function of training iterations at an SNR of 15 dB

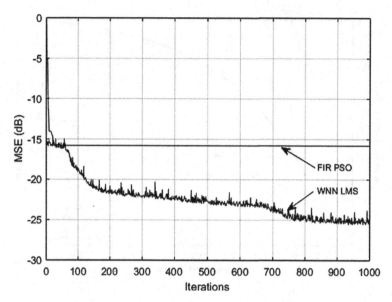

compares MSE performance of WNN equalizer with FIR PSO algorithm at different values of SNR. In the table, both training and testing MSE are shown. It can be seen that MSE obtained by the WNN equalizer algorithm is significantly less compared to the reference scheme for all compared SNR values. Similar results and conclusion can be drawn for channel with Ghorbani nonlinear model and is shown in Table 2.

Table 1. Comparison of MSE for channel with Saleh model of nonlinearity

SNR (dB)	WNN Algorithm		FIR PSO Algorithm	
	MSE Training	MSE Testing	MSE Training	MSE Testing
8	0.0062	0.0148	0.1159	0.1197
10	0.0085	0.0101	0.0767	0.0780
12	0.0030	0.0035	0.0493	0.0512
14	0.0024	0.0027	0.0316	0.0320

CONCLUSION

In this chapter, wavelet neural network architectures and their learning algorithm were presented. Architecture of different types of networks, namely wavelet networks and

Table 2. Comparison of MSE for channel with Ghorbani model of nonlinearity

SNR (dB)	WNN Algorithm		FIR PSO Algorithm	
	MSE Training	MSE Testing	MSE Training	MSE Testing
6	0.0304	0.0399	0.1307	0.1353
8	0.0060	0.0074	0.0864	0.0898
10	0.0022	0.0064	0.0564	0.0585
12	0.0052	0.0075	0.0362	0.0377

wavenet were discussed. Difference between single dimensional and multidimensional wavelet networks was also given. This chapter also explained backpropagation training algorithm for multidimensional wavelet networks. Finally, a novel application of WNN in the form of equalization of nonlinear satellite communication channel was presented. The proposed WNN equalizer was trained using backpropagation algorithm and evaluated over different types of nonlinear channels. Simulation results show that proposed WNN equalizer perform significantly better compared to other equalizer scheme in literature.

REFERENCES

Al-Shaikhi, A. A., Khan, A. H., Al-Awami, A. T., & Zerguine, A. (2019). A Hybrid Particle Swarm Optimization Technique for Adaptive Equalization. *Arabian Journal for Science and Engineering, 44*(3), 2177–2184. doi:10.100713369-018-3387-8

Alexandridis, A. K., & Zapranis, A. D. (2013). Wavelet neural networks: A practical guide. *Neural Networks, 42*, 1–27. doi:10.1016/j.neunet.2013.01.008 PMID:23411153

Chen, S., Gibson, G. J., & Cowan, C. F. N. (1990). Adaptive channel equalisation using a polynomial-perceptron structure. *IEE Proceedings. Part I. Communications, Speech and Vision, 137*(5), 257–264. doi:10.1049/ip-i-2.1990.0036

Chen, S., Gibson, G. J., Cowan, C. F. N., & Grant, P. M. (1990). Adaptive equalization of finite non-linear channels using multilayer perceptrons. *Signal Processing, 20*(2), 107–119. doi:10.1016/0165-1684(90)90122-F

Doucoure, B., Agbossou, K., & Cardenas, A. (2016). Time series prediction using artificial wavelet neural network and multi-resolution analysis: Application to wind speed data. *Renewable Energy, 92*, 202–211. doi:10.1016/j.renene.2016.02.003

Ghorbani, A., & Sheikhan, M. (1991, September). The effect of solid state power amplifiers (SSPAs) nonlinearities on MPSK and M-QAM signal transmission. In *1991 Sixth International Conference on Digital Processing of Signals in Communications* (pp. 193-197). IET.

Goswami, J. C., & Chan, A. K. (2011). *Fundamentals of wavelets: theory, algorithms, and applications* (Vol. 233). John Wiley & Sons. doi:10.1002/9780470926994

Ibnkahla, M., & Yuan, J. (2004). A neural network MLSE receiver based on natural gradient descent: Application to satellite communications. *EURASIP Journal on Advances in Signal Processing, 2004*(16), 394715. doi:10.1155/S1110865704405010

Iqbal, N., Zerguine, A., & Al-Dhahir, N. (2014). Adaptive equalisation using particle swarm optimisation for uplink SC-FDMA. *Electronics Letters, 50*(6), 469–471. doi:10.1049/el.2013.4091

Jafarmadar, S., Khalilaria, S., & Saraee, H. S. (2018). Prediction of the performance and exhaust emissions of a compression ignition engine using a wavelet neural network with a stochastic gradient algorithm. *Energy, 142*, 1128–1138. doi:10.1016/j.energy.2017.09.006

Jantunen, P. (2004). *Modelling of nonlinear power amplifiers for wireless communications* (Master's thesis).

Ludwig, O., & Nunes, U. (2010). Novel maximum-margin training algorithms for supervised neural networks. *IEEE Transactions on Neural Networks, 21*(6), 972–984.

Nanda, S. J., & Garg, S. (2019). Design of Supervised and Blind Channel Equalizer Based on Moth-Flame Optimization. *Journal of The Institution of Engineers (India): Series B, 100*(2), 105-115.

Nanda, S. J., & Jonwal, N. (2017). Robust nonlinear channel equalization using WNN trained by symbiotic organism search algorithm. *Applied Soft Computing, 57*, 197–209. doi:10.1016/j.asoc.2017.03.029

Oussar, Y., Rivals, I., Personnaz, L., & Dreyfus, G. (1998). Training wavelet networks for nonlinear dynamic input–output modeling. *Neurocomputing, 20*(1-3), 173–188. doi:10.1016/S0925-2312(98)00010-1

Panda, S., Mohapatra, P. K., & Panigrahi, S. P. (2015). A new training scheme for neural networks and application in non-linear channel equalization. *Applied Soft Computing, 27*, 47–52. doi:10.1016/j.asoc.2014.10.040

Panda, S., Sarangi, A., & Panigrahi, S. P. (2014). A new training strategy for neural network using shuffled frog-leaping algorithm and application to channel equalization. *AEÜ. International Journal of Electronics and Communications, 68*(11), 1031–1036. doi:10.1016/j.aeue.2014.05.005

Pandey, R. (2005). Fast blind equalization using complex-valued MLP. *Neural Processing Letters, 21*(3), 215–225. doi:10.100711063-005-1085-5

Park, D. C., & Jeong, T. K. J. (2002). Complex-bilinear recurrent neural network for equalization of a digital satellite channel. *IEEE Transactions on Neural Networks, 13*(3), 711–725. doi:10.1109/TNN.2002.1000135 PMID:18244467

Patel, V., Gandhi, V., Heda, S., & George, N. V. (2016). Design of adaptive exponential functional link network-based nonlinear filters. *IEEE Transactions on Circuits and Systems. I, Regular Papers, 63*(9), 1434–1442. doi:10.1109/TCSI.2016.2572091

Patra, J. C., Meher, P. K., & Chakraborty, G. (2009). Nonlinear channel equalization for wireless communication systems using Legendre neural networks. *Signal Processing, 89*(11), 2251–2262. doi:10.1016/j.sigpro.2009.05.004

Pradhan, A. K., Meher, S. K., & Routray, A. (2006). Communication channel equalization using wavelet network. *Digital Signal Processing, 16*(4), 445–452. doi:10.1016/j.dsp.2005.06.001

Saleh, A. A. (1981). Frequency-independent and frequency-dependent nonlinear models of TWT amplifiers. *IEEE Transactions on Communications, 29*(11), 1715–1720. doi:10.1109/TCOM.1981.1094911

Siu, S., Gibson, G. J., & Cowan, C. F. N. (1990). Decision feedback equalisation using neural network structures and performance comparison with standard architecture. *IEE Proceedings I-Communications, Speech and Vision, 137*(4), 221-225.

Swayamsiddha, S., & Thethi, H. (2018). Performance comparison of adaptive channel equalizers using different variants of differential evolution. *Journal of Engineering Science and Technology, 13*(8), 2271–2286.

Tivive, F. H. C., & Bouzerdoum, A. (2005). Efficient training algorithms for a class of shunting inhibitory convolutional neural networks. *IEEE Transactions on Neural Networks, 16*(3), 541–556. doi:10.1109/TNN.2005.845144 PMID:15940985

Veitch, D. (2005). *Wavelet Neural Networks and their application in the study of dynamical systems.* Department of Mathematics University of York UK.

Wang, G., Wu, Y., Jiang, H., Zhang, Y., Quan, J., & Huang, F. (2019). Physical and chemical indexes of synthetic base oils based on a wavelet neural network and genetic algorithm. *Industrial Lubrication and Tribology*, *72*(1), 116–121. doi:10.1108/ILT-03-2019-0101

Wang, X., & Huang, Y. (2011). Convergence study in extended Kalman filter-based training of recurrent neural networks. *IEEE Transactions on Neural Networks*, *22*(4), 588–600. doi:10.1109/TNN.2011.2109737 PMID:21402512

Zhang, Q. (1997). Using wavelet network in nonparametric estimation. *IEEE Transactions on Neural Networks*, *8*(2), 227–236. doi:10.1109/72.557660 PMID:18255627

Zhang, Q., & Benveniste, A. (1992). Wavelet networks. *IEEE Transactions on Neural Networks*, *3*(6), 889–898. doi:10.1109/72.165591 PMID:18276486

Zhao, H., Zeng, X., Zhang, X., Zhang, J., Liu, Y., & Wei, T. (2011). An adaptive decision feedback equalizer based on the combination of the FIR and FLNN. *Digital Signal Processing*, *21*(6), 679–689. doi:10.1016/j.dsp.2011.05.004

Chapter 10
Meta–Heuristic Parameter Optimization for ANN and Real–Time Applications of ANN

Asha Gowda Karegowda
Siddaganga Institute of Technology, India

Devika G.
ⓘ https://orcid.org/0000-0002-2509-2867
Government Engineering College, Mandya, India

ABSTRACT

Artificial neural networks (ANN) are often more suitable for classification problems. Even then, training of ANN is a surviving challenge task for large and high dimensional natured search space problems. These hitches are more for applications that involves process of fine tuning of ANN control parameters: weights and bias. There is no single search and optimization method that suits the weights and bias of ANN for all the problems. The traditional heuristic approach fails because of their poorer convergence speed and chances of ending up with local optima. In this connection, the meta-heuristic algorithms prove to provide consistent solution for optimizing ANN training parameters. This chapter will provide critics on both heuristics and meta-heuristic existing literature for training neural networks algorithms, applicability, and reliability on parameter optimization. In addition, the real-time applications of ANN will be presented. Finally, future directions to be explored in the field of ANN are presented which will of potential interest for upcoming researchers.

DOI: 10.4018/978-1-7998-4042-8.ch010

INTRODUCTION

There are umpteen number of standard machine learning algorithms that are developed during previous decades to cater the day to day activities in various domains which demand pattern recognition, prediction, decision making and many others. But still there is a gap between the domain specific applications and solving algorithms. Furthermore, there is need for parameter optimization of various machine learning algorithms, so as to achieve faster convergence with minimum iterations, which in turn increases the efficiency of an algorithm, both in terms of execution time and accuracy. In recent years, many nature-inspired meta-heuristic optimization algorithms (MHOA) were developed, which have been successfully applied for optimization of various machine learning algorithms like artificial neural network (ANN), extreme learning machine, deep learning machine, support vector machine, Radial basis neural network, etc. Few of the MHOAs use memory to keep track of the search process and find the optimal solution based on the previous solutions stored in the memory. Based on the search process, these MHOAs are broadly classified as single solution based and population based algorithms. The search process in the single solution based algorithm starts with one candidate solution (search agent/ object) and progresses over a specific number of iterations. Contrary to single solution, in the population based solution, the search process starts with a set of candidate solutions which gets upgraded in next iterations and finally the best fit candidate is chosen as the optimal solution. This chapter mainly focuses on how MHOAs can be applied to optimize various parameters of ANN in particular connection weights. Furthermore, various applications of ANN in the field of textile, tourism and educations are elaborated. In addition, applications of MHOA optimized ANN are also elucidated.

ANNs has significant advantages over statistical models when both are relatively compared. There is no prerequisite demand of hypothesis for testing as needed for statistical methods. In addition, ANNs are robust enough to handle noisy data, provide desired results, are scalable and suitable for handling nonlinear data. ANN processing is reassuring in numerous areas including medical analysis, (Catalogna, 2012, Raval, 2018), education, agriculture, industry, weather forecasting, tourism, textile, manufacturing industry, defense and many more. Surveys provided on ANN till date is limited to tools survey or ANN with specific application. Comparatively this chapter will provide a deeper insights of design techniques of ANN with respects to parameter optimization of ANN using meta heuristic method and also will discuss applications of ANN and MHOAs optimized ANN for umpteen number of real time applications.

Highlights of the chapter are briefed below:

- An overview of ANN weights optimization using two meta-heuristic algorithms: Genetic algorithm and Particle swarm optimization is provided.
- Brief discussion on ANN for few applications namely education, textile, tourism is provided which is not commonly found in literature. Most of the work published covers common applications of ANN restricted to medical field and agriculture domain.
- GA optimized ANN and PSO optimized ANN is covered in detail for umpteen numbers of applications.
- Summarized information of various meta heuristic methods for optimizing ANN and its applications is also deliberated.
- Recent advances and future applications of NNs are briefed.

OVERVIEW OF ANN

The ANN is a feed forward neural network (FFNN) structure which mostly has three layers namely input layer, hidden layer and output layer (figure 1). The training of ANN is the continuous optimization which is the mapping of input layer to output layer by setting the optimal set of weights and biases so as solve the problem in minimum number of iterations and minimum classification error. The outcome of the training a ANN is the connection weight matrix/ synaptic weights which decides the perfomance of ANN during test phase(Fan, 2012; Saravan, 2014). The back-propagation network (BPN) is the most popular traditional learning algorithm that is gradient-based used to train the ANN by back propagating the error estimated as the difference between the actual output and expected output at the output layer . The major loopholes of BPN are getting trapped in local minimum and slow convergence rates (Porchas, 2016;Abid, 2014). Other popularly used training methods include Newton method, Conjugate gradient, Quasi-Newton method and Levenberg-Marquardt algorithm.

For ANN modeling, the first and foremost operation is to define ANN topology/ architecture. It comprises of deciding the number of nodes in input layer (which is usually the number of input features for the given data set), number of hidden layers, number of nodes in each hidden layer, number of nodes in the output layer(representing the number of class labels for given data or the values to be predicted). Apart from topology, we need to set bias and connection weights based (usually set randomly) on defined ANN topology, momentum and the learning rate. The commonly used approach to train the ANN is back propagation, which involves updating the initially assigned random weights by back propagating the error at the output layer in the reverse order. The training process is repeated till the ANN produces desired minimum classification/prediction error or the user specified

Figure 1. Feed forward neural network of 3-4-1 topology

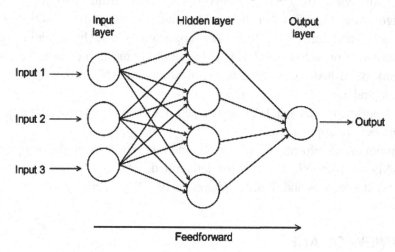

number of iterations(epochs) are reached. The variants of ANN include multilayer feed forward neural networks (MLFNN), time-delay neural networks (TDNN), recurrent neural networks (RNN), convolution neural networks (CNN), deep belief networks (DBN), radial basis function neural networks (RBFNN), wavelet neural networks (WNN), fuzzy neural networks (FNN) and many more.

META-HEURISTIC APPROACH TO OPTIMIZE ANN

The various ANN parameters can be optimized using MHOA which include: number of nodes in input layer (identify significant features which will decide the size of input layer), number of hidden layers, number of nodes in each hidden layer, bias, connection weights, momentum and learning rate. Learning most often is modeled as an optimization process, wherein the error is minimized as the learning takes place. Various nature inspired or soft computing-based algorithms have resolved intricate optimization problems where traditional or classical problem-solving methods fail. In recent years, enormous work has been done to optimize connection weights of ANNs using evolutionary algorithms, especially Evolution Strategy, Differential Evolution, and swarm-intelligent based approaches (Sharma, 2015). Green II et al. proposed a Central Force Optimization (CFO) method for training ANNs and found it performed better than PSO in terms of algorithm design, computational complexity, and natural basis. (Bolaji, 2016) proposed the fireworks algorithm and compared it against other established algorithms using different benchmark datasets. Faris et al. proposed the Lightening Search Algorithm (LSA) for finding optimal results and tested it with different measurements. (Karaboga, 2007) contributed Artificial Bee Colony (ABC) for optimizing weights in ANNs. (Aljarah,2016), developed the whale optimization algorithm to find optimal connection weights in MLP ANNs, which showed superior performance to those of other benchmark algorithms.

In this section, we will attempt to understand how MHOA are used to optimize connection weights for simple feed forward NN using (i) Genetic algorithm and (ii) particle swam optimization. In general, population based algorithm of MHOA is used to optimize the connection weights. The type of population depends on the optimization algorithm selected. Each member or search agent (P) of the population is considered as a K-dimensional vector (indicating K connection weights) and K is calculated as, $K = (I * H) + (H * O)$, where $I, H \, and \, O$ are the number of nodes in input layer, hidden layer and output layer; (I*H) indicates the number of connection weights between input layer and output layer; $(H * O)$ indicates the number of connection weights between the hidden and output layer. If we want to optimize the bias, leaning rate and momentum in addition to weights then the dimension of population member or agent will be

$$K = (I * H) + (H * O) + (H + O) + 2;$$

where $(I * H) + (H * O)$ is number of connection weights as explained above, $(H + O)$ for number of bias in hidden nodes and output layer, and 2 is one each for momentum and learning rate. The good optimization algorithm should maintain a proper trade-off between exploration and exploitation while maintaining its efficient search behavior to find "global" most optimal solution. The major objective of MHOA is to make sure that, the ANN does not get entangled in local optimum and avoid premature convergence. Since lot of literature exist on fundamentals of GA and PSO, henceforth details of working of GA and PSO is not covered in this chapter, instead a direct explanation of GA and PSO for optimizing FFN weights is explicated.

GA Optimized FFN Connection Weights (GAFFN)

GA has been used for optimizing the NN parameters which include: architecture (deciding the number of hidden layers and number of nodes in each hidden layer), and connections weights, bias, significant feature selection, activation function, learning rate, momentum and numbers of iterations. (Asha, 2013) have applied GA for optimizing the connection weights of FFN: GAFFN for diagnosis of PIMA diabetic dataset. The functioning of GAFFN for optimizing connection weights of FFN is briefed as follows.

1. The original population is a set of randomly generated N chromosomes. For a FFN with single hidden layer with H hidden nodes, I inputs nodes and O output nodes, the number of connection weights is equal to $(I* H) + (H*O)$. Each chromosome is made up of number of genes equal to total number of connection weights of FFN. Genes are represented by real number encoding method. For example, Figure 2 shows sample chromosome with 10 genes representing (3*2+2*2) connection weights for 3-2-2 topology network.

2. Repeat steps (c) - (f) until termination condition (80% of the chromosomes converge to the same fitness value or user set maximum iterations is reached.

3. Fitness of each chromosome is computed by maximum fitness method. For optimal connection weights, Fitness function is computed $(Ci) = 1 /E$, for each chromosome Ci of the population, where E is the error computed as mean square error (MSE) at the output layer. Less the MSE, more fit is the chromosome.

4. The best-fit chromosomes (lowest MSE) replace the worst fit chromosomes (Reproduction step).

5. Crossover step is implemented using single point crossover, two-point crossover and multi point crossover and mixed crossover is used. In mixed crossover, given M number of generation, multipoint crossover is applied for the first 60% of generation, followed by two point crossover for the next 20% generation and finally one point crossover for the remaining generations.

6. Mutation is applied by changing the weights of randomly selected chromosomes by multiplying it with a random number to generate the new population.

Figure 2. Chromosome in GA / Particle in PSO representing weights for 3-2-2 topology

W14	W15	W16	W24	W25	W26	W46	W47	W56	W57

The weights represented by the fittest chromosome (with least MSE) in the final population are the optimized connection weights of the FFN. Functioning of GAFFN is shown in Figure. 3(a).

Particle Swarm Optimization Algorithm (PSO)

For a FFN with single hidden layer with m nodes in hidden layer, I inputs nodes and O output nodes, the number of connection weights is given by $(I *H) +(H* O)$. The total number of connection weights of the FFN decides the number of dimensions of the PSO particle. The proposed PSOFFN algorithm is explained below (Asha 2013).

1. Initialize the original population as set of N particles (each particle representing connection Weights of NN), which is initially generated randomly.
2. Train the NN using particle (set connection weights using each particle figure 2).
3. Compute the learning error at output layer of NN. Fitness of each particle is computed by maximum optimization method. Compute Fitness $(Pi) = 1/E$ for each particle of the population, where E is the error computed as *MSE* at the output layer of NN as the difference between expected and estimated output.
4. Compare the particles current fitness value with particles *Pbest*. If the current fitness value of particle is better than the previous *Pbest* then set *Pbest* as current fitness value. If the current best fitness value is better than the previous *Gbest* then set *Gbest* as best current fitness value.
5. Compute the velocity and update position of each particle based on *Gbest* value (lowest learning error found in entire learning process so far) and *Pbest* value (each particles lowest learning error so far)
6. Repeat steps (b) - (e) until terminating condition is reached (user defined maximum iterations or minimum error criterion).

The *Gbest* positioned particle, represents the optimized connection weights for FFN. The performance of PSOFFN is measured using percentage of correctly classified test data. Functioning of PSOFFN is shown in Figure. 3(b)

FEW APPLICATIONS OF ANN IN EDUCATION SECTOR, TEXTILE AND TOURISM INDUSTRY

Having understood the basic functioning of ANN, in previous sections, this section covers ANN application to real-world problem in education sector, textiles and tourism Industry all of which play a vital role in national economy.

Application of ANN in Education

It is found that a substantial percentage of students are dropping out from colleges for various causes, which include lack of finance, family background, lack of interest, poor academic background etc. This results in loss of revenue to the institutes as well as reducing the percentage of graduates for the nation as whole. Hence in this regard lot of research is employed to study the student data so as to predict enrollment rates,

Figure 3. (a) GA optimized of FFN weights (b) PSO optimized FFN weights (Asha 2013)

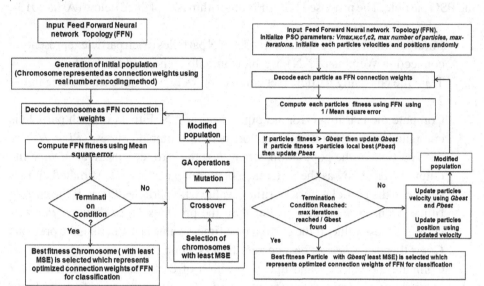

perseverance rates, and/or graduation rates. The educational performance of students is one of the major benchmark to associate the eminence of university students. ANN can play a major role in education to improve the proficiency of students in attaining high academic which in turn improves the ranking of the institution and standard of nation at global level.

In (Barker, 2004), ANNs and Support Vector Machines are applied to classify graduation rate of students at a 4-year course at an institution using total of 59 input features to describe each student in terms of demographic, academic, and attitudinal information. Both SVM and ANN resulted in accuracy rate of 63.4% for test data.

In (Stamos, 2008), authors have applied ANN with the following 11 input parameters: Ethnic Code, Gender, Current Age, Graduated High schools Code, Intention for enrolling college as intent code, Disability, Boolean variables Need disability services and Need support services, Zip code, Country, Age during high school graduation, Student's major while enrolling to college; hidden layer and with two nodes at output layer indicating Successful or not Successful case for student. The test data resulted in an accuracy of 70.27%.

In (Suknovic, 2014), authors have used six different methods for building neural network models: Quick, Dynamic, Multiple, Prune, RBFN and Exhaustive Prune with 15 input features (student gender, high school GPA and high school type, entrance exam points, individual grades at 11 examinations of the first year of elementary studies to predict GPA at the end their studies. They further experimented the work by identifying the top 6 relevant (which included grades at 11 exam, high school GPA and high school type) among the total 15 input features to get improved results. Among the six different methods of building NN model, the Exhaustive Prune method showed superior results with 0.253, 0.317, and 0.890 as absolute average error, standard deviation, and Linear correlation respectively with top six relevant features.

In (Oancea, 2017) ANN is used with 7 nodes input layer representing students age, gender (0/1 for M/F), part time/ full time (0/1), points scored at high school, break in number of years between high school and higher education; two hidden layers and output layer with three nodes, to predict GPA (as poor, medium or good) in the first year of study of higher education. Authors have adopted various training algorithms: backpropagation, quick propagation, classical resilient propagation, scaled conjugate gradient and got superior results using version of Resilient backpropagation called RPROP with an overall accuracy of 86%.

In (Mason,2017), authors aim to adopt probabilistic neural network (PNN) to study engineering student attrition. This data consist of student attributes related to demographics and academic background of engineering student attrition. Among the various attributes collected, the following 14 selected were selected: First term end exam Cumulative GPA, Maths GPA, total credit, highest math course, cumulative earned hours at the end of first term, Summation score, ACT math imputed, Age, total expenses for first term, Financial aid semester award amount, Financial aid offer accepted (yes/no), Income levels Scale and College division of major Categorical. Results are compared with logistic regression, a multi-layer perceptron artificial neural network, and PNN. Performance is measured using accuracy, sensitivity, specificity and overall results. The sensitivity (detecting non-retained students) was found to be 65.4%, 72.2% and 76.9% for the logistic regression model, MLP and PNN respectively. Prediction accuracy of PNN was found be less compared to other two models, but PNNs better sensitivity was more important to detect a student who will, without intervention, eventually leave engineering.

In (Lau, 2019), the ANN with 11-30-30-1 topology with hyperbolic tangent function is used with following 11 input nodes in input layer pertaining to students background information like gender, location, repeating or not repeating students, earlier school location, occupation of parents, and entrance exam results for five subjects: Chinese, English, Maths, Comprehensive Science and Proficiency test and one single node in output layer for prediction of students CGPA. The principle component analysis is used to reduce the dimensionality and for this data resulted in five best components so to avoid over-fitting. The performance was measured using Mean Square Error (MSE), regression analysis, error histogram, the area under the ROC curve (AUC) and confusion matrix. Levenberg–Marquardt algorithm is used to determine the optimal weights of ANN during training phase and resulted in prediction accuracy of 84.8% and AUC value of 0.86.

In (AYbek, 2018), authors have used MLP and RBF for predicting the final exam scores and pass/fail rates of the students taking the Basic Information Technologies Basic Information Technologies course as part of Open Education System (OES) of Anadolu University. The following input features were identified for the work which included: Demographic(Year of birth, TR identity no, Nationality, Gender, Province), Educational Background (Year of Graduation from the High School, University entrance score (UES), High school type, High school code, High School GPA, Foreign Language, UES Score type, Quota type, University placement ranking), Open education system(Mid-term exam, final exam, letter grade), and Other (Mid-term exam, final exam, letter grade). 12 MLPs were executed with different combination of six parameters which include number of hidden layers, number of nodes in hidden layer, batch training (weights updates at end of all training data) or online training (weights updates at end of each training record), activation function: hyperbolic tangent and sigmoidal, data standardized (data range [0,1] or normalized (data range in [-1,1]). The RBF was also executed with four various combinations of three parameters: Hidden Layer, Activation Function and scaling of Continuous Variables. Importance levels, correlation and determination coefficients of the independent variables are used to evaluate the performance of both MLP and RBF. MLP was found to make better prediction of pass/fail rates of students compared to RBF. It was also observed that few of input features namely mid-term exam scores, university entrance scores and secondary school graduation year proved to play a vital role in elucidation of prediction of final exam scores and pass/fail rates of the students.

Teaching professional career need to acquire large number of competencies and skills, pressure to handle various students and their parents, completion with peers leads to lot of physical and mental stress and hence resulting in teacher's burnout Syndrome. (Ilda, 2017) have applied ANN to predict professional burnout issues related to teachers. They collected the various parameters related to science teachers which include: Sureness on the field information of science teachers, Sureness on the performance of science teacher, Sureness on the lab knowledge of science teacher, Competence of science teacher, Depersonalization in science teachers and Personal achievement in science teachers. The work resulted in performance of ANN network with 40%, 50%, 20% and 80% for prediction of Emotional exhaustion, Personal success, Depersonalization and Competence respectively.

There is tremendous hike in the percentage of students involved in online learning. MLP has been used by (Zacharis, 2016) to predict students performance and resulted in an accuracy of 98.3% using four learning activities as inputs from the Moodle server: communication via emails, collaborative content creation with wiki, content interaction measured by files viewed and self-evaluation through online quizzes.

The authors claim that the model can be further extended to help the instructors to plan accordingly to enhance the success rates of students based on predicted results.

RBF, MLP, PNN, and SVM has been applied to predict the learning performances of medical students (Dharmasaroja, 2016). The data related to medical neuroscience course, in two academic years was garnered which includes demographics -gender, high-school backgrounds, first-year grade-point averages, and composite scores of examinations (normalized T-scores of raw scores of MCQ examinations, laboratory examinations, laboratory post-tests, and post-tests of small-group/PBL/TBL sessions) during the course have been applied to predict the learning performance of medical students. Performance is measured in terms of accuracy, sensitivity, specificity, positive predictive value (PPV), negative predictive value (NPV), F-measure, and areas under the receiver operating characteristic (ROC) curves (AUC). Accuracies of RBF, MLP, PNN, and SVM were almost same (in between 98.1 to 99.5%).

ANN Applications in Textiles Industry

ANN and logistic regression have been extensively used by research fraternity for predicting different kinds of yarn and fabric properties. Drape is the ability of a fabric to fall under its own weight into wavy folds. From the designer point of view, the drape property has a vital role in aesthetic appeal of fabric and hence of great importance in textile market. Drapability of fabric is accessed manually and hence differs based on individual skill and experience. In (Amine, 2018), ANN has been used to predict fabric drapability using fabric mechanical properties measured by the Fabric Assurance by Simple Testing (FAST). The following seven input features: Warp count (tex), Weft count (tex), Picks per centimeter, Ends per centimeter, Weight (g/m2), Formability on weft direction in mm2 and Formability on warp direction in mm2 were provided to ANN to predict the five grades of the Drapability from 1 as low drapability to 5 as excellent drapability. A high positive correlation coefficient of 0.86 was obtained between actual and ANN predicted drapability.

Tensile strength is the key characteristic that discriminates it from non-woven and knitted fabric. The more is the crimp in the yarn, the more extensible is the fabric. The air permeability, is mainly dependent on fabrics weight, thickness and porosity, and is equally vital factor to access the quality of few textile materials and is in particular given more importance for clothing which include parachutes, sails, vacuum cleaner, fabrics for air bags and industrial filter fabrics. Tensile properties, breaking extension and air permeability of woven fabrics were anticipated using ANN and regression models (Ghada, 2015). The input layer has three variables: weft yarn count (Ne), twist multiplier and weft density (ppi). Dependent variables used to predict the tensile strength, breaking extension and air permeability. The outcomes of the work clearly states that ANN outperformed regression modes in terms of RMSE, absolute error and correlation coefficient R2 value. The RMSE was found to be 4.477 and 1.08; and R2 as 0.951 and 1.0 for regression model and ANN respectively for prediction of air permeability of the woven fabrics. In addition the RMSE was found to be 1.24 and 0.0006; and R2 as 0.67 and 0.99 for regression model and ANN respectively for prediction of breaking extension of the woven fabrics. Furthermore, the RMSE was found to be 3.072 and 0.0; and R2 as 0.87 and 1.0 for regression model and ANN respectively for prediction of tensile strength.

Core-spun yarns are structures entailing 2 constituent fibers: corn yarn (marks the mechanical properties of yarn, enhances yarn strength) and sheath or covering (causes surface physical and esthetic properties). The tensile properties of core-spun yarn is widely used to measure the performance various post-spinning operations like warping, weaving, knitting, final textile products etc., henceforth there is need for precise prediction of tensile properties. ANN and logistic regression has been used (Almetwally, 2014) to predict the tensile properties of cotton core-spun. ANN model with 3-12-1 topology with one-neuron output layer at a time, aiming on tensile properties of cotton/spandex corespun yarn, i.e. breaking strength (cN), breaking elongation (%), and work of rupture (N cm). The input layer has three nodes representing: linear density of core part (spandex linear density, dtex), drawing ratio of the spandex filament (%), and twist multiplier. The RMSE was 4.87 and 27.45 ; Mean bias error (MBE) was 1.35 and 1.81; and correlation coefficient was 0.99 and 0.71 for ANN and multiple regression model respectively.

In addition to food industry, textile industry also plays a vital role in the increase of foreign exchange. Manual assessment of fabric quality is done with human eye which is not only time consuming but also erroneous. The manual inspection volume may not balance with production volume and hence has impact on the consumer demand. Image processing and ANN is used to classify defects in the fabric as substitute for human inspection and henceforth reduces the inspection time and upsurge the accuracy level of defect identification. ANN has been applied to classify the fabric as normal, wrap defect, empty feed defect and oil defect by using GLCM features (Mulyana, 2017). Accuracy result obtained for test data was 88.75% with an average inspection time for classification of 80 data in real time as 0.56 seconds when compared to average manual scanning time of 19.87 seconds.

Woven fabric properties mainly include yarn parameters: yarn count, twist factor, twist direction, spinning type, and the fabric constructional parameters: weave structure, warp density, cover factor, weft yarn density and tightness factor. Among these parameters, the Tightness factor also known fabric firmness is the key parameter which prominently affects the woven fabric properties. (Nassif, 2018) attempted to predict the tightness degree of cotton-spandex stretchable woven fabric at various levels of spandex ratio and linear density using ANN (3-20-1 topology), linear and logarithmic regression models. A total of 36 woven cotton stretchable fabrics with different weave structures (plain 1/1, twill 2/2 and satin 5), spandex draw ratio (four different draw ratios, i.e. 2, 3, 4 and 5 y) and spandex linear density were woven (20,40 and 80 dtex) was identified as input to ANN to predict the tightness factor The learning method of the ANN is accomplished using Levenberg–Marquardt algorithm, sigmoid as activation function. RMSE values 0.00013, 0.02825 and 0.0268; correlation coefficient R2 values 0.999, 0.867 and 0.891; and MBE of 0.00009, 0.02431 and 0.0239 was obtained with ANN, multiple regression and logarithmic regression respectively.

Even though fabrics are distributed to garment manufacturers from finishing facilities with the desired values, it is found that during the cloth take-up process and cloth spreading process throughout garment manufacturing increase total internal tensions in the fabric and henceforth the garment manufacturers complain about the dimensional change issues. In this context, ANN has been used to correctly estimate the dimensional changes in fabrics and accordingly estimate dimensional changes in a garment. Kalkanci(2017) used dimensional measure properties of T-shirts using ANN. The ANN has 5 nodes in the input layer representing fabric type, fabric code, measurement table for sizes, ironed, measurement point. The fabric type were of four types (S[Single, jersey], LS[single,sersey, lykra], INT[interlock], LINT[interlock/lykra]) coded as 1,2,3,4). The fabric code was represented as numbers in the range of 1 to 18 and measurement size as XS, M and XL represented as 37, 41 and 47. The ironed parameter was taken as 1 and 2 for before ironing and after ironing so as determining the ironing effect. The measurement point such as chest, waist, hips, Length from shoulder, Shoulder to shoulder, Arm hole, Arm length, Sleeve hem, Collar pit, Front collar drop, Back collar drop, were replaced with numerical values of 1, 2, 3, 4, 5, 6, 7, 8, 9, 10 and 11, respectively. ANN resulted in correlation coefficient R2 of 0.99872 and MSE of 0.60535.

Yarn strength depends on roving's characteristics and spinning process. During yarn spinning process one of the vital parameters to be controlled is yarn strength. Technicians predict the Yarn strength using knowledge about various fiber parameters like fiber strength, the fiber length, the twist yarn, the yarn count, and the fineness. The laborious task is solved by (Furferi, 2010) using ANN for predicting the yarn strength and achieved a mean error less than 4%. The data considered for work has 6 different families of roving's for different type of fabrics with values of fiber strength, fiber length, twist yarn, and yarn. Results proved to better that multiple regression model.

Bleach washing and use of enzymatic treatment are two conventional technologies used in fabric industry to create design by fading of color. Cotton Denim fabric used for jeans uses cellulase as part of enzymatic treatment to create good color. This method has various drawback, to list a few are difficult to apply, time consuming, not easy to create new design, difficult to get the color effect to all textile surface and in application, and resulting in poor quality fabric if the process is out of control. An ANN with Bayesian regulation back propagation (Kan, 2013) was applied to predict the color properties and color yield of cotton denim fabric after undergoing the cellulase treatment. The fabric yarn twist level and the following cellulase treatment processing factors: treatment temperature (temperature), treatment time (time), pH (pH), and mechanical agitation (MA) formed the input layer of the ANN model. The output layer had six nodes representing color-ks, color-l, color-a, color-b, color-candcolor-h to be predicted. Work was done with changing the number of hidden nodes and adopting both one and two hidden layers. The ANN results proved to excellent compared to that of linear regression model. Figure 4 illustrate how ANN model predicted are matching with and actual values for color-l compared to that of linear regression model prediction. Similar results were obtained for the other colors also.

Figure 4. (a) ANN model fitting for color-l (b) Linear regression model fitting for color-l
(Kan, 2013)

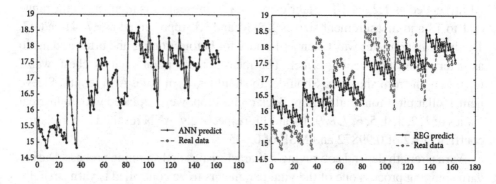

Applications of ANN for Tourism

In addition to food industry, fabric industry, and many more applications, Tourism also plays a vital role in national economy. In fact, tourism industry is one of the world largest employer option. Hence there is tremendous need for development strategy for Tourism to accurately predict the tourism demand. There are many factors affecting the tourism demand which include: population, gross national product, financial status, Qualification, age, weather, travel distance and time, prices, etc. Xiaofeng(2019) have used the following factors as input to ANN model Number of inbound tourists, Currency exchange rate, Per capita GDP of both source and destination countries, Total import and export of goods, Population, Virtual variables(special events), Per capita GDP of the destination country to predict the tourism demand. Performance is measured using MSE and determination coefficient R2. ANN (trained using back propogation) model results outperformed results of support vector machine (SVM) and autoregressive integrated moving average (ARIMA) model at a regional level.

Cankurt (2016) have compared the performance of 3 methods: multiple linear regression (MLR), MLP regression, and support vector regression (SVR) for multivariate tourism forecasting for Turkey. The dataset was collected during Jan 1996 to Dec 2013 (67 time series) with respect to Turkey for 26 major tourism clients. SVR resulted in better results with relative absolute error (RAE) of 12.34% and root relative squared error (RRSE) of 14.02% (figure 5).

Figure 5. ANN model fitting for number of tourists using MLR, MLP, SVR and Actual (Cankurt, 2016)

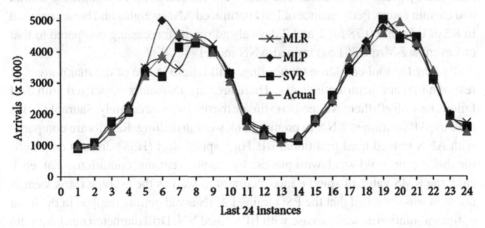

Panarat(2017) have applied feed forward network of 8-1-1 topology to forecast the airline passengers. Data during 1993-2016 was collected with input parameters of world GDP, world population growth, world jet fuel prices, world air fares (proxy for air travel cost), Australia's tourism attractiveness, outbound flights, Australia's unemployment levels, the Australian and United States foreign exchange rate and three dummy variables (Sydney Olympics, 9/11 and the 2006 Commonwealth Games) to predict the Australia's Outbound Passenger Air Travel Demand. The following five measures were used in the present study: mean square error (MSE), the root mean square error (RMSE), mean absolute error (MAE), mean absolute percentage error (MAPE), and correlation coefficient (R) goodness-of-fit measures:

mean absolute error (MAE), mean square error (MSE), root mean square errors (RMSE), AND mean absolute percentage errors (MAPE). ANN obtained R-value of 0.99733 proving its efficient predictive capability.

APPLICATIONS OF PSO OPTIMIZED ANN

This section covers few of applications of PSO optimized ANN.

Since several water bodies are drying, Iran faces water scarcity problem, henceforth there was a need to develop precise model to simulate the rainfall -runoff processing in Karaj basin so as to support the related administrations to handle water scarcity problem. The proper water resource planning depends on the precise forecasting of river flow on daily basis. In (Hamed, 2017), ANN has been applied for reliable rainfall runoff model which can provide information for water planning and supervision for Kajra river in Iran. The 5 years data pertaining to daily precipitation and runoff recorded by gauges were used. The data were collected from hydrometric station and the rain gauge. Performance of PSO optimized ANN weights and biases resulted in R2 of 0.88 and 0.78 for 1 and 2 days ahead runoff forecasting compared to that of Levenberg-Mrquadt(LM) trained ANN model.

Among the tool condition monitoring, drill failure is one of the major areas of research in manufacturing industry. There are various factors associated with drill failure, henceforth there is a need to estimate the drill were accurately. Saurabh(2014) have used PSO trained ANN to predict flank wear in drilling. Results are compared with ANN trained used traditional BP. High speed steel (HSS) drills is employed for drilling on mild steel workpieces, by varying cutting conditions. For each case, the RMS value of spindle motor current as well as the average flank wear is noted. It was observed that the PSO trained ANN avoid getting trapped in the local optimum solution as was the case with BP trained NN. Drill diameter(mm), Spindle speed(rpm), Feed rate (mm/rev), Motor current sensor value (rpm) are input nodes.

Zhang(2000), have adopted two interleaved PSO: outer PSO (particle with integer values) for architecture optimization (to optimize the number of nodes in the hidden layer) and inner PSO for MLP weight optimization. (Marcio, 2000) also have used two interleaved PSO as used by Zhang(2000) with a small alteration done in use of weight decay heuristic in the inner PSO for the MLP weight adjustment. Work is carried out on commonly used benchmark medical data for classification problems of Cancer, Diabetes and Heart from machine learning repository. 50% training data was used for inner PSO to optimize weights, 25% validation data was used by outer PSO for architecture optimization (with one hidden layer) and remaining 25% for testing the MLP network. Results obtained by (Marcio, 2000) are better compared to those obtained by Zhang(2000). Results were also compared with other methods which include Evolutionary Programming (EP), Genetic Algorithm trained MLP, Tabu Search(TS), Simulated Annealing(SA) and Yamazaki Methodology(TS +SA). The proposed method results were in between those obtained by EP and GA. Performance was evaluated using Mean Classification Error Percentage (CEP) and standard deviation (σ) for each algorithm.

The slope stability can used as measure to ensure a safe and low cost design of the various structures. Hence prediction of slope stability is one the major concern in geotechnical engineering during earthquake. (Behrouz, 2016) have used PSO trained ANN to predict factor of safety (FOS) of homogenous slope. The input for the PSO-ANN model was slope height, gradient, cohesion, friction angle and peak ground acceleration. The performance of proposed PSO-ANN was compared with ANN using RMSE, VAF and R2 measures. R2 values obtained was 0.915 and 0.986 for ANN and PSO–ANN model.

One of the major subjects of interest for investors and decision makers in predicting failures in financial sector. Fathima(2019) proposed solution for banking sector bankruptcy prediction using ANN trained via 3 different combination of PSO and Simulated Annealing (SA) as depicted in figure 6. In all the three methods, the outer PSO is used to find the optimal number of hidden nodes for ANN. In PSO-PSO method, inner PSO for ANN weight optimization. In PSO-PSO-SA method, the inner PSO with SA is used to find optimal ANN weights. In PSO-improved PSO-SA, the inner improved PSO with SA is used to find the ANN optimal weights. The improved PSO is based on the assumption that learning process is based on bad experiences in addition to good experiences. Multivariate Discriminant Analysis (MDA), Logistic Regression (LR) and Decision Tree (DT) are used to find significant features as input for input layer of ANN. Number of features selected by DA, LR and DT was 8, 13 and 16 respectively. Among the different combination, the best results for Bankrupt and Non-bankrupt prediction was found to be 73.5% and 92.2% respectively using PSO-improved PSO-SA with DT identified features.

Metal Bending is one of the activities which consumes lot of time. Springback happens owing to residual stress in the metal sheet while bending process. After removal of punch on the metal, the springback takes place and the change in the wall angle 'a', is defined to be a measure of distortion. Therefore, a suitable prediction method is required to predict the springback angle. Springback is subjective to various parameters like thickness of the sheet, grease conditions, tooling geometry and material properties. Sathish(2018) have used PSO optimized ANN weights for predicting the springback effect of metal sheet while bending of the sheet (Sathish, 2018)

The plastic injection cost comprises of design/R&D cost, mold cost, and molding products cost. Che(2010) have used amalgamation of factor analysis (FA), PSO and ANN with 2 BPNs (shown in figure 7) called FAPSO-TBP (shown in figure 8) and

Figure 6. PSO & SA based ANN optimization with features extracted by MDA, LR & DT
(Fathima, 2019)

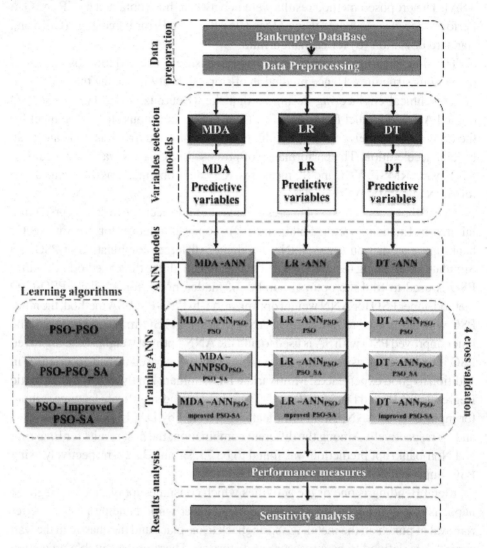

one BPN called FAPSO-SBP to predict the mold cost and molding product cost for plastic injection molding. FAPSO-TBP showed better and stable results (shown in figure 9,10) in terms of cost Percentage error compared to FAPSO-SBP and ANN trained using BP (Che, 2010).

Huge amount of chlorophenol compounds which are exceedingly toxic and resistant to biological degradation are found in wastewater produced from various industry. Electro-oxidation is very costly but rapid, efficient, environment friendly

Figure 7. FAPSO with two BPN using total of 16 input features to predict product and mold cost
(Che,2010)

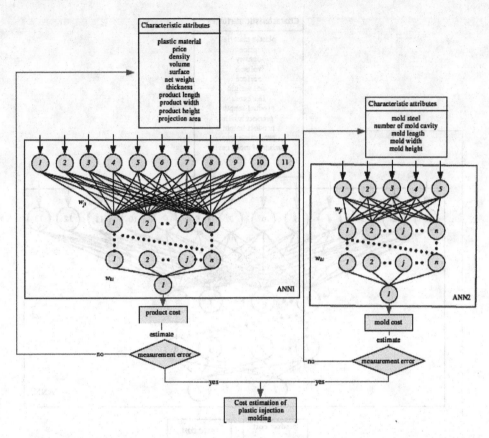

method, and doesn't use extra reagents to remove chlorophenol compounds from wastewater. Compared to traditional mathematical models, ANN model are found to be more reliable for predicting the behavior of electrochemical oxidation processes at low energy cost. Yu Mei(2019) have used PSO trained ANN to predict (i) COD removal efficiency & (ii) total energy consumption (TEC) of electro-oxidation (Mei, 2019). The proposed PSO-ANN model (figure 11) provide appreciable results with R2 of 0.99 and 0.9944 for COD removal efficiency and TEC, and MSE values of 0.0015526 and 0.0023456 respectively for the testing dataset. The weight matrix of PSO-ANN provided the relative importance of input variables (with current density: 18.85%, original pH:21.11%, electrolyte concentration: 19.69%, electro-oxidation time: 21.30%, ORP 19.05%) on the value of COD removal efficiency and TEC.

Tourist wish to cover maximum tourist spots on each day of trip in tourist city. It is important to have proper selection of tourist spots, in order to visit those

Figure 8. FAPSO with single BPN using 13 input features to predict product & mold cost (Che,2010)

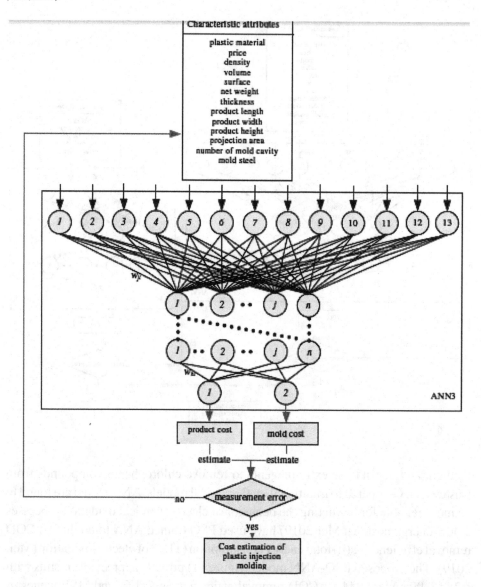

spots and optimal route to those spots to make trip worth for the tourist. In this context, Sehrish Malik(2019) have proposed optimal route recommendation to (i) predict the next tourist attraction using ANN using input parameters: past routes, season, day, time & vehicles on route and (ii) predict the optimal route (with input parameters as distance, road congestion, weather conditions, route popularity, and

Figure 9. Cost Percentage Errors of FAPSO-SBP and FAPSO-TBP for product cost (Z.H. Che(2010)

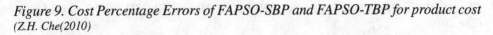

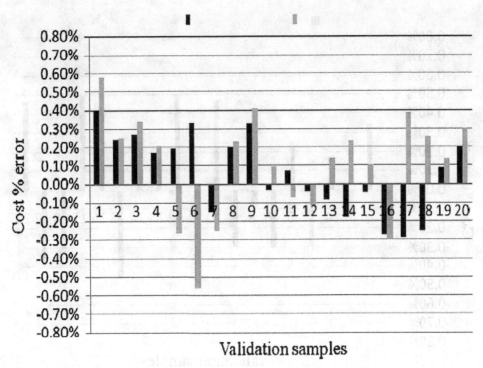

user preference) to the foretold location by ANN using PSO. These can be used in navigation applications by drivers to get better routes for their trips. Distance, road congestion, weather conditions, route popularity, and user preference are used as route parameters as input to objective function for the route Optimization. In this work PSO, is not used to optimize ANN parameters but an amalgamation of ANN (to predict optimal tourist spot) and PSO (to find optimal route to ANN predicted tourist spot) is done to assist tourist to cover maximum spots in minimum time. Work is carried on tourism data form 2016-17 of Jeju Island of South Korea. The data used is the tourism data of Jeju Island from December. Overall model is presented in figure 12. Detailed design of ANN for prediction of next tourist spot is shown in figure 13. Detailed design of optimal route to ANN predicted next tourist spot is shown in figure 14. Both the algorithms gave same optimized route as output using the proposed objective function. Prediction accuracy of next tourist spot of PSO optimized ANN was superior than ANN, SVM, random forest, (RF), and naive Bayes (NB). In the similar lines they have used GA optimized ANN to find optimal path to the next tourist spot. Performance of both GA and PSO were good. Compared to PSO, GA took more number of iterations and hence more time to find optimal route.

Figure 10. Cost percentage errors of FAPSO-SBP and FAPSO-TBP for mold cost (Che, 2010)

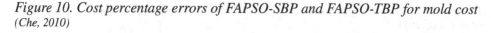
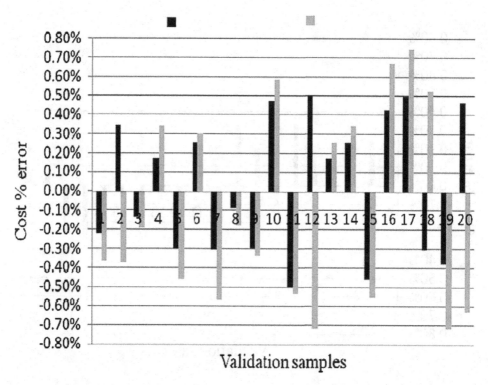

Validation samples

APPLICATIONS OF GA OPTIMIZED ANN

Monjenzi (2012) have used GA optimized ANN to predict fly rock and back break in blasting operation of the Sungun copper mine, Iran. Fly rock and back break are the most adverse happenings of the blasting operations. The following parameters of ANN: number of nodes in hidden layer (1-30), the learning rate (0 to1), and the momentum (0-1) is represented as genes in a chromosome string of GA. The GA identified optimal number of hidden layer was nodes found to be 16 with 0.58 and 0.46 learning rate and momentum. The following 9 parameters are the inputs: Hole diameter (mm) as D, Hole length (m) as L, Spacing (m) as S, Burden (m) as B, Stemming (m) as T, Powder factor (kg/ton) as Pf, Specific drilling(m/m3) as SD, Charge per Delay (kg) as Ch and RMR) Output Fly rock (m) Fly rock 20–100 to GA-ANN model to predict fly rock and back break (figure 15). Performance was measured using MSE, NMSE, and determination coefficient R2. Multivariable regression analysis resulted in R2 value of 0.58 showing poor correlation between the parameters and flyrock ; and 0.42 for backbreak. Contrary to this, GA-ANN

Figure 11. PSO-ANN model for predicting COD removal efficiency and total energy consumption
(Yu Mei, 2019)

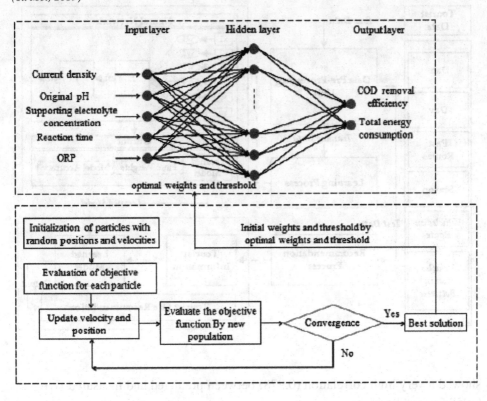

Figure 12. Overall proposed model for Site prediction using ANN & route optimization using PSO
(Sehrish Malik, 2019)

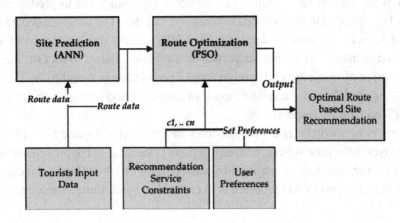

Figure 13. Detailed model for predicting next tourist spot using ANN
(Sehrish Malik, 2019)

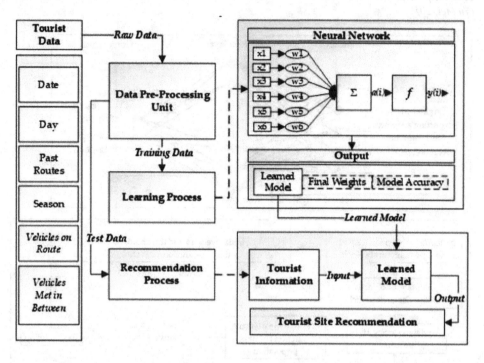

showed a very high correlation (0.978) between predicted and measured flyrock ; 0.958 for backbreak.

International standard refers high speed rails as the one with speed above 250km/hr. China aims to achieve 38000 km by 2025 to strengthen the connection between provinces, cities and countries. Since the traditional means of tourism demand prediction cannot meet the precision requirements of the high-speed railway era, Meiyu Wang (2019) have applied GA based ANN (figure 16) to predict tourism demand by optimizing the threshold values and weights. The time series data (1990 to 2014 samples as training data and 2015-2016 as test data) is used to forecast the tourist demand and economic growth of Sanjiang County. With GA, the ANN relative error of domestic and foreign tourist population is found to be 12.23 and 4.95% respectively and the relative error of domestic and foreign tourism income as 1.84% and 1.82% respectively.

There is noteworthy rise of ultraviolet radiation (UVR) due to depletion of Ozone layer in the atmosphere; henceforth there is increase in the prevalence of skin cancers in countries like Australia and South Africa which have high solar exposure. One of the solutions to this problem is to cover skin by clothing. There are various

Figure 14. Detailed route optimization using PSO to tourist spot predicted by ANN (Sehrish Malik, 2019)

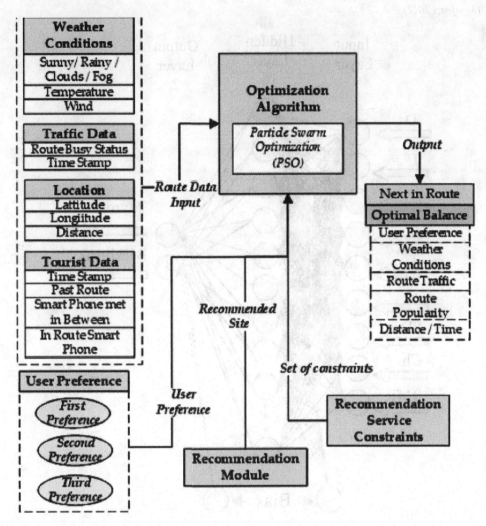

parameters which influence the UV protection capacity which include fiber type, yarn structure, fabric cover factor, fabric areal density, fabric thickness, finishing process, coloration process and presence of UVR absorbers. Ultraviolet protection factor (UPF) indicates the UV protective capacity of fabric. A comfortable fabric must allow transmission of air permeability (AP) and moisture vapor transmission rate (MVTR) in addition to UV protective property. The major problem is by increasing UPF, reduces the fabric comfort factor of AP and MVTR. Thus Fabric designing is a multi-objective problem to have sought after levels of conflicting to each other parameter: UPF, AP and MVTR simultaneously. Abhijit(2015) have endeavored the

Figure 15. GA-ANN (optimized number of hidden nodes, learning rate and momentum) to predict flyrock and backbreak
(Monjenzi 2012)

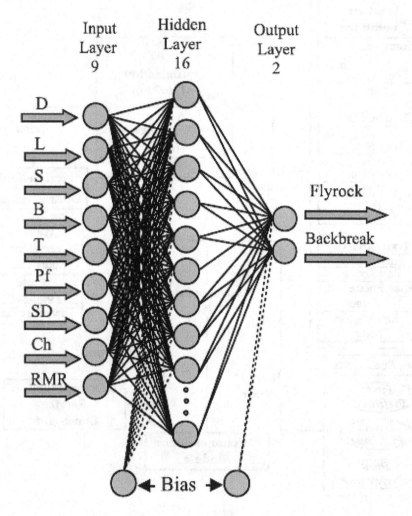

above mentioned fabric multi objective problem by finding optimal combination of UPF, AP and MVTR using GA based ANN (figure 17) with following input parameters: fiber blend proportion in yarn, yarn count (warp and weft) and thread density (ends per inch and picks per inch). Separate ANN models with one hidden layer (4 hidden nodes) was trained by Levenberg–Marquardt algorithm. The result of ANN was compared with GA trained ANN. The encoding of GA chromosome representing the search space with five input variables (each of 14 bits) indicating the overall proportion of polyester in fabric. Example of the 30 bit binary encoded chromosome indicating the binary values of five inputs is shown in figure 18.

Figure 16. Meiyu Wang (2019) proposed GA-ANN to optimize weights and thresholds to predict tourist demand and economic growth

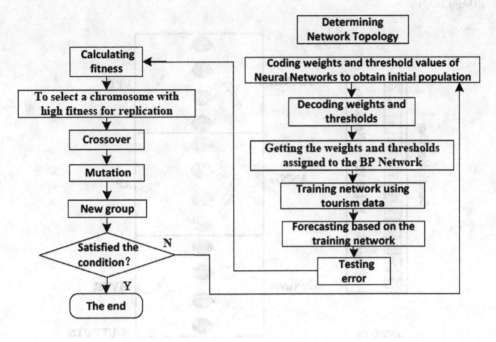

Results prove, the hybrid ANN–GA system was precise in attaining targeted fabric functional properties.

Noersasongko(2016) have used GA to optimize the 3 parameters of BPNN: learning rate, training cycle and momentum to predict tourist arrival. The findings reveal that GA-ANN resulted in very small RMSE compared to BPNN, K-Nearest Neighbor (KNN) and Multiple Linier Regression (MLR).

One of the major sources of electric power industry which is both low cost as well as environment friendly is wind power. Precise prediction of wind power production is used for various tasks which include optimal generation scheduling, maintenance scheduling, load shedding and various diction making process. Yordanos (2018) have proposed hybrid GA and PSO algorithms to optimize the weights and bias of ANN model for predicting wind power. The dataset has wind speed and the corresponding turbine output power data of the aforesaid period. Initially the ANN model starts with randomly generated weights and bias which decide the size of candidate solution for both PSO and GA. The fitness function of both GA and PSO are compared. If PSO best particle is better than the GA best chromosome, then the genes of best chromosome is replaced by PSO solution. If GA solution is best then, best particle's variables are replaced by the genes of best GA chromosome. In either case for the next new iteration, both GA and PSO begin with the best global

Figure 17. Hybrid ANN–GA Model to predict the optimal combination of UPF, AP and MVTR
(Abhijit 2015)

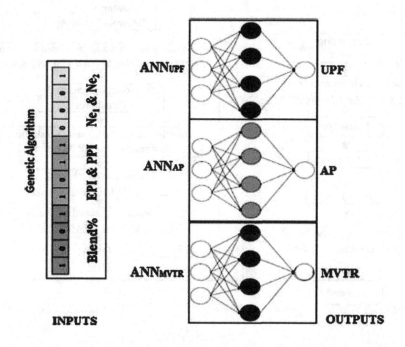

solution among the both. Mean squared error (MSE), root mean square error (RMSE), mean absolute error (MAE), normalized mean absolute error (NMAE), and mean absolute percentage error (MAPE) are used as performance evaluation measures. Results prove that prediction of wind power using hybrid PSO-GA-ANN are better

Figure 18. Sample binary encoded chromosome of size 30 representing the five genes of 6 bits each for five input features
(Abhijit 2015).

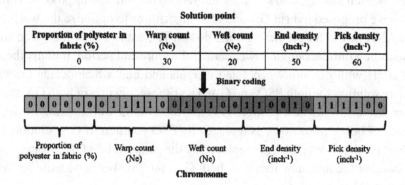

(with highest and lower errors of 12.55% and 1.2% respectively) than PSO-ANN and GA-ANN model. The proposed hybrid model yielded highest and lowest errors of 12.55% and 1.2% respectively

Arya (2018) have used GA to optimize the ANN weights to predict rainfall for Goa region. As part of data pre-processing, the missing values in the time series data was handled using List wise deletion method followed by use PCA to extract five significant input features: SST, SLP, Humidity, U-wind, V-wind of IO region. SOM and k-mediods are used to cluster rainfall values. SOM resulted in better clusters than k-mediods. Finally the GA-ANN is used to predict the rainfall. The accuracy of BPNN and GA-NN was found to be 92.78 and 98.78

Lalita(2009) applied GA to optimize the various parameters of ANN to predict yarn properties in spinning process of Textile industry. Each chromosome is encoded as to include the following NN parameters to be optimized: number of nodes in hidden layers, transfer function, learning rate, momentum and number of epochs with MSE as the fitness function. GA resulted in NN which can predict the fiber properties from given yarn properties Uniformity Ratio, Tenacity, Elongation, Count, Thin, Thick, Neps and CSP respectively. The quality of any yarn spun from cotton depends on fiber quality chiefly, Span Length(SL), Uniformity Ratio(UR), Short Fibre Index(SFI), Micronaire(MIC), Strength(STR) and Trash(TR), henceforth selection of cotton is very important for a better end product design.

In textile industry, yarn tenacity is most vital property of yarn production. Dasti(2014) have used GA to find the optimal input values to obtain desired yarn tenacity keeping minimum production cost. Seven fibers characteristics are used as input: Fiber Tenacity (CN/Tex), Fiber Elongation, %50 Average Length, length uniformity, Micronaire Reflection Degree, Yellownes. Firstly, the ANN is trained independent of GA using backpropagation to find the optimal NN topology. As part of second step, GA is used on NN topology of first step to determine optimal input values to attain the desired yarn tenacity at minimum production cost. Performance is measured error value and coefficient determination. The fitness function of GA is multigoal problem, keeping the production cost as minimum and attaining the tenacity of produced yarn to be equal and more than the desired tenacity. One can use the proposed model by first determining the desired tenacity of yarn, followed by assigning the weights of input material propositional to the cost of material. The GA will be used to predict the amount of input material needed for yarn production keeping two goals: minimum production cost and produced yarn has desired yarn tenacity. GA is not used to optimize the ANN weights in the proposed method.

Eutrophication is excess contents of nutrients in water body which leads to growth of aquatic plants, henceforth create problems for water supply, fishery etc. Nitrogen and phosphorus are the two major controllable nutrients loads used to control eutrophication. Jan-Tai (2006) have applied ANN to simulate watershed nutrient model based on data from nutrient loads, average and maximum rainfall in the watershed, and outflow to forecast phosphorus concentration in the reservoir. The GA is applied with ANN model to optimize nutrient control from the watershed to forecast the total phosphorus concentration in the reservoir and compared with total phosphorus (TP) model figure 19. The fitness of each chromosome is assessed using an objective function which comprises of one measure to represent the minimum treatment level (i.e. sum of the square of the phosphorus reduction rates is the

Figure 19. GA based ANN for water quality model

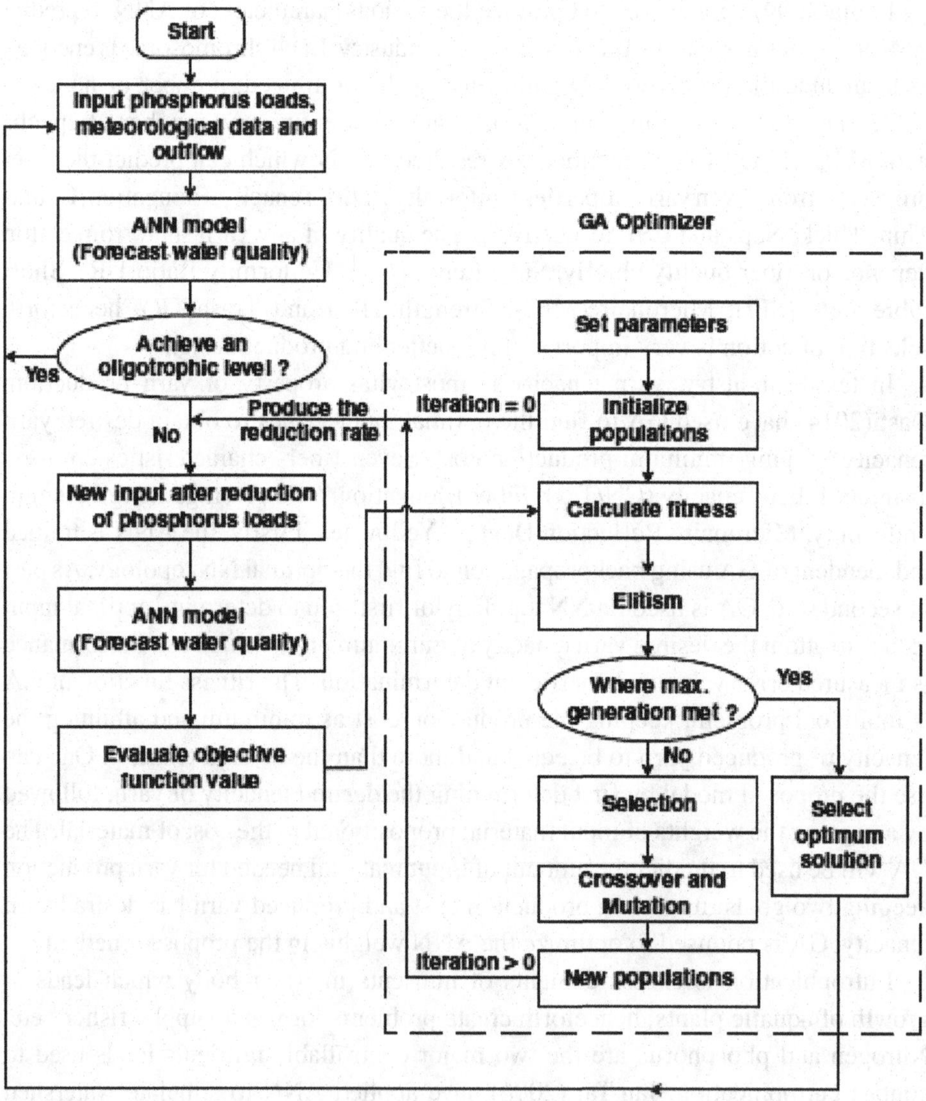

minimum). The GA-ANN method provides precise information which can be used by decision makers to manage reservoir eutrophication control.

Dezdemona(2014) have applied GA optimized neural network to forecast the tourist number and to regulate the trends of the future tourist inflow; henceforth serving Albania tourism agencies in financial decision. A total of 99 months data (number of tourist) from Jan 2005 to June 2013, was collected for the work. Results of both ANN and GA-ANN were compared with Exponential Smoothing model to validate their accuracy. Han-chen(2017) applied GA to find the optimal number of hidden nodes of ANN to predict Air ticket sales revenue (T month). GA identified ANN optimal network architecture was 12-142-1. The 12 input nodes represented NTD/USD exchange rate, the number of people traveling abroad from Taiwan each month, the international oil price, the Taiwan stock market weighted index, Taiwan's monthly monitor indicator, Taiwan's monthly composite leading index, Taiwan's monthly composite coincident index, and W travel agency's monthly air ticket sales(T-1~T-18). The GA identified optimal number of hidden nodes for ANN resulted in mean absolute relative error (MARE) of 10.51% and correlation coefficient of 0.913.

Brief applications of few more MHOA for optimizing ANN parameters in summarized in table 1.

FUTURE DIRECTIONS

There are still many more MHOA algorithms which are yet to explored to optimize the various parameters of ANN, and other machine learning algorithms for solving diverse applications. The upcoming research scholars can focus on the few of the imminent research areas in machine learning listed below.

- Integration of fuzzy logic and ANN: Fuzzy logic is a type of logic that recognizes more than simple true and false values, hence better simulating the real world. For example, the statement today is sunny might be 100% true if there are no clouds, 80% true if there are a few clouds, 50% true if it's hazy, and 0% true if rains all day. Hence, it takes into account concepts like -usually, somewhat, and sometimes. Fuzzy logic and neural networks have been integrated for uses as diverse as automotive engineering, applicant screening for jobs, the control of a crane, and the monitoring of glaucoma.
- In recent years, data from neurobiological experiments have made it increasingly clear that biological neural networks, which communicate through pulses, use the timing of the pulses to transmit information and perform computation. This realization has stimulated significant research

Table 1. Summary of MHOA optimized ANN for various applications

Author &Year	Meta Heuristic Approach	Purpose	Application	Function/DATASET
Conforth, 2014	Ant Colony Optimization +PSO	Ant Colony Optimization(ACO) is applied to optimize ANN topology, Particle Swarm Optimization (PSO) is applied to adjust ANN connection weights.	reinforcement learning	SWIRL, the XOR and double pole balance Problem
Ojha, 2017	Ant Colony Optimization	To explore the impact of The optimization of the individual transfer function parameters On the performance of NN.	Classification	Iris, Breast Cancer (Wdbc) and Wine
Weingaertner, 2002	Artificial Bee colony (ABC)	Means of choosing various transfer function at the hidden Layers and the output layers of a NN	Pattern classification	Heart
Sheg, 2010	ABC	Means of choosing various transfer function at the hidden Layers and the output layers of a NN	Activation function optimization	Xor, Decoder-Encoder and 3-Bit Parity Problems
Ozturk, 2011	ABC+LM(Levenberq-Marquardt)	To find global Optimistic result	Training	Xor, Decoder-Encoder and 3-Bit Parity problems.
Karaboga, 2007	ABC	To train feed-forward artificial neural Networks for classification purpose	Classification	XOR, 3-Bit Parity and 4-Bit Encoder-Decoder problems
Johm, 2007	ABC	To optimize two key neural network BP learning parameters, Namely the random initial weight range and the single learning rate	Weight optimization and Comparison	Thyroid, heart, horse, soybean, gene, digits
Noor, 2017	ABC+PSO	To train neural networks using optimal weight set to obtain better results	pattern-classification	Iris, Cancer, Diabetes and Glass
Ozkan, 2011	ABC+LM(Levenberq-Marquardt)	To Train feed-forward neural networks on classi¨cation	oil spill detection	132 Oil pollution Radarsat-1 images of Lebanese coast, 2007
Cheg,2007	ACO	To construct the relationship function among response, inputs And parameters of a dynamic system, which is then used to predict the responses of the System.	Parameter design with dynamic charcteristics	crystal nanobalance (QCN) gas sensor, motor controller test circuit
Suamn, 2010	Binary ACO	To achieve the Optimal FNN model in terms of neural complexity minimization of hidden layers and cross-entropy error	classification	Iris, Liver disorders Diabetes, Yeast, Breast Cancer, Wine Hepatitis, Thyroid, Mushroom Horse colic, Ionosphere, Arcene
Meil, 2009	ACO	To achieve continuous optimization, which includes Global searching, local searching and definite searching	Find relation function	Two exponential functions
Michalis, 2013	ACO	To use global optimization algorithms to provide BP with good initial connection weights	Prediction	Cancer, Diabetes, Heart
Salman, 2014	ACO	To achieve Topological improvement	Construct topology of FNN	20 benchmark pattern classification datasets, from UCI
Michalis, 2014	ACO	To train feed-forward neural networks for pattern classification	Pattern classification	Cancer, Diabetes, Heart

continued on following page

Table 1. Continued

Author &Year	Meta Heuristic Approach	Purpose	Application	Function/DATASET
Rahul, 2007	ACO	To eliminate the variables that produce noise Or, are strictly correlated with other already selected variables	feature subset selection	Thyroid, Dermatology, breast cancer
Socha, 2007	ACO	To achieve continuous optimization	Pattern classification	Cancer, diabetes, heart
Valiant, 2011	Cuckoo search	To adopted best fitness function	Optimization of parameters	20 benchmark pattern classification datasets, from UCI
Nawi, 2013	Cuckoo search	For faster convergence and local minima avoidance	classification	Heart
Nawi, 2014	Cuckoo search + Levenberg Marquardt	To adopted improved fitness function	classification	Wisconsin Breast Cancer D
Yi, 2014	Cuckoo search	to simultaneously optimize the initial weights and bias of BP network	classification	Wine data
Nandy, 2012	Firefly Optimization Algorithm (FOA)	to optimize its performance index	classification	Iris, wine, liver
Mirjalili,, 2015	Grey wolf optimizer	To adopted improved fitness function	Function approximation and classification	3 XOR, balloon, iris, breast cancer, heart
Brajevic, 2013	Firefly Optimization Algorithm (FOA)	To improve function	Activation function optimization	Sin, sigmoid
Alweshah, 2014	Firefly Optimization Algorithm (FOA)	To improve fitness function for better classification	Parameter optimization	UCR time series characteristics
Tang, 2014	Wolf search algorithm	to produce the weight values for BPN to train	Activation function optimization	Griewangk, sphere, rastrign, moved axis parallel hyper, Bohachevsky, Michalewiz, Rosenbrook function
Saha, 2014	Gravitational search algorithm (GSA)	for the faster convergence towards global optima	classification	Iris, glass, wine, cancer, crab
Mirjalili, 2014	Gravitational search algorithm (GSA)	To generate adaptive weight	Function approximation and classification	3 XOR, balloon, iris, breast cancer, heart
Rashedi, 2009	Gravitational search algorithm (GSA)	To minimization of MSE is the objective function	Optimization of activation function	3 Linear Functions
Hadi, 2016	Bacterial foraging optimization algorithm	To improve activation function	Parameter estimation	Cancer, balloon
Kaur, 2014	Bacterial foraging optimization algorithm	To improve weights	Classification of software defect	Ant 1.7
Nawi, 2014	Bat inspired	To improve activation function	Parameter optimization	2-bit XOR, 3-bit XOR, 4-OR
Jaddi, 2014	Bat inspired	Optimize ANN structure	Function optimization	
Mirjalili, 2014	Biogeography-based optimization	To optimize fitness function To optimize the number of weights and biases	Classification	Iris, Breast Cancer (Wdbc) and Wine
Askarzadeh, 2013	Bird mating optimizer	to identify the weights for training ANN	Parameter optimization	UCR time series characteristics
Yu, 2011	Chemical reaction optimization	To improve fitness function and to achieve local minima in minimum duration	?????	Functions of ANN
Yumany, 2015	Moth-flame optimization algorithm	the objective function used to find the optimal solution	Classification	XOR, balloons, iris, heart, breast cancer
Cuves, 2013	Social Spider optimization	the objective function used to find the optimal solution to reduce mean square error	Search agents	
Balamurugan, 2018	social spider optimization	to separate the categorical and non-categorical data pre-processing	Classification of micro array data as normal or abnormal data	breast cancer, leukemia, lung cancer, lymphoma and ovarian
Kose, 2018	Ant-lion optimization	the objective function used to find the optimal solution to reduce mean square error and mean absolute error	Electroencephalogram (EEG) Prediction	10 different EEG datasets recorded at State Hospital, Isparta, Turkey

continued on following page

Table 1. Continued

Author & Year	Meta Heuristic Approach	Purpose	Application	Function/DATASET
Saghatforoush, 2007	Ant colony optimization (ACO)	for prediction and optimization of flyrock and back-break induced by blasting,	Mining prediction	data from the mine, burden, spacing, hole length, stemming, and powder factor were selected as input parameters. The R2 values of 0.994 and 0.832 for testing datasets of flyrock and back-break
Li, 2019	Firefly Optimization algorithm (FOA)	the objective function used to find the optimal solution	Daily Tourism Demand Forecasting with Web Search Data	validated with the data of bus line Jiading 3 in Shanghai, China
Haitao, 2019	Glowworm	the objective function used to find the optimal solution, adn parameters set methods	Traffic prediction	Yangjiang inbound tourism
Mais, 2018	Dragon fly and ABC	To optimize NN weights	Medical data classification	Cleveland Clinic heart disease, the hepatitis, diabetes, Wisconsin Diagnostic breast cancer and blood donations dataset from the Blood Transfusion Service Center in Taiwan

on pulsed neural networks, including theoretical analyses and model development, neurobiological modeling, and hardware implementation.

- Amalgamation of two or more MHOA to optimize the NN parameters
- Apply MHOA to optimize various machine learning algorithms apart from ANN: SVM, RBF etc.
- Apply MHOA to find the best input feature set for machine learning algorithms
- Apply MHOA to optimize parameters of Convolutional Neural Network (CNN), Long short-term memory (type is an artificial recurrent neural network (RNN) architecture) and other deep learning algorithms.
- Apply MHOA to optimize unsupervised algorithms.

CONCLUSION

ANN has been widely used for classification and prediction in umpteen number of fields since it is robust to handle voluminous, noisy and nonlinear data. The performance of the ANN depends on various parameters among which the connection weights play a vital role. This chapter elucidates how ANN weights optimization can be obtained using two most common MHOA: GA and PSO. Various real time applications of ANN for textile, education and tourism is also briefed. Real time applications of GA optimized ANN, PSO optimized ANNs, and many more MHOA are covered. These applications will definitely help the research fraternity to carry out further work using MHOA optimized ANN for further more domains. There is lot of scope for optimizing many more ANN parameters using emerging MHOA; as well for optimizing the upcoming deep learning algorithms.

REFERENCES

Abid, F., & Hamami, L. (2018). A survey of neural network based automated systems for human chromosome classification. *Artificial Intelligence Review, 49*(1), 41–56. doi:10.100710462-016-9515-5

Abou-Nassif. (2015). Predicting the Tensile and Air Permeability Properties of Woven Fabrics Using Artificial Neural Network and Linear Regression Models. *J Textile Sci Eng, 5*(5). DOI: . doi:10.4172/2165-8064.1000209

Abou-Nassif, A. (2018). Comparison among artificial neural network, linear and logarithmic regression models as predictors of stretchable woven fabric tightness. *International Journal of Chemtech Research, 11*(01), 41–49.

Admuthe, L., Apte, S., & Admuthe, S. (2009). Topology and Parameter Optimization of ANN Using Genetic Algorithm for Application of Textiles. *IEEE International Workshop on Intelligent Data Acquisition and Advanced Computing Systems: Technology and Applications*, 21-23. 10.1109/IDAACS.2009.5342981

Al-Hadi & Hashim. (2016). Bacterial foraging optimization algorithm for neural network learning enhancement. *Int. J. of Innovative Computing, 1*(1), 8–14.

Al Nuaimi & Abdullah. (2017). Neural network training using hybrid particle-move artificial bee colony algorithm for pattern classification. *Journal of ICT, 16*(2), 314–334.

Aljarah, I., Faris, H., & Mirjalili, S. (2016). Optimizing connection weights in neural networks using the whale optimization algorithm. *Soft Computing, 22*(1), 1–15. doi:10.100700500-016-2442-1

Almetwally, A. A., Idrees, H. M. F., & Hebeish, A. A. (2014). Predicting the tensile properties of cotton/spandex core-spun yarns using artificial neural networkand linear regression models. *Journal of the Textile Institute, 105*(11), 1221–1229. doi :10.1080/00405000.2014.882043

Alweshah, M. (2014). Firefly Algorithm with Artificial Neural Network for Time Series Problems. *Research Journal of Applied Sciences, Engineering and Technology, 7*(19), 3978–3982. doi:10.19026/rjaset.7.757

Arya & Pai. (2018). Rainfall Prediction Using an Optimised Genetic-Artificial Neural Network Model. *National Journal of Pure and Applied Mathematics, 119*(10), 669-678.

Asha Gowda Karegowda, M.A. (2013). Significant Feature Set Driven and Optimized FFN for Enhanced Classification. *International Journal of Computational Intelligence and Informatics, 2*(4), 248–255.

Askarzadeh, A., & Rezazadeh, A. (2013). Artificial neural network training using a new efficient optimization algorithm. *Applied Soft Computing, 13*(2), 1206–1213. doi:10.1016/j.asoc.2012.10.023

Azayite, F., & Achchab, S. (2019). A hybrid neural network model based on improved PSO and SA for bankruptcy prediction. *International Journal of Computer Science Issues, 16*(1).

Balamurugan & Nanc. (2018). Basis Function Neural Network. *International Journal of Uncertainty, Fuzziness and Knowledge-Based Systems, 26*(5), 695–715. Doi:10.1142/S0218488518500320695

Barker, K., Trafalis, T., & Rhoads, T. R. (2004). Learning from Student Data. *Proceedings of the 2004 IEEE Symposium on Systems and information Engineering Design*, 79-86. 10.1109/SIEDS.2004.239819

Bolaji, A. L., Ahmad, A. A., & Shola, P. B. (2016). Training of neural network for pattern classification using fireworks algorithm. *Int. J. Syst. Assur. Eng. Manag., 9*(1), 208–215. doi:10.100713198-016-0526-z

Brajevic, I., & Tuba, M. (2013). Training feed-forward neural networks using firefly algorithm. *Recent Advances in Knowledge Engineering and Systems Science: Proc. of the 12th Int. Conf. Artificial Intelligence, Knowledge Engineering and Data Bases (AIKED'13)*, 156-161.

Bullinaria & Alyahya. (2014). Artificial Bee Colony Training of Neural Networks: Comparison with Back-Propagation. *Journal Memetic Computing.* Doi:10.100712293-014-0137-7

Cankurt, S., & Subas, A. (2016). Tourism demand modeling and forecasting using data mining techniques in multivariate time series: A case study in Turkey. *Turkish Journal of Electrical Engineering and Computer Sciences, 24*, 3388–3404. doi:10.3906/elk-1311-134

Carvalho, M. (2000). Particle Swarm Optimization of Neural Network Architectures and Weights. Academic Press.

Catalogna,, M., Cohen,, F., & Fishman,, S., Halpern, Nevo, U., & Ben-Jacob, E. (.(2012). ANN based controller for gloucose monitoring during, clamp test. *PLoS One, 7*, e44587. doi:10.1371/journal.pone.0044587 PMID:22952998

Chang, Chen, & Chen. (2007). Dynamic parameter design by ant colony Optimization and neural networks. *Asia-Pacific Journal of Operational Research, 24*(3), 333–351.

Che, Z. H. (2010). PSO-based back-propagation artificial neural network for product and mold cost estimation of plastic injection molding. *Computers & Industrial Engineering, 58*(4), 625–637. doi:10.1016/j.cie.2010.01.004

Conforth & Meng. (2014). *Toward Evolving Neural Networks using Bio-Inspired Algorithms*. Academic Press.

Cuevas, E., Cienfuegos, M., Zald'ıvar, D., & P'erez-Cisnero, M. (2013). A swarm optimization algorithm inspired in the behavior of the social-spider. *Expert Systems with Applications, 40*(16), 6374–6384. doi:10.1016/j.eswa.2013.05.041

Dashti, M., Derhami, V., & Ekhtiyari, E. (2014). Yarn tenacity modeling using artificial neural networks and development of a decision support system based on genetic algorithms. *Journal of Artificial Intelligence and Data Mining, 2*(1), 73–78.

Dharmasaroja, P., & Kingkaew, N. (2016). Application of Artificial Neural Networks for Prediction of Learning Performances. *12th International Conference on Natural Computation, Fuzzy Systems and Knowledge Discovery (ICNC-FSKD)*. 10.1109/FSKD.2016.7603268

Fan, W., Bouguila, N., & Ziou, D. (2012). Variational learning for finite Dirichlet mixture models and applications. *IEEE Transactions on Neural Networks and Learning Systems, 23*(5), 762–774. doi:10.1109/TNNLS.2012.2190298 PMID:24806125

Furferi, Gelli, & Yarn. (2010). Strength Prediction: A Practical Model Based on Artificial Neural Networks. *Advances in Mechanical Engineering*. doi:10.1155/2010/640103

Garg, S., Patra, K., & Pal, S. K. (2014). Particle swarm optimization of a neural network model in a machining process. *Sadhana, 39*(3), 533–548. doi:10.100712046-014-0244-7

Gjylapi & Durmishie. (2014). Albania Artificial neural networks in forecasting tourists' flow, an intelligent technique to help the economic development of tourism in Albania. *Academicus - International Scientific Journal, 10*(14). Doi:10.7336/academicus.2014.10.14

Gordan, B., Armaghani, D. J., Hajihassani, M., & Monjezi, M. (2016). Prediction of seismic slope stability through combination of particle swarm optimization and neural network. *Engineering with Computers, 32*(1), 85–97. doi:10.100700366-015-0400-7

Haykin, S. S. (2001). Kalman Filtering and Neural Networks. Wiley.

Hilal, S. Y. A., & Okur, M. R. (2018). Predicting Achievement with Artificial Neural Networks: The Case of Anadolu University Open Education System. *International Journal of Assessment Tools in Education*, *5*(3), 474–490. doi:10.21449/ijate.435507

Huang, H.-C., & I Hou, C. (2017). Tourism Demand Forecasting Model Using Neural Network. *International Journal of Computer Science & Information Technology*, *9*(2), 19–29. doi:10.5121/ijcsit.2017.9202

Jaddi, N. S., Abdullah, S., & Hamdan, A. R. (2015). Multi-population cooperative bat algorithm-based optimization of artificial neural network model. *Journal of Information Science*, *294*, 628–644. doi:10.1016/j.ins.2014.08.050

Kalkanci, M., Kurumer, G., Öztürk, H., Sinecen, M., & Kayacan, Ö. (2017). Artificial Neural Network System for Prediction of Dimensional Properties of Cloth in Garment Manufacturing: Case Study on a T-Shirt. *Fibres & Textiles in Eastern Europe*, *4*(14), 135–140. doi:10.5604/01.3001.0010.2859

Kan, C. W., Wong, W. Y., Song, L. J., & Law, M. C. (2013). Prediction of Color Properties of Cellulase-Treated 100% Cotton Denim Fabric. *Journal of Textiles*. Advance online publication. doi:10.1155/2013/962751

Karaboga, D., Akay, B., & Ozturk, C. (2007). Artificial bee colony (ABC) optimization algorithm for training feed-forward neural networks. In *Modeling Decisions for Artificial Intelligence* (pp. 318–329). Springer. doi:10.1007/978-3-540-73729-2_30

Karaboga, D., Akay, B., & Ozturk, C. (2007). Artificial Bee Colony (ABC) Optimization Algorithm for Training Feed-Forward Neural Networks. *LNAI*, *4617*, 318–329.

Kaur, R., & Kaur, B. (2014). Artificial neural network learning enhancement using bacterial foraging optimization algorithm. *International Journal of Computers and Applications*, *102*(10), 27–33. doi:10.5120/17852-8812

Kose, U. (2018). An Ant-Lion Optimizer-Trained Artificial Neural Network System for Chaotic Electroencephalogram (EEG). *Prediction. Appl. Sci.*, *8*(9), 1613. Advance online publication. doi:10.3390/app8091613

Kuoa, J.-T., Wanga, Y.-Y., & Lungb, W.-S. (2006). A hybrid neural–genetic algorithm for reservoir water quality management. *Water Research*, *40*(7), 1367–1376. doi:10.1016/j.watres.2006.01.046 PMID:16545860

Lau, Sun, & Yang. (2019). SN Modelling, prediction and classification of student academic performance using artificial neural networks. *Applied Sciences*, *1*, 982-989. doi:10.100742452-019-0884-7

Li, H. (2019). Network traffic prediction of the optimized BP neural network based on Glowworm Swarm Algorithm. *Systems Science & Control Engineering.*, 7(2), 64–70. doi:10.1080/21642583.2019.1626299

Li, K., Lu, W., Liang, C., & Wang, B. (2019). Intelligence in Tourism Management: A Hybrid FOA-BP Method on Daily Tourism Demand Forecasting with Web Search Data. *Mathematics*, 7(6), 531–542. doi:10.3390/math7060531

Majumdar, A., Das, A., Hatua, P., & Ghosh, A. (2015). *Optimization of woven fabric parameters for ultraviolet radiation protection and comfort using artificial neural network and genetic algorithm*. Neural Comput & Applic. doi:10.100700521-015-2025-6

Malik, S. (2019). Optimal Travel Route Recommendation Mechanism Based on Neural Networks and Particle Swarm Optimization for Efficient Tourism Using Tourist. *Sustainability*, *11*, 3357. doi:10.3390u11123357

Martínez-Porchas, M., Villalpando-Canchola, E., & Vargas-Albores, F. (2016). Significant loss of sensitivity and specificity in the taxonomic classification occurs when short 16S rRNA gene sequences are used. *Heliyon*, 2(9), e00170. doi:10.1016/j.heliyon.2016.e00170 PMID:27699286

Mason, C., Twomey, J., Wright, D., & Whitman, L. (2017). Predicting Engineering Student Attrition Risk Using a Probabilistic Neural Network and Comparing Results with a Backpropagation Neural Network and Logistic Regression. *Research in Higher Education*. Advance online publication. doi:10.100711162-017-9473-z

Mavrovouniotis & Yang. (2014). *Training neural networks with ant colony optimization algorithms For pattern classification*. Springer-Verlag.

Mei, Y., Yang, J., Lu, Y., Hao, F., Xu, D., Pan, H., & Wang, J. (2019). BP–ANN Model Coupled with Particle Swarm Optimization for the Efficient Prediction of 2-Chlorophenol Removal in an Electro-Oxidation System. *International Journal of Environmental Research and Public Health*, *16*(14), 2454. doi:10.3390/ijerph16142454 PMID:31295918

Mei & Wang. (2009). Ant Colony Optimization for Neural Network. *Key Engineering Materials, 392*, 677-681.

Mirjalili, S. (2015). How effective is the Grey Wolf optimizer in training multi-layer perceptrons. *Applied Intelligence*, *43*(1), 150–161. doi:10.100710489-014-0645-7

Mirjalili, S., Mirjalili, S. M., & Lewis, A. (2014). Grey wolf optimizer. *Advances in Engineering Software*, *69*, 46–61. doi:10.1016/j.advengsoft.2013.12.007

Mirjalili, S., Mirjalili, S. M., & Lewis, A. (2014). Let a biogeography-based optimizer train your Multi- Layer Perceptron. *Information Sciences, 269*, 188–209. doi:10.1016/j.ins.2014.01.038

Monjezi, Amini Khoshalan, Yazdian, Arab, & Geosci. (2012). Prediction of flyrock and backbreak in open pit blasting operation. *A Neuro-Genetic Approach, 5*, 441–448. DOI doi:10.100712517-010-0185-3

Motahari. (2017, January). Development of a PSO-ANN Model for Rainfall-Runoff Response in Basins, Case Study: Karaj Basin, Civil. *Engineering Journal (New York), 3*(1), 35–44.

Nandy, S., Sarkar, P. P., & Das, A. (2012). Analysis of a nature inspired firefly algorithm based back-propagation neural network training. *International Journal of Computers and Applications, 43*, 8–16. doi:10.5120/6401-8339

Nawi, N. M., Khan, A., & Rehman, M. Z. (2013). New back-propagation neural network optimized with cuckoo search algorithm. *Proc. Int. conf. Computational Science and Its Applications, ICCSA-2013*, 413–426. 10.1007/978-3-642-39637-3_33

Nawi, N. M., Khan, A., & Rehman, M. Z. (2014). *Data classification using metaheuristic Cuckoo Search technique for Levenberg Marquardt back propagation (CSLM) algorithm.* AIP Conference Proceedings.

Nawi, N. M., Rehman, M. Z., & Khan, A. (2014). A new bat based back-propagation (BAT-BP) algorithm. In J. Swiatek, A. Grzech, P. Swiatek, & J. Tomczak (Eds.), *Advances in Systems Science, Advances in Intelligent Systems and Computing* (pp. 395–404). Springer. doi:10.1007/978-3-319-01857-7_38

Noersasongko, E., Julfia, F. T., Syukur, A., Purwanto, R. A. P., & Supriyanto, C. (2016, January). A Tourism Arrival Forecasting using Genetic Algorithm based Neural Network. *Indian Journal of Science and Technology, 9*(4). Advance online publication. doi:10.17485/ijst/2016/v9i4/78722

Oancea, B., Dragoescu, R., & Ciucu, S. (2017). *Predicting students' results in higher education using a neural network.* https://mpra.ub.uni-muenchen.de/72041/

Obeid. (2018). Optimizing Neural Networks using Dragonfly Algorithm for Medical Prediction. *2018 8th International Conference on Computer Science and Information Technology (CSIT).*

Ojha, Abraham, & Sn'a˘sel. (2017). *Simultaneous Optimization of Neural Network Weights and Active Nodes using Metaheuristics.* arxiv:1707.01810v1

Özdemir & Polat. (2017). Forecasting With Artificial Neural Network Of Science Teachers. *Professional Burnout Variables. Int. J. Educ. Stud.*, *04*(03), 49–64.

Ozkan, Ozturky, Sunarz, & Karaboga. (2011). The artificial bee colony algorithm In training artificial neural Network for oil spill detection. *ICS AS CR 2011*.

Ozturk & Karaboga. (2011). *Hybrid Artificial Bee Colony Algorithm For Neural Network Training*. IEEE.

Rashedi, E., Nezamabadi-pour, H., & Saryazdi, S. (2009). GSA: A gravitational search algorithm. *Information Sciences*, *179*(13), 2232–2248. doi:10.1016/j.ins.2009.03.004

Raval, D., Bhatt, D., Kumhar, M. K., Parikh, V., & Vyas, D. (2016). Medical diagnosis system using machine learning. *International Journal of Computer Science & Communication*, *7*(1), 177–182.

Sadeghyan & Asadi. (2010). *Ms-baco: a new model selection algorithm using binary ant Colony optimization for neural complexity and error reduction*. Academic Press.

Saghatforoush, A., Monjezi, M., Shirani, R., & Faradonbeh, D. J. A. (2007). Combination of neural network and ant colony optimization algorithms for prediction and optimization of flyrock and back-break induced by blasting. *Engineering with Computers*. Advance online publication. doi:10.100700366-015-0415-0

Saha, S., Chakraborty, D., & Dutta, O. (2014). Guided convergence for training feed-forward neural network using novel gravitational search optimization. *Proc. 2014 International Conference on High Performance Computing and Applications (ICHPCA)*, 1-6. 10.1109/ICHPCA.2014.7045348

Salama, K., & Abdelbar, A. M. (2014). A Novel Ant Colony Algorithm for Building Neural Network Topologies. *Springer International Publishing Switzerland LNCS*, *8667*, 1–12. doi:10.1007/978-3-319-09952-1_1

Saravanan, K., & Sasithra, S. (2014). Review on classification based on artificial neural networks. *Int. J. Ambient Syst. Appl.*, *2*(4), 11–18.

Sathish, T. (2018). Prediction of springback effect by the hybridisation of ANN with PSO in wipe bending process of sheet metal. Progress in Industrial Ecology –. *International Journal (Toronto, Ont.)*, *12*(1), 112–119.

Semero, Y. K., Zhang, J., Zheng, D., & Wei, D. (2018). A GA-PSO Hybrid Algorithm Based Neural Network Modeling Technique for Short-term Wind Power Forecasting. *Distributed Generation & Alternative Energy Journal*, *33*(4), 26–43. doi:10.1080/21563306.2018.12029913

Shadika & Rendra. (2017). Optimizing Woven Curtain Fabric Defect Classification using Image Processing with Artificial Neural Network Method at PT Buana Intan Gemilang. *MATEC Web of Conferences, 135*. Doi:10.1051/matecconf/201713500052

Sharma, K., Gupta, P., & Sharma, H. (2015). Fully informed artificial bee colony algorithm. *Journal of Experimental & Theoretical Artificial Intelligence, 281*, 403–416.

Sheng, Z., Xiuyu, S., & Wei, W. (2010). An ann model of optimizing activation Functions based on constructive algorithm and gp. In *Computer Application And System Modeling (ICCASM), 2010 International Conference On*, 420–424.

Shi, X. (2019). Tourism culture and demand forecasting based on BPNN mining algorithms. *Personal and Ubiquitous Computing*. Advance online publication. doi:10.100700779-019-01325-x

Sivagaminathan, R. K., & Ramakrishnan, S. (2007). A hybrid approach for feature subset selection using neural Networks and ant colony optimization. *Expert Systems with Applications, 33*(1), 49–60. doi:10.1016/j.eswa.2006.04.010

Socha & Blum. (2007). An ant colony optimization algorithm for continuous Optimization: application to feed-forward neural network. *Neural Comput & Applic.*, (16), 235–247. DOI doi:10.100700521-007-0084-z

Srisaeng, P., & Baxter, G. (2017). Modelling Australia's Outbound Passenger Air Travel Demand Using An Artificial Neural Network Approach. *International Journal for Traffic and Transport Engineering, 7*(4), 406–423. doi:10.7708/ijtte.2017.7(4).01]

Stamos, T. Karamouzis and Andreas Vrettos. (2008). An Artificial Neural Network for Predicting Student Graduation Outcomes. *Proceedings of the World Congress on Engineering and Computer Science*.

Suknovic, M., & Isljamovic, S. (2014). Predicting Students' Academic Performance Using Artificial Neural Network: A Case Study From Faculty Of Organizational Sciences. *The Eurasia Proceedings of Educational & Social Sciences (EPESS)*, 68-72.

Taieb, A. H., Mshali, S., & Sakli, F. (2018). Predicting Fabric Drapability Property by Using an Artificial Neural Network. *Journal of Engineered Fibers and Fabrics, 13*(3). Advance online publication. doi:10.1177/155892501801300310

Tang, R., Fong, S., Yang, X. S., & Deb, S. (2014). Wolf search algorithm with ephemeral memory. *Proc. Seventh International Conference on Digital Information Management (ICDIM 2012)*, 165-172.

Valian, E., Mohanna, S., & Tavakoli, S. (2011). Improved cuckoo search algorithm for feedforward neural network training. *Int. J. of Artificial Intelligence & Applications, 2*. Advance online publication. doi:10.5121/ijaia.2011.2304

Wang, M., Zhang, H., & Wu, Z. (2019). Forecast and Application of GA Optimization BP Neural Network Tourism Demand in High-speed Railway Era. *IOP Conf. Series: Materials Science and Engineering, 569*. doi:10.1088/1757-899X/569/4/042053

Weingaertner, D., Tatai, V. K., Gudwin, R. R., & Von Zuben, F. J. (2002). Hierarchical evolution of heterogeneous neural networks. in Evolutionary Computation, CEC'02. *Proceedings of the 2002 Congress On, 2*, 1775–1780.

Yamany, W., Fawzy, M., Tharwat, A., & Hassanien, A. E. (2015). Moth-flame optimization for training Multi-Layer Perceptrons. *Proc. 2015 11th International Computer Engineering Conference (ICENCO)*, 267-272. 10.1109/ICENCO.2015.7416360

Yang. (2013). *Evolving Neural Networks using Ant Colony Optimization with Pheromone Trail Limits*. IEEE.

Yi, Xu, & Chen. (2014). *Novel Back Propagation Optimization by Cuckoo Search Algorithm*. Hindawi Publishing Corporation. doi:10.1155/2014/878262

Yu, J. J. Q., Lam, A. Y. S., & Li, V. O. K. (2015). Evolutionary artificial neural network based on chemical reaction optimization. *Proc. IEEE Congress of Evolutionary Computation (CEC)*, 2083-2090.

Yu, W., He, H., & Zhang, N. (2009). Advances in Neural Networks. *ISNN 2009 6th International Symposium*.

Zacharis, N. Z. (2016). Predicting Student Academic Performance In Blended Learning Using Artificial Neural Networks. *International Journal of Artificial Intelligence and Applications, 7*(5). Advance online publication. doi:10.5121/ijaia.2016.7502

Zhang, C., & Shao, H. (2000). An ANN's Evolved by a New Evolutionary System and Its Application. *Proceedings of the 39th IEEE Conference on Decision and Control, 4*(1), 3562-3563. 10.1109/CDC.2000.912257

Chapter 11
Latest Technology and Future Trends

Meghna Babubhai Patel
Ganpat University, India

Jagruti N. Patel
Ganpat University, India

Upasana M. Bhilota
Ganpat University, India

ABSTRACT

ANN can work the way the human brain works and can learn the way we learn. The neural network is this kind of technology that is not an algorithm; it is a network that has weights on it, and you can adjust the weights so that it learns. You teach it through trials. It is a fact that the neural network can operate and improve its performance after "teaching" it, but it needs to undergo some process of learning to acquire information and be familiar with them. Nowadays, the age of smart devices dominates the technological world, and no one can deny their great value and contributions to mankind. A dramatic rise in the platforms, tools, and applications based on machine learning and artificial intelligence has been seen. These technologies not only impacted software and the internet industry but also other verticals such as healthcare, legal, manufacturing, automobile, and agriculture. The chapter shows the importance of latest technology used in ANN and future trends in ANN.

DOI: 10.4018/978-1-7998-4042-8.ch011

DEEP LEARNING

A deep neural network (DNN), it is actually a part of artificial neural network (ANN) which is having multiple layers basically those are residing between the input layer and the output layers. The DNN searches for the right mathematical manipulation and it transforms the inputs into the outputs, whether it can be any relationship, can be a linear relationship or can be a non-linear relationship. The network will proceed in between the layers and calculate the possibilities for each and every output

Applications of ANN in deep learning

- Automated Machine Translations
- Image reorganization
- Automatic images caption generation
- Prediction of earthquakes
- Neural networks in health services
- Neural network for Finances
- Energy Market Cost Prediction
- Behavior Analysis

Convolutional Neural Networks

CNNs adversely designed in comparison to a normal neural network. In a normal neural network, each layer merges all set of neurons. Each layer is linked to all neurons in the preceding layer. Convolutional neural networks acts like it have 3-dimensional layers like width, height and depth. All neurons in a specific layer are not linked to the neurons in the preceding layer. Instead, a layer is only affixed to a small part of neurons in the preceding layer (Flat World Solutions, n.d.).

- Decoding Facial Recognition
- Analyzing Documents
- Historic and Environmental Collections
- Understanding Climates
- Grey Areas

Long Short Term Memory Networks

Long Short Term Memory is basically a kind of recurrent neural network. In RNN output from the final step is acts as an input to the next or present step. LSTM was designed by Hochreiter & Schmidhuber. LSTM sort out the problem of long-term dependencies of RNN as RNN cannot forecast the word saved in the long term memory but it can provide more precise forecasts from the current information. As the distance grows RNN cannot provide effective performance. LSTM can by default keep the information for much time. It is generally used for processing, forecasting and categorizing on the basis of time seriesdata.

LSTM is basically a distinctive kind of Recurrent Neural Network (RNN) it is able to learning the long-term dependencies, those are helpful for some kind of forecasting that needs the network will keep information for long time periods, and it is a task that conventional RNNs are struggling with(Missing Link, n.d.).

Applications of LSTM (Missing Link, n.d.)

- Text Prediction
- Stock Market Prediction

Hybrid Systems

A Hybrid system we can say basically a smart system and it enclosed by joining two smart mechanisms can be like the Fuzzy Logic and the neural network as well as the Genetic algorithm and the reinforcement Learning and many more. It is basically the mixture of different kind of technologies residing in one computational model which make these systems to own an expanded scope of much capabilities. These type of systems are much capable of reasoning as well as learning in the undetermined and the unspecific environment. These are the systems that will provide human alike expertise, those can be regarding domain knowledge as well as adaptation in type of noisy environment (Geeks for Geeks, n.d.).

- Neuro Fuzzy Hybrid Systems
- Neuro Genetic Hybrid Systems
- Fuzzy Genetic Hybrid Systems

Hybrid Neural Network

A hybrid neural network is type of first principles modeling strategy and it is reinforced and that can be used to model a kind offed batch bioreactor. It joins type of partial first principle model, it basically integrates the already available preceding information of types of processes those are basically being modeled along the use of artificial neural network and it provide a predictor for non-measured process parameters, these parameters are tough to model by first principles. This kind of hybrid model is having far greater characteristics as compare to the traditional type of "black-box" neural network as it is capable of interpose and can extrapolate more precisely as well as it is much more easy to analyze as well as translate, and it also needs less training instances. Two options state as well as parameters predictions approaches and it is an expanded Kalman filtering as well as the NLP optimization, they are too can be included. When there is no an earlier well-known model of unseen processes parameter is accessible, the hybrid network model serves great approximations of all the parameters, as comparing to these all methods. By giving the basic model for these kind of non-measured parameters, the hybrid neural network can do forecasts as well as it may can be utilized for the processes optimizations. These final outcomes can be applied on both when the complete state as well as the partial state assessments are there, but for further situation the state regeneration technique have to be utilized for the first principles as it is segment of a hybrid model (University of Pennsylvania, n.d.).

Time Series Forecasting on basis of HNN. Time series forecasting is basically use as a predictions of future values. The future variables are those which can be measured in time. Those can be measured as discrete as well as on continuous base (Jain & Kumar, 2007).

REFERENCES

1. Flat World Solutions. (n.d.). https://www.flatworldsolutions.com/data-science/articles/7-applications-of-convolutional-neural-networks.php

3. Geeks for Geeks. (n.d.). https://www.geeksforgeeks.org/introduction-ann-artificial-neural-networks-set-3-hybrid-systems/

5. Jain, A., & Kumar, A. M. (2007). Hybrid neural network models for hydrologic time series forecasting. *Applied Soft Computing*, 7(2), 585–592. doi:10.1016/j.asoc.2006.03.002

2. Missing Link. (n.d.). https://missinglink.ai/guides/neural-network-concepts/deep-learning-long-short-term-memory-lstm-networks-remember/

4. University of Pennsylvania. (n.d.). https://www.cis.upenn.edu/~ungar/papers/OLD/psichogios_AICHE.pdf

274

Compilation of References

Abid, F., & Hamami, L. (2018). A survey of neural network based automated systems for human chromosome classification. *Artificial Intelligence Review*, *49*(1), 41–56. doi:10.100710462-016-9515-5

Aboelmaged, M., & Gebba, T. R. (2013). Mobile banking adoption: An examination of technology acceptance model and theory of planned behavior. *International Journal of Business Research and Development*, *2*(1), 35–50. doi:10.24102/ijbrd.v2i1.263

Abou-Nassif. (2015). Predicting the Tensile and Air Permeability Properties of Woven Fabrics Using Artificial Neural Network and Linear Regression Models. *J Textile Sci Eng, 5*(5). DOI: . doi:10.4172/2165-8064.1000209

Abou-Nassif, A. (2018). Comparison among artificial neural network, linear and logarithmic regression models as predictors of stretchable woven fabric tightness. *International Journal of Chemtech Research, 11*(01), 41–49.

Admuthe, L., Apte, S., & Admuthe, S. (2009). Topology and Parameter Optimization of ANN Using Genetic Algorithm for Application of Textiles. *IEEE International Workshop on Intelligent Data Acquisition and Advanced Computing Systems: Technology and Applications*, 21-23. 10.1109/IDAACS.2009.5342981

Ajzen, I., & Fishbein, M. (1980). *Understanding attitudes and predicting social behaviour.* Prentice Hall.

Ajzen, I., & Madden, T. J. (1986). Prediction of goal-directed behavior: Attitudes, intentions, and perceived behavioral control. *Journal of Experimental Social Psychology*, *22*(5), 453–474. doi:10.1016/0022-1031(86)90045-4

Akgül, Y. (2017a). Integrating e-trust antecedents into TAM to explain mobile banking behavioral intention: A SEM-neural network modeling. *4th International Conference on Business and Economics Studies (Özet Bildiri/Sözlü Sunum).* (Yayın No:4406728)

Akgül, Y. (2018c). Predicting determinants of Mobile banking adoption: A two-staged regression-neural network approach. *8th International Conference of Strategic Research on Scientific Studies and Education (ICoSReSSE) 2018 (Özet Bildiri/Sözlü Sunum).* (Yayın No:4405980)

Akgül, Y. (2019). Understanding and Predicting the Determinants of the Facebook Usage in Higher Education: A Two Staged Hybrid SEM-Neural Networks Approach. *11th International Conference of Strategic Research on Scientific Studies and Education (ICoSReSSE).*

Akgül, Y. (2019a). A social commerce investigation of the role of trust in a social networking site on purchase intentions: A Multi-Analytical Structural Equation Modeling and Neural Network Approach. *11th International Conference of Strategic Research on Scientific Studies and Education (ICoSReSSE) (Tam Metin Bildiri/Sözlü Sunum).* (Yayın No:5486037)

Akgül, Y., & Tunca, M. Z. (2019). Strategic Orientation and Performance of Istanbul Stock Market Businesses: Empirical Studies Based on Business, Information Systems, and Knowledge Strategic Orientation. In Strategy and Superior Performance of Micro and Small Businesses in Volatile Economies (pp. 94-114). IGI Global.

Akgül, Y., Öztürk, T., & Varol, Z. (2019). Investigation of Internet Banking Users' Perceptions and Factors Affecting Internet Banking Benchmarks: Expanded With Unified Theory of Acceptance and Use of Technology 2 (UTAUT2) Risk. In Structural Equation Modeling Approaches to E-Service Adoption (pp. 64-82). IGI Global.

Akgül, Y. (2017). *A multi-analytical approach for predicting antecedents of m-commerce adoption. In Academic Studies about communication, business and economics. Strategic Researches Academy Strategic Researches Academic Publishing.*

Akgül, Y. (2018a). An Analysis of Customers' Acceptance of Internet Banking: An Integration of E-Trust and Service Quality to the TAM–The Case of Turkey. In *E-Manufacturing and E-Service Strategies in Contemporary Organizations* (pp. 154–198). IGI Global. doi:10.4018/978-1-5225-3628-4.ch007

Akgül, Y. (2018b). A SEM-Neural Network Approach for Predicting Antecedents of Factors Influencing Consumers' Intent to Install Mobile Applications. In *Mobile Technologies and Socio-Economic Development in Emerging Nations* (pp. 262–308). IGI Global. doi:10.4018/978-1-5225-4029-8.ch012

Akgül, Y., Yaman, B., Geçgil, G., & Yavuz, G. (2019). The Influencing Factors for Purchasing Intentions in Social Media by Utaut Perspective. In *Structural Equation Modeling Approaches to E-Service Adoption* (pp. 254–267). IGI Global. doi:10.4018/978-1-5225-8015-7.ch013

Akhand, K., Nizamuddin, M., & Roytman, L. (2018). Wheat Yield Prediction in Bangladesh using Artificial Neural Network and Satellite Remote Sensing Data. *Global Journal of Science Frontier Research: D Agriculture and Veterinary, 18*(2).

Akhand, K., Nizamuddin, M., & Roytman, L. (2018). An Artificial Neural Network-Based Model for Predicting Boro Rice Yield in Bangladesh Using AVHRR-Based Satellite Data. *International Journal of Agriculture and Forestry, 8*(1), 16–25. doi:10.5923/j.ijaf.20180801.04

Akturan, U., & Tezcan, N. (2012). Mobile banking adoption of the youth market. *Marketing Intelligence & Planning, 30*(4), 444–459. doi:10.1108/02634501211231928

Al Ahmar, E. (2010). *Advanced Signal Processing Techniques for Fault Detection and Diagnosis in a Wind Turbine Induction Generator Drive Train: A Comparative Study. IEEE Energy Conversion Congress and Exposition.* ECCE.

Al Nuaimi & Abdullah. (2017). Neural network training using hybrid particle-move artificial bee colony algorithm for pattern classification. *Journal of ICT, 16*(2), 314–334.

Al-Ahmar, E. (2008). Wind Energy Conversion Systems Fault Diagnosis Using Wavelet Analysis. *International Review of Electrical Engineering, 3*(4), 646–652.

Alalwan, A. A., Dwivedi, Y. K., Rana, N. P., & Simintiras, A. C. (2016). Jordanian consumers' adoption of telebanking: Influence of perceived usefulness, trust, and self-efficacy. *International Journal of Bank Marketing, 34*(5), 690–709. doi:10.1108/IJBM-06-2015-0093

AlAlwan, A., Dwivedi, Y. K., & Rana, N. P. (2017). Factors influencing adoption of mobile banking by jordanian bank customers: Extending UTAUT2 with trust. *International Journal of Information Management, 37*(3), 99–110. doi:10.1016/j.ijinfomgt.2017.01.002

Alexandridis, A. K., & Zapranis, A. D. (2013). Wavelet neural networks: A practical guide. *Neural Networks, 42*, 1–27. doi:10.1016/j.neunet.2013.01.008 PMID:23411153

Al-Hadi & Hashim. (2016). Bacterial foraging optimization algorithm for neural network learning enhancement. *Int. J. of Innovative Computing, 1*(1), 8–14.

Aljarah, I., Faris, H., & Mirjalili, S. (2016). Optimizing connection weights in neural networks using the whale optimization algorithm. *Soft Computing, 22*(1), 1–15. doi:10.100700500-016-2442-1

Almetwally, A. A., Idrees, H. M. F., & Hebeish, A. A. (2014). Predicting the tensile properties of cotton/spandex core-spun yarns using artificial neural networkand linear regression models. *Journal of the Textile Institute, 105*(11), 1221–1229. doi:10.1080/00405000.2014.882043

Al-Shaikhi, A. A., Khan, A. H., Al-Awami, A. T., & Zerguine, A. (2019). A Hybrid Particle Swarm Optimization Technique for Adaptive Equalization. *Arabian Journal for Science and Engineering, 44*(3), 2177–2184. doi:10.100713369-018-3387-8

Alshare, K. A., & Mousa, A. A. (2014). *The moderating effect of espoused cultural dimensions on consumer's intention to use mobile payment devices.* Paper presented at the 35th International Conference on Information Systems "Building a Better World through Information Systems", ICIS 2014, Auckland: Association for Information Systems.

Alshare, K., Grandon, E., & Miller, D. (2004). Antecedents of computer technology usage: Considerations of the technology acceptance model in the academic environment. *Journal of Computing Sciences in Colleges, 19*(4), 164–180.

Al-Somali, S., Gholami, R., & Clegg, B. (2009). An investigation into the acceptance of online banking in Saudi Arabia. *Technovation, 29*(2), 130–141. doi:10.1016/j.technovation.2008.07.004

Alweshah, M. (2014). Firefly Algorithm with Artificial Neural Network for Time Series Problems. *Research Journal of Applied Sciences, Engineering and Technology, 7*(19), 3978–3982. doi:10.19026/rjaset.7.757

Apanasevic, T., Markendahl, J., & Arvidsson, N. (2016). Stakeholders' expectations of mobile payment in retail: Lessons from Sweden. *International Journal of Bank Marketing, 34*(1), 37–61. doi:10.1108/IJBM-06-2014-0064

Arvidsson, N. (2014). Consumer attitudes on mobile payment services - results from aproof of concept test. *International Journal of Bank Marketing, 32*(2), 150–170. doi:10.1108/IJBM-05-2013-0048

Arya & Pai. (2018). Rainfall Prediction Using an Optimised Genetic-Artificial Neural Network Model. *National Journal of Pure and Applied Mathematics, 119*(10), 669-678.

Asha Gowda Karegowda, M.A. (2013). Significant Feature Set Driven and Optimized FFN for Enhanced Classification. *International Journal of Computational Intelligence and Informatics, 2*(4), 248–255.

Askarzadeh, A., & Rezazadeh, A. (2013). Artificial neural network training using a new efficient optimization algorithm. *Applied Soft Computing, 13*(2), 1206–1213. doi:10.1016/j.asoc.2012.10.023

Aslam, W., Ham, M., & Arif, I. (2017). Consumer Behavioral Intentions towards Mobile Payment Services: An Empirical Analysis in Pakistan. *Market-Trziste, 29*(2), 161–176. doi:10.22598/mt/2017.29.2.161

Astya, P. (2017, May). Sentiment analysis: approaches and open issues. In *2017 International Conference on Computing, Communication and Automation (ICCCA)* (pp. 154-158). IEEE.

Ayoubi. (2011). Application of Artificial Neural Network (ANN) to Predict Soil Organic Matter Using Remote Sensing Data in Two Ecosystems. In *Biomass and Remote Sensing of Biomass*. InTech.

Azad, M. A. K. (2016). Predicting mobile banking adoption in Bangladesh: A neural network approach. *Transnational Corporations Review, 8*(3), 207–214. doi:10.1080/19186444.2016.1233726

Azayite, F., & Achchab, S. (2019). A hybrid neural network model based on improved PSO and SA for bankruptcy prediction. *International Journal of Computer Science Issues, 16*(1).

Bagozzi, R. Y., & Yi, Y. (1988). On the evaluation of structural equation models. *Journal of the Academy of Marketing Science, 16*(1), 74–94. doi:10.1007/BF02723327

Balamurugan & Nanc. (2018). Basis Function Neural Network. *International Journal of Uncertainty, Fuzziness and Knowledge-Based Systems, 26*(5), 695–715. Doi:10.1142/S0218488518500320695

Baptista, G., & Oliveira, T. (2016). A weight and a meta-analysis on mobile banking acceptance research. *Computers in Human Behavior, 63*, 480–489. doi:10.1016/j.chb.2016.05.074

Barclay, D., Higgins, C., & Thompson, R. (1995). The partial least squares (PLS) approach to causal modeling: Personal computer adoption and use as an illustration (with commentaries). *Technology Studies*, 2(2), 285–324.

Barker, K., Trafalis, T., & Rhoads, T. R. (2004). Learning from Student Data. *Proceedings of the 2004 IEEE Symposium on Systems and information Engineering Design*, 79-86. 10.1109/SIEDS.2004.239819

Baroni, M., & Zamparelli, R. (2010, October). Nouns are vectors, adjectives are matrices: Representing adjective-noun constructions in semantic space. In *Proceedings of the 2010 conference on empirical methods in natural language processing* (pp. 1183-1193). Academic Press.

Bashir, Z. A., & El-Hawary, M. E. (2009). Applying wavelets to short-term load forecasting using PSO-based neural networks. *IEEE Transactions on Power Systems*, 24(1), 20–27. doi:10.1109/TPWRS.2008.2008606

Basu, J. K., Bhattacharyya, D., & Kim, T. H. (2010). Use of artificial neural network in pattern recognition. *International Journal of Software Engineering and Its Applications*, 4(2).

Bauer, H. H., Reichardt, T., Barnes, S. J., & Neumann, M. M. (2005). Driving consumer acceptance of mobile marketing: A theoretical framework and empirical study. *Journal of Electronic Commerce Research*, 6(3), 181.

Belanger, F., & Carter, L. (2008). Trust and risk in e-government adoption. *The Journal of Strategic Information Systems*, 17(2), 165–176. doi:10.1016/j.jsis.2007.12.002

Bezdek, J. C., & Pal. (1992). Fuzzy Models for Pattern Recognition. IEEE Press.

Blödt, M. (2010). Mechanical Fault Detection. In F. Detection & W. Zhang (Eds.), Induction Motor Drives Through Stator Current Monitoring-Theory and Application Examples. Academic Press.

Blunsom, P., Kocik, K., & Curran, J. R. (2006, August). Question classification with log-linear models. In *Proceedings of the 29th annual international ACM SIGIR conference on Research and development in information retrieval* (pp. 615-616). ACM.

Bolaji, A. L., Ahmad, A. A., & Shola, P. B. (2016). Training of neural network for pattern classification using fireworks algorithm. *Int. J. Syst. Assur. Eng. Manag.*, 9(1), 208–215. doi:10.100713198-016-0526-z

Bonaldi. (2012). *Predictive Maintenance by Electrical Signature Analysis to Induction Motors*. InTech.

Bouazizi, Mondher, & Ohtsuki. (2019). Multi-class sentiment analysis on twitter: classification performance and challenges. *Big Data Mining and Analytics*, 2(3), 181-194.

Bouchon-Meunier, B. (1995). *La Logique Floue et ses Applications*. Addison-Wesley.

Boureau, Y. L., Ponce, J., & LeCun, Y. (2010). A theoretical analysis of feature pooling in visual recognition. In *Proceedings of the 27th international conference on machine learning (ICML-10)* (pp. 111-118). Academic Press.

Bourguet & Antsaklis. (1994). *Artificial Neural Networks In Electric Power Industry*. Technical Report of the ISIS Group at the University of Notre Dame ISIS-94-007.

Brajevic, I., & Tuba, M. (2013). Training feed-forward neural networks using firefly algorithm. *Recent Advances in Knowledge Engineering and Systems Science: Proc. of the 12th Int. Conf. Artificial Intelligence, Knowledge Engineering and Data Bases (AIKED'13)*, 156-161.

Bullinaria & Alyahya. (2014). Artificial Bee Colony Training of Neural Networks: Comparison with Back-Propagation. *Journal Memetic Computing*. Doi:10.100712293-014-0137-7

Burns, R. S. (1995). The use of artificial neural networks for the intelligent optimal control of surface ships. *IEEE Journal of Oceanic Engineering*, 20(1), 65–72. doi:10.1109/48.380245

Campos, B. R. (2009). *Character recognition in natural images*. VISAPP.

Cankurt, S., & Subas, A. (2016). Tourism demand modeling and forecasting using data mining techniques in multivariate time series: A case study in Turkey. *Turkish Journal of Electrical Engineering and Computer Sciences*, 24, 3388–3404. doi:10.3906/elk-1311-134

Carton, F., Hedman, J., Damsgaard, J., Tan, K.-T., & McCarthy, J. (2012). Framework for mobile payments integration. *The Electronic Journal of Information Systems Evaluation*, 15(1), 14–25.

Carvalho, M. (2000). Particle Swarm Optimization of Neural Network Architectures and Weights. Academic Press.

Catalogna,, M., Cohen,, F., & Fishman,, S., Halpern, Nevo, U., & Ben-Jacob, E. (.(2012). ANN based controller for gloucose monitoring during, clamp test. *PLoS One*, 7, e44587. doi:10.1371/journal.pone.0044587 PMID:22952998

Chakkor, Mostafa, & Hajraoui. (2014). ESPRIT Method Enhancement for Real-time Wind Turbine Fault Recognition. *International Journal of Power Electronics and Drive System*, 5(4).

Chakkor, S., Mostafa, B., & Hajraoui, A. (2014). Performance Analysis of Faults Detection in Wind Turbine Generator Based on High-Resolution Frequency Estimation Methods. International Journal of Advanced Computer Science and Applications. *SAI Publisher*, 5(4), 139–148.

Chakkor, S., Mostafa, B., & Hajraoui, A. (2014). Wind Turbine Fault Detection System in Real Time Remote Monitoring. *Iranian Journal of Electrical and Computer Engineering*, 4(6), 1495–1502.

Chandra, A., Mitra, P. S. K., Dubey, & Ray. (2019). *Machine Learning Approach For Kharif Rice Yield Prediction Integrating Multi-Temporal Vegetation Indices And Weather And Non-Weather Variables*. The International Archives of the Photogrammetry, Remote Sensing and Spatial Information Sciences, New Delhi, India.

Chandra, S., Srivastava, S. C., & Theng, Y. L. (2010). Evaluating the role of trust in consumer adoption of mobile payment systems: An empirical analysis. *Communications of the Association for Information Systems*, *27*(29), 561–588. doi:10.17705/1CAIS.02729

Chandrasekhar, U., & Nandagopal, R. (2016). Mobile payment usage intent in an Indian context: An exploratory study. *Asian Journal of Information Technology*, *15*(3), 542–552.

Chang, Chen, & Chen. (2007). Dynamic parameter design by ant colony Optimization and neural networks. *Asia-Pacific Journal of Operational Research*, *24*(3), 333–351.

Chaouali, W. I., Ben Yahia, I., & Souiden, N. (2016). The interplay of counter-conformity motivation, social influence, and trust in customers' intention to adopt Internet banking services: The case of an emerging country. *Journal of Retailing and Consumer Services*, *28*, 209–218. doi:10.1016/j.jretconser.2015.10.007

Chen. (2008). Neural Network Electrical Machine Faults Diagnosis Based On Multi-Population GA. *IEEE International Joint Conference on Neural Networks*.

Cheng, T. C. E., Lam, D. Y. C., & Yeung, C. L. (2006). Adoption of internet banking: An empirical study in Hong Kong. *Decision Support Systems*, *42*(3), 1558–1572. doi:10.1016/j.dss.2006.01.002

Cheng, V. C., Leung, C. H., Liu, J., & Milani, A. (2013). Probabilistic aspect mining model for drug reviews. *IEEE Transactions on Knowledge and Data Engineering*, *26*(8), 2002–2013. doi:10.1109/TKDE.2013.175

Chen, H. R., & Tseng, H. F. (2012). Factors that influence acceptance of web-based e-learning systems for the in-service education of junior high school teachers in Taiwan. *Evaluation and Program Planning*, *35*(3), 398–406. doi:10.1016/j.evalprogplan.2011.11.007 PMID:22321703

Chen, L.-D. (2008). A model of consumer acceptance of mobile payment. *International Journal of Mobile Communications*, *6*(1), 32–52. doi:10.1504/IJMC.2008.015997

Chen, S., Gibson, G. J., & Cowan, C. F. N. (1990). Adaptive channel equalisation using a polynomial-perceptron structure. *IEE Proceedings. Part I. Communications, Speech and Vision*, *137*(5), 257–264. doi:10.1049/ip-i-2.1990.0036

Chen, S., Gibson, G. J., Cowan, C. F. N., & Grant, P. M. (1990). Adaptive equalization of finite non-linear channels using multilayer perceptrons. *Signal Processing*, *20*(2), 107–119. doi:10.1016/0165-1684(90)90122-F

Cheong, S. N., Ling, H. C., & Teh, P. L. (2014). Secure encrypted steganography graphical password scheme for near field communication smartphone access control system. *Expert Systems with Applications*, *41*(7), 3561–3568. doi:10.1016/j.eswa.2013.10.060

Che, Z. H. (2010). PSO-based back-propagation artificial neural network for product and mold cost estimation of plastic injection molding. *Computers & Industrial Engineering*, *58*(4), 625–637. doi:10.1016/j.cie.2010.01.004

Chin, W. W. (1998). The Partial Least Squares Approach to Structural Equation Modeling. In G. A. Marcoulides (Ed.), *Modern Methods for Business Research* (pp. 295–358). Lawrence Erlbaum Associates.

Chong, A. Y. L. (2013). A two-staged SEM-neural network approach for understanding and predicting the determinants of m-commerce adoption. *Expert Systems with Applications, 40*(4), 1240–1247. doi:10.1016/j.eswa.2012.08.067

Chong, A. Y. L. (2013). Predicting m-commerce adoption determinants: A neural network approach. *Expert Systems with Applications, 40*(2), 523–530. doi:10.1016/j.eswa.2012.07.068

Chong, A. Y. L., Liu, M. J., Luo, J., & Keng-Boon, O. (2015). Predicting RFID adoption in healthcare supply chain from the perspectives of users. *International Journal of Production Economics, 159*, 66–75. doi:10.1016/j.ijpe.2014.09.034

Chong, A. Y. L., Ooi, K. B., Lin, B., & Bao, H. (2012). An empirical analysis of the determinants of 3G adoption in China. *Computers in Human Behavior, 28*(2), 360–369. doi:10.1016/j.chb.2011.10.005

Chow, T. W. S., & Leung, C. T. (1996). Neural network based short-term load forecasting using weather compensation. *IEEE Transactions on Power Systems, 11*(4), 1736–1742. doi:10.1109/59.544636

Cireşan, D., Meier, U., Masci, J., & Schmidhuber, J. (2011, July). A committee of neural networks for traffic sign classification. In *The 2011 international joint conference on neural networks* (pp. 1918–1921). IEEE. doi:10.1109/IJCNN.2011.6033458

Clark, L., & Watson, D. (1995). Constructing validity: Basic issues in objective scale development. *Psychological Assessment, 7*(3), 309–319. doi:10.1037/1040-3590.7.3.309

Clavel, C., & Callejas, Z. (2015). Sentiment analysis: From opinion mining to human-agent interaction. *IEEE Transactions on Affective Computing, 7*(1), 74–93. doi:10.1109/TAFFC.2015.2444846

Cobanoglu, C., Yang, W., Shatskikh, A., & Agarwal, A. (2015). Are consumers ready for mobile payment? An examination of consumer acceptance of mobile payment technology in restaurant industry. *Hospitality Review, 31*(4), 6.

Cohen, J. (1988). *Statistical Power Analysis for the Behavioral Sciences*. Lawrence Erlbaum.

Conforth & Meng. (2014). *Toward Evolving Neural Networks using Bio-Inspired Algorithms*. Academic Press.

Cuevas, E., Cienfuegos, M., Zald'ıvar, D., & P'erez-Cisnero, M. (2013). A swarm optimization algorithm inspired in the behavior of the social-spider. *Expert Systems with Applications, 40*(16), 6374–6384. doi:10.1016/j.eswa.2013.05.041

Dahlberg, T., Mallat, N., Ondrus, J., & Zmijewska, A. (2008). Past, present and future of mobile payments research: A literature review. *Electronic Commerce Research and Applications, 7*(2), 165–181. doi:10.1016/j.elerap.2007.02.001

Danisman, K., Dalkiran, I., & Celebi, F. V. (2006). Design of a high precision temperature measurement system based on artificial neural network for different thermocouple types. *Measurement, 39*(8), 695–700. doi:10.1016/j.measurement.2006.03.015

Dashti, M., Derhami, V., & Ekhtiyari, E. (2014). Yarn tenacity modeling using artificial neural networks and development of a decision support system based on genetic algorithms. *Journal of Artificial Intelligence and Data Mining, 2*(1), 73–78.

Dave, V. S., & Dutta, K. (2014). Neural network-based models for software effort estimation: A review. *Artificial Intelligence Review, 42*(2), 295–307.

Davis, F. D. (1989). Perceived usefulness, perceived ease of use, and user acceptance of information technology. *Management Information Systems Quarterly, 13*(3), 319–340. doi:10.2307/249008

de Sena Abrahão, R., Moriguchi, S. N., & Andrade, D. F. (2016). Intention of adoption of mobile payment: An analysis in the light of the Unified Theory of Acceptance and Use of Technology (UTAUT). *RAI Revista de Administração e Inovação, 13*(3), 221–230. doi:10.1016/j.rai.2016.06.003

Dennehy, D., & Sammon, D. (2015). Trends in mobile payments research: A literature review. *Journal of Innovation Management, 3*(1), 49–61. doi:10.24840/2183-0606_003.001_0006

Detection and Classification of Induction Motor Faults Using Motor Current Signature Analysis and Multilayer Perceptron. (2014). *IEEE 8th International Power Engineering and Optimization Conference (PEOCO2014)*.

Devin, C., Gupta, A., Darrell, T., Abbeel, P., & Levine, S. (2017, May). Learning modular neural network policies for multi-task and multi-robot transfer. In *2017 IEEE International Conference on Robotics and Automation (ICRA)* (pp. 2169-2176). IEEE. 10.1109/ICRA.2017.7989250

Dewan, S. G., & Chen, L. D. (2005). Mobile payment adoption in the USA: A crossindustry, cross-platform solution. *Journal of Information Privacy & Security, 1*(2), 4–28. doi:10.1080/15536548.2005.10855765

Dharmasaroja, P., & Kingkaew, N. (2016). Application of Artificial Neural Networks for Prediction of Learning Performances. *12th International Conference on Natural Computation, Fuzzy Systems and Knowledge Discovery (ICNC-FSKD)*. 10.1109/FSKD.2016.7603268

Di Pietro, L., Guglielmetti Mugion, R., Mattia, G., Renzi, M. F., & Toni, M. (2015). The integrated model on mobile payment acceptance (IMMPA): An empirical application to public transport. *Transportation Research Part C, Emerging Technologies, 56*, 463–479. doi:10.1016/j.trc.2015.05.001

Doucoure, B., Agbossou, K., & Cardenas, A. (2016). Time series prediction using artificial wavelet neural network and multi-resolution analysis: Application to wind speed data. *Renewable Energy, 92*, 202–211. doi:10.1016/j.renene.2016.02.003

Duane, A., O'Reilly, P., & Andreev, P. (2014). Realising M-payments: Modelling consumers' willingness to M-pay using smart phones. *Behaviour & Information Technology, 33*(4), 318–334. doi:10.1080/0144929X.2012.745608

Dubois, D., & Prade, H. (1980). Fuzzy Sets and Systems: Theory and Applications. Academic Press.

Duygulu, P., Barnard, K., de Freitas, J. F., & Forsyth, D. A. (2002, May). Object recognition as machine translation: Learning a lexicon for a fixed image vocabulary. In *European conference on computer vision* (pp. 97-112). Springer.

Dwivedi, Y. K., Rana, N. P., Janssen, M., Lal, B., Williams, M. D., & Clement, R. M. (2017). B). an empirical validation of a Unified Model of Electronic Government Adoption (UMEGA). *Government Information Quarterly, 34*(2), 211–230. doi:10.1016/j.giq.2017.03.001

Dwivedi, Y. K., Shareef, M. A., Simintiras, A. C., Lal, B., & Weerakkody, V. (2016). A generalised adoption model for services: A cross-country comparison of mobile health (mhealth). *Government Information Quarterly, 33*(1), 174–187. doi:10.1016/j.giq.2015.06.003

El Bouchikhi, E. H. (2012). Induction Machine Fault Detection Enhancement Using a Stator Current High Resolution Spectrum. *IECON - IEEE 38th Annual Conference on Industrial Electronics Society*, 3913-3918 10.1109/IECON.2012.6389267

El Bouchikhi, E. H. (2013). A Parametric Spectral Estimator for Faults Detection in Induction Machines. *The IEEE 39th Annual Conference on Industrial Electronics Society.* 10.1109/IECON.2013.6700357

El Bouchikhi, E. H., Choqueuse, V., & Benbouzid, M. (2015). Induction Machine Faults Detection Using Stator Current Parametric Spectral Estimation. Original Research Article, Elsevier. *Journal of Mechanical Systems and Signal Processing, 52–53*, 447–464. doi:10.1016/j.ymssp.2014.06.015

El-Jawad, M. H. A., Hodhod, R., & Omar, Y. M. (2018, December). Sentiment Analysis of Social Media Networks Using Machine Learning. In *2018 14th International Computer Engineering Conference (ICENCO)* (pp. 174-176). IEEE. 10.1109/ICENCO.2018.8636124

Emre Celebi, M. (2015). *Partitional Clustering Algorithms*. Springer International Publishing Switzerland.

Falk, R. F., & Miller, N. B. (1992). *A primer for soft modeling*. University of Akron Press.

Fan, W., Bouguila, N., & Ziou, D. (2012). Variational learning for finite Dirichlet mixture models and applications. *IEEE Transactions on Neural Networks and Learning Systems, 23*(5), 762–774. doi:10.1109/TNNLS.2012.2190298 PMID:24806125

Featherman, M., & Pavlou, P. (2003). Predicting e-services adoption: A perceived risk facets perspective. *International Journal of Human-Computer Studies*, *59*(4), 451–474. doi:10.1016/S1071-5819(03)00111-3

Felipe, C. M., Roldán, J. L., & Leal-Rodríguez, A. L. (2017). Impact of organizational culture values on organizational agility. *Sustainability*, *9*(12), 2354. doi:10.3390u9122354

Fitriani, F., Suzianti, A., & Chairunnisa, A. (2017). Analysis of factors that affect nfc mobile payment technology adoption:(case study: telkomsel cash). *Proceedings of the 2017 International Conference on Telecommunications and Communication Engineering*, 103-109. 10.1145/3145777.3145778

Fornell, C. I. J. (1994). Partial Least Squares. *Advanced Methods of Marketing Research*, 52-78.

Fornell, C., & Larcker, D. F. (1981). Evaluation Structural Equation Models with Unobservable Variables and Measurement Error. *JMR, Journal of Marketing Research*, *18*(1), 39–50. doi:10.1177/002224378101800104

Francisco, J. V. S. (2013). *Diagnosis of Electric Induction Machines in Non-Stationary Regimes Working in Randomnly Changing Conditions* (Thesis Report). Universitat Politècnica de València.

Furferi, Gelli, & Yarn. (2010). Strength Prediction: A Practical Model Based on Artificial Neural Networks. *Advances in Mechanical Engineering*. doi:10.1155/2010/640103

Garcia-Moya, L., Anaya-Sánchez, H., & Berlanga-Llavori, R. (2013). Retrieving product features and opinions from customer reviews. *IEEE Intelligent Systems*, *28*(3), 19–27. doi:10.1109/MIS.2013.37

Garg, Pulkit, Garg, & Ranga. (2017). Sentiment analysis of the uri terror attack using twitter. In *2017 international conference on computing, communication and automation (ICCCA)*. IEEE.

Garg, S., Patra, K., & Pal, S. K. (2014). Particle swarm optimization of a neural network model in a machining process. *Sadhana*, *39*(3), 533–548. doi:10.100712046-014-0244-7

Gbongli, K., Xu, Y., & Amedjonekou, K. M. (2019). Extended Technology Acceptance Model to Predict Mobile-Based Money Acceptance and Sustainability: A Multi-Analytical Structural Equation Modeling and Neural Network Approach. *Sustainability*, *11*(13), 3639. doi:10.3390u11133639

Gefen, D., Ridgon, E. E., & Straub, D. W. (2011). Editor's Comments: An Updated and Extension to SEM Guidelines for Administrative and Social Science Research. *Management Information Systems Quarterly*, *35*(2), iii–xiv. doi:10.2307/23044042

Geisser, S. (1974). A predictive approach to the random effect model. *Biometrika*, *61*(1), 101–107. doi:10.1093/biomet/61.1.101

Geisser, S. (1975). The predictive sample reuse method with applications. *Journal of the American Statistical Association*, *70*(350), 320–328. doi:10.1080/01621459.1975.10479865

Gerpott, T., & Kornmeier, K. (2009). Determinants of customer acceptance of mobile payment systems. *International Journal of Electronic Finance, 3*(1), 1–30. doi:10.1504/IJEF.2009.024267

Ghorbani, A., & Sheikhan, M. (1991, September). The effect of solid state power amplifiers (SSPAs) nonlinearities on MPSK and M-QAM signal transmission. In *1991 Sixth International Conference on Digital Processing of Signals in Communications* (pp. 193-197). IET.

Giri, F. (2013). *AC Electric Motors Control: Advanced Design Techniques and Applications.* John Wiley & Sons. doi:10.1002/9781118574263

Gjylapi & Durmishie. (2014). Albania Artificial neural networks in forecasting tourists' flow, an intelligent technique to help the economic development of tourism in Albania. *Academicus - International Scientific Journal, 10*(14). Doi:10.7336/academicus.2014.10.14

Go, A., Bhayani, R., & Huang, L. (2009). Twitter sentiment classification using distant supervision. CS224N Project Report, Stanford, 1(12), 2009.

Göktaş, P., & Akgül, Y. (2019). The Investigation of Employer Adoption of Human Resource Information Systems at University Using TAM. In *Structural Equation Modeling Approaches to E-Service Adoption* (pp. 1–27). IGI Global. doi:10.4018/978-1-5225-8015-7.ch001

Gold, A. H., Malhotra, A., & Segars, A. H. (2001). Knowledge management: An organizational capabilities perspective. *Journal of Management Information Systems, 18*(1), 185–214. doi:10.1080/07421222.2001.11045669

Gordan, B., Armaghani, D. J., Hajihassani, M., & Monjezi, M. (2016). Prediction of seismic slope stability through combination of particle swarm optimization and neural network. *Engineering with Computers, 32*(1), 85–97. doi:10.100700366-015-0400-7

Goswami, J. C., & Chan, A. K. (2011). *Fundamentals of wavelets: theory, algorithms, and applications* (Vol. 233). John Wiley & Sons. doi:10.1002/9780470926994

Gregor, K., Danihelka, I., Graves, A., Rezende, D. J., & Wierstra, D. (2015). *Draw: A recurrent neural network for image generation.* arXiv preprint arXiv:1502.04623

Gu, J., Lee, S., & Suh, Y. (2009). Determinants of behavioral intention to mobile banking. *Expert Systems with Applications, 36*(9), 11605–11616. doi:10.1016/j.eswa.2009.03.024

Guo, K. (2017). An Empirical Examination of Initial Use Intention of Mobile Payment. *Boletrn Tecnico, 55*(10).

Hagger, M. S., Chatzisarantis, N. L., & Biddle, S. J. (2002). A metaanalytic review of the theories of reasoned action and planned behavior in physical activity: Predictive validity and the contribution of additional variables. *Journal of Sport & Exercise Psychology, 24*(1), 3–32. doi:10.1123/jsep.24.1.3

Hair, J. F., Ringle, C. M., & Sarstedt, M. (2011). PLS-SEM: Indeed a Silver Bullet. *Journal of Marketing Theory and Practice, 18*(2), 139–152. doi:10.2753/MTP1069-6679190202

Hai, Z., Chang, K., Kim, J. J., & Yang, C. C. (2013). Identifying features in opinion mining via intrinsic and extrinsic domain relevance. *IEEE Transactions on Knowledge and Data Engineering*, *26*(3), 623–634. doi:10.1109/TKDE.2013.26

Ha, K. H., Canedoli, A., Baur, A. W., & Bick, M. (2012). Mobile banking: Insights on its increasing relevance and most common drivers of adoption. *Electronic Markets*, *22*(4), 217–227. doi:10.100712525-012-0107-1

Hampshire, C. (2017). A mixed methods empirical exploration of UK consumer perceptions of trust, risk and usefulness of mobile payments. *International Journal of Bank Marketing*, *35*(3), 354–369. doi:10.1108/IJBM-08-2016-0105

Hanafizadeh, P., Behboudi, M., Koshksaray, A. A., & Tabar, S. J. M. (2014). Mobile banking adoption by Iranian bank clients. *Telematics and Informatics*, *31*(1), 62–78. doi:10.1016/j.tele.2012.11.001

Harris, M. A., Brookshire, R., & Chin, A. G. (2016). Identifying factors influencing consumers' intent to install mobile applications. *International Journal of Information Management*, *36*(3), 441–450. doi:10.1016/j.ijinfomgt.2016.02.004

Hassan, A. U., Hussain, J., Hussain, M., Sadiq, M., & Lee, S. (2017, October). Sentiment analysis of social networking sites (SNS) data using machine learning approach for the measurement of depression. In *2017 International Conference on Information and Communication Technology Convergence (ICTC)* (pp. 138-140). IEEE. 10.1109/ICTC.2017.8190959

Haykin, S. S. (2001). Kalman Filtering and Neural Networks. Wiley.

Henseler, J., Ringle, C., & Sarsted, M. (2014). A new criterion for assessing discriminant validity in variance-based structural equation modeling. *Journal of the Academy of Marketing Science*, *43*(1), 115–135. doi:10.100711747-014-0403-8

Henseler, J., Ringle, C., & Sinkovics, R. (2009). The Use Of Partial Least Squares Path Modeling In International Marketing. *Advances in International Marketing*, *20*(1), 277–319. doi:10.1108/S1474-7979(2009)0000020014

Hew, T. S., Leong, L. Y., Ooi, K. B., & Chong, A. Y. L. (2016). Predicting drivers of mobile entertainment adoption: A two-stage SEM artificial-neural-network analysis. *Journal of Computer Information Systems*, *56*(4), 352–370. doi:10.1080/08874417.2016.1164497

Hilal, S. Y. A., & Okur, M. R. (2018). Predicting Achievement with Artificial Neural Networks: The Case of Anadolu University Open Education System. *International Journal of Assessment Tools in Education*, *5*(3), 474–490. doi:10.21449/ijate.435507

Hongxia, P., Xianhao, X., & Weidan, L. (2011). Drivers and barriers in the acceptance of mobile payment in China. In *International conference on E-business and E-government*. 10.1109/ICEBEG.2011.5887081

Hossain, R., & Mahmud, I. (2016). *Influence of cognitive style on mobile payment system adoption: An extended technology acceptance model.* Paper presented at the 2016 International Conference on Computer Communication and Informatics, ICCCI 2016, 10.1109/ICCCI.2016.7479973

Hsu, C., Wang, C., & Lin, J. C. (2011). Investigating customer adoption behaviors in mobile financial services. *International Journal of Mobile Communications, 9*(5), 477–494. doi:10.1504/IJMC.2011.042455

Hsu, H. S., & Kulviwat, S. (2006). An integrative framework of technology acceptance model and personalisation in mobile commerce. *International Journal of Technology Marketing, 1*(4), 393–410. doi:10.1504/IJTMKT.2006.010734

Huang. (2017). Imitating the brain with neurocomputer a "new" way towards artificial general intelligence. *Int. J. Autom. Comput., 14*(5), 520-531.

Huang, H.-C., & I Hou, C. (2017). Tourism Demand Forecasting Model Using Neural Network. *International Journal of Computer Science & Information Technology, 9*(2), 19–29. doi:10.5121/ijcsit.2017.9202

Hussein, D. M. E. D. M. (2018). A survey on sentiment analysis challenges. *Journal of King Saud University-Engineering Sciences, 30*(4), 330–338. doi:10.1016/j.jksues.2016.04.002

Husson, R. (2009). *Control Methods for Electrical Machines.* ISTE Ltd and John Wiley & Sons, Inc. doi:10.1002/9780470611760

Ibnkahla, M., & Yuan, J. (2004). A neural network MLSE receiver based on natural gradient descent: Application to satellite communications. *EURASIP Journal on Advances in Signal Processing, 2004*(16), 394715. doi:10.1155/S1110865704405010

Insider, B. (2015). The mobile payments report: Forecasts, user trends, and the companies vying to dominate mobile payments. *BI Intelligence.* https://www.businessinsider.com/the-free-mobile-payments-report-2015-06

Iqbal, F., Hashmi, J. M., Fung, B. C., Batool, R., Khattak, A. M., Aleem, S., & Hung, P. C. (2019). A Hybrid Framework for Sentiment Analysis Using Genetic Algorithm Based Feature Reduction. *IEEE Access: Practical Innovations, Open Solutions, 7*, 14637–14652. doi:10.1109/ACCESS.2019.2892852

Iqbal, N., Zerguine, A., & Al-Dhahir, N. (2014). Adaptive equalisation using particle swarm optimisation for uplink SC-FDMA. *Electronics Letters, 50*(6), 469–471. doi:10.1049/el.2013.4091

Jaddi, N. S., Abdullah, S., & Hamdan, A. R. (2015). Multi-population cooperative bat algorithm-based optimization of artificial neural network model. *Journal of Information Science, 294*, 628–644. doi:10.1016/j.ins.2014.08.050

Jafarmadar, S., Khalilaria, S., & Saraee, H. S. (2018). Prediction of the performance and exhaust emissions of a compression ignition engine using a wavelet neural network with a stochastic gradient algorithm. *Energy, 142*, 1128–1138. doi:10.1016/j.energy.2017.09.006

Jantunen, P. (2004). *Modelling of nonlinear power amplifiers for wireless communications* (Master's thesis).

Jiang, Yang, Clinton, & Wang. (2004). An artificial neural network model for estimating crop yields using remotely sensed information. *International Journal of Remote Sensing*. http://www.tandf.co.uk/journals

John, A., John, A., & Sheik, R. (2019, April). Context Deployed Sentiment Analysis Using Hybrid Lexicon. In *2019 1st International Conference on Innovations in Information and Communication Technology (ICIICT)* (pp. 1-5). IEEE. 10.1109/ICIICT1.2019.8741413

Jr, J. F., Hult, G. T. M., Ringle, C., & Sarstedt, M. (2016). *A primer on partial least squares structural equation modeling (PLS-SEM)*. Sage Publications.

Juneja, P., & Ojha, U. (2017, July). Casting online votes: to predict offline results using sentiment analysis by machine learning classifiers. In *2017 8th International Conference on Computing, Communication and Networking Technologies (ICCCNT)* (pp. 1-6). IEEE. 10.1109/ICCCNT.2017.8203996

Kaitawarn, C. (2015). Factor influencing the acceptance and use of M-payment in Thailand: A case study of AIS mPAY rabbit. *Rev. Integr. Bus. Econ. Res.*, *4*(3), 222.

Kalchbrenner, N., Grefenstette, E., & Blunsom, P. (2014). *A convolutional neural network for modelling sentences*. arXiv preprint arXiv:1404.2188

Kalkanci, M., Kurumer, G., Öztürk, H., Sinecen, M., & Kayacan, Ö. (2017). Artificial Neural Network System for Prediction of Dimensional Properties of Cloth in Garment Manufacturing: Case Study on a T-Shirt. *Fibres & Textiles in Eastern Europe*, *4*(14), 135–140. doi:10.5604/01.3001.0010.2859

Kan, C. W., Wong, W. Y., Song, L. J., & Law, M. C. (2013). Prediction of Color Properties of Cellulase-Treated 100% Cotton Denim Fabric. *Journal of Textiles*. Advance online publication. doi:10.1155/2013/962751

Kangas, J. A., Kohonen, T. K., & Laaksonen, J. T. (1990). Variants of self-organizing maps. *IEEE Transactions on Neural Networks*, *1*(1), 93–99. doi:10.1109/72.80208 PMID:18282826

Kapoor, K., Dwivedi, Y., & Williams, M. (2014). Examining the role of three sets of innovation attributes for determining adoption of the interbank mobile payment service. *Information Systems Frontiers*. Advance online publication. doi:10.100710796-014-9484-7

Karaboga, D., Akay, B., & Ozturk, C. (2007). Artificial bee colony (ABC) optimization algorithm for training feed-forward neural networks. In *Modeling Decisions for Artificial Intelligence* (pp. 318–329). Springer. doi:10.1007/978-3-540-73729-2_30

Karaboga, D., Akay, B., & Ozturk, C. (2007). Artificial Bee Colony (ABC) Optimization Algorithm for Training Feed-Forward Neural Networks. *LNAI*, *4617*, 318–329.

Kaur, R., & Kaur, B. (2014). Artificial neural network learning enhancement using bacterial foraging optimization algorithm. *International Journal of Computers and Applications*, *102*(10), 27–33. doi:10.5120/17852-8812

Kennedy, A., & Inkpen, D. (2006). Sentiment classification of movie reviews using contextual valence shifters. *Computational Intelligence*, *22*(2), 110–125. doi:10.1111/j.1467-8640.2006.00277.x

Keramati, A., Taeb, R., Larijani, A. M., & Mojir, N. (2012). A combinative model of behavioural and technical factors affecting 'Mobile'-payment services adoption: An empirical study. *Service Industries Journal*, *32*(9), 1489–1504. doi:10.1080/02642069.2011.552716

Khalilzadeh, J., Ozturk, A. B., & Bilgihan, A. (2017). Security-related factors in extended UTAUT model for NFC based mobile payment in the restaurant industry. *Computers in Human Behavior*, *70*, 460–474. doi:10.1016/j.chb.2017.01.001

Khan, A. N., & Ali, A. (2018). Factors affecting Retailer's Adopti on of Mobile payment systems: A SEM-neural network modeling approach. *Wireless Personal Communications*, *103*(3), 2529–2551. doi:10.100711277-018-5945-5

Khan, A. N., Cao, X., & Pitafi, A. H. (2019). Personality Traits as Predictor of M-Payment Systems: A SEM-Neural Networks Approach. *Journal of Organizational and End User Computing*, *31*(4), 89–110. doi:10.4018/JOEUC.2019100105

Kiang, M. Y. (2001). Extending the Kohonen self-organizing map networks for clustering analysis. *Computational Statistics & Data Analysis*, *38*(2), 161–180. doi:10.1016/S0167-9473(01)00040-8

Kim, C., Mirusmonov, M., & Lee, I. (2010). An empirical examination of factors influencing the intention to use mobile payment. *Computers in Human Behavior*, *26*(3), 310–322. doi:10.1016/j.chb.2009.10.013

Kim, G., Shin, B., & Lee, H. G. (2009). Understanding dynamics between initial trust and usage intentions of mobile banking. *Information Systems Journal*, *19*(3), 283–311. doi:10.1111/j.1365-2575.2007.00269.x

Kim, Y., Choi, J., & Park, Y., & Yeon, J. (2016). The adoption of mobile payment services for "fintech". *International Journal of Applied Engineering Research*, *11*(2), 1058–1061.

Kline, R. (2011). *Principles and Practice of Structural Equation Modeling* (3rd ed.). Guilford Press.

Klir, G. J., & Yuan, B. (1996). Fuzzy Sets, Fuzzy Logic, and Fuzzy Systems: Selected Papers by Lotfi Asker Zadeh. World Scientific Publishing Co. Pte. Ltd.

Ko, E., Kim, E., & Lee, E. (2009). Modeling consumer adoption of mobile shopping for fashion products in Korea. *Psychology and Marketing*, *26*(7), 669–687. doi:10.1002/mar.20294

Koenig-Lewis, N., Marquet, M., Palmer, A., & Zhao, A. L. (2015). Enjoyment and social influence: Predicting mobile payment adoption. *Service Industries Journal*, *35*(10), 537–554. doi:10.1080/02642069.2015.1043278

Koeni-Lewis, N., Palmer, A., & Moll, A. (2010). Predicting young consumers' take up of mobile banking services. *International Journal of Bank Marketing, 28*(5), 410–432. doi:10.1108/02652321011064917

Kohonen, T., & Honkela, T. (2007). Kohonen network. *Scholarpedia, 2*(1), 1568. doi:10.4249cholarpedia.1568

Korovkinas, K., Danėnas, P., & Garšva, G. (2019). SVM and k-Means Hybrid Method for Textual Data Sentiment Analysis. *Baltic Journal of Modern Computing, 7*(1), 47–60. doi:10.22364/bjmc.2019.7.1.04

Kose, U. (2018). An Ant-Lion Optimizer-Trained Artificial Neural Network System for Chaotic Electroencephalogram (EEG). *Prediction. Appl. Sci., 8*(9), 1613. Advance online publication. doi:10.3390/app8091613

Kourakos, G., & Mantoglou, A. (2009). Pumping optimization of coastal aquifers based on evolutionary algorithms and surrogate modular neural network models. *Advances in Water Resources, 32*(4), 507–521. doi:10.1016/j.advwatres.2009.01.001

Kulkarni & Rodd. (2018). Extensive study of text based methods for opinion mining. In *2018 2nd international conference on inventive systems and control (ICISC)*. IEEE.

Kumar, Gupta, Mishra, & Prasad. (2015). Comparison of support vector machine, artificial neural network, and spectral angle mapper algorithms for crop classification using LISS IV data. *International Journal of Remote Sensing, 36*(6).

Kumar, P., Prasad, R., Prashant, K., & Srivasta. (2015). Artificial neural network with different learning parameters for crop classification using multispectral datasets. In *International Conference on Microwave, Optical and Communication Engineering (ICMOCE)*. IEEE.

Kumara, P., Prasada, R., Mishraa, V. N., Guptaa, D. K., & Singhb, S. K. (2016). Artificial Neural Network for Crop Classification Using C-band RISAT-1 Satellite Datasets. *Russian Agricultural Sciences, 42*(3-4), 281–284.

Kuoa, J.-T., Wanga, Y.-Y., & Lungb, W.-S. (2006). A hybrid neural–genetic algorithm for reservoir water quality management. *Water Research, 40*(7), 1367–1376. doi:10.1016/j.watres.2006.01.046 PMID:16545860

Kuwataa, K. R., & Shibasakib. (2016), Estimating Corn Yield In The United States With Modis EVI And Machine Learning Methods. *ISPRS Annals Of The Photogrammetry, Remote Sensing And Spatial Information Sciences, 8*.

Lau, Sun, & Yang. (2019). SN Modelling, prediction and classification of student academic performance using artificial neural networks. *Applied Sciences, 1*, 982-989. doi:10.100742452-019-0884-7

Laukkanen, T. (2016). Consumer adoption versus rejection decisions in seemingly similar service innovations: The case of the Internet and mobile banking. *Journal of Business Research, 69*(7), 2432–2439. doi:10.1016/j.jbusres.2016.01.013

Laukkanen, T., & Kiviniemi, V. (2010). The role of information in mobile banking resistance. *International Journal of Bank Marketing*, *28*(5), 372–388. doi:10.1108/02652321011064890

Lawrence, S., Giles, C. L., Tsoi, A. C., & Back, A. D. (1997). Face recognition: A convolutional neural-network approach. *IEEE Transactions on Neural Networks*, *8*(1), 98–113. doi:10.1109/72.554195 PMID:18255614

Lee, C. (1990). Fuzzy Logic in Control Systems: Fuzzy Logic Controller. *IEEE Transactions on Systems, Man, and Cybernetics*, *20*, 404–435.

Leong, L.-Y., Hew, T.-S., Tan, G. W.-H., & Ooi, K. B. (2013). Predicting the determinants of the NFC-enabled mobile credit card acceptance: A neural network approach. *Expert Systems with Applications*, *40*(14), 5604–5620. doi:10.1016/j.eswa.2013.04.018

Le, T. H. (2011). Applying artificial neural networks for face recognition. *Advances in Artificial Neural Systems*, *2011*, 15. doi:10.1155/2011/673016

Lewellen, M. (1998, August). Neural network recognition of spelling errors. In *Proceedings of the 36th Annual Meeting of the Association for Computational Linguistics and 17th International Conference on Computational Linguistics-Volume 2* (pp. 1490-1492). Association for Computational Linguistics.

Li, H., Liu, Y., & Heikkilä, J. (2014). Understanding the factors driving NFC-enabled mobile payment adoption: an empirical investigation. PACIS 2014 Proceedings, 231.

Liébana-Cabanillas, F., Marinkovic, V., de Luna, I. R., & Kalinic, Z. (2018). Predicting the determinants of mobile payment acceptance: A hybrid SEM-neural network approach. *Technological Forecasting and Social Change*, *129*, 117–130. doi:10.1016/j.techfore.2017.12.015

Liébana-Cabanillas, F., Marinković, V., & Kalinić, Z. (2017b). A SEM-neural network approach for predicting antecedents of m-commerce acceptance. *International Journal of Information Management*, *37*(2), 14–24. doi:10.1016/j.ijinfomgt.2016.10.008

Liébana-Cabanillas, F., Munoz-Leiva, F., & Sánchez-Fernandez, J. (2015b). Payment systems in new electronic environments: Consumer behavior in payment systems via SMS. *International Journal of Information Technology & Decision Making*, *14*(02), 421–449. doi:10.1142/S0219622015500078

Liébana-Cabanillas, F., Muñoz-Leiva, F., & Sánchez-Fernández, J. (2017a). A global approach to the analysis of user behavior in mobile payment systems in the new electronic environment. *Service Business*, 1–40.

Liébana-Cabanillas, F., Ramos de Luna, I., & Montoro-Ríos, F. (2017c). Intention to use new mobile payment systems: A comparative analysis of SMS and NFC payments. *Economic Research Journal*, *30*(1), 892–910. doi:10.1080/1331677X.2017.1305784

Liébana-Cabanillas, F., Ramos de Luna, I., & Montoro-Ríos, F. J. (2015a). User behaviour in QR mobile payment system: The QR payment acceptance model. *Technology Analysis and Strategic Management*, *27*(9), 1031–1049. doi:10.1080/09537325.2015.1047757

Liébana-Cabanillas, F., Sánchez-Fernández, J., & Muñoz-Leiva, F. (2014). Antecedents of the adoption of the new mobile payment systems: The moderating effect of age. *Computers in Human Behavior*, *35*, 464–478. doi:10.1016/j.chb.2014.03.022

Li, H. (2019). Network traffic prediction of the optimized BP neural network based on Glowworm Swarm Algorithm. *Systems Science & Control Engineering.*, *7*(2), 64–70. doi:10.1080/216425 83.2019.1626299

Li, K., Lu, W., Liang, C., & Wang, B. (2019). Intelligence in Tourism Management: A Hybrid FOA-BP Method on Daily Tourism Demand Forecasting with Web Search Data. *Mathematics*, *7*(6), 531–542. doi:10.3390/math7060531

Lin, F. H. (2011). An empirical investigation of mobile banking adoption: The effect of innovation attributes and knowledge based trust. *International Journal of Information Management*, *31*(3), 252–260. doi:10.1016/j.ijinfomgt.2010.07.006

Liu, Y., & Bazzi, A. M. (2017). A review and comparison of fault detection and diagnosis methods for squirrel-cage induction motors: State of the art. *ISA Transactions.*

Luarn, P., & Lin, H. H. (2005). Toward an understanding of the behavioral intention to use mobile banking. *Computers in Human Behavior*, *21*(6), 873–891. doi:10.1016/j.chb.2004.03.003

Ludwig, O., & Nunes, U. (2010). Novel maximum-margin training algorithms for supervised neural networks. *IEEE Transactions on Neural Networks*, *21*(6), 972–984.

Lu, Y., Yang, S., Chau, P. Y. K., & Cao, Y. (2011). Dynamics between the trust transfer process and intention to use mobile payment services: A cross-environment perspective. *Information & Management*, *48*(8), 393–403. doi:10.1016/j.im.2011.09.006

Majumdar, A., Das, A., Hatua, P., & Ghosh, A. (2015). *Optimization of woven fabric parameters for ultraviolet radiation protection and comfort using artificial neural network and genetic algorithm*. Neural Comput & Applic. doi:10.100700521-015-2025-6

Malaquias, F. R., & Hwang, Y. (2016). An empirical study on trust in mobile banking: A developing country perspective. *Computers in Human Behavior*, *54*, 453–461. doi:10.1016/j.chb.2015.08.039

Malik, S. (2019). Optimal Travel Route Recommendation Mechanism Based on Neural Networks and Particle Swarm Optimization for Efficient Tourism Using Tourist. *Sustainability*, *11*, 3357. doi:10.3390u11123357

Mallat, N. (2007). Exploring consumer adoption of mobile payments–a qualitative study. *The Journal of Strategic Information Systems*, *16*(4), 413–432. doi:10.1016/j.jsis.2007.08.001

Mallat, N., Rossi, M., & Tuunainen, V. K. (2004). Mobile banking services. *Communications of the ACM*, *47*(5), 42–46. doi:10.1145/986213.986236

Mallat, N., & Tuunainen, V. K. (2008). Exploring merchant adoption of mobile payment systems: An empirical study. *e-Service Journal*, *6*(2), 24–57. doi:10.2979/esj.2008.6.2.24

Mani, N., & Srinivasan, B. (1997, October). Application of artificial neural network model for optical character recognition. In *1997 IEEE International Conference on Systems, Man, and Cybernetics. Computational Cybernetics and Simulation* (Vol. 3, pp. 2517-2520). IEEE. 10.1109/ICSMC.1997.635312

Manoj, Semwal, & Verma. (2019). *An Artificial Neural Network Model For Estimating Mentha Crop Biomass Yield Using Landsat 8 OLI.* Precision Agriculture. Https://Doi.Org/10.1007/S11119-019-09655-1

Mansour, A. H., Zen, G., Salh, A., Hayder, H., & Alabdeen, Z. (2015). *Voice recognition Using back propagation algorithm in neural networks.* Academic Press.

Mansour, I. H. F., Eljelly, A. M., & Abdullah, A. M. (2016). Consumers' attitude towards e-banking services in Islamic banks: The case of Sudan. *Review of International Business and Strategy, 26*(2), 244–260. doi:10.1108/RIBS-02-2014-0024

Martens, M., Roll, O., & Elliott, R. (2017). Testing the technology readiness and acceptance model for mobile payments across Germany and South Africa. *International Journal of Innovation and Technology Management, 14*(6), 1750033. Advance online publication. doi:10.1142/S021987701750033X

Martínez-Porchas, M., Villalpando-Canchola, E., & Vargas-Albores, F. (2016). Significant loss of sensitivity and specificity in the taxonomic classification occurs when short 16S rRNA gene sequences are used. *Heliyon, 2*(9), e00170. doi:10.1016/j.heliyon.2016.e00170 PMID:27699286

Martins, C. T. O., & Popovič, A. (2014). Understanding the internet banking adoption: A unified theory of acceptance and use of technology and perceived risk application. *International Journal of Information Management, 34*(1), 1–13. doi:10.1016/j.ijinfomgt.2013.06.002

Masamila, B., Mtenzi, F., Said, J., & Tinabo, R. (2010). A secured mobile payment model for developing markets. In *International Conference on Networked Digital Technologies.* Springer. 10.1007/978-3-642-14292-5_20

Mason, C., Twomey, J., Wright, D., & Whitman, L. (2017). Predicting Engineering Student Attrition Risk Using a Probabilistic Neural Network and Comparing Results with a Backpropagation Neural Network and Logistic Regression. *Research in Higher Education.* Advance online publication. doi:10.100711162-017-9473-z

Mavrovouniotis & Yang. (2014). *Training neural networks with ant colony optimization algorithms For pattern classification.* Springer-Verlag.

Mei & Wang. (2009). Ant Colony Optimization for Neural Network. *Key Engineering Materials, 392*, 677-681.

Meixin, X., & Wei, L. (2014). *A Study on the Intention to Use NFC Mobile Phone Payment and Strategies to Expand the NFC Market—Based on Users' Perspective.* Academic Press.

Mei, Y., Yang, J., Lu, Y., Hao, F., Xu, D., Pan, H., & Wang, J. (2019). BP–ANN Model Coupled with Particle Swarm Optimization for the Efficient Prediction of 2-Chlorophenol Removal in an Electro-Oxidation System. *International Journal of Environmental Research and Public Health, 16*(14), 2454. doi:10.3390/ijerph16142454 PMID:31295918

Michou, A., Matsagouras, E., & Lens, W. (2014). Dispositional achievement motives matter for autonomous versus controlled motivation and behavioral or affective educational outcomes. *Personality and Individual Differences, 69*, 205–211. doi:10.1016/j.paid.2014.06.004

Mikolov, T., Karafiát, M., Burget, L., Černocký, J., & Khudanpur, S. (2010). Recurrent neural network based language model. In *Eleventh annual conference of the international speech communication association.* Academic Press.

Miltgen, C. L., Popovič, A., & Oliveira, T. (2013). Determinants of end-user acceptance of biometrics: Integrating the "Big 3" of technology acceptance with privacy context. *Decision Support Systems, 56*, 103–114. doi:10.1016/j.dss.2013.05.010

Mirjalili, S. (2015). How effective is the Grey Wolf optimizer in training multi-layer perceptrons. *Applied Intelligence, 43*(1), 150–161. doi:10.100710489-014-0645-7

Mirjalili, S., Mirjalili, S. M., & Lewis, A. (2014). Grey wolf optimizer. *Advances in Engineering Software, 69*, 46–61. doi:10.1016/j.advengsoft.2013.12.007

Mirjalili, S., Mirjalili, S. M., & Lewis, A. (2014). Let a biogeography-based optimizer train your Multi- Layer Perceptron. *Information Sciences, 269*, 188–209. doi:10.1016/j.ins.2014.01.038

Mishra. (2016). Applications of Machine Learning Techniques in Agricultural Crop Production: A Review Paper. *Indian Journal of Science and Technology, 9*(38). www.indjst.org

Mishra, S., Mishra, D., & Santra, G. H. (2016). Applications of Machine Learning Techniques in Agricultural Crop Production: A Review Paper. *Indian Journal of Science and Technology, 9*(38). doi:10.17485/ijst/2016/v9i38/95032

Mitchell, T. M. (1997). *Machine Learning* (International Edition). McGraw-Hill.

Mohanty, A. R. (2015). *Machinery Condition Monitoring Principles and Practices.* CRC Press Taylor& Francis.

Monjezi, Amini Khoshalan, Yazdian, Arab, & Geosci. (2012). Prediction of flyrock and backbreak in open pit blasting operation. *A Neuro-Genetic Approach, 5*, 441–448. DOI doi:10.100712517-010-0185-3

Moodley, T., & Govender, I. (2016). Factors influencing academic use of internet banking services: An empirical study. *African Journal of Science, Technology, Innovation and Development, 8*(1), 43–51. doi:10.1080/20421338.2015.1128043

Moore, G. C., & Benbasat, I. (1991). Development of an instrument to measure the perceptions of adopting an information technology innovation. *Information Systems Research, 2*(3), 192–222. doi:10.1287/isre.2.3.192

Morosan, C., & DeFranco, A. (2016a). It's about time: Revisiting UTAUT2 to examine consumers' intentions to use NFC mobile payments in hotels. *International Journal of Hospitality Management*, *53*, 17–29. doi:10.1016/j.ijhm.2015.11.003

Morosan, C., & DeFranco, A. (2016b). Investigating American iPhone users' intentions to use NFC mobile payments in hotels. In *Information and Communication Technologies in Tourism 2016* (pp. 427–440). Springer International Publishing. doi:10.1007/978-3-319-28231-2_31

Motahari. (2017, January). Development of a PSO-ANN Model for Rainfall-Runoff Response in Basins, Case Study: Karaj Basin, Civil. *Engineering Journal (New York)*, *3*(1), 35–44.

Mun, Y. P., Khalid, H., & Nadarajah, D. (2017). Millennials' Perception on Mobile Payment Services in Malaysia. *Procedia Computer Science*, *124*, 397–404. doi:10.1016/j.procs.2017.12.170

Nanda, S. J., & Garg, S. (2019). Design of Supervised and Blind Channel Equalizer Based on Moth-Flame Optimization. *Journal of The Institution of Engineers (India): Series B*, *100*(2), 105-115.

Nanda, S. J., & Jonwal, N. (2017). Robust nonlinear channel equalization using WNN trained by symbiotic organism search algorithm. *Applied Soft Computing*, *57*, 197–209. doi:10.1016/j.asoc.2017.03.029

Nandy, S., Sarkar, P. P., & Das, A. (2012). Analysis of a nature inspired firefly algorithm based back-propagation neural network training. *International Journal of Computers and Applications*, *43*, 8–16. doi:10.5120/6401-8339

Nawi, N. M., Khan, A., & Rehman, M. Z. (2013). New back-propagation neural network optimized with cuckoo search algorithm. *Proc. Int. conf. Computational Science and Its Applications*, *ICCSA-2013*, 413-426. 10.1007/978-3-642-39637-3_33

Nawi, N. M., Khan, A., & Rehman, M. Z. (2014). *Data classification using metaheuristic Cuckoo Search technique for Levenberg Marquardt back propagation (CSLM) algorithm*. AIP Conference Proceedings.

Nawi, N. M., Rehman, M. Z., & Khan, A. (2014). A new bat based back-propagation (BAT-BP) algorithm. In J. Swiatek, A. Grzech, P. Swiatek, & J. Tomczak (Eds.), *Advances in Systems Science, Advances in Intelligent Systems and Computing* (pp. 395–404). Springer. doi:10.1007/978-3-319-01857-7_38

Noersasongko, E., Julfia, F. T., Syukur, A., Purwanto, R. A. P., & Supriyanto, C. (2016, January). A Tourism Arrival Forecasting using Genetic Algorithm based Neural Network. *Indian Journal of Science and Technology*, *9*(4). Advance online publication. doi:10.17485/ijst/2016/v9i4/78722

Nunnally, J., & Bernstein, I. (1994). *Psychometric Theory* (3rd ed.). McGraw Hill.

O'Connor, Y., & O'Reilly, P. (2016). Examining the infusion of mobile technology by healthcare practitioners in a hospital setting. *Information Systems Frontiers*, 1–21.

Oancea, B., Dragoescu, R., & Ciucu, S. (2017). *Predicting students' results in higher education using a neural network*. https://mpra.ub.uni-muenchen.de/72041/

Obeid. (2018). Optimizing Neural Networks using Dragonfly Algorithm for Medical Prediction. *2018 8th International Conference on Computer Science and Information Technology (CSIT)*.

Ojha, Abraham, & Sn'aˇsel. (2017). *Simultaneous Optimization of Neural Network Weights and Active Nodes using Metaheuristics*. arxiv:1707.01810v1

Oliveira, T., Thomas, M., Baptista, G., & Campos, F. (2016). Mobile payment: Understanding the determinants of customer adoption and intention to recommend the technology. *Computers in Human Behavior, 61*, 404–414. doi:10.1016/j.chb.2016.03.030

Ondrus, J., & Pigneur, Y. (2006). Towards a holistic analysis of mobile payments: A multiple perspectives approach. *Electronic Commerce Research and Applications, 5*(3), 246–257. doi:10.1016/j.elerap.2005.09.003

Ooi, K., & Tan, G. W.-H. (2016). Mobile technology acceptance model: An investigation using mobile users to explore smartphone credit card. *Expert Systems with Applications, 59*, 33–46. doi:10.1016/j.eswa.2016.04.015

Oussar, Y., Rivals, I., Personnaz, L., & Dreyfus, G. (1998). Training wavelet networks for nonlinear dynamic input–output modeling. *Neurocomputing, 20*(1-3), 173–188. doi:10.1016/S0925-2312(98)00010-1

Özdemir & Polat. (2017). Forecasting With Artificial Neural Network Of Science Teachers. *Professional Burnout Variables. Int. J. Educ. Stud., 04*(03), 49–64.

Ozkan, Ozturky, Sunarz, & Karaboga. (2011). The artificial bee colony algorithm In training artificial neural Network for oil spill detection. *ICS AS CR 2011*.

Ozturk & Karaboga. (2011). *Hybrid Artificial Bee Colony Algorithm For Neural Network Training*. IEEE.

Ozturk, A. B., Bilgihan, A., Salehi-Esfahani, S., & Hua, N. (2017). Understanding the mobile payment technology acceptance based on valence theory: A case of restaurant transactions. *International Journal of Contemporary Hospitality Management, 29*(8), 2027–2049. doi:10.1108/IJCHM-04-2016-0192

Pal, D., Vanijja, V., & Papasratorn, B. (2015). An empirical analysis towards the adoption of NFC mobile payment system by the end user. *Procedia Computer Science, 69*, 13–25. doi:10.1016/j.procs.2015.10.002

Pamungkas, Wahyu, & Putri. (2016). An experimental study of lexicon-based sentiment analysis on Bahasa Indonesia. In *2016 6th international annual engineering seminar (INAES)*. IEEE.

Panda, S., Mohapatra, P. K., & Panigrahi, S. P. (2015). A new training scheme for neural networks and application in non-linear channel equalization. *Applied Soft Computing, 27*, 47–52. doi:10.1016/j.asoc.2014.10.040

Panda, S., Sarangi, A., & Panigrahi, S. P. (2014). A new training strategy for neural network using shuffled frog-leaping algorithm and application to channel equalization. *AEÜ. International Journal of Electronics and Communications, 68*(11), 1031–1036. doi:10.1016/j.aeue.2014.05.005

Pandey, R. (2005). Fast blind equalization using complex-valued MLP. *Neural Processing Letters, 21*(3), 215–225. doi:10.100711063-005-1085-5

Pant, G., & Srinivasan, P. (2010). Predicting web page status. *Information Systems Research, 21*(2), 345–364. doi:10.1287/isre.1080.0231

Pao, Y. (1989). *Adaptive pattern recognition and neural networks.* Academic Press.

Park, D. C., & Jeong, T. K. J. (2002). Complex-bilinear recurrent neural network for equalization of a digital satellite channel. *IEEE Transactions on Neural Networks, 13*(3), 711–725. doi:10.1109/TNN.2002.1000135 PMID:18244467

Park, E., & Kim, K. J. (2013). User acceptance of long-term evolution (LTE) services: An application of extended technology acceptance model. *Program, 47*(2), 188–205. doi:10.1108/00330331311313762

Patel, V., Gandhi, V., Heda, S., & George, N. V. (2016). Design of adaptive exponential functional link network-based nonlinear filters. *IEEE Transactions on Circuits and Systems. I, Regular Papers, 63*(9), 1434–1442. doi:10.1109/TCSI.2016.2572091

Patra, J. C., Meher, P. K., & Chakraborty, G. (2009). Nonlinear channel equalization for wireless communication systems using Legendre neural networks. *Signal Processing, 89*(11), 2251–2262. doi:10.1016/j.sigpro.2009.05.004

Pavlou, P. A. (2003). Consumer acceptance of electronic commerce: Integrating trust and risk with the technology acceptance model. *International Journal of Electronic Commerce, 7*(3), 101–131. doi:10.1080/10864415.2003.11044275

Peng, H., Xu, X., & Liu, W. (2011). Drivers and barriers in the acceptance of mobile payment in China. *Communications in Information Science and Management Engineering, 1*(5), 73–78.

Peng, R., Xiong, L., & Yang, Z. (2012). Exploring tourist adoption of tourism mobile payment: An empirical analysis. *Journal of Theoretical and Applied Electronic Commerce Research, 7*(1), 21–33. doi:10.4067/S0718-18762012000100003

Pham, T. T. T., & Ho, J. C. (2015). The effects of product-related, personal-related factors and attractiveness of alternatives on consumer adoption of NFC-based mobile payments. *Technology in Society, 43*, 159-172.doi: .techsoc.2015.05.004 doi:10.1016/j

Phonthanukitithaworn, C., Sellitto, C., & Fong, M. (2015). User intentions to adopt mobile payment services: A study of early adopters in Thailand. *Journal of Internet Banking and Commerce, 20*(1), 1–29.

Phonthanukitithaworn, C., Sellitto, C., & Fong, M. W. L. (2016). An investigation of mobile payment (m-payment) services in Thailand. *Asia-Pacific Journal of Business Administration*, *8*(1), 37–54. doi:10.1108/APJBA-10-2014-0119

Poria, S., Gelbukh, A., Hussain, A., Howard, N., Das, D., & Bandyopadhyay, S. (2013). Enhanced SenticNet with affective labels for concept-based opinion mining. *IEEE Intelligent Systems*, *28*(2), 31–38. doi:10.1109/MIS.2013.4

Pousttchi, K., & Wiedemann, D. G. (2007). What influences consumers' intention to use mobile payments. *Proceedings of the 6th Annual Global Mobility Roundtable*.

Pradeep, J., Srinivasan, E., & Himavathi, S. (2011, March). Neural network based handwritten character recognition system without feature extraction. In 2011 international conference on computer, communication and electrical technology (ICCCET) (pp. 40-44). IEEE. doi:10.1109/ICCCET.2011.5762513

Pradhan, A. K., Meher, S. K., & Routray, A. (2006). Communication channel equalization using wavelet network. *Digital Signal Processing*, *16*(4), 445–452. doi:10.1016/j.dsp.2005.06.001

Qasim, H., & Abu-Shanab, E. (2016). Drivers of mobile payment acceptance: The impact of network externalities. *Information Systems Frontiers*, *18*(5), 1021–1034. doi:10.100710796-015-9598-6

Ramos-de-Luna, I., Montoro-Rios, F., & Liebana-Cabanillas, F. (2016). Determinants of the intention to use NFC technology as a payment system: An acceptance model approach. *Information Systems and e-Business Management*, *14*(2), 293–314. doi:10.100710257-015-0284-5

Rana, N. P., Dwivedi, Y. K., Lal, B., Williams, M. D., & Clement, M. (2017). Citizens' adoption of an electronic government system: Towards a unified view. *Information Systems Frontiers*, *19*(3), 549–568. doi:10.100710796-015-9613-y

Rana, N. P., Dwivedi, Y. K., Williams, M. D., & Weerakkody, V. (2016). Adoption of online public grievance redressal system in India: Toward developing a unified view. *Computers in Human Behavior*, *59*, 265–282. doi:10.1016/j.chb.2016.02.019

Rashedi, E., Nezamabadi-pour, H., & Saryazdi, S. (2009). GSA: A gravitational search algorithm. *Information Sciences*, *179*(13), 2232–2248. doi:10.1016/j.ins.2009.03.004

Rathi, M., Malik, A., Varshney, D., Sharma, R., & Mendiratta, S. (2018, August). Sentiment Analysis of Tweets Using Machine Learning Approach. In *2018 Eleventh International Conference on Contemporary Computing (IC3)* (pp. 1-3). IEEE. 10.1109/IC3.2018.8530517

Raval, D., Bhatt, D., Kumhar, M. K., Parikh, V., & Vyas, D. (2016). Medical diagnosis system using machine learning. *International Journal of Computer Science & Communication*, *7*(1), 177–182.

Ren, F., & Wu, Y. (2013). Predicting user-topic opinions in twitter with social and topical context. *IEEE Transactions on Affective Computing*, *4*(4), 412–424. doi:10.1109/T-AFFC.2013.22

Ringle, C. M., Sarstedt, M., Mitchell, R., & Gudergan, S. P. (2018). Partial least squares structural equation modeling in HRM research. *International Journal of Human Resource Management*, 1–27.

Rogers, E. M. (1995). Diffusion of Innovations. Academic Press.

Rogers, E. M. (1983). *Diffusion of innovations* (3rd ed.). Free Press of Glencoe.

Roldán, J. L., & Sánchez-Franco, M. J. (2012). Variance-based structural equation modeling: Guidelines for using partial least squares in information systems research. In *Research methodologies, innovations and philosophies in software systems engineering and information systems* (pp. 193–221). IGI Global. doi:10.4018/978-1-4666-0179-6.ch010

Ross, T. J. (2010). *Fuzzy Logic with Engineering Applications* (3rd ed.). John Wiley & Sons. doi:10.1002/9781119994374

Rouibah, K. P. B. L., & Hwang, Y. (2016). The effects of perceived enjoyment and perceived risks on trust formation and intentions to use online payment systems: New perspectives from an Arab country. *Electronic Commerce Research and Applications, 19*, 33–43. doi:10.1016/j.elerap.2016.07.001

Ryan, R. M., & Deci, E. L. (2000). Intrinsic and extrinsic motivations: Classic definitions and new directions. *Contemporary Educational Psychology, 25*(1), 54–67. doi:10.1006/ceps.1999.1020 PMID:10620381

Sadeghyan & Asadi. (2010). *Ms-baco: a new model selection algorithm using binary ant Colony optimization for neural complexity and error reduction.* Academic Press.

Saghatforoush, A., Monjezi, M., Shirani, R., & Faradonbeh, D. J. A. (2007). Combination of neural network and ant colony optimization algorithms for prediction and optimization of flyrock and back-break induced by blasting. *Engineering with Computers.* Advance online publication. doi:10.100700366-015-0415-0

Saha, S., Chakraborty, D., & Dutta, O. (2014). Guided convergence for training feed-forward neural network using novel gravitational search optimization. *Proc. 2014 International Conference on High Performance Computing and Applications (ICHPCA),* 1-6. 10.1109/ICHPCA.2014.7045348

Saini, R. S. K., & Ghosh. (2018). *Crop Classification On Single Date Sentinel-2 Imagery Using Random Forest And Suppor Vector Machine.* The International Archives of the Photogrammetry, Remote Sensing and Spatial Information Sciences, Dehradun, India.

Salama, K., & Abdelbar, A. M. (2014). A Novel Ant Colony Algorithm for Building Neural Network Topologies. *Springer International Publishing Switzerland LNCS, 8667,* 1–12. doi:10.1007/978-3-319-09952-1_1

Saleh, A. A. (1981). Frequency-independent and frequency-dependent nonlinear models of TWT amplifiers. *IEEE Transactions on Communications, 29*(11), 1715–1720. doi:10.1109/TCOM.1981.1094911

Salloum, S. A., Al-Emran, M., Khalaf, R., Habes, M., & Shaalan, K. (2019). An Innovative Study of E-Payment Systems Adoption in Higher Education: Theoretical Constructs and Empirical Analysis. *International Journal of Interactive Mobile Technologies, 13*(6), 68. doi:10.3991/ijim.v13i06.9875

San Martín, H., & Herrero, Á. (2012). Influence of the user's psychological factors on the online purchase intention in rural tourism: Integrating innovativeness to the UTAUT framework. *Tourism Management, 33*(2), 341–350. doi:10.1016/j.tourman.2011.04.003

Saravanan, K., & Sasithra, S. (2014). Review on classification based on artificial neural networks. *Int. J. Ambient Syst. Appl., 2*(4), 11–18.

Sathish, T. (2018). Prediction of springback effect by the hybridisation of ANN with PSO in wipe bending process of sheet metal. Progress in Industrial Ecology –. *International Journal (Toronto, Ont.), 12*(1), 112–119.

Schierz, P. G., Schilke, O., & Wirtz, B. W. (2010). Understanding consumer acceptance of mobile payment services: An empirical analysis. *Electronic Commerce Research and Applications, 9*(3), 209–216. doi:10.1016/j.elerap.2009.07.005

Schürmann, J. (1996). *Pattern classification: a unified view of statistical and neural approaches.* Wiley.

Semero, Y. K., Zhang, J., Zheng, D., & Wei, D. (2018). A GA-PSO Hybrid Algorithm Based Neural Network Modeling Technique for Short-term Wind Power Forecasting. *Distributed Generation & Alternative Energy Journal, 33*(4), 26–43. doi:10.1080/21563306.2018.12029913

Sermanet, P., Chintala, S., & LeCun, Y. (2012). *Convolutional neural networks applied to house numbers digit classification.* arXiv preprint arXiv:1204.3968

Shadika & Rendra. (2017). Optimizing Woven Curtain Fabric Defect Classification using Image Processing with Artificial Neural Network Method at PT Buana Intan Gemilang. *MATEC Web of Conferences, 135.* Doi:10.1051/matecconf/201713500052

Shaikh, A. A., & Karjaluoto, H. (2015). Mobile Banking adoption: A literature review. *Telematics and Informatics, 32*(1), 129–142. doi:10.1016/j.tele.2014.05.003

Shareef, M. A., Baabdullah, A., Dutta, S., Kumar, V., & Dwivedi, Y. K. (2018). Consumer Adoption of Mobile Banking Services: An Empirical Examination of Factors According to Adoption Stages. *Journal of Retailing and Consumer Services, 43*(July), 54–67. doi:10.1016/j.jretconser.2018.03.003

Shareef, M. A., Dwivedi, Y. K., Kumar, V., & Kumar, U. (2017). Content design of advertisement for consumer exposure: Mobile marketing through short messaging service. *International Journal of Information Management, 37*(4), 257–268. doi:10.1016/j.ijinfomgt.2017.02.003

Sharma, K., Gupta, P., & Sharma, H. (2015). Fully informed artificial bee colony algorithm. *Journal of Experimental & Theoretical Artificial Intelligence, 281,* 403–416.

Sharma, S. K. (2015). Adoption of e-Government services: The role of service quality dimensions and demographic variables. *Transforming Government: People, Process and Policy, 9*(2), 207–222. doi:10.1108/TG-10-2014-0046

Sharma, S. K. (2017). Integrating cognitive antecedents into TAM to explain mobile banking behavioral intention: A SEM-neural network modeling. In *Information Systems Frontiers* (pp. 1–13). Springer Nature.

Sharma, S. K. (2019). Integrating cognitive antecedents into TAM to explain mobile banking behavioral intention: A SEM-neural network modeling. *Information Systems Frontiers*, *21*(4), 815–827. doi:10.100710796-017-9775-x

Sharma, S. K., Al-Badi, A. H., Govindaluri, S. M., & Al-Kharusi, M. H. (2016). Predicting motivators of cloud computing adoption: A developing country perspective. *Computers in Human Behavior*, *62*, 61–69. doi:10.1016/j.chb.2016.03.073

Sharma, S. K., Govindaluri, S. M., & Al Balushi, S. M. (2015). Predicting determinants of Internet banking adoption. *Management Research Review*, *38*(7), 750–766. doi:10.1108/MRR-06-2014-0139

Sharma, S. K., Govindaluri, S. M., Al-Muharrami, S., & Tarhini, A. (2016). Predicting mobile banking adoption: A neural network approach. *Journal of Enterprise Information Management*, *29*, 222–237.

Sharma, S. K., Govindaluri, S. M., Al-Muharrami, S., & Tarhini, A. (2017). A multi-analytical model for mobile banking adoption: A developing country perspective. *Review of International Business and Strategy*, *27*(1), 133–148. doi:10.1108/RIBS-11-2016-0074

Sharma, S. K., Joshi, A., & Sharma, H. (2016). A multi-analytical approach to predict the Facebook usage in higher education. *Computers in Human Behavior*, *55*, 340–353. doi:10.1016/j.chb.2015.09.020

Sharma, S. K., Sharma, H., & Dwivedi, Y. K. (2019). A Hybrid SEM-Neural Network Model for Predicting Determinants of Mobile Payment Services. *Information Systems Management*, *36*(3), 1–19. doi:10.1080/10580530.2019.1620504

Sheng, S., & Guo, Y. (2015). An Integrated Approach Using Condition Monitoring and Modeling to Investigate Wind Turbine Gearbox Design. In *ASME Turbo Expo: Turbine Technical Conference and Exposition Montréal, Canada, 2015*. National Renewable Energy Laboratory (NREL) Publications. 10.1115/GT2015-43888

Sheng, S. (2015). *Improving Component Reliability Through Performance and Condition Monitoring Data Analysis*. NREL-Wind Farm Data Management & Analysis North America.

Sheng, Z., Xiuyu, S., & Wei, W. (2010). An ann model of optimizing activation Functions based on constructive algorithm and gp. In *Computer Application And System Modeling (ICCASM), 2010 International Conference On*, 420–424.

Shin, D. (2009). Towards an understanding of the consumer acceptance of mobile wallet. *Computers in Human Behavior*, *25*(6), 1343–1354. doi:10.1016/j.chb.2009.06.001

Shin, D.-H. (2010). Modelling the interaction of users and mobile payment system: Conceptual framework. *International Journal of Human-Computer Interaction, 26*(10), 917–940. doi:10.1 080/10447318.2010.502098

Shi, X. (2019). Tourism culture and demand forecasting based on BPNN mining algorithms. *Personal and Ubiquitous Computing.* Advance online publication. doi:10.100700779-019-01325-x

Shmueli, G. (2010). To explain or to predict? *Statistical Science, 25*(3), 289–310. doi:10.1214/10-STS330

Shmueli, G., & Koppius, O. R. (2011). Predictive analytics in information systems research. *Management Information Systems Quarterly, 35*(3), 553–572. doi:10.2307/23042796

Shmueli, G., Ray, S., Estrada, J. M. V., & Chatla, S. B. (2016). The elephant in the room: Predictive performance of PLS models. *Journal of Business Research, 69*(10), 4552–4564. doi:10.1016/j.jbusres.2016.03.049

Shmueli, G., Sarstedt, M., Hair, J. F., Cheah, J. H., Ting, H., Vaithilingam, S., & Ringle, C. M. (2019). Predictive model assessment in PLS-SEM: Guidelines for using PLSpredict. *European Journal of Marketing, 53*(11), 2322–2347. doi:10.1108/EJM-02-2019-0189

Sinha, I., & Mukherjee, S. (2016). Acceptance of technology, related factors in use of off branch e-banking: An Indian case study. *The Journal of High Technology Management Research, 27*(1), 88–100. doi:10.1016/j.hitech.2016.04.008

Siu, S., Gibson, G. J., & Cowan, C. F. N. (1990). Decision feedback equalisation using neural network structures and performance comparison with standard architecture. *IEE Proceedings I-Communications, Speech and Vision, 137*(4), 221-225.

Sivagaminathan, R. K., & Ramakrishnan, S. (2007). A hybrid approach for feature subset selection using neural Networks and ant colony optimization. *Expert Systems with Applications, 33*(1), 49–60. doi:10.1016/j.eswa.2006.04.010

Slade, E. L., Dwivedi, Y. K., Piercy, N. C., & Williams, M. D. (2015b). Modeling consumers' adoption intentions of remote mobile payments in the united kingdom: Extending UTAUT with innovativeness, risk, and trust. *Psychology and Marketing, 32*(8), 860–873. doi:10.1002/mar.20823

Slade, E. L., Williams, M. D., & Dwivedi, Y. K. (2013). Mobile payment adoption: Classification and review of the extant literature. *The Marketing Review, 13*(2), 167–190. doi:10.1362/14693 4713X13699019904687

Slade, E., Williams, M., Dwivedi, Y., & Piercy, N. (2014). Exploring consumer adoption of proximity mobile payments. *Journal of Strategic Marketing*, 1–15.

Socha & Blum. (2007). An ant colony optimization algorithm for continuous Optimization: application to feed-forward neural network. *Neural Comput & Applic.*, (16), 235–247. DOI doi:10.100700521-007-0084-z

Spencer, J., & Uchyigit, G. (2012, September). Sentimentor: Sentiment analysis of twitter data. In SDAD@ ECML/PKDD (pp. 56-66). Academic Press.

Sreekanth, J., & Datta, B. (2010). Multi-objective management of saltwater intrusion in coastal aquifers using genetic programming and modular neural network based surrogate models. *Journal of Hydrology (Amsterdam), 393*(3-4), 245–256. doi:10.1016/j.jhydrol.2010.08.023

Srisaeng, P., & Baxter, G. (2017). Modelling Australia's Outbound Passenger Air Travel Demand Using An Artificial Neural Network Approach. *International Journal for Traffic and Transport Engineering, 7*(4), 406–423. doi:10.7708/ijtte.2017.7(4).01]

Stamos, T. Karamouzis and Andreas Vrettos. (2008). An Artificial Neural Network for Predicting Student Graduation Outcomes. *Proceedings of the World Congress on Engineering and Computer Science.*

Statista.com. (2015). *Mobile phone users worldwide 2013-2019.* Retrieved from https://www.statista.com/statistics/274774/forecast-of-mobile-phone-users-worldwide/

Stone, M. (1974). Cross-validatory choice and assessment of statistical predictions. *Journal of the Royal Statistical Society. Series B. Methodological, 36*(2), 111–133. doi:10.1111/j.2517-6161.1974.tb00994.x

Sugeno, M. (1985). An Introductory Survey of Fuzzy Control. *Information Sciences, Prentice-Hall, 36*(1-2), 59–83. doi:10.1016/0020-0255(85)90026-X

Suknovic, M., & Isljamovic, S. (2014). Predicting Students' Academic Performance Using Artificial Neural Network: A Case Study From Faculty Of Organizational Sciences. *The Eurasia Proceedings of Educational & Social Sciences (EPESS),* 68-72.

Sun, T. Y., Liu, C. C., Lin, C. L., Hsieh, S. T., & Huang, C. S. (2009). A radial basis function neural network with adaptive structure via particle swarm optimization. In *Particle Swarm Optimization.* IntechOpen. doi:10.5772/6763

Su, P., Wang, L., & Yan, J. (2018). How users' Internet experience affects the adoption of mobile payment: A mediation model. *Technology Analysis and Strategic Management, 30*(2), 186–197. doi:10.1080/09537325.2017.1297788

Swayamsiddha, S., & Thethi, H. (2018). Performance comparison of adaptive channel equalizers using different variants of differential evolution. *Journal of Engineering Science and Technology, 13*(8), 2271–2286.

Szopiński, T. S. (2016). Factors affecting the adoption of online banking in Poland. *Journal of Business Research, 69*(11), 4763–4768. doi:10.1016/j.jbusres.2016.04.027

Taieb, A. H., Mshali, S., & Sakli, F. (2018). Predicting Fabric Drapability Property by Using an Artificial Neural Network. *Journal of Engineered Fibers and Fabrics, 13*(3). Advance online publication. doi:10.1177/155892501801300310

Taj, S., Shaikh, B. B., & Meghji, A. F. (2019, January). Sentiment Analysis of News Articles: A Lexicon based Approach. In *2019 2nd International Conference on Computing, Mathematics and Engineering Technologies (iCoMET)* (pp. 1-5). IEEE. 10.1109/ICOMET.2019.8673428

Tan, G. W., Ooi, K.-B., Chong, S.-C., & Hew, T.-S. (2014). NFC mobile credit card: The next frontier of mobile payment? *Telematics and Informatics, 31*(2), 292307. doi:10.1016/j.tele.2013.06.002

Tang, R., Fong, S., Yang, X. S., & Deb, S. (2014). Wolf search algorithm with ephemeral memory. *Proc. Seventh International Conference on Digital Information Management (ICDIM 2012)*, 165-172.

Taşdemir & Wirnhardt. (2012). Neural network-based clustering for agriculture management. *EURASIP Journal on Advances in Signal Processing*, 200.

Tavner, P. (2008). Condition Monitoring of Rotating Electrical Machines. The Institution of Engineering and Technology IET.

Teo, A. C., Tan, G. W. H., Ooi, K. B., Hew, T. S., & Yew, K. T. (2015). The effects of convenience and speed in m-payment. *Industrial Management & Data Systems, 115*(2), 311–331. doi:10.1108/IMDS-08-2014-0231

Teo, T., Srivastava, S., & Jiang, L. (2008). Trust and electronic government success: An empirical study. *Journal of Management Information Systems, 25*(3), 99–132. doi:10.2753/MIS0742-1222250303

Thakur, R. (2013). Customer adoption of mobile payment services by professionals across two cities in India: An empirical study using modified technology acceptance model. *Business Perspectives and Research, 1*(2), 17–30. doi:10.1177/2278533720130203

Thakur, R., & Srivastava, M. (2014). Adoption readiness, personal innovativeness, perceived risk and usage intention across customer groups for mobile payment services in India. *Internet Research, 24*(3), 369–392. doi:10.1108/IntR-12-2012-0244

Tian, Y., & Dong, H. (2013). *An analysis of key factors affecting user acceptance of mobile payment*. Paper presented at the 2013 2nd International Conference on Informatics and Applications, ICIA 2013. 10.1109/ICoIA.2013.6650263

Ting, H., Yacob, Y., Liew, L., & Lau, W. M. (2016). Intention to use mobile payment system: A case of developing market by ethnicity. *Procedia: Social and Behavioral Sciences, 224*, 368–375. doi:10.1016/j.sbspro.2016.05.390

Tivive, F. H. C., & Bouzerdoum, A. (2005). Efficient training algorithms for a class of shunting inhibitory convolutional neural networks. *IEEE Transactions on Neural Networks, 16*(3), 541–556. doi:10.1109/TNN.2005.845144 PMID:15940985

Toliyat, H. A. (2013). *Electric Machines Modeling, Condition Monitoring, and Fault Diagnosis*. CRC Press Taylor & Francis Group NW.

Trachuk, A., & Linder, N. (2017). The adoption of mobile payment services by consumers: An empirical analysis results. *Business and Economic Horizons, 13*(3), 383–408. doi:10.15208/beh.2017.28

Trigeassou, J.-C. (2011). *Electrical Machines Diagnosis*. ISTE Ltd and John Wiley & Sons, Inc. doi:10.1002/9781118601662

Tyagi, Priyanka, & Tripathi. (2019). A review towards the sentiment analysis techniques for the analysis of twitter data. Academic Press.

Unar, M. A., & Murray-Smith, D. J. (1999). Automatic steering of ships using neural networks. *International Journal of Adaptive Control and Signal Processing, 13*(4), 203–218. doi:10.1002/(SICI)1099-1115(199906)13:4<203::AID-ACS544>3.0.CO;2-T

Valdivia, Luzión, & Herrera. (2017). Neutrality in the sentiment analysis problem based on fuzzy majority. In *2017 IEEE international conference on fuzzy systems (FUZZ-IEEE)*. IEEE.

Valian, E., Mohanna, S., & Tavakoli, S. (2011). Improved cuckoo search algorithm for feedforward neural network training. *Int. J. of Artificial Intelligence & Applications, 2*. Advance online publication. doi:10.5121/ijaia.2011.2304

Van der Heijden, F. (2004). *Classification, Parameter Estimation and State Estimation an Engineering Approach using MATLAB*. John Wiley & Sons Ltd. doi:10.1002/0470090154

Vansteenkiste, M., Neyrinck, B., Niemiec, C. P., Soenens, B., Witte, H., & Broeck, A. (2007). On the relations among work value orientations, psychological need satisfaction and job outcomes: A selfdetermination theory approach. *Journal of Occupational and Organizational Psychology, 80*(2), 251–277. doi:10.1348/096317906X111024

Varshney, U., & Vetter, R. (2002). Mobile commerce: Framework, applications and networking support. *Mobile Networks and Applications, 7*(3), 185–198. doi:10.1023/A:1014570512129

Vas. (1999). *Artificial-Intelligence-Based Electrical Machines and Drives Application of Fuzzy, Neural, Fuzzy-Neural, and Genetic-Algorithm-Based Techniques*. Oxford University Press. doi:10.1049/PBPO056E

Veitch, D. (2005). *Wavelet Neural Networks and their application in the study of dynamical systems*. Department of Mathematics University of York UK.

Venkatesh, V., & Davis, F. D. (2000). A theoretical extension of the technology acceptance model: Four longitudinal field studies. *Management Science, 46*(2), 186–204. doi:10.1287/mnsc.46.2.186.11926

Venkatesh, V., Morris, M. G., Davis, G. B., & Davis, F. D. (2003). User acceptance of information technology: Toward a unified view. *Management Information Systems Quarterly, 27*(3), 425–478. doi:10.2307/30036540

Venkatesh, V., Ramesh, V., & Massey, A. P. (2003). Understanding usability in mobile commerce. *Communications of the ACM, 46*(12), 53–56. doi:10.1145/953460.953488

Venkatesh, V., Thong, J. Y., & Xu, X. (2012). Consumer acceptance and use of information technology: Extending the unified theory of acceptance and use of technology. *MIS Quartely*, *36*(1), 157–178. doi:10.2307/41410412

Veríssimo, J. M. C. (2016). Enablers and restrictors of mobile banking app use: A fuzzy set qualitative comparative analysis (fsQCA). *Journal of Business Research*, *69*(11), 5456–5460. doi:10.1016/j.jbusres.2016.04.155

Vroom, V. H. (1964). *Work and Motivation*. Jossey-Bass.

Wang, M., Zhang, H., & Wu, Z. (2019). Forecast and Application of GA Optimization BP Neural Network Tourism Demand in High-speed Railway Era. *IOP Conf. Series: Materials Science and Engineering, 569.* doi:10.1088/1757-899X/569/4/042053

Wang, G., Wu, Y., Jiang, H., Zhang, Y., Quan, J., & Huang, F. (2019). Physical and chemical indexes of synthetic base oils based on a wavelet neural network and genetic algorithm. *Industrial Lubrication and Tribology*, *72*(1), 116–121. doi:10.1108/ILT-03-2019-0101

Wang, L., & Yi, Y. (2012). The impact of use context on mobile payment acceptance: An empirical study in China. In A. Xie & X. Huang (Eds.), *Advances in computer science and education* (pp. 293–300). Springer. doi:10.1007/978-3-642-27945-4_47

Wang, X., & Huang, Y. (2011). Convergence study in extended Kalman filter-based training of recurrent neural networks. *IEEE Transactions on Neural Networks*, *22*(4), 588–600. doi:10.1109/TNN.2011.2109737 PMID:21402512

Wang, Y. M., & Elhag, T. M. (2007). A comparison of neural network, evidential reasoning and multiple regression analysis in modelling bridge risks. *Expert Systems with Applications*, *32*(2), 336–348. doi:10.1016/j.eswa.2005.11.029

Wang, Y. S., Wu, M. C., & Wang, H. Y. (2009). Investigating the determinants and age and gender differences in the acceptance of mobile learning. *British Journal of Educational Technology*, *40*(1), 92–118. doi:10.1111/j.1467-8535.2007.00809.x

Weingaertner, D., Tatai, V. K., Gudwin, R. R., & Von Zuben, F. J. (2002). Hierarchical evolution of heterogeneous neural networks. in Evolutionary Computation, CEC'02. *Proceedings of the 2002 Congress On, 2,* 1775–1780.

Wei, T. T., Marthandan, G., Chong, A. Y. L., Ooi, K. B., & Arumugam, S. (2009). What drives Malaysian m-commerce adoption? An empirical analysis. *Industrial Management & Data Systems*, *109*(3), 370–388. doi:10.1108/02635570910939399

Wessels, L., & Drennan, J. (2010). An investigation of consumer acceptance of m-banking. *International Journal of Bank Marketing*, *28*(7), 547–568. doi:10.1108/02652321011085194

Westland, J. C. (2010). Lower bounds on sample size in structural equation modeling. *Electronic Commerce Research and Applications*, *9*(6), 476–487. doi:10.1016/j.elerap.2010.07.003

Wetzels, M., Odekerken-Schroder, G., & Van Oppen, C. (2009). Using PLS path modeling for assessing hierarchical construct models: Guidelines and empirical illustration. *Management Information Systems Quarterly, 33*(1), 33177–33195. doi:10.2307/20650284

Wilamowski, B. M., & David Irwin, J. (2011). *The Industrial Electronics Handbook Intelligent systems* (2nd ed.). CRC Press Taylor & Francis Group.

Wold, H. (1982). Soft modeling: the basic design and some extensions. *Systems Under Indirect Observation, 2*, 343.

Wong, T. C., Wong, S. Y., & Chin, K. S. (2011). A neural network-based approach of quantifying relative importance among various determinants toward organizational innovation. *Expert Systems with Applications, 38*(10), 13064–13072. doi:10.1016/j.eswa.2011.04.113

Wu, J. H., & Wang, S. C. (2005). What drives mobile commerce?: An empirical evaluation of the revised technology acceptance model. *Information & Management, 42*(5), 719–729. doi:10.1016/j.im.2004.07.001

Wu, U., & Kaohsiung, T., & Yang. (2007). Using UTAUT to explore the behavior of 3G mobile communication users. *2007 IEEE International Conference on Industrial Engineering and Engineering Management*, 199–203. 10.1109/IEEM.2007.4419179

Xu, X., Cheng, X., Tan, S., Liu, Y., & Shen, H. (2013). Aspect-level opinion mining of online customer reviews. *China Communications, 10*(3), 25–41. doi:10.1109/CC.2013.6488828

Yadav, R., Sharma, S. K., & Tarhini, A. (2016). A multi-analytical approach to understand and predict the mobile commerce adoption. *Journal of Enterprise Information Management, 29*(2), 222–237. doi:10.1108/JEIM-04-2015-0034

Yamany, W., Fawzy, M., Tharwat, A., & Hassanien, A. E. (2015). Moth-flame optimization for training Multi-Layer Perceptrons. *Proc. 2015 11th International Computer Engineering Conference (ICENCO)*, 267-272. 10.1109/ICENCO.2015.7416360

Yan, F., Gong, Y., & Feng, Z. (2015). Combination of Artificial Neural Network with Multispectral Remote Sensing Data as Applied in Site Quality Evaluation in Inner Mongolia. *Croatian Journal of Forest Engineering, 36*, 2.

Yang. (2013). *Evolving Neural Networks using Ant Colony Optimization with Pheromone Trail Limits*. IEEE.

Yang, Q. C., Pang, C., Liu, L., Yen, D. C., & Michael Tarn, J. (2015). Exploring consumer perceived risk and trust for online payments: An empirical study in China's younger generation. *Computers in Human Behavior, 50*, 9–24. doi:10.1016/j.chb.2015.03.058

Yang, S., Lu, Y., Gupta, S., Cao, Y., & Zhang, R. (2012). Mobile payment services adoption across time: An empirical study of the effects of behavioral beliefs, social influences, and personal traits. *Computers in Human Behavior, 28*(1), 129–142. doi:10.1016/j.chb.2011.08.019

Yao, C. (2017). *Application of convolutional Neural Network in classification of high resolution Agricultural Remote Sensing Images*. The International archives of the photogrammetry, remote sensing and spatial information sciences, Wuhan, China.

Yao, C., Zhang, Y., Zhang, Y., & Liu, H. (2017). Application of convolutional Neural Network in classification of high resolution Agricultural Remote Sensing Images. The International archives of the photogrammetry, remote sensing and spatial information sciences, Wuhan, China.

Yen, J., & Langari, R. (1999). *Fuzzy Logic: Intelligence, Control, and Information*. Prentice Hall, Inc.

Yi, Xu, & Chen. (2014). *Novel Back Propagation Optimization by Cuckoo Search Algorithm*. Hindawi Publishing Corporation. doi:10.1155/2014/878262

Yi, M. Y., Jackson, J. D., Park, J. S., & Probst, J. C. (2006). Understanding information technology acceptance by individual professionals: Toward an integrative view. *Information & Management*, *43*(3), 350–363. doi:10.1016/j.im.2005.08.006

Yu, W., He, H., & Zhang, N. (2009). Advances in Neural Networks. *ISNN 2009 6th International Symposium*.

Yu, J. J. Q., Lam, A. Y. S., & Li, V. O. K. (2015). Evolutionary artificial neural network based on chemical reaction optimization. *Proc. IEEE Congress of Evolutionary Computation (CEC)*, 2083-2090.

Yu, X., Liu, Y., Huang, X., & An, A. (2010). Mining online reviews for predicting sales performance: A case study in the movie domain. *IEEE Transactions on Knowledge and Data Engineering*, *24*(4), 720–734. doi:10.1109/TKDE.2010.269

Zacharis, N. Z. (2016). Predicting Student Academic Performance In Blended Learning Using Artificial Neural Networks. *International Journal of Artificial Intelligence and Applications*, *7*(5). Advance online publication. doi:10.5121/ijaia.2016.7502

Zaremba, W., Sutskever, I., & Vinyals, O. (2014). *Recurrent neural network regularization*. arXiv preprint arXiv:1409.2329

Zarmpou, T., Saprikis, V., Markos, A., & Vlachopoulou, M. (2012). Modeling users' acceptance of mobile services. *Electronic Commerce Research*, *12*(2), 225–248. doi:10.100710660-012-9092-x

Zhang, C., & Shao, H. (2000). An ANN's Evolved by a New Evolutionary System and Its Application. *Proceedings of the 39th IEEE Conference on Decision and Control*, *4*(1), 3562-3563. 10.1109/CDC.2000.912257

Zhang, Q. (1997). Using wavelet network in nonparametric estimation. *IEEE Transactions on Neural Networks*, *8*(2), 227–236. doi:10.1109/72.557660 PMID:18255627

Zhang, Q., & Benveniste, A. (1992). Wavelet networks. *IEEE Transactions on Neural Networks*, *3*(6), 889–898. doi:10.1109/72.165591 PMID:18276486

Zhang, X., Cui, L., & Wang, Y. (2013). Commtrust: Computing multi-dimensional trust by mining e-commerce feedback comments. *IEEE Transactions on Knowledge and Data Engineering, 26*(7), 1631–1643. doi:10.1109/TKDE.2013.177

Zhao. (2017). Weakly-supervised deep embedding for product review sentiment analysis. *IEEE Transactions on Knowledge and Data Engineering, 30*(1), 185-197.

Zhao, H., Zeng, X., Zhang, X., Zhang, J., Liu, Y., & Wei, T. (2011). An adaptive decision feedback equalizer based on the combination of the FIR and FLNN. *Digital Signal Processing, 21*(6), 679–689. doi:10.1016/j.dsp.2011.05.004

Zhou, M. (2016). Chinese university students' acceptance of MOOCs: A self-determination perspective. *Computers & Education, 92*, 194–203. doi:10.1016/j.compedu.2015.10.012

Zhou, T. (2011). The effect of initial trust on user adoption of mobile payment. *Information Development, 27*(4), 290–300. doi:10.1177/0266666911424075

Zhou, T. (2014). Understanding the determinants of mobile payment continuance usage. *Industrial Management & Data Systems, 114*(6), 936–948. doi:10.1108/IMDS-02-2014-0068

About the Contributors

Hiral Ashil Patel, is an Assistant Professor in Department of Computer Science, Ganpat University, Gujarat, India. She did her Ph.D. from Ganpat University. She completed her Ph.D. under the Faculty of Computer Applications. Her research title is "Prediction Model for Financial Products". Her research area of interest is in Machine Learning. She is Gold Medalist in Master of Computer Science and B.C.A. from Ganpat University. She has 10 years of experience in academic. Recently, she has received "Ganpat University Presidential Award of Staff Excellence" under Research - Early Career Researcher category for the year 2019. She is awarded as "Young Scientist" in May 2017 by International Science Community Association in 3rd International Young Scientist Congress. She is recipient of "Best Conceptual Paper" in GFJMR 2012. She has published research papers in well known and globally indexed journals. She has been working with Web Application Development, Mobile Application Development, Database Management System, Data Mining and Machine Learning.

A. V. Senthil Kumar has to his credit 7 Book Chapters, 95 papers in International Journals, 2 papers in National Journals, 25 papers in International Conferences, 5 papers in National Conferences, and edited four books in Data Mining, Mobile Computing, Fuzzy Expert Systems and Web Mining (IGI Global, USA). He is an Editor-in-Chief for International Journal titled "International Journal of Data Mining and Emerging Technologies", "International Journal of Image Processing and Applications", "International Journal of Advances in Knowledge Engineering & Computer Science", "International Journal of Advances in Computers and Information Engineering" and "International Journal of Research and Reviews in Computer Science".. Key Member for India, Machine Intelligence Research Lab (MIR Labs).

* * *

Yakup Akgül was born on March 22, 1977. He studied Department of Information Management at the university of Hacettepe, Ankara (Turkey), from which he graduated in 2001. He received Master (2010) and Ph.D. (2015) in Business Administration at Süleyman Demirel University, Isparta, Turkey. He works as a Ass.Prof. at the Alanya Alaaddin Keykubat University, Alanya/ANTALYA, Turkey.

Mostafa Baghouri was born in Tangier Morocco. He is a member in the Physics department, Communication and detection Systems laboratory, Faculty of sciences, University of Abdelmalek Essaâdi, Tetouan Morocco, his research area is: routing and real time protocols for energy optimization in wireless sensors networks. He obtained a Master's degree in Electrical and Computer Engineering from the Faculty of Science and Techniques of Tangier, Morocco in 2002. He graduated enabling teaching computer science for secondary qualifying school in 2004. In 2006, he graduated from DESA in Automatics and information processing at the same faculty. He works as a teacher of computer science in the high school.

Saad Chakkor was born in Tangier, Morocco. He is member with LabTIC laboratory and Communication and Information Systems department, ENSA of Tangier, University of Abdelmalek Essaadi, Morocco. His research areas are: Intelligent Telecommunications Systems, IoT, Signal Processing Methods, Fault detection and Diagnosis systems. He obtained the Master's degree in Electrical and Computer Engineering from the Faculty of Sciences and Techniques of Tangier, Morocco in 2002. In 2003, he obtained his pedagogical habilitation diploma, from the Higher Normal School in Rabat, for teaching computer science to qualifying secondary education in Morocco. In 2006, he graduated from the DESA (Diploma of Advanced Studies) in automatic and information processing from the FST of Tangier. He obtained the doctorate degree in Automatic and Telecommunications from the Faculty of Sciences of Tetouan in 2015. Currently, he works as professor of Telecommunications at ENSA of Tangier.

Devika G. is working as Assistant Professor in GEC, KRPet, Mandya, Karnataak, India since 8years. has teaching experience of about 15 years, industry experience of 1 year and research experience of 6 years. interested in subjects like computer networks, artificial intelligence, machine learning.

Abderrahmane Hajraoui is a professor of the Higher Education at University of Abdelmalek Essaâdi. He is a director thesis in the Physics department, Communication and detection Systems laboratory, Faculty of sciences, University of Abdelmalek Essaâdi, Tetouan, Morocco. His research areas are: Signal and image processing, automation systems, simulation systems, antennas and radiation, microwave devices and intelligent wireless sensors networks.

Asha Karegowda is currently working as Associate Professor, Dept of MCA, Siddaganga Institute of Technology form last 20 years. Have authored few books on C and Data structures using C, currently writing books on Python, Data mining and Data structures using C++. Area of interest include Data mining, WSN, Remote sensing, Bio inspired computing. Have published papers both in international conferences and journals. Guiding 3 research scholars in the area of image processing and remote sensing. Handling subjects for both PG and UG students: Python, Data structures C and C++, Data mining, Data Analytics.

Geetha M. completed MCA from Gulbarga University in the year 2001. Since 2006 working as Assistant Professor in the Dept. of Master of Computer Applications, Bapuji Institute of Engineering and Technology(BIET), Davangere, Karnataka. She holds life membership of ISTE, New Delhi. Her areas of interest include Data Mining, Java Programming, Operations Research, Design and Analysis of Algorithms, Data Structures. Pursuing Ph.D in the area of Remote Sensing and Image processing from Visvesvaraya Technological University, Belgaum, Karnataka. Published a debut research review paper in IJARCS.

Index

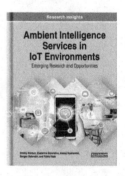

Ensure Quality Research is Introduced to the Academic Community

Become an IGI Global Reviewer for Authored Book Projects

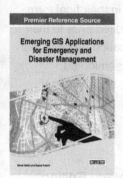

Premier Reference Source

Emerging GIS Applications for Emergency and Disaster Management

Premier Reference Source

Managerial Strategies and Green Solutions for Project Sustainability

Premier Reference Source

Comparative Approaches to Using R and Python for Statistical Data Analysis

Premier Reference Source

Solutions for High-Touch Communications in a High-Tech World

The overall success of an authored book project is dependent on quality and timely reviews.

In this competitive age of scholarly publishing, constructive and timely feedback significantly expedites the turnaround time of manuscripts from submission to acceptance, allowing the publication and discovery of forward-thinking research at a much more expeditious rate. Several IGI Global authored book projects are currently seeking highly-qualified experts in the field to fill vacancies on their respective editorial review boards:

Applications and Inquiries may be sent to:
development@igi-global.com

Applicants must have a doctorate (or an equivalent degree) as well as publishing and reviewing experience. Reviewers are asked to complete the open-ended evaluation questions with as much detail as possible in a timely, collegial, and constructive manner. All reviewers' tenures run for one-year terms on the editorial review boards and are expected to complete at least three reviews per term. Upon successful completion of this term, reviewers can be considered for an additional term.

If you have a colleague that may be interested in this opportunity, we encourage you to share this information with them.

IGI Global's Transformative Open Access (OA) Model:
How to Turn Your University Library's Database Acquisitions Into a Source of OA Funding

In response to the OA movement and well in advance of Plan S, IGI Global, early last year, unveiled their OA Fee Waiver (Offset Model) Initiative.

Under this initiative, librarians who invest in IGI Global's InfoSci-Books (5,300+ reference books) and/or InfoSci-Journals (185+ scholarly journals) databases will be able to subsidize their patron's OA article processing charges (APC) when their work is submitted and accepted (after the peer review process) into an IGI Global journal.*

How Does it Work?

1. When a library subscribes or perpetually purchases IGI Global's InfoSci-Databases including InfoSci-Books (5,300+ e-books), InfoSci-Journals (185+ e-journals), and/or their discipline/subject-focused subsets, IGI Global will match the library's investment with a fund of equal value to go toward subsidizing the OA article processing charges (APCs) for their patrons.

   Researchers: Be sure to recommend the InfoSci-Books and InfoSci-Journals to take advantage of this initiative.

2. When a student, faculty, or staff member submits a paper and it is accepted (following the peer review) into one of IGI Global's 185+ scholarly journals, the author will have the option to have their paper published under a traditional publishing model or as OA.

3. When the author chooses to have their paper published under OA, IGI Global will notify them of the OA Fee Waiver (Offset Model) Initiative. If the author decides they would like to take advantage of this initiative, IGI Global will deduct the US$ 1,500 APC from the created fund.

4. This fund will be offered on an annual basis and will renew as the subscription is renewed for each year thereafter. IGI Global will manage the fund and award the APC waivers unless the librarian has a preference as to how the funds should be managed.

Hear From the Experts on This Initiative:

"I'm very happy to have been able to make one of my recent research contributions, 'Visualizing the Social Media Conversations of a National Information Technology Professional Association' featured in the *International Journal of Human Capital and Information Technology Professionals*, freely available along with having access to the valuable resources found within IGI Global's InfoSci-Journals database."

– Prof. Stuart Palmer,
Deakin University, Australia

For More Information, Visit: www.igi-global.com/publish/contributor-resources/open-access or contact IGI Global's Database Team at eresources@igi-global.com

Printed in the United States
By Bookmasters